Environmental Policy:
Implementation and Enforcement

NEIL HAWKE
De Montfort University, UK

ASHGATE

Published by
Ashgate Publishing Limited
Gower House
Croft Road
Aldershot
Hampshire GU11 3HR
England

Ashgate Publishing Company
131 Main Street
Burlington, VT 05401-5600 USA

Ashgate website: http://www.ashgate.com

British Library Cataloguing in Publication Data
Hawke, Neil
    Environmental Policy : Implementation and Enforcement
    1. European Union 2. Environmental law - European Union
    countries 3. Environmental law - Great Britain
    4. Environmental law - North America
    I. Title
    344.4'046

Library of Congress Cataloging-in-Publication Data
Hawke, Neil.
    Environmental policy : implementation and enforcement/ Neil Hawke.
        p. cm
    Includes biographical references and index.
    ISBN 0-7546-2067-0 - ISBN 0-7546-2311-4 (pbk.)
        1. Environmental law--European Union countries. 2. Environmental
       policy--European Union countries. 3. Environmental law 4.
    Environmental policy. I. Title.

    KJE6242 .H39 2002
    341.7'62'094--dc21

2002024027

ISBN 0 7546 2067 0 (HBK)
ISBN 0 7546 2311 4 (PBK)

Printed and bound in Great Britain by MPG Books Ltd, Bodmin, Cornwall

Contents

Table of Cases

Table of Canadian Legislation

Table of EC Decisions

Table of EC Directives

Table of EC Regulations

Table of EC Treaty Provisions

Table of International Treaties and Conventions

Table of United Kingdom Primary Legislation

Table of United Kingdom Secondary Legislation

Table of United States Legislation

Preface and Acknowledgements

The theme of this book is the dynamic that drives the development of Community policy, its further development into Community law on the environment and its final realisation – through transposition – in the national law of each member state. That national law is referred to here as 'municipal' law. Matters of implementation and enforcement are dealt with by reference to the essential nature of Community law and the apparent freedom ceded to national governments of the member states in transposing much of that law through directives. Although the experience in the United Kingdom is of particular interest, the opportunity has been taken to look also at the experience of implementation and enforcement in certain other member states. Against this general background consideration is given also to the usually elusive line which divides Community law and policy on the environment from those areas of law and policy in member states which do not owe their authority to the European Community. One area of particular significance here relates to Economic Instruments where member states have enjoyed considerable freedom from control at the centre of the Community. Chapter Six looks at Economic Instruments and it will not go unnoticed that it is the longest of the ten chapters. The growing significance of such instruments is in itself an indication of the changing face of environmental control and management through the medium of the law. Indeed, the growing sophistication of such instruments is a powerful piece of evidence of the presence at a crossroads of environmental law and policy in the European Community. A number of areas covered in the chapters of this book point to the likely way ahead, based in part on the experience of at least three decades of Community law and policy on the environment. The direction to be followed will no doubt continue to be influenced considerably by member state culture and practice in approaches to management and control of the environment, another central theme of this book. By way of contrast frequent reference is made to the experiences of the United States and Canada. The final chapter attempts to encapsulate the issues, variables and controversies which are likely to affect environmental management and control under the law through a case study. This case study draws on many of the areas of law and policy examined elsewhere in the book.

I am pleased to be able to acknowledge my debt to a number of individuals and organisations whose support and expertise has proved invaluable. In no particular order I would like to thank my many contacts in the United Kingdom, in other parts of the European Community, and in the United States and Canada for their time and patience in helping me with the research for the book. I am particularly grateful for the financial support which came from a Canadian Studies Faculty Research Program grant, enabling me to spend time in Canada in 2000. I am happy also to express my appreciation of colleagues and postgraduate students in the Department of Law at De Montfort University. Without the active support of the Department, time management for writing and research would have been very much more difficult. Last, but by no means least, I have to thank my wife, Mary, for her unfailing support throughout the preparation of the book.

Neil Hawke
Brighton

Chapter One

The Development of Law and Policy

Background to Law and Policy Development

It is the task of this book to look at the factors and variables which shape the evolution of policy and its crystallisation in law. Prior to accession to membership of the European Community by the United Kingdom such a task would generally have had a very different character, for reasons which will unfold in this first chapter and beyond. Indeed, much environmental law that is now implemented and enforced in the United Kingdom started life as a policy ambition of the European Community. Nevertheless there are some laws which do not owe their parentage to such policy, directly at least. Within this framework and its European emphasis there is a fundamental concern for the way in which policy's dynamic character sees its evolution into law and, in turn, its enforcement in the United Kingdom. A major concern for this purpose is the extent to which member states of the European Community may be seen to have discretion in the style, extent and emphasis of their transposition of Community law. In so far as any discretion does exist here it arises from the fundamental status of the legislative instruments of the Community. More particularly, the main instrument of environmental law, the directive, often allows that discretion in transposition.

Evolution and Development

The 1990s were notable for the fact that a central concern of the European Community was with the process of implementation affecting member states. The years leading to this point can be characterised as being bound up with the process of creating the policy which in many instances flowered into law for implementation and enforcement in member states. This preoccupation appears to have represented an inward-looking exercise where little thought was given to the efficiency of the process overall. In other words, the appearance is of a regime with only a marginal preoccupation with whether the objectives behind the law and policy are being realised. Arguably, in a period of such rapid development where the status of the environment in the constitutional structure of the European Community was still beset with uncertainty, attention to effectiveness and efficiency in the implementation and enforcement process was never likely to be towards the top of any list of priorities. The development of environmental law and policy in this period up to the 1990s is usually characterised as involving a 'top-down' approach. The 5th Environmental Action Programme signalled a potentially important shift to what is often characterised as a 'bottom-up' approach.

The 5th Environmental Action Programme[1]

This and the other programmes of the same name are essentially declarations of intent, as well as being discussion documents. In addition proposals for action may be prescribed by reference to a timetable for action. Nevertheless, the programmes have no legally binding status. Perhaps most importantly, the programmes and the 5th in particular provide something of a marker against which the progress of implementation and enforcement can be measured. The 5th Environmental Action Programme set out an ambitious strategy for environmental management at Community level, with quantified targets as well as the means of achieving them. Five target areas were selected for particular attention: industry, energy, transport, agriculture and tourism.[2] Within this framework the intention was to address procedures, to maximise public participation, to promote voluntary agreements, to stress horizontal rather than vertical policy development and enforcement, and to promote self-regulation. However, it was the 4th Environmental Action Programme (addressed below) which set the scene in relation to matters of environmental policy implementation.

The 'Bottom-up' Approach

One attractive argument in favour of this approach is that there is potential for bringing matters of implementation and enforcement rather closer to the point, on the ground, where environmental law and policy has to have its impact. In turn there is the potential for better accountability as well as the potential for environmental policy integration, which will be examined later in this chapter. For the moment though, environmental policy integration seeks a better and more effective representation in the other policies of the European Community by means of horizontal rather than vertical policy development and enforcement.

One increasingly significant example of the 'bottom-up' approach is the development and implementation of policy on self-regulation through the

Community Regulation allowing voluntary participation in the eco-management and audit scheme.[3] Here local government (an important environmental regulator) has been notable for its pro-active involvement in adoption and implementation of what is usually referred to as EMAS.[4] Whatever the context there are important matters of principle to be realised through the bottom-up implementation and enforcement of environmental policy, not least the appearance of greater credibility of the law that emerges from the foundation of that policy. In Chapter Six, where economic instruments are addressed, it will be seen that a bottom-up approach is particularly crucial since it is from this direction that markets and market-based instruments will gather their momentum as well as the synergy which allows flexible change as one of the outstanding characteristics of these instruments.

Increasing reliance on the foregoing bottom-up approach will tend to reduce reliance on the more traditional 'command and control' techniques of regulatory control. Although it is tempting to pose the question whether bottom-up approaches are more effective than command and control, such a question is probably naïve, for two reasons. First, there is little doubt that economic instruments are for the foreseeable future complementary to the command and control approach to environmental regulation. Second, any enquiry into effectiveness is fraught with complexity and difficulty: any such enquiry is certainly beyond the scope of this book.

The 4th Environmental Action Programme[5]

This Programme stressed the need to deal with matters of implementation. As such this programme was an important marker in the progress from law and policy creation to realisation of environmental objectives in member states. Considerable stress was placed on environmental protection policy as an essential ingredient of economic, social and agricultural policy. The priority of policy integration (which is further developed towards the end of this chapter) was more clearly articulated than it had been in the 3rd Environmental Action Programme. Where agriculture is concerned, the 4th Action Programme emphasised the specific problems confronting agricultural policy, such as overproduction and variable soil quality.[6] The 3rd Environmental Action Programme also represented an important, incremental building block in the development of environmental law and policy.

The 3rd Environmental Action Programme[7]

Environmental policy integration was first adverted to in this programme, as well as the significance of preventative action for the protection of the environment. Agriculture was one area mentioned as being in need of greater environmental awareness. The need to recognise and address the causes of environmental damage were adverted to also against the background of a need for a 'rational' management of landed resources.

Wisely, the Programme points to the fact that the way in which land is used very largely conditions environmental quality. Accordingly attention is directed to the need for reinforcement of policy priorities both at member state and Community level for the purpose of more successful protection and conservation of those areas which fulfil important ecological functions.

The 3rd Environmental Action Programme appeared just ten years after the accession of the United Kingdom to membership of the European Community. The environmental law and policy of the United Kingdom in the years up to 1973 will be examined later in this chapter and elsewhere in this book. More immediately though, the United Kingdom's accession can be characterised by very significant changes in the style and emphasis of applicable environmental law and policy. In the years to 1973 the United Kingdom was used to arrangements which were less than transparent and far from objective, in part as a result of a devolved system. This picture is well worth stressing as developments in the European Community are dealt with.

The Shaping and Management of Policy Creation

There is no easy way of defining the variables which affect the creation of environmental policy. One critical issue is that some elements of such policy will be intended to crystallise into the law of the Community before being implemented by transposition in member states. In principle, therefore, policy creation necessitates attention to the practicalities of the transition into law that is both capable of effective implementation and enforcement in member states. In theory that path should be smooth enough to facilitate that process. In practice there are various factors which stand in the way of the effective realisation of that process, not least the blurring of the edges that occurs where (typically) a directive finally agreed is the product of political compromise following often tortuous negotiation within the Community. Against this background it is possible to generalise for the purpose of suggesting that five variables will tend to predominate in the creation and shaping of policy on the environment: science, technology, economics, risk and geography. For present purposes the first three of these will be examined in a little more detail. To a large extent these variables are recognised in the EC Treaty, as will be seen below.

Science

It is not unreasonable to surmise that the very nature of the environment, its regulation, management and control suggest the centrality of science and scientific principles. The fundamental shortcoming of science is that it may not deliver the certainties that policy-makers hanker after. In order to cope with this uncertainty there may be resort to devices such as the 'precautionary' principle which is examined in Chapter Three. Furthermore, the Royal Commission on Environmental Pollution in its 21st Report on 'Setting Environmental Standards' had this to say:

> The requirement for sound science as the basis for environmental policy is not a requirement for absolute knowledge or certainty and should not be interpreted as such. Rather ... its limitations should be made explicit.[8]

The Royal Commission indicates that, in setting an environmental standard, the starting point should be scientific understanding of the problem or potential problem being addressed. Whether pollutants should be released to the environment raises issues which go well beyond scientific evidence in many cases. Should the (assumed) assimilative capacity of the marine environment be relied upon? Should there be a presumption in favour of precaution? These and very many other issues and variables lie beyond the scientific boundary. It is here that, as will be seen in Chapter Three, the precautionary and preventative principles at the centre of much European Community environmental law and policy-making provide opportunities for the balancing of all sorts of factors before the final decision is forthcoming on the shape and extent of environmental law and policy. One of these factors may well be technology.

Technology

Reference will be made elsewhere in this book to criteria such as 'BATNEEC' (best available technology not entailing excessive cost) and 'BPEO' (best practicable environmental option), both of which are now well-entrenched in important areas of environmental law in the European Community and its member states. Beyond these criteria for decision-making in member states other dimensions affecting this variable may require development in the early years of the twenty-first century. The possibility that 'technology' for present purposes may be indicative of a rather wider constituency is adverted to by the Royal Commission on Environmental Pollution.[9] The Royal Commission suggests that assessments of technological options ought to have a broader perspective, examining the whole supply chain to determine whether it may be managed in a less environmentally-damaging way. In other words, life-cycle analysis should be a constituent of this technological variable in law and policy-making.

Economics

A crude recognition of economic variables occurs through an identification of the costs and benefits of the implementation and enforcement of environmental requirements. Simple examples come to mind: for example, what are the consequences of a cessation of sea-dumping of sewage sludge in the North Sea? Are any indirect consequences of a prohibition on sea-dumping acceptable? Are there net benefits here, in terms of the alternative management and disposal of sewage sludge through incineration, treatment and land-spreading? These questions beg many other fundamental questions en route to any meaningful analysis of costs and benefits. For example, what value can be placed on the technology necessary and the externalities relied on for the purpose of managing huge quantities of sewage sludge accruing as a result of a prohibition of sea-dumping? One simple generalisation here may suggest that replacement of sea-dumping with incineration, treatment and land-spreading is a good deal more expensive. If this is the case and economic or financial variables are part of the decision-making equation, how is the externality now protected (the North Sea) to be represented? No doubt its value takes account of the absence of sewage dumping with (no doubt) a resulting improvement in water quality affecting all sorts of other environmental indicators, over varying periods of time, that take account of recovery times, for example. These valuation exercises, despite their inherent uncertainties, reflect an absence of any market mechanisms through which values might otherwise be determined. The importance of modelling along these lines is driven increasingly by principles of sustainable development, which is dealt with in Chapter Six. Whatever the limitations of cost-benefit criteria, statute has not ignored their value in environmental decision-making.

The Environment Agency in England and Wales (as well as the Scottish Environment Agency) is bound by section 39 of the Environment Act 1995 to take account of likely costs and benefits arising from any exercise or non-exercise of its very considerable powers. More specifically, the section requires the Agency, in considering whether or not to exercise *any* power conferred upon it by or under *any* enactment or in deciding the manner in which to exercise any such power, to take into account the *likely* costs and benefits of the exercise or non-exercise of the subject power in the manner in question. However, the duty does not apply if it is considered unreasonable to enter into this calculation by reference to the nature or purpose of the power in question or in the circumstances of the particular case. Furthermore, the Act stipulates that the duty cannot compromise or eliminate any obligation of the Agency to discharge any duties, to comply with any requirements or to pursue any objectives as a result of requirements arising beyond section 39. Therefore, the so-called 'conservation' duties arising elsewhere in the Act are not excluded by the section 39 duty.[10]

The Environment Agency's position in relation to the section 39 duty is that a fully quantified analysis will be carried out only

> ... where there is a reasonably acceptable way of putting monetary value on the non-financial costs and benefits of the alternatives [and that] ... where there are additional features which means that monetary valuation is inappropriate or unacceptable, ... multi-attribute analysis may be used. Because of the expense involved, a fully quantified analysis of costs and benefits, or multi-attribute analysis, is regarded as justifiable only if a policy would involve the Agency and those affected by it, in estimated total expenditure of at least £1 million.[11]

Overall, it can be seen that section 39 is heavily qualified. Such qualification, as can be seen, arises both from the statute itself as well as the Agency's own policy on deployment of cost-benefit criteria.

EC Treaty and Policy Variables

The foregoing variables are recognised in the EC Treaty[12] although there may be apparent overlap on occasions, as where Article 174 of the EC Treaty requires any proposed action on the environment to take account of (*inter alia*) '... the potential benefits and costs of action or lack of action'. The requirement is that all Community institutions shall take into account these variables for present purposes although they have no binding legal status as such and are, for the most part, submerged in the formative process of policy development. Science is represented in a list of four variables. The assumption at the outset is that account will be taken of available scientific data, whatever its source. The precautionary principle, already referred to, recognises that the law and policy-making regime cannot be tied to a strict precondition of comprehensive science. In the meantime, the European Environment Agency has the function of generating uniform scientific data across the Community, as will be seen later in this chapter. The three other variables recognised in the EC Treaty relate to regional variations ('geography'), so-called 'advantages and charges' (costs and benefits), and economic and social development.

The directive may allow a member state to choose the means by which the legislative object is achieved in relation to regional variations and characteristics. As will be seen elsewhere in later chapters, this legislative vehicle permits numerous factors to influence the nature of member state transposition through its own law. For example, a member state may choose between civil and criminal law as a means of enforcing the legislation in question. In the same way the Community is not prescriptive in addressing the matter of regional environmental variations: derogations are not directed towards such variations, for example. On the other hand the ability of a member state to address these regional variations may be manifested in rather more subtle terms. The Urban Waste Water Directive (Directive 91/271), for example, allows for varying levels of treatment according to whether effluent is being discharged into sensitive or less-sensitive waters.[13]

So-called 'advantages and charges' effectively translate as 'costs and benefits' and their manifestation in European policy-making serves to confirm just how crude the approach is to this matter, at least in the absence of any scientifically reliable equation from economics through which valuation of environmental externalities (for example) might be possible. Politically the tendency is to see costs in terms of the cost impact of environmental law and policy on industry in member states. Nevertheless there are routes out of this arguably unsatisfactory state of affairs, via reliance on the preventative principle (addressed in Chapter Three) and the policy objective of environmental improvement.

Economic and social development is again an ill-defined category which is tied more to the concern of some less well developed member states to avoid any undue compromise to economic development. Indeed, much of what was said previously in connection with regional matters should apply here also. Nevertheless, there are instances where this variable is of potential significance, as where the financial implications of nature conservation on a member state may be seen to be disproportionate giving the scale of its resources and the undue extent of its obligations under emerging Community law.

Transforming Policy into Law

The foregoing variables will be explored and investigated by the Commission en route to the preparation of a draft proposal for a directive, for example. The Commission has the pivotal role in bringing forward proposals for legislation. Indeed, the Commission's position is distinctive since there is both a right to bring proposals forward as well as an obligation so to do.[14] The likelihood is that, at an early stage, a decision will be taken as to the appropriate legislative vehicle. Environmental legislation is characterised by reliance on the directive although there may be good reason why a directly applicable regulation may be appropriate, albeit exceptionally.

Initial Processes

The Commission will undertake an investigation of a range of matters before a draft proposal is brought forward. As indicated previously, attention will be given to factors and variables such as scientific data, costs and benefits, as well as the legal position (if any) in member states. Thereafter the draft proposal and supporting material is put forward for consultation with member states as well as representatives of industrial and environmental interests before any revised proposal (which will be published in the Official Journal) starts its journey through the Commission's adoption process.

Processes beyond the Commission

The Council, Parliament, Economic and Social Committee and the Committee of the Regions receive the proposed measure and have an opportunity to convey their respective opinions. The Council and the Parliament are the two significant participants at this stage and the 'interplay' between them through the co-decision procedure[15] is complex as progress is made towards final adoption. In the simplest case the Council's agreement with Parliament's amendments leads to formal adoption of the measure. A rather more difficult situation arises where such agreement on amendments cannot be reached. Here formal conciliation between the parties is provided for: agreement at this stage indicates adoption on those conciliated terms. In the absence of such agreement the measure is treated as being rejected.

Co-decision and Majority Voting

The co-decision procedure outlined above is clearly complex. Politically co-decision is important in providing the Parliament with greater influence as an elected assembly at least since the Treaty of Amsterdam which introduced the new regime. Until the arrival of the co-decision procedure the relationship between the Council and the Parliament was allegedly a cooperative relationship which in reality never really gave much influence to the Parliament. It cannot be assumed that all environmental legislation will be subject to this procedural template. Article 6 of the EC Treaty, which will be dealt with later in the chapter, emphasises that environmental issues are considered in the context of other areas of activity in the Community. Accordingly, environmental provisions emanating from what may be overlapping policy concerns may well be generated through a legislative process other than that prescribed by Article 175. Since 1993 the Maastricht Treaty has provided for majority voting in a number of areas of competence, including the environment.[16] Nevertheless, certain areas such as those relating to town and country planning are still subject to unanimous voting.

Overlapping Policy Concerns

A frequent overlap giving rise to likely controversy is the process of seeing policy mature into law as it relates to trade priorities within the European Community. Indeed, there are of course real possibilities that any initial tension may ultimately be the subject of litigation. A particularly significant example occurs in relation to the matter of packaging and packaging waste.

Directive 85/339[17] (subsequently repealed and replaced by Directive 94/62[18]) dealt with containers for liquids used for human consumption. Among other things, the Directive dealt also with restrictions affecting schemes, such as those in Denmark, for the return and replenishment of drinks containers whereby imports may be adversely affected. Indeed, likely constraints on imports formed the basis for the Commission's case against Denmark, in 1998.

Ultimately, the European Court of Justice decided that such deposit and return schemes are not disproportionate to environmental objectives.[19] Denmark was prohibited from insisting on prescribed bottle design for the purpose of such schemes. Not surprisingly, the tensions here surfaced during the passage of the repealing measure, Directive 94/62. Was the measure an environmental measure or was it in fact a trade measure? Similar questions have occurred elsewhere. For example, Regulation 3093/94[20] seeks to regulate substances which deplete the ozone layer. Although the Regulation was made under Article 175 EC as an environmental measure, there is in fact a cogent argument that there should have been resort instead to Article 95 and its concern with goods, services and (in this case, arguably) product specification for the purpose of eliminating or reducing products relying on the proscribed substances, such as refrigerators. Had Article 95 been used as the legal basis for the Regulation there would not now be any particular prejudice to the environmental credentials of the Regulation. The reason for this position is that Article 6 now insists that environmental factors are integrated into other policies: one reason why choice of legal basis is perhaps not so critical as it once was.

The Policy Process Illustrated

Four areas which overlap to a considerable extent are used here to illustrate the dynamic of the policy process: air pollution, volatile organic compounds, climate change and (finally) eco-management and audit.

Air Pollution

The European Community over the last two decades has shown a very active involvement in addressing the environmental issues surrounding emissions to the atmosphere. Acid rain and ozone depletion have featured very prominently in the agenda for action through policy and law. The Community was an active participant in international fora concerned with a global response to these problems. One of many challenging problems concerns the approach to implementation of standards in member states for the purpose of dealing with ambient air quality. Effective implementation will often depend on the ease or otherwise of transposition of the relevant directives. Early efforts here were fraught with difficulty through uncertainties and infelicities in drafting. Awareness of the shortcomings of these early attempts to crystallise law from the policy background led in turn to a refinement of approach. As a result Directive 96/62[21] dealing with ambient air quality management operates as a so-called 'framework' directive with daughter directives filling out technical standards and limits in respect of specific pollutants. In due course this collection of directives will replace the existing provisions which gave rise to the foregoing problems. However, the regulation of emissions to the atmosphere enjoys a rather wider part in the regulatory framework. In particular, the Directive on Integrated Pollution Prevention and Control (96/61) (IPPC)[22] sees atmospheric emissions as an important element in what is a far more integrated measure of control over industrial installations.

Volatile Organic Compounds

The policy response of the European Community and its programme of legislation on VOCs provides an important example of the way in which there is a concern to relate to international standard-setting and, in turn, to rationalise those standards in member states. The international convention in question is the UNECE Convention on Long-range Transboundary Air Pollution, its VOC Protocol and the so-called 5th Action Programme on VOC target reductions. Directive 94/63[23] on the control of VOC emissions is the first in a series of Community laws here, followed by Directive 99/13[24] which addresses emission limits in relation to the use of organic solvents in certain industrial sectors. Interestingly, this Directive operates only where an installation operates above prescribed solvent consumption levels. Again, as was seen in the previous section on air pollution, some installations may be subject to this and the IPPC regulatory regime. Otherwise there are two significant characteristics of this Directive. First, throughout the consultation which preceded transposition in the United Kingdom, it was recognised by the . Department of the Environment (now the Department for Environment, Food and Rural Affairs) that because there are so many sources of volatile organic compounds, only some of those can sensibly be subject to regulatory control. Second, where regulatory control *does* apply, three methods of solvent emission reduction are allowed, through (1) uniform emission limits; (2) schemes for solvent reduction; and (3) national plans.

Climate Change

Climate change policy may be seen in retrospect as a policy area where the early initiative appeared to be with certain of the more influential member states of the European Community. Nevertheless, there has been some 'parallel running' by the European Community, particularly as a partner in international negotiations. Effective interest on the part of the European Community appears to date back to 1986 and a resolution of the Parliament.[25] Two years later the

Commission published its report *The Greenhouse Effect and the Community*.[26] Thereafter, in 1990, the Council sought an expedited adoption of targets and strategies for the purpose of addressing greenhouse gas emissions. Interestingly, policy integration is manifested in the Community's position at this stage, prior to the Second World Conference on Climate Change at the end of that year.

Attempts at an integrated strategy appear in the deliberations of the Environment and Energy Councils. Those deliberations were to prove to be particularly influential on the world stage against the background of an agreement that carbon dioxide emissions from the Community would be stabilised at 1990 levels if other major industrialised countries were willing to subscribe to stabilisation on comparable terms. This most important stage in the gestation of climate policy was not however characterised by legally binding commitments to stabilisation.

The Convention on Climate Change was signed at the Rio Conference on Environment and Development in June 1992. The United Nations Convention was ratified by the European Community and the United Kingdom in December 1993. Significantly, the Convention contained no legally binding obligation to stabilise greenhouse gas emissions at 1990 levels by 2000. Instead, Article 4 of the Convention refers to such stabilisation as a desirable aim. Elsewhere in the Convention there is a rather bland reference to fulfilment of this aim in the Community at large by the Community and member states within the respective competence of each.[27] The Kyoto Protocol adopted in December 1997 seeks to reduce emissions of carbon dioxide and its equivalents by 5 per cent below 1990 levels from 2008 to 2012. The Protocol was signed by the European Community and the United Kingdom in the following year. At the time of writing the issue in the United Kingdom is how best to meet the 12.5 per cent reduction required of this member state within the legally binding target set for the European Community in a joint agreement under the Kyoto Protocol.

Originally the Commission had concluded a strategy as a vehicle for realisation of the commitments that had found their way into the Framework Convention signed at Rio.[28] That strategy includes a range of instruments such as a framework directive on energy efficiency which provides a reminder of the fact that much of the policy in this area is in fact European energy policy rather than environmental policy. Out of the range of instruments chosen by the Commission for the realisation of Community policy, perhaps one of the more significant items is a Decision (93/389)[29] on the monitoring and limitation of greenhouse gas emissions, requiring member states to submit inventories to the Commission annually. The Commission is obliged to compile a report whose preparation is to be assisted by the European Environment Agency, with particular reference to the sufficiency of member states' progress towards the targets set under the Kyoto Protocol. Subsequently this Decision was modified by Decision 99/296[30] in order to take account of member states' obligations to limit or reduce other greenhouse gases not subject to the Montreal Protocol.

There is little doubt that the Commission's strategy was overshadowed by the proposal – part of the overall package – for what is often referred to as a 'carbon-energy' tax.[31] Resistance was strong among several member states, including the United Kingdom. The House of Lords Select Committee on the European Communities published a report on 'Carbon/Energy Tax' in the early 1990s, stressing two reservations:

> ... it is a unilateral response to a global problem: the Community is responsible for only some 13 per cent of global emissions [of carbon dioxide]. The second is that the behavioural characteristics of energy consumers and the distorted nature of energy markets mean that to achieve a perceptible result we believe the tax would need to be much higher than $10 per barrel of oil equivalent proposed and would cause great economic disruption.[32]

Subsequently, the United Kingdom government has introduced a so-called 'Climate Change Levy' from April 2001. The proposal was that the levy would be revenue neutral, seeking to reduce employers' national insurance contributions. Some of the levy will be devoted to benefits for smaller businesses through advice on energy audits and developments in new carbon technology. The objective is to reduce carbon dioxide emissions by a modest 1.5 tonnes by 2010: Kyoto assumes cuts of 28.5 million tonnes in the United Kingdom by that date, albeit the levy is but one device available for this purpose. Implementation of the levy is addressed in Chapter Six.

Eco-management and Audit

Reference has been made already to the Regulation governing eco-management and audit.[33] This area of policy as manifested in the law is of particular note since it is based on voluntary participation by interested corporations and businesses. However, the longer-term prospects for this area are a matter of some interest by virtue of the fact that there may be opportunities to streamline regulatory control over the environment based on risk, for example. Clearly, a corporation's subscription to environmental management standards may tend to suggest that a lighter touch is justified where the regulatory agencies are concerned. The evolution of a streamlined regulatory strategy along these lines may not necessitate further policy intervention by the European Community, at least as long as there is evidence that member states are inclined to realise any sustainable benefits here. For the moment therefore, streamlining the environmental regulatory process appears to invite consideration of the essential principles of subsidiarity, a subject that is taken up in the next chapter.

Developed and Developing Law and Policy

References to developed and developing law and policy are references to the essential dynamic through which a complex process can be identified and analysed. Essentially that complex process is centred on implementation of those elements of environmental policy crystallised for the most part in the European Community, contained in its legislation, and transposed through the legislation of the member states. That process of transposition in the United Kingdom is by no means a straightforward process. Some of complexities are illustrated below, in Chapter Two and elsewhere in this book. Furthermore, across all member states of the European Community there are enormous variables, cultural and otherwise, which determine often distinctive styles of transposition, some of which will be touched on from time to time throughout the book. For the moment, though, attention is given to the moulding of national law to facilitate transposition, to the development of policy surrounding and accompanying the law, to the evolution of law and policy following new legislative developments in the European Community as well as any other relevant developments at member state level. This alone suggests the scale of the complexity just referred to. For present purposes, this section of the chapter is divided into two. In the first section, expert influences on the development of law and policy are addressed while in the second section policy guidance is examined.

Influences on the Development of Law and Policy

There is little doubt that expert influence in particular operates both within and across borders. In other words, the development of environmental law and policy is amenable to what might be described as a two-way process with Community expertise (and priorities) playing an essential part in matters of development and evolution at the centre and at the devolved member state level. In perhaps a rather different way, member state expert influence serves not only to advise development and evolution within its territory, albeit within the jurisdictional limits imposed by membership of the European Community, but may also contribute to deliberations at the centre where a mixture of informed, well-respected expertise and political influence is undoubtedly a potentially powerful catalyst. This axis is characterised by a large number of processes, including consultations, strategies, expert reports and recommendations, participatory devices, and international conventions and treaties. Even in this selection of factors there are likely to be significant overlaps: strategies for example are almost always subject to a consultation process prior to finalisation, as will be seen below.

Consultation

Consultation may be initiated by any number of agencies at Community and member state level although commonly encountered examples include the Department for Environment, D-G XI (the Environment Directorate of the European Commission) and the Environment Agency. Agencies like these engage in consultation for four main purposes: to ensure compliance with the law, to allow debate on proposals and strategies for implementation, to anticipate policy despite uncertainty whether such policy might be crystallised in law, and to anticipate the operation of a formal, national strategy.

Ensuring compliance with the law Ensuring compliance with the law may necessitate consultation either in anticipation of legislation or following its passage into force. The Landfill Directive,[34] for example, was subject to formal compliance by July 2001, even though provision is made for numerous other target dates for compliance in respect of waste reduction.

In an important consultation paper *The Implementation of Council Directive 1999/31*[35] the then Department of the Environment sought to ensure adequate compliance with the new law as the compliance dates drew nearer. Although attention was drawn to the considerable overlap between existing regulatory arrangements and those anticipated by the Directive, nevertheless there was recognition of some landfilling practices in need of attention in the United Kingdom.

Because some landfills will be subject to the IPPC regime referred to previously[36] the prospect is one of a dual system with some landfills being subject to the waste management licensing regime of the Environmental

Protection Act 1990. Accordingly, the consultation paper proposes that all landfills be governed by the IPPC regime although this raises two questions, whether the IPPC regime is compatible with the requirements of the Directive, and whether transference of all landfills to IPPC increases the regulatory burden for those not otherwise included. The problems do not end here because reference is made to the landfills previously licensed under the Control of Pollution Act 1974: legislation which, unlike the Landfill Directive, did not require financial security prior to landfilling operations. These matters are returned to, in Chapter Two.

Debate on proposals and strategies for implementation Debate on proposals and strategies for implementation through consultation in the United Kingdom is dominated by the requirements, or likely requirements, of European Community law. This is a particularly important process since it allows a member state like the United Kingdom to put its own stamp on style and emphasis, within the four corners of the objectives set by the subject directive.

On occasions though an issue of municipal concern may be seen to have an impact on an obligation arising under European Community law. This was the case, for example, in the consultation paper dealing with the *Review of Water Abstraction Licensing* published by the former Department of the Environment in 1998.[37] The paper recognises the damage being sustained by Sites of Special Scientific Interest as well as other sites designated under the Habitats and Birds Directive as a result of water abstraction. Consultations of this sort are necessarily alive to the increasingly comprehensive coverage of European Community legal requirements: evidence of growing integration of regulatory and other regimes affecting the environment.

In its consultation paper on *The Shellfish Waters Directive*[38] the former Department of the Environment was concerned with the need to meet the legal obligations flowing from Directive 79/923[39] on the quality standards applicable to waters used for shellfisheries, in anticipation of the designation of new waters. Against this background, the Department of the Environment stressed the influence of the licensing of discharges by the Environment Agency under the Urban Waste Waters Directive (91/271[40]) as well as the influence of principles emerging from recent litigation before the European Court of Justice in connection with member states' noncompliance with the Directive.

Having sought to implement a directive, the transposition may give rise to anxiety about failures of compliance and, in turn, consultation for the purpose of attempting to correct matters. Directive 94/62 on Packaging Waste[41] includes in Article 15 a provision empowering a member state to use economic instruments as a means of realising the packaging waste recycling targets prescribed, in the absence of any initiative by the European Community. The transposition provided for what is essentially a voluntary industry-based scheme using 'PRNs': packaging recovery notes, one of whose primary objectives was to create sustainable revenue flows as an incentive for the encouragement of recycling. The revenue flow was found to be inadequate. It was this inadequacy that was addressed by the Department of the Environment's consultation paper *Packaging Waste*.[42]

Consultation though may indicate the likely way forward in the enforcement of the law. The Environment Agency for example set out its proposals for the *Consenting of Dangerous Substances in Discharges to Surface Waters*.[43] Those proposals show very clearly how the objectives of a Directive (76/464)[44] may require careful transposition, particularly where (as here) that Directive contains a good deal of detailed prescription. In these circumstances it is necessary to limit the agenda for consultation. As environmental policy from the centre develops with greater emphasis on subsidiarity and more reliance on sustainable development principles, where member states may be allowed to create their own economic instruments, the consultation process may be seen to widen its boundaries quite radically.

The anticipation of policy development The anticipation of policy development is a matter which, not surprisingly throws up opportunities for consultation at the centre, through the structures of the European Community. This of course is a function of the very significant proportion of environmental law and policy that emanates from the centre. Nevertheless, at member state level, policy formation continues to generate consultation also. A notable example occurs in connection with the fact that the Community does not have a policy on contaminated land, as a result of which the government of the United Kingdom was able to turn to policy formation here, culminating in the legislation of Part IIA of the Environmental Protection Act after extensive consultation over many years. Two interesting examples of consultation from the centre relate to greenhouse gas emissions trading in the European Community and a proposal for a framework Directive on Environmental Liability.

The Green Paper on greenhouse gas emission[45] stresses the concern of the European Community to be pro-active in addressing developing international requirements, in this case the Kyoto emissions trading regime, due to operate from 2008. The Green Paper anticipates the launch of an emissions trading scheme in the Community by the year 2005 for two purposes: to ensure compatibility with Kyoto, and to gain experience ahead of the Kyoto trading regime. The Green Paper is a potentially valuable instrument, even for purposes beyond formal consultation since from this particular document there is an opportunity for public notice of the fact that various member states are actively developing their own trading schemes. Of course, a Green Paper probably acts as a political catalyst so that any final translation of policy into law may well recognise the merit of allowing member states a measure of independence in developing their own regimes. While the Green Paper may well provide an important foundation en route to the creation of law and policy it will point up in this case, implicitly at least, the fact that member states will be constrained in their own schemes by competition and state-aid requirements. A member state may (for example) seek to discount tradable permits as a means of protecting vulnerable businesses. Furthermore, where a member state seeks to base its system of tradable permits on energy efficiency criteria there may well be future problems in the context of developed law and policy from the European Community where more traditional mandatory limits may characterise such a system.

A Commission White Paper on Environmental Liability adopted in February 2000[46] represents the latest attempt to legislate a pan-European regime in this area. That the debate has been running since 1976 and indicates that there are political and other problems in arriving at any coherent policy view on the matter. Although some characteristics have changed little through the consultation processes over the years, there are numerous uncertainties about other elements of the proposal. So, while strict liability seems to be a fixed feature, it is by no means clear what defences should be available to a defendant, what damage threshold should trigger liability, what remediation requirements should apply to environmental damage, and how those strictly liable here might be identified. While these shortcomings in the proposal have been one product of the long-running consultation on the liability proposal, it seems clear also that there are other, considerable objections which are well characterised in the following observation:

> ... the concept of compensating for environmental damage seems too far removed from environmental needs. In short, the environment is sick, rather than suffering from specific, punctual disasters (or accidents). The liability concept, which stems from compensation for bodily injury and was extended to economic loss, and later to damages for pain and suffering, only adapts with difficulty to progressive deterioration, legalised contamination and the disappearance of species.[47]

The on-going consultation here illustrates again the interplay of political and expert opinion. Consultation inviting expert input to a proposal may have the effect of identifying or even confirming political misgivings. For present purposes such misgivings have to be seen against a preference for minimal regulation of liability. This is particularly noticeable in relation to the European Community's Directive on the Deliberate (Environmental) Release of Genetically Modified Organisms.[48] This Directive (90/220) fails to address liability issues where damage occurs through the release of genetically modified organisms, leaving the matter to litigation by reference to common law principles in the United Kingdom. Essentially, as long as there is a lacuna here, damage, loss or injury in member states will depend on the compensation rules which are extant by virtue of their respective legal systems.

The anticipation of a formal, national strategy A national strategy may of course be a creature of the exclusive environmental law and policy of a member state, untouched by that of the European Community. Of course this is increasingly less likely as the initiative for many areas of environmental law and policy shifts away from member states. Nevertheless, it may be the case that, by virtue of the transposition of directives, a member state sees the opportunity to realise its own policy and priorities in relation to Community law even though that law may not yet be in force. Refining a national strategy here will undoubtedly require a good measure of consultation if law and policy are to stand a chance of working effectively in context.

It has been seen already that an increasingly important catalyst for action on environmental law and policy is international initiative on the environment. For example, the global strategy for sustainable development that emerged from the Rio Conference prompted the publication of a consultation paper on a *U.K. Strategy for Sustainable Development*[49] which pointed up the challenges in putting sustainability into practice. Only after a number of revisions and considerable debate did a final strategy emerge: *Sustainable Development: The U.K. Strategy*.[50] The progress from consultation to final strategy showed the extent to which the exercise was necessary, if only to rationalise a number of disparate initiatives that had appeared previously. Part of the strategy relates to waste and waste management. Indeed, the 1993 consultation had recognised that there are many ways to combine economic activity with environmental protection, including improved technology and management, waste minimisation and sound decision-making in land use planning. This strategy has affected the development of policy on waste, best evidenced by the *Waste Strategy for England and Wales 2000*.[51] The strategy has through its evolution been subject to considerable consultation, as ever a process that requires that targets and related matters from the relevant directives are factored into the exercise. Furthermore, consultation will also necessarily have to take note of emerging policy and law. In January 1995 for example, the then Department of the Environment launched a consultation exercise in anticipation of an earlier strategy, taking account of, among other things, the Seventeenth Report of the Royal Commission on Environmental Pollution on the *Incineration of Waste*[52] involving standards and targets which were at that time binding in law or likely to become so.

Even where standards and targets are finally binding by virtue of a directive in force, it is often feasible for a member state to choose, through the regulatory agency responsible, a preferred strategy. Such a preferred strategy, depending on the scope of discretion allowed by the directive, may be put out to consultation, often accompanied by other options. A good example of this approach appears in the consultation paper *Controlling Pollution from Existing Coal- and Oil-fired power Stations*.[53] The strategy set out in the document is heavily dependent on 'FGD' (flue gas desulphurisation), taking account of a preference for greater flexibility in relation to the regulation of sulphur dioxide emissions. The strategy presented for consultation has to be seen against the background of the Directive (88/609)[54] on emission limits of certain pollutants into the atmosphere from large combustion plants. The Environment Agency proposed an allocation of emission limits to generators on a company-wide basis, with variables affecting such limits through incentives in favour of resort to FGD. In turn, any generator looking to increase market share would be permitted to increase company-wide emissions, but only proportionately through commitment to, and investment in, FGD.

Strategies

A good deal has been said already about strategies, in the previous section on consultation. However, it is instructive to see a strategy as an operative instrument, effectively breathing life into a legal framework which should owe its existence to the law as manifested in the relevant directive and the municipal legislation as the vehicle for transposition. A significant example of this process in action is to be found in the *Air Quality Strategy for England, Scotland, Wales and Northern Ireland*.[55]

The strategy describes the plans drawn up by government as well as devolved administrations to improve and protect ambient air quality in the United Kingdom in the medium term. The intention is to protect health and the environment, without imposing unacceptable economic or social costs.

Objectives are set for eight main air pollutants and performance against them will be monitored. There are two new objectives to protect vegetation and ecosystems. Under local air quality management, local authorities will work towards achieving the objectives prescribed for seven of the pollutants, excluding ozone, which is affected by pollutants produced outside the United Kingdom. Equally, local authorities will have no statutory responsibility for the two new objectives affecting vegetation and ecosystems. Some objectives will be achieved through measures such as tighter vehicle emissions while others may require local authorities to act locally in pursuit of the objectives, including local air quality strategies, smoke control and local traffic powers. Land use planning and new local transport plans will also have a direct effect on the improvement of air quality.

The standards informing the foregoing objectives are based on medical and scientific evidence relating to health effects. The inclusion of standards and objectives does not in itself impose obligations on local authorities in respect of the designation of air quality management areas and their duties in relation to designated areas. This occurs only where there are standards and/ or objectives prescribed by regulation under section 87 of the Environment Act 1995.

The Environment Act anticipates that where objectives are unlikely to be met through national action, there should be complementary action at local level. The objectives included in the 1997 strategy were (with the exception of ozone) included in the Air Quality Regulations 1997 as objectives capable of triggering the designation of air quality management areas as well as further assessment of air quality and the preparation of the action plans provided for under sections 83 and 84 of the Act.

Objective-setting for present purposes depends on the likely feasibility and practicability of measures to move towards recommended standards as well as achievement of those standards. Accordingly, it is well recognised (along with some of the relevant directives) that 100 per cent compliance is not feasible. Nevertheless, there is always the possibility that some objectives will exceed the limits prescribed by European Community legislation.

One of the pollutants referred to in the strategy is benzene where the objective is to reduce atmospheric concentrations to as low as is reasonably practicable, such that they represent an exceedingly small risk to human health. Benzene is a well recognised genotoxic human carcinogen, as well as being a volatile organic compound. In the United Kingdom the main atmospheric source is the combustion and distribution of petrol.

Expert Reports and Recommendations

The Commission relies very heavily on expertise from an enormous range of sources such as the European Environment Agency. However, policy development is shaped inexorably by many other such influences. Indeed, many expert contributions to debates about science, economics and the other variables affecting environmental policy will contribute indirectly and even quite subtly to other, related strands of policy development. However, it is clearly a mistake to assume that the only object of this process is the policy formulator at the centre: the Commission in particular. Given the mechanics of policy implementation and enforcement, involving in large part transposition by law in each member state, much expertise is routinely concerned not with the 'front end' of the process but rather with the later part of the process. Accordingly, any illustration of the impact of expertise on the policy process throws up a complex pattern which includes expert dialogue in and out of recognised fora which is referred to next. There is no doubt that in the United Kingdom the deliberations of the Royal Commission on Environmental Pollution are of considerable importance and certainly influential both here and in the Commission. The Commission itself is necessarily involved in commissioning and compiling expert reports along with bodies such as the European Environment Agency whose status and role is examined later in this chapter. For the moment though it is clear that there may be considerable differences in the significance accorded to the product of expert deliberation. For example, the status of Council and Commission recommendations is claimed to be very marginal.[56]

Council and Commission recommendations have no binding force. A number of such recommendations[57] have covered quite a wide field. Nevertheless, it would appear that even if a recommendation graduates beyond a proposal, its force is still marginal, at best. In so far as a recommendation can be legitimately categorised as an expert report for present purposes, its force is compromised, not only because it is a nonbinding instrument but because it may be perceived to be running against the grain of developing policy in particular. Arguably this is the case with the Proposal for a Council Recommendation on *Minimum Criteria for Environmental Inspections in Member States*.[58] The objective of the proposal was the raising of consistency and standards of effectiveness in the implementation and enforcement of environmental law across the Community. The draft Proposal set out criteria for the preparation of inspection plans and for the making public of those plans, the execution of site visits, the arrangements for reporting on inspection visits and publicising those reports, and the content of reports to the Commission. Thereafter the Commission was invited to develop the criteria further. Despite a disappointing response to the Standardised Reporting Directive (91/692[59]) through which implementation reporting to the Commission by member states is required the Commission does not support an administrative structure dedicated to inspections in member states, at least in the area of the environment. Furthermore, an inspectorate operating in member states is clearly inconsistent with the principle of subsidiarity. This and the Standardised Reporting Directive are examined in the following chapter.

Apart from the fact that the law in Article 211 requires the Commission to see that environmental law is applied, it is concerned also to raise and maintain awareness of law and policy on the environment. For this purpose the Commission may consider it necessary to publish appropriate expert reports. Just one example is the report *Towards Environmental Pressure Indicators for the EU*[60] which notes interestingly that the quality of the data behind the report is variable. Nevertheless, the report is of importance, particularly within the expanding area of sustainable development policy. One indicator relates to nitrous oxide emissions. The main purpose of this indicator is to facilitate the monitoring of total anthropogenic emissions. The report provides a reminder that nitrous oxide is a major greenhouse gas, that its radiative force is high and that its global warming potential is 310 bigger than that of carbon dioxide. Emissions are stated to be produced mainly by denitrification processes in anaerobic environments with a high nitrate load, such as soils and sediments in polluted waterbodies. Limited quantities are released also through the use of fossil fuels. Half the anthropogenic emissions arise from agriculture, land-use change and forestry (50 per cent), followed by industrial processes (29 per cent). This Commission report typifies not only the matter of awareness-raising but provides a potentially valuable resource for those member states less well able to address developments in these and similar fields. By contrast, the United Kingdom is representative of several member states with a wide range of resources enabling pressing environmental issues to be addressed both with a view to influencing wider consideration at the centre within the European Community, as well approaches to transposition at national level. An important example of expert influence is the Royal Commission on Environmental Pollution.

The Royal Commission's Report on *Transport and the Environment* was published in 1994[61] and in several important respects seems to have anticipated some important sections of the Environment Act 1995. Among the recommendations was that local authorities should have new duties to assess ambient air quality, sources of air pollution in their areas, and risks of pollutant concentrations exceeding threshold levels to be set by government to enable action to be taken to prevent air quality from deteriorating to a dangerous level. In turn, such authorities should be subject to a duty to implement an air quality management plan if it is considered necessary in order to prevent a breach of the foregoing thresholds. The reduction of carbon dioxide emissions features very significantly in a number of the recommendations. For example, it was recommended that emissions from surface transport be reduced in 2020 to no more than 80 per cent of the 1990 level. Climate change was the topic of the Royal Commission's 22nd report *Energy – The Changing Climate.*[62] Carbon dioxide is again recognised as the principal cause of climate change. Against this background the Royal Commission suggested that the most promising and just basis for any long term agreement on controls is to issue emission rights to nations on a *per capita* basis, enshrining the idea that every human is entitled to release into the atmosphere the same quantities of greenhouse gases. The potential of international emissions trading is recognised, as is the potential of partnerships between industrialised and industrialising nations. The Royal Commission considered that the United Kingdom faces difficulty in seeking to make further, substantial cuts in carbon dioxide emissions after 2010. It is observed that the government's goal of a 20 per cent reduction in carbon dioxide emissions by that date, compared with 1990 levels, is much more ambitious than the United Kingdom's Kyoto legal obligation at 12.5 per cent.

Participatory Devices

Again in this case it is difficult to generalise about the matter of influence on policy development. For present purposes 'participatory devices' refers to parliamentary and governmental institutions (and quasi-governmental institutions), as well as non-governmental organisations which facilitate public participation, not all of which is necessarily characterised as 'expert'. There is a clear overlap with the previous concern with expert reports and recommendations. Accordingly, the reference to the deliberations of the Royal Commission on Environmental Pollution could equally well appear here. A perhaps tenuous distinction is drawn by reference to the concern for dialogue as a policy priority in favour of participation on a wider scale than that which may be seen to apply to the foregoing 'expert' deliberations. Such preferences in favour of wider participation are best characterised by the 5th Environmental

Action Plan[63] which gave rise to two bodies, the Implementation Network on EU Environmental Policy (IMPEL) and an Environmental Policy Review Group. At about the same time the Commission created the European Consultative Forum on the Environment and Sustainable Development.[64] Additionally, at member state level parliamentary institutions can be seen to foster wider participation despite the fact they will often attract the specialised expertise referred to previously. In the United Kingdom it is possible to point to a number of relevant parliamentary institutions, such as the House of Commons Environment, Transport and Regional Affairs Committee and the House of Lords Select Committee on the European Communities, both of whom have contributed significantly to policy development and, at the other end of the axis, policy transposition at member state level.

IMPEL seeks to facilitate exchanges of information and experience on an intergovernmental basis in connection with matters of implementation. As such, this informal grouping created by the Commission has the opportunity to influence its approaches to policy creation and implementation. The Environmental Policy Review Group on the other hand is another informal forum where senior Commission officials meet with equally senior officials from the relevant ministries in the member states. The Consultative Forum is made up of a widely-defined constituency which includes representatives of local and regional authorities, environmental organisations, trade unions, and so on, and whose essential task is to act as a consultee to the Commission.

The parliamentary committees in the United Kingdom just referred to are responsible for the publication of some often influential reports on policy implementation and enforcement. However, it is perhaps important at this point to stress the very considerable influence at the centre, of the Environmental Committee of the European Parliament whose tasks are more widely defined than those of the parliamentary committees, examples of whose work is now described.[65] Among the more significant questions raised by these committees in the recent past is whether draft directives are sufficiently robust and lacking in ambiguity, whether sustainable development objectives are capable of effective implementation and enforcement, and whether subsidiarity is sufficiently exploited through effective penalties and incentives according to the form of transposition chosen. There seems little doubt that one of the more important functions of such committees is the scrutiny of draft European legislation from the centre. For example, the House of Lords Select Committee on the European Communities reported on *Community Water Policy* in 1997.[66] In its report the Committee looked at the proposed rationalisation of Community water policy through the need for all waters to be brought up to or maintained at what was described as 'good status'. The Committee was critical of the ambiguity of this term. Elsewhere in its report the Committee called for full cost recovery for the provision of water services as well as the need to ensure full consistency between the respective directives. Arguably, one of the more important functions of parliamentary committees increasingly is to point out the priorities and practicalities arising from the well-recognised need to move beyond traditional 'command and control' regulatory techniques into market-based and similar approaches, particularly in aid of sustainable development priorities. Parliamentary committees have not been slow to point out inadequacies in legislative proposals. For example, the same House of Lords Select Committee reported on *Sustainable Landfill* in 1997[67] and suggested that the (then) draft Landfill Directive contained no truly sustainable, internalised costs in the minimum amount to be charged to landfill operators. The Select Committee's criticism stressed the absence from the draft of a recognition of the full cost of the environmental externalities arising from landfill operations.

International Treaties and Conventions

The need for international conventions and treaties is justified by various requirements, not least of which may be the global proportions of particular environmental problems. On occasions the environmental dimension of a treaty or convention may be confused by trade priorities. Whatever the emphasis of this variety of lawmaking there is little doubt that member states and the European Community have often been actively involved in the development of treaties and conventions, such as Kyoto, which has been referred to previously. To that extent their influence is clear where policy development, implementation and enforcement are concerned. Even if the criticism of treaties and conventions were sustainable, that they are less than effective than possible because of policy fragmentation, institutional coherence and weakness in implementation,[68] the existence of an entity like the European Community may provide for such deficiencies, at least where there is a political will to develop and realise policy in the area concerned. Furthermore, where the Community is a party to a convention or treaty there will be a strong presumption in favour of supporting legislation enabling implementation and enforcement in member states, as indeed occurred where the Vienna Convention on the Protection of the Ozone Layer was followed by legislation of a Regulation (3322/88[69]) which effectively enabled member states themselves to ratify the Montreal Protocol.[70] Finally, where a treaty or convention is effectively influencing the development of European Community policy, passage to implementation and enforcement is essentially a three stage process from the entry into force of the international instrument to transposition in the member state. Assuming that transposition is via a directive, allowing cultural and other variables to influence implementation and enforcement, there is of course a danger that the treaty or convention may 'lose something in translation', as it were. Accordingly the Community may view the directive as something of a luxury, seeing a directly applicable regulation as the only vehicle available which will allow the 'hard edges' of the international instrument to be implemented with minimal danger of compromise through transposition.

Policy Guidance

In large part it seems clear that policy guidance is essentially a member state function. As such it is a function that operates in two main areas. In the first place, a member state may within the flexibility allowed in the transposition of a directive proceed on the basis of implementation through discretion. Policy guidance here is quite legitimate as long as it remains within the *vires* of the Community legislation. Secondly, policy guidance may be essential in the eyes of the member state where there is a need for coexistence between an area of municipal law and Community law. The first area just described may involve either overt or what may be termed 'discreet' policy although the latter is undoubtedly exceptional in contemporary government in the United Kingdom. The environmental strategy is an important example of the overt policy just referred to: notable examples are the waste and air quality strategies addressed previously in the chapter.[71] The second area admits of many examples although one of the more significant is the Planning Policy Guidance on Planning and Pollution Control.[72] The evolution of policy guidance here is characterised not so much by the boldly defined limits of European Community law as by the need to draw a distinct line between planning and pollution control powers. En route to final effect, the Department of the Environment commissioned research[73] and the Policy Guidance appeared in draft form for the purpose of consultation. The consultative exercise demonstrated the increasing scope and effectiveness of regulatory control of pollution in reducing the need for reliance on planning conditions and obligations. Altogether, the Policy Guidance here provides an opportunity to put down markers showing the territory within which Community law and policy is open to legitimate implementation and enforcement. Nevertheless, in an area like waste management there remain areas where there is congruence, demanding careful navigation between requirements according to whether their source is Community law or municipal law.

Environmental Policy Integration

Much of the present chapter has been preoccupied with the policy creation process which is characterised by initiative from the centre of the Community and movement downwards through the governmental hierarchy. From time to time that process has been reinforced by references to so-called 'top-down' processes although in recent times, greater interest has been shown in so-called 'bottom-up' processes. On the other hand, there appears to be little evidence of horizontal pressures spreading environmental policy through other areas of competence within the European Community. Such pressures have been very largely absent even though it was the 3rd Environmental Action Programme in 1983 that first recognised the potential significance of environmental policy integration. The position is described very succinctly by the Environmental Audit Committee of the House of Commons in its Report on *EU Policy and the Environment: An Agenda for the Helsinki Summit*:[74]

> Policy making throughout the EU tends to be sectoral and vertical rather than horizontal. It is important therefore that the process of integration also involves the Commission developing systems to produce more integrated policy proposals for the Council and Parliament to consider. The Commission has already committed itself to a number of measures intended to ensure a better integration of environmental considerations into its policy making and management.[75]

To date there is little doubt that horizontal policy initiatives have had little impact. This was particularly evident from a review of the 5th Environmental Action Programme.[76] This progress report examined the state of play in five target sectors, including agriculture,[77] by reference to six elements that make up the approach to sustainable development, including (for present purposes) the integration of environmental considerations into other policy areas. The conclusion was that such integration had made progress, but at varying speeds. That integration was observed to be generally most advanced in the manufacturing sector but least apparent in agriculture and tourism. The case of agriculture is addressed below, before attention turns back to the review of the 5th Action Programme.

The Case of Agriculture

The two Directorates of the European Commission dealing with agriculture (XVI) and the environment (XI) provide a vivid illustration of the continuing barriers to environmental policy integration. Despite a number of agri-environmental policy initiatives in recent years, many of which have given rise to important law for implementation in member states, environmental policy integration gives the appearance of being, at best, marginal.[78] Although there have been high-profile initiatives since 1992 extending from the so-called accompanying agri-environmental measures to the more recent Rural Development Regulation, such initiatives have to be put into perspective. That perspective is dominated by structures in the agricultural market overseen by the largest and probably most influential Directorate-General, D-G XVI.

Further Reflections on Policy Integration

The Commission's review of the 5th Action Programme stresses that traditional policy promotion of improved technology as well as stricter regulatory control is insufficient for the purpose of reversing the adverse impact of social and economic development. It is against such a background that environmental policy is seen as being complementary and contributory to sustainability for the purpose of starting to reverse that adverse impact. Clearly though, as was recognised by the Cardiff Council, integration of policy necessitates considerable political leadership as well as the appropriate political will. Accordingly, one of the crucial products of that Cardiff Council meeting was the apparent will to embrace sectoral integration strategies. However, initiative from members states may serve to force progress here. The United Kingdom government for example has produced its own policy guide here: *Policy Appraisal and the Environment.*[79]

Articles 2 and 6 of the Treaty of Amsterdam is a fundamentally important structural reform to the extent that there is now formal legal provision in favour of a integration of environmental matters into all European Community policy as well as a positive signal to member states that sustainable development should drive initiatives in relation to environmental law and policy. Where policy is under scrutiny therefore, environmental well-being and enhancement are intended to be focal points as well as social and economic development priorities. Again, initiative from member states is probably crucial in this context. The Local Government Act 2000 is a recent piece of legislation which obliges English local authorities, for example, to address environmental well-being in the discharge of their functions.

Nevertheless, a negative element in any attempt by the European Community to develop strategies for policy integration is the fact that it has little, if any, control over many of those activities that provide the adverse impacts referred to previously. A clear example is the remaining jurisdiction of member states over planning and development control, despite Community legislation on environment impact assessment. For the moment it appears that the Commission in particular may address those adverse impacts on an *ad hoc* basis. That approach is illustrated by the agreement negotiated between European car manufacturers and the Commission in the context of what appears to have been a veiled threat to reduce carbon dioxide emission levels for motor vehicles. However, addressing those adverse impacts may be an equally important function of member states, albeit against a background of legal and other targets set at the centre in the Community.

As an example of member state initiative here the United Kingdom government has sought to drive an important element of its measures in relation to the Climate Change levy by encouraging agreements for emissions reductions between it and different industries. In return those industries and their constituent companies should qualify for a rebate in respect of the levy. Furthermore, the government seeks to encourage industries and their constituent companies to opt for more stringent regulatory control under the Integration Pollution Prevention and Control (IPPC) regime, in return for rebates in respect of the levy of up to 80 per cent. These are not the only examples of voluntary agreements: in 1996 the government concluded agreements with certain industries and their constituent companies when it was realised that alternatives to CFCs were damaging to the ozone layer. Those alternatives – HFCs (hydroflourocarbons) – are greenhouse gases and it was agreed with the subject industries that they should not be used if there are practicable alternatives.[80]

Enough has been seen here to stress the fundamental limitations of environmental policy integration. The critical limitations are those which arise from underdevelopment of what is often seen to be a political will in favour of horizontal policy engagement, as well as the absence of control by the centre of those member state functions and activities which need to be harnessed for the purposes of effective integration. Although these are characterised as critical limitations, the underlying limitations of information management affecting the environment also need to be appreciated. This limitation and how it might be addressed are the subject of the next section.

Information Management

In the absence of effective information management within the European Community there is little chance that accurate, timely data will be available for all sorts of purposes, including environmental policy integration. 'Information management' seems to require a suitably wide definition here. For example, it is not unreasonable to assume that access to information should be a fundamental part of the equation. Efficiency of access in this context is equated with transparency, which is clearly a policy priority in what was seen earlier in the chapter where public participation emerges as an important element of the 5th Environmental Action Plan. Transparency though is probably one of the more significant badges of progress arising from accession to membership of the European Community, at least in the case of the United Kingdom and no doubt in other member states also. In terms of the implementation and enforcement of environmental law and policy the United Kingdom has progressed from a largely closed, discretionary style often dependent on voluntary compliance, to a regime based on rather more objective criteria centred on directives whose objectives often provide a clearer benchmark against which to measure implementation and enforcement. The culture of greater transparency at the centre is seen also in Article 255 (introduced by the Treaty of Amsterdam) which defines rights of access to documents generated by the Parliament, the Council and the Commission. Indeed, many of these institutions will be subject to explicit rights of access when the United Nations Convention on Access to Information, Public Participation and Access to Justice in Environmental Matters – the so-called Aarhus Convention of 1998 – comes into effect. This will represent a considerable shift in the law of the European Community. Nevertheless it is possible to detect incremental increases in transparency from initiatives within the Community in recent years. Some of the more significant developments are set out below in approximate chronological order.

The 'Corine' Decision

This Decision[81] gave rise to an experimental programme. That programme was aimed at assembling basic information on the environment in certain specific areas following the 3rd Environmental Action Programme. This important network is now subsumed and expanded within the functions and responsibilities of the European Environment Agency.

The European Environment Agency

The essential function of the Agency is to provide the European Union and member states with information on the environment which is suitably standardised and comparative, otherwise referred to as 'best available information' (BAI). The essential goal of the Agency is to provide such information for policy development and implementation. The Agency was established under Regulation 1210/90.[82] An interesting limitation under that Regulation is that the Agency's jurisdiction extends to Community environmental policy but not the law and policy of member states and international agencies. In undertaking its functions, the Agency depends largely on the so-called EIONET: the European Information and Observation Network operative in the member states. The founding Regulation was amended in 1999 and the effect is to clarify the Agency's function in monitoring environmental law and policy implementation in member states. In turn, the extension of European Community objectives to include the achievement of 'balanced and sustainable development' as a result of Article 2 of the Treaty on European Union means a yet wider function for the Agency.

The Regulation goes on to stipulate that the Agency has corporate personality giving it the power to sue and be sued. The possibility arises therefore that the Agency might be vulnerable to litigation in respect of adverse consequences arising from the function of collecting and processing relevant environmental data. Whether this has a constraining effect on Agency reporting is difficult to say. Nevertheless, there may be the possibility that a too prescriptive interpretation of a matter such as causation in relation to the impact of an environmental pollutant may generate the sort of reliance which gives rise to loss, damage or injury that could render the Agency vulnerable in litigation. Whether the court would be willing to proceed where the data in question is then used for a legislative purpose within the Community must be doubtful.

The exposure of the Agency to liability in law is not however an issue of any immediate consequence. What is of immediate consequence is what has been described by the House of Commons Audit Committee in its report on *EU Policy and the Environment* (quoting from a conference on the subject[83]) as a monitoring system which is inefficient and wasteful.[84] Furthermore, this system is seen to generate excessive amounts of data on subjects which do not need it, and failing to provide timely and relevant information where there is an urgent policy need. At the time of its report, the House of Commons Audit Committee noted that two measures were being addressed for the purpose of dealing with inefficient and wasteful monitoring systems.

The two measures just referred to are described as the development of new sector reporting mechanisms the first of which is for transport with areas such as agriculture to follow, and analyses by the Agency of the returns from the so-called 'reporting Directives' requiring member states to report environmental data to the Commission. The latter measure will be returned to later. More immediately this review of the development of information management turns to a Directive on access to environmental information.

Directive 90/313 on Freedom of Access to Environmental Information[85]

This Directive deals with freedom of access to information on the environment. At the time of writing the Directive is under review following the signing by the European Community (and the United Kingdom) of the Aarhus Convention referred to previously. It is clear that the Directive is ripe for amendment, on two fronts. In the first place, the Aarhus Convention anticipates quite radical developments in environmental information management. Secondly, the Community appears to have recognised the limitations of the law here during the decade of its existence.

The Aarhus Convention, apart from subjecting the institutions of the European Community to access requirements, appears to give rise to important opportunities in environmental enforcement in facilitating challenges to the substance of decisions, and realising the objective of 'fair, equitable, timely and not prohibitively expensive' access to justice. Furthermore, the Convention refers to a rather more expansive 'right' to information which contrasts with the rather more modest 'freedom' of information.

Some of the thinking behind the Aarhus Convention appears to find its way into European Community proposals for modification of Directive 90/313, the 'right' to information in particular. Otherwise, the intention is that any amending directive will extend to include public utilities, for example. In turn, decisions on applications for information access will be subject to a public interest test which will no doubt make it more difficult to deny access. Strategic matters represented by policies, plans and programmes are likely to be included in a new directive as are provisions to permit member states to take a more pro-active position in facilitating access to environmental information. Where the United Kingdom is concerned, the Freedom of Information Act 2000 omits any new substantive provision on access to environmental information except an enabling power to make regulations, in anticipation of the foregoing proposal by the Community to legislate a new directive. For the moment, the existing regime under Directive 90/313 serves to illustrate how broadly drafted and (arguably) ill-considered legislation from the centre can allow member states considerable extra freedom in implementation and enforcement. Indeed, the uncertainties in the Directive on matters such as discretionary access are reflected in the government's guidance[86] on the application of the Environmental Information Regulations 1992[87] which seek to implement the Directive in Great Britain.

Directive 91/692: the Standardised Reporting Directive[88]

Reference was made previously to the Standardised Reporting Directive in the discussion on the European Environment Agency. Reference to other aspects of the operation of the Directive will be made in the following chapter. The essence of the Directive is the harmonisation and improvement of the reporting obligations which arise from certain directives on the environment. Those obligations occur at three-yearly intervals although there are directives affecting surface and drinking water quality and air quality which feature an annual reporting obligation. The efficiency of enforcement of this rationalisation of reporting obligations will be taken up again in Chapter Two. In the meantime it seems clear that the number of directives subject to the reporting obligations of this Directive will reduce over time as streamlined reporting requirements find their place in newer directives affecting the environment.

The Monitoring of Carbon Dioxide and Other Greenhouse Gas Emissions

Decision 93/389[89] gives the Commission the task of monitoring carbon dioxide and other greenhouse gases emissions in member states. On the basis of data collected the Commission reports on the incidence of these gases and their emission to the atmosphere. This measure has to be seen in the broader context addressed previously whereby member states are bound by programmes for the reduction of carbon dioxide and greenhouse gas emissions by reference to the targets set by the European Community and Kyoto. Where information of the sort in issue here is reported to the Commission and the competent authority in a member state there is no certainty, for the moment at least, that that information will be in the public domain. A significant example of the confidentiality of information in favour of producers and others providing the required data is Regulation 3093/94[90] governing substances that deplete the ozone layer.

Environmental Statistics

Decision 94/808[91] provided for a four year development plan between 1994 and 1997 in relation to the environmental components of statistics generated in the European Community. The development plan owes its origins to the 5th Environmental Action Programme and the perceived need for a distinct environmental 'edge' to economic and social statistics.

Information Exchange and Availability

The Directive on Integrated Pollution Prevention and Control[92] facilitates information exchange between member states on 'best available techniques' assessments and emission limits. This facility is primarily a reflection of the variables affecting authorisations in member states. Transparency is an important characteristic of this Directive: decisions and authorisations must be in the public domain, unless protected from disclosure by the terms of Directive 90/313. A further example of transparency is to be found in the Framework Directive on Ambient Air Quality Assessment and management: Directive 96/62.[93] In this case the public must be advised on any occasion where the so-called 'alert thresholds' are exceeded.

The Mechanics of Implementation

This final section of the chapter deals with six interrelated issues: development of European Community competence in relation to the environment; modes of implementation; constraints on implementation; implementation in the United Kingdom; directives and discretion in implementation; and (finally) so-called 'marginal' implementation in the United Kingdom.

Community Competence

Up to the early 1980s there was no clearly explicit constitutional competence in relation to the environment where the European Community was concerned although environmental competence was clearly boosted by the creation of D-G XI in 1981. Nevertheless, in the previous decade the Commission had pointed to Article 308 as a vehicle for dealing with environmental problems. Indeed, this Article and Article 94 became the formal legal and constitutional vehicles for the limited number of initiatives on the environment occurring in the 1970s. Throughout the European Court of Justice has been influential in shaping some of the important limits to Community jurisdiction here. Article 308 (formerly Article 235) confers general powers to act to further the objectives of the Treaty where no other specific power exists. Thereafter the Single European Act of 1987 provided far more constitutional formality than hitherto where matters of environmental competence were concerned. From that reform the potential for environmental policy integration was realised through what is now Article 174. In this respect the Article provides that '… environmental protection requirements shall be a component of the Community's other policies'. The Single European Act also provided that a '… high level of protection' be realised in what is now Article 95. The same Article clarifies member states' competence in seeking to apply more stringent standards than those operating in other member states, subject to safeguards in relation to trade. Article 174 goes on to require action on the environment where relevant objectives '… can be attained better at Community level than at the level of the individual member states': this requirement is now further developed by the Maastricht Treaty. The cooperation procedure provided for in Article 175 has been dealt with earlier in this chapter. All of this though is supported on the twin foundations of European Community law and policy on the environment through what may be described as the 'implementation base' and 'policy objectives and principles'.

The implementation base This first foundation is created from the Treaty requirements that legislation is implemented in member states through the terms of Articles 174 and 175 as well as the Article 6 requirement that environmental protection be integrated into other policies. The second foundation leads on from the first and is seen in Article 2 which demands achievement of a balanced and sustainable development of economic activity.

Policy objectives and principles Article 174 stipulates that Community environmental action is governed by four objectives: (1) preservation, protection and improvement of the quality of the environment; (2) protection of human health; (3) prudent and rational utilisation of natural resources; and (4) the promotion of measures at international level to deal with regional or worldwide environmental problems. The first of these objectives appears to extend to cover past, present as well as future environmental damage. Such damage may often be characterised as physical damage although the second objective clearly widens the target for action. The third objective appears to suggest that sustainable development is at least an implicit objective. The fourth objective is reflection of the need to base action on international measures such as international conventions, as seen earlier in this chapter.

These objectives have to be read in conjunction with four principles: (1) the precautionary principle; (2) the need for preventative action; (3) the priority for environmental damage to be remedied at source: the so-called 'proximity' principle; and (4) the 'polluter pays' principle. These principles will be examined in rather greater depth in Chapter Three.

These objectives and principles are accompanied by other elements to be taken into account in environmental policy preparation and (presumably) the development of any resulting legislation, prescribed by Article 174. Some of these have been encountered already. These elements are as follows: (1) available scientific and technical data; (2) prevailing environmental conditions in the regions of the European Union; (3) cost-benefit analysis as a prerequisite to action on the environment; and (4) economic and social development as well as the balanced development of the regions. The first of these elements is nebulous in failing to prescribe threshold data standards, for example. The second recognises the variables affecting conditions in the regions, arguably necessitating different regulatory approaches, for example. The cost-benefit basis of the third element appears to give implicit recognition to the principle of proportionality, itself a central element of Article 5 of the EC Treaty. Finally, the recognition of economic and social development and of the need for balanced regional development necessitates a variable approach if it is perceived (say) that regulatory requirements will stifle economic development. Indeed, Article 175 empowers the Council to provide derogations or even financial assistance where it is the case that implementation in a member state would attract disproportionate financial burdens.

Modes of Implementation

Given that the directive is the principal legislative vehicle where Community environmental law and policy is concerned it is by no means easy to generalise about the mode of implementation across member states. In crude terms it can be asserted that as long as a member state achieves the objectives set by a directive there is effective, complete transposition. Unfortunately there are a host of variables at work which make reliable judgements by the Commission for these purposes extremely problematic. Some of those variables have been seen earlier in this chapter. A particular difficulty is the availability of reliable, objective data and other information, a matter of great moment if the developments mapped in the remainder of this section of the chapter are to be realised effectively. Even if such data and information are available, judgements about effective transposition will be rendered virtually impossible where the directive itself is replete with ambiguities and uncertainties. This is graphically illustrated in Directive 90/313 on freedom of access to environmental information which was dealt with earlier.[94]

'Measuring' transposition Hitherto transposition has been characterised in large part through regulatory measures. Accordingly, the starting point in any quest to determine whether there has been effective and, by definition, lawful transposition is whether institutional and instrumental measures are consistent with the Commission's view of the relevant objectives. Of course, the Commission's view cannot ultimately override or be superior to the court's view of the transposition process in any individual case. This thumbnail sketch does not reveal the relative difficulty in 'measuring' transposition in the case of traditional regulatory measures although information failures referred to previously provide some inkling of the limitations of the process. Chapter Six will deal with the emerging challenges associated with so-called 'economic instruments'. Such instruments represent a rather different approach to the implementation and enforcement of environmental policy. Rather than being a 'top-down' process like the regulatory model of implementation and enforcement, economic instruments tend to be characterised as bringing a 'bottom-up' approach to such matters.

Economic instruments Economic instruments appear to enjoy several advantages over the traditional regulatory model, not least of which is the ability of such instruments to provide very much more flexibility. That flexibility is characterised through close identification with the market variables affecting those whose activities are (or may be) prejudicial to the environment. A good example of the apparent dichotomy between traditional regulatory control and the deployment of economic instruments is seen in relation to the legal control of volatile organic compounds and their associated solvents.[95] The practical difficulty of enforcing regulatory control over sometimes quite small businesses in the printing industry (for example) suggests in turn, a regulatory threshold below which the aggregated emissions may be seen to be a considerable proportion of total emissions. It is here, below that threshold, that market-based approaches might be capable exerting control of total emissions. Increasingly there are different methods of realising such market-based economic instruments: in the present case there is for example the opportunity to deploy tax incentives in favour of the use of water-based products in the printing industry. Where such tax incentives are in use it is possible to see another advantage of the economic instrument whose terms and impact can be adjusted quite quickly and sensitively to address emerging problems and priorities.

All of the foregoing reflections on economic instruments suggest that matters of definition for the purpose of effective implementation represent a considerable challenge. As will be seen later in Chapter Six, this is an area of Community law and policy that will unfold in the next decade or two particularly by reference to policies on sustainable development, begging a myriad of questions about matters such as subsidiarity and the extent to which member states should be permitted to determine the shape and local impact of such instruments. For the moment though economic instruments are seen as complementary to traditional regulatory control of the environment. However, it is a mistake to see developments beyond such regulatory control only in terms of economic instruments, important though they are. Reference has been made, earlier in the chapter, to environmental management schemes.[96] The law on the subject of such schemes as well as the emerging law on pollution prevention and control[97] shows that the 'bottom-up' approach just referred to extends rather more widely than economic instruments alone. Pollution prevention and control for example, is concerned with 'installations', stressing again an important opportunity to tailor controls which are referable to the individual plant. It is here that the complementary nature of environmental management systems becomes clear, even though at the time of writing the take-up of such schemes in the United Kingdom and elsewhere is slow.

Environmental management schemes EMAS and similar schemes undoubtedly force companies and others whose activities pollute or have the potential to pollute the environment (*inter alia*) to confront and manage liability issues which are the product of laws affecting the environment. Like economic instruments however, environmental management schemes are in an early state of evolution. While economic instruments are likely to evolve into a very significant vehicle for the transposition of Community environmental law and policy, what is the future significance of the environmental management scheme adopted by the typically regulated industrial company? Is that future significance tied to formal requirements for lawful transposition in member states such as the United Kingdom?

These two questions seem to invite two answers. On the one hand there may be a future trend in favour of an increasingly clearer regime of subsidiarity where member states may be encouraged to regard environmental management schemes as a prime opportunity to streamline regulatory control where there is satisfaction about the robustness of a company's processes for environmental and pollution management. According to existing assumptions, Commission enforcement by reference to this model becomes rather more difficult unless reporting by member states becomes that much more reliable. Transposition as a result will tend to become a rather less well-defined process compared with the relatively well-defined hard edges of existing and recent regulatory regimes affecting environmental control.

A second answer is that, already, there is evidence of an evolution towards a less dogmatic enforcement of regulatory regimes. Drawing on experience from the Netherlands, the Organisation for Economic Cooperation and Development has pointed to a four-phased development of a rather more streamlined regulatory process where environmental management schemes have allowed significant 'bottom-up' responsibility to be devolved to industrial companies.[98] The first phase was characterised by inadequate compliance with environmental law where the regulatory agency relied heavily on command and control techniques where the company in question regarded such techniques as a commercial burden. The second phase saw corporate compliance as the company's primary environmental objective with some organisational measures introduced for this purpose. Compliance was now acceptable and bearable with lighter regulatory controls placing greater stress on the company's development of its own management systems. The third phase saw compliance developed to the point of being a matter of course with corporate ethos and procedures closely attuned, against a background of well-developed management systems where the regulatory agency operates largely by reference to information generated by the company, as well as sampling. The final phase sees assurance of compliance through the company's adoption of a certified environmental management system where the company regards good environmental performance as being self-motivated and an integral corporate objective with the regulatory agency tailoring what is essentially self-regulatory compliance to the management system though a process of mutual trust.[99]

Constraints on Implementation

It is at least arguable that the foregoing possibilities in relation to 'bottom-up' approaches are motivated by the realisation at the centre of the Community that effective and enforceable implementation is not possible without addressing a number of shortcomings such as the lack of reliable data and information across member states, and the incidence of badly drafted legislation. Such shortcomings are compounded by the increased complexity of transposition as a result of devolution in the United Kingdom and elsewhere. References previously to transposition of regulatory control regimes indicated difficulties in 'measuring' lawful transposition in member states despite the tendency for there to be crystallised limit values (for example) which in turn represent a disincentive to any continuous tightening of targets, subject to what is said below about so-called 'guide values' in directives. Indeed, target dates for transposition and derogations emerging from negotiated compromise may be so generous that statutory requirements may have reduced impact. The need for radical reform is of course compounded by the further emerging developments outlined in the previous section of this chapter.

Implementation in the United Kingdom

The position in the United Kingdom has been touched on from time to time earlier in the chapter. However, it is necessary to look at some of the variables affecting the development of Community environmental law and policy as it has been received through transposition, particularly in relation to waste management. At the outset there is no doubt that in the present context, accession to membership of the European Community facilitated the development of a very different regime of environmental law to that which existed previously. There were very few obviously transparent standards in the law, serving to emphasise the extent of governmental discretion where matters of implementation and enforcement were concerned. Indeed, the constituent administrative agencies – local authorities in particular – shared this discretionary and decentralised freedom, often with the consequence that uniformity of enforcement was lacking. This body of law and policy was developed, implemented and enforced largely within a rather parochial vacuum without much reference to international standard-setting or other external pressure to tighten those standards and limits (which were usually referable to pollution sources) or indeed without much reference to defining objectives.

Against this background it is perhaps surprising to find that the Control of Pollution Act 1974 was legislated, Part I of which addressed the need for a far more coherent statutory regime in relation to waste management. In turn, this legislation may have been influential in shaping the European Community's own legislative programme in the same area subsequently, as represented by the Framework Directive on Waste: 75/442.[100]

Part I of the Control of Pollution Act was eventually superseded by Part II of the Environmental Protection Act 1990 and illustrates very well what may be described, from the foregoing picture of the pre-accession position, as something akin to a cultural change of approach in the United Kingdom. Interestingly there were claims from the government that Part II of the Act anticipated the amending Directive 91/156.[101] The accompanying Waste Management Licensing Regulations 1994[102] represent a really very detailed and elaborate transposition of the technical requirements flowing from the amending Directive. The essential background to Part II of the Act shows the extent of the cultural change mentioned above. A duty of care is now enforceable against waste producers and others who are legal accountable for subject waste from cradle to grave. Waste transporters are subject to registration. Regulatory and operational functions are separated, the net effect being that (with the Environment Agency as the waste regulatory authority) local authorities are considerably marginalised, although they maintain a function as waste collection authorities and may operate waste treatment facilities. Waste policies and strategies as described previously are a good deal more coherent and transparent and clearly referable to the standards generated from the centre of the European Community. This most significant example of implementation tends to reinforce the view expressed by the Royal Commission on Environmental Pollution in its 21st Report, that the adoption and implementation of policies based on particular values have a powerful effect in reinforcing those values, as well as bringing about their practical realisation.[103]

International obligations may be adopted which again demand implementation although increasingly this is a function of the Community on behalf of member states. The United Kingdom Management Plan for Exports and Imports of Waste is a notable example here, taking account as it does of obligations arising under the Basel Convention on the Control of Transboundary Movements of Hazardous Wastes and their Disposal. The Plan is legally binding and seeks to implement government policy on self-sufficiency in waste disposal from the date of operation: 1 June 1996. While preserving legitimate trade in wastes moving for recovery, the Plan contains guidance to combat 'sham' recovery. The main policies include a ban on all exports for disposal, to allow exports for recovery to OECD countries, and to some non-OECD countries in limited circumstances consistent with obligations under the Basel Convention, and to ban most imports for disposal.

Directives and Discretion in Implementation

As the principal vehicle for the environmental law of the Community directives have (for example) often set limit values and guide values. These guide values are values to which a member may aspire beyond its strict legal obligation to achieve the prescribed limit values. For the moment it is possible to generalise by characterising limit values as the essential objective of compliance in any member state when the directive is in force and assuming that no derogations apply. Fundamentally, it a matter for the discretion of the member state as to how that objective is achieved although the prescriptive detail of a directive may narrow or broaden that perceived implementation discretion. The Waste Strategy 2000 for England and Wales[104] is a good example of discretionary implementation where (for example) it is shown that tradable permits will be used as a means of dealing with landfilling while at the same time contributing to sustainable development strategies. These latter strategies[105] fill a considerable vacuum, as long as the Community does not itself have very prescriptive policies and priorities beyond the Treaty recognition of sustainable development as a priority, a matter addressed previously in this chapter. Member state discretion and freedom of action in meeting directive objectives will therefore be determined by the terms of the directive. Additionally, that freedom of action may be widened further in the relevant municipal legislation. The Pollution Prevention and Control Act 1999 is a statute in point here, providing as it does an enabling framework for the government to use subordinate legislation as a means of implementation, a matter that draws the criticism that such an approach renders government lawmaking less accountable than it should be if primary legislation were the main substantive framework for implementation.

Marginal Implementation

In a small number of cases it can be said that the law of the European Community has had only a marginal influence on municipal law in the United Kingdom. A prime example is Directive 79/409[106] – the Birds Directive – which came into force as the government was actively considering incorporation of international conventions into municipal law for the purpose of enhancing provision in relation to habitats and the wider countryside. The seminal legislation here – the Wildlife and Countryside Act 1981 – came into force very shortly after member states were obliged to implement the Birds Directive. Despite the transposition of the directive requirements in terms just as elaborate as those that found their way into the Waste Management Licensing Regulations 1994 from Directive 91/156 just referred to, pre-existing statutory provision and attitudes to that provision may justify the label of 'marginal' implementation. However, pre-existing provision based on a particular culture can lead to accusations of failure lawfully to effect transposition according to law. With the benefit of hindsight that conclusion may be justified, particularly by reference to previous heavy reliance on voluntary management agreements as the principal measure to secure nature conservation. Furthermore, the protection of species in Part I of the Act did not mention the matter of derogations, a clear requirement of the Birds Directive: only 14 years later was the Act amended to secure compliance. The Birds Directive was followed by Directive 92/43[107] – the Habitats Directive – where, again there were problems in implementation. Among several problems arising from marginal implementation was the alleged failure to address the need for an adequate environmental assessment (indicating possible alternative solutions) where a drought order is sought by a water company under the Water Industry Act 1991.

Notes

1   OJ C485, 18.3.92.
2   Franklin, D., Hawke, N. and Lowe, M. (1995), *Pollution in the UK*, Sweet and Maxwell, London, pp. 167–9.
3   Reg. 1836/93: OJ L168, 10.7.93.
4   Morphet, J. (1998), 'Local Authorities', in P. Lowe and S. Ward (eds), *British Environmental Policy and Europe*, Routledge, London, p. 150.
5   OJ C328, 19.10.87.
6   Hawke, N. and Kovaleva, N. (1998), *Agri-Environmental Law and Policy*, Cavendish Publishing, London, pp. 2–4.
7   OJ C46, 17.2.83.
8   Cm 4053 (1998), The Stationery Office, London, para. 2.73.
9   *Ibid.*, para. 3.46.
10   See, for example, the general environmental and recreational duties arising from section 7 of the Environment Act.
11   Environment Agency (1996), *Taking Account of Costs and Benefits*, Sustainable Development Publication DS3, paras 4.4 and 5.1–5.2.
12   Article 174(3).
13   OJ L135, 30.5.91.
14   Articles 192(2) and 175(3) EC.
15   Article 175 E.C.
16   *Ibid.*
17   OJ L176, 6.7.85.

18 OJ L365, 31.12.94.
19 *Commission v. Denmark* [1988] ECR 4607.
20 OJ L333, 22.12.94.
21 OJ L296, 21.11.96.
22 OJ L257, 10.10.96.
23 OJ L365, 31.12.94.
24 OJ L85, 29.3.99.
25 OJ C255, 13.10.86.
26 COM (88) 656.
27 Decision 94/69: OJ L33, 7.2.94.
28 COM (92) 246.
29 OJ L167, 9.7.93.
30 OJ L117, 5.5.99.
31 COM (92) 226.
32 8th Report (Session 1991–92), para. 97.
33 *Supra*, n. 3.
34 OJ L182, 16.7.99.
35 Department of the Environment, October 2000.
36 *Supra*, n. 22.
37 Department of the Environment, June 1998.
38 Department of the Environment, July 1998.
39 OJ L281, 10.11.79.
40 *Supra*, n. 13.
41 OJ L365, 31.12.94.
42 Department of the Environment, July 1998.
43 Environment Agency, August 2000.
44 OJ L129, 18.5.76.
45 COM (2000) 87.
46 EU Document 6055/00.
47 Kramer, L. (2000), *EC Environmental Law*, Sweet and Maxwell, London, p. 123.
48 OJ L117, 8.5.90.
49 Department of the Environment, July 1993.
50 Department of the Environment, May, 1999.
51 Cm 4693, May 2000.
52 Cm 2181, May 1993.
53 Environment Agency, 1999.
54 OJ L336, 7.12.88.
55 Cm 4548, 2000.
56 Kramer, *op. cit.*, n. 47, at pp. 42–3.
57 *Ibid.*
58 COM (1990) 772 Final.
59 OJ L377, 31.12.91.
60 European Commission, 1999.
61 Cm 2674, October 1994.
62 Cm 4749, June 2000.
63 *Supra*, n. 1.
64 Kramer, *op. cit.*, note 47, at p. 31.

65 Kramer, *op. cit.*, n. 47, at p. 32.
66 8th Report (Session 1997–98).
67 17th Report (Session 1997–98).
68 United Nations Environment Programme, (1998), 'Policy Effectiveness and Multilateral Environmental Agreements', UNEP/98/6: Environment and Trade Paper 17, Geneva, p. 12.
69 OJ L297, 31.10.88.
70 Haigh, N. (ed.) (2000), *Manual of Environmental Policy*, Institute for European Environmental Policy, London, pp. 6.12–3 and 13.2–12.
71 *Supra*, notes 51 and 55, respectively.
72 PPG 23, Department of the Environment, 1994.
73 Department of the Environment (1992), 'Planning, Pollution and Waste Management' for example.
74 1st Report (Session 1999–2000).
75 *Ibid.*, para. 36 at p. xv. *Cf.* Commission press release IP/97/636, 11 July 1997.
76 COM (95), 10 January 1996.
77 Hawke and Kovaleva, *op. cit.*, n. 6, at p. 4.
78 *Ibid.*, at pp. 8–10. *Cf.* House of Lords Select Committee on the European Communities 'Fifth Environmental Action Programme: Integration of Community Policies', 8th Report (Session 1992–93).
79 Department of the Environment, March 1998.
80 Department of the Environment press release, 'Voluntary agreements on the use of HFCs between Government and Industry' (23 January 1996).
81 Decision 85/338: OJ L176, 6.7.85.
82 OJ L120, 11.5.90.
83 1st Report (Session 1999–2000).
84 *Ibid.*, para. 1.
85 OJ L158, 23.6.90.
86 Department of the Environment (1992), 'Guidance on the Implementation of the Environmental Information Regulations'.
87 SI 1992, No.3240. *Cf.* comments on the operation of the Regulations in the White Paper (1997) 'Your right to know: the Government's proposals for a Freedom of Information Act', Cm 3818.
88 OJ L377, 31.12.92.
89 OJ L167, 9.7.93.
90 *Supra*, n. 20.
91 OJ L328, 20.12.94.
92 *Supra*, n. 22.
93 *Supra*, n. 21.
94 *Supra*, n. 85.
95 *Supra*, nn. 23 and 24.
96 *Supra*, nn. 3, 4 and 33.
97 *Supra*, n. 22.
98 OECD (1997), *Reforming Environmental Regulation in OECD Countries*, p. 21.
99 For the wider context, see Hawke, N. (2000), *Corporate Liability*, Sweet and Maxwell, London, pp. 240–41.
100 OJ L194, 25.5.75.

101 OJ L78, 26.3.91.
102 SI 1994, No. 1056.
103 *Supra*, n. 8, at para. 6.3.
104 *Supra*, n. 51.
105 *Supra*, n. 50.
106 OJ L103, 25.4.79.
107 OJ L206, 22.7.92.

Chapter Two

Structures for Policy Implementation and Enforcement

Hierarchical Structures

Despite evidence of a policy ambition on the part of the European Community to develop policy on a horizontal axis, as represented in Chapter One, environmental policy structures remain fundamentally vertical. Along this vertical line runs the constitutional dynamic (and authority) which enables implementation and enforcement of policy. In turn, it is of course the axis of implementation and enforcement by law that provides the essential theme of this and the other chapters.

The present chapter and its concern for structural matters seeks to build on Chapter One by addressing a small number of additional issues concerning central policy and other decision-making processes. The substantial theme of this chapter however is the development and operation of structural arrangements for implementation and enforcement in member states, and the United Kingdom in particular. Accordingly, early attention is given to the matter of subsidiarity. Subsidiarity is followed by a consideration of devolution, and environmental standard and target-setting in member states. Traditionally, much of the implementation and enforcement process has been encased in 'command and control' regulatory arrangements and while these will be addressed, there is a concern also for other, developing techniques affecting implementation and enforcement. A particular point of emphasis here will be the functions, in England and Wales, of the Environment Agency and local authorities. Another major player in the implementation and enforcement process, the Secretary of State and other responsible ministers, will be seen to have implementation and enforcement functions which extend widely and include crucial functions relating to guidance, review, advisory and broad strategic processes.

Having travelled down the vertical line running from the centre, the present chapter goes on to deal with the integrity and effectiveness of the constitutional structure in terms of the accountability of the centre for the realisation of policy on the environment. Accordingly some attention is given to standardised reporting on directives as well as the developing structural arrangements for so-called 'sector' reporting. Such reporting is an important part of the Commission's enforcement responsibilities (in the absence of any inspection capacity) where the objects of those responsibilities – the member states – are themselves the suppliers of the vital information. Those member states are obliged to report the detailed arrangements for transposition to the Commission through so-called 'compliance letters'. In turn, the extensive monitoring required of member states has generated further policy and law where gaps have been discovered in the range of environmental protection.

Finally in this chapter there is a concern for comparative approaches to the process of implementing and enforcing environmental policy through law. For this purpose there is a necessary interest in comparative environmental law emerging from individual member states as revealed throughout the chapters. That comparative law is particularly important in understanding what may be described as cultural variables which influence the style of transposition of directives in those member states. However, a wider perspective is necessary if an effective evaluation of the European Community's framework for environmental policy implementation and enforcement is to be achieved. For this reason the final sections of this chapter are taken up with an examination of the structures for policy implementation and enforcement in the United States of America and Canada.

The National and Local Context

There is no better summary of the central issue in this chapter than the words of one commentator who observes that:

> ... while at one level, the process of Europeanisation engenders, whether intentionally or otherwise, a certain rapprochement of institutional models and policy styles, national and local contexts remain, for the time being, the defining feature of environmental policy style.[1]

Reference has been made in Chapter One to the formal, constitutional structures at the centre of the European Community, as well as the competence of the Community to legislate in the area of the environment. It will be seen later in this chapter that subsidiarity is crucial to the question whether such competence remains at the centre or is devolved to member states. For the moment, though, it is necessary to look again at the Treaty of Amsterdam, this time to note the way it deals with the amendment of Article 95, widening the boundary within which more stringent member state legislation may be implemented despite the existence of harmonised European Community legislation. The effect of the Treaty amendment is to allow the application of such member state legislation even though there had been unanimous adoption of the harmonised Community legislation. Even where that member state legislation comes into force after the adoption of the Community measures it may still operate to apply its more stringent requirements. However, such an effect does depend on the member state legislation being based on new scientific evidence relating to protection of the environment and being referable to problems peculiar to that member state which arise after adoption of the Community legislation. Whether member state legislation satisfies this test demands persuasion of the Commission.

Legislative Provision

Community legislation may be explicit in allowing member states to prescribe requirements more stringent than those found in a particular directive. Directive 85/203[2] on air quality standards relating to nitrogen dioxide for example, refers to values which apply in areas deemed to require special protection, permitting a member state to prescribe more demanding values in such locations. Similarly, in Directive 94/63[3] relating to volatile organic compounds from petrol, a member state is empowered to prescribe more demanding requirements for health and environmental protection. Indeed, a member state is empowered to depart from the regulatory framework of the Directive, on the assumption that its regulatory control is as efficient as that provided for in the Community legislation. There is however no guarantee that Community legislation will be so explicit, in which case it will no doubt be a task for the court and judicial interpretation to determine the scope of any freedom and discretion available to the member state.

Judicial Interpretation

Two cases decided by the European Court of Justice provide an insight into the process of judicial interpretation, through which apparent legislative intention is manifested. In *Kemikalieinspekionen v. Toolex Alpha AB*[4] the European Court of Justice addressed the legality of national measures affecting the use of specific chemical substances. Under the relevant Swedish law it is unlawful to sell, transfer or use trichloroethylene (TCH) subject to exemptions that may be granted by a regulatory agency. Toolex was refused consent to continue use of TCH but without any plan for discontinuation. It was contended that such a decision was inconsistent with European Community law. Before the Court it was recognised that regulatory requirements exist under Community law, that such Community law is not intended to harmonise use restrictions affecting TCH but to impose minimum requirements and procedures so that, accordingly, the member state is not restricted in its competence to regulate its marketing and use. The second of the cases (a joined case) – *ARCO Chemie Nederland and Epon*[5] – started from the premise that the meaning of the term 'waste' in Community law turns on the interpretation of the word 'discard' as it appears in the Waste Framework Directive, a term which has to be interpreted by reference to its essential objectives: protection of human health and the environment based on precaution and preventive action. This, the Court suggested, indicated the need for the term 'waste' to be subject to a wide interpretation and (crucially for present purposes) for the mode of proof to be open to the choice of the member state.

Information Transparency

The reality of implementation and enforcement in the member state, allied to the jurisdiction of the Commission further up the vertical line of hierarchy, stresses the fundamental importance of arrangements for effective enforcement at the centre which necessitates reliable, transparent information generated at member state level. Whether that is the reality is very doubtful, as will be seen later in this chapter. In the meantime, it appears that an effective 'bottom up' approach as represented towards the beginning of Chapter One serves the fundamental purpose of ensuring that there is generation of information closer to the point of local implementation and enforcement. In part that information management process is one of the outstanding functions of the European Environment Agency. However, the task of generating effective, transparent information for this purpose involves responsibilities extending rather more widely for the benefit both of the Commission and the member state. This task suggests a need to encourage greater public participation in structures for information creation where such participation may include increasing resort to contractual arrangements of the sort described later, in Chapter Seven. Some of the overall problems here have been encountered already in Chapter One, in relation to information management.

Reciprocal arrangements for information generation by reference to a widely-defined network already exist: Decision 97/101[6] is an important example even if the public participation just referred to is not incorporated in the structures. The essential intention here is to generate a reciprocal information exchange where data on prescribed air pollutants is passed between member states, the Commission and the European Environment Agency. The Agency has an important management function in making this data available in the public domain.

Further developments whereby information becomes more transparent are anticipated by the Aarhus Convention on Access to Information, Public Participation and Access to Justice in Environmental Matters. It was seen in Chapter One that the Convention (which has been signed by the European Union) will open up European Community institutions to information access requirements thus enabling greater opportunities for environmental law enforcement. Criticism of structures at the centre is not new in the present context. In recent times it has been observed by the House of Lords Select Committee on the European Communities that the Commission consults little – and late – in relation to new legislation. This was seen as being allied to a lack of transparency in relation to scientific and technical advice.[7] Indeed, an earlier report of the same Select Committee[8] dealing with *Implementation and Enforcement of Environmental Legislation* advocated structures for early consultation of those most affected by legislation in order to create a positive climate for implementation for the benefit of enforcement agencies and commercial organisations. The importance of consultation is also to be seen in the next section, dealing with subsidiarity. Here the Commission in particular is obliged to justify its decision-making on whether Community action comes from the centre or can be generated by member states.

Subsidiarity

Since 1987 and the Single European Act there has been a recognition of subsidiarity in the European Community. In essence, the principle of subsidiarity attempts to establish criteria by reference to which it can be determined whether action is better taken at the centre through the Community or locally, through the intervention of member states. In its original formulation in 1987 subsidiarity operated through a narrow focus in determining the appropriate level for action on the environment. However, the Maastricht and Amsterdam treaties have taken subsidiarity forward, quite dramatically. These most recent constitutional developments have seen the principle graduate to apply to Community law and policy at large, through the terms of Article 5:

> In areas which do not fall within its exclusive competence, the Community shall take action, in accordance with the principle of subsidiarity, only if and in so far as the objectives of the proposed action cannot be sufficiently achieved by the Member States and can therefore, by reason of the scale or effects of the proposed action, be better achieved by the Community.

These words are a source of difficulty, as will be seen below. Essentially, that difficulty arises from a tension that exists between, on the one hand, the Community's attempts to provide guidance on the operation of the principle and the range of meaning that may be drawn from the words of Article 5.

Community Guidance

In 1992 the Council agreed the terms on which the principle applies to the institutions of the Community, an agreement which was followed the next year by an Interinstitutional Declaration on Democracy, Transparency and Subsidiarity.[9] That Declaration focuses on the Commission's competence to initiate legislation, the need to take account of subsidiarity and to account for observation of the principle. This matter of accountability appears to assume that the consultative processes which form part of the legislative structures referred to in Chapter One will be explicit on the merits and mechanics of subsidiarity affecting not only the Commission but the Council and Parliament as well. Manifestation of this process will be seen in various ways, not least of which will be the rehearsal of the principle, as appropriate, in legislative preambles. Where the Council is concerned there is a recognition of what may described as 'legislative proportionality' which lays stress on the need to legislate only as far as is reasonable necessary, as well as on the merit of legislation by directive or (ideally) framework directive. Nevertheless there is also recognition of a preference for those measures which do not carry the force of law. Subsequently, the Treaty of Amsterdam has developed rather more formal requirements against a background of legal enforceability, as will be seen below.

Article 5

A reading of Article 5 raises doubts about its constitutional and legal integrity. Arguably, the Article begs more questions than it answers. In particular, it may be asked what is meant by the references to 'exclusive competence', failure of sufficient achievement by member states, and better achievement by the Community. Matters of exclusive competence are difficult to define but refer essentially to an absence of shared competence between the Community and member states. The equally difficult question is to determine where shared competence ends and the Community's exclusive competence begins. Arguably, the key to any answer here is whether, hitherto, the Community has exercised its legislative competence in a particular area. Accordingly there can be no generalised position on matters of shared or exclusive competence: everything depends on a reading (for present purposes) of Community environmental legislation. The issue is brought into sharp relief where Community agricultural policy is concerned: the policy is referred to as the 'Common Agricultural Policy'. As such agricultural policy allows the Community exclusive competence so excluding the subsidiarity principle and Article 5. Any attempt therefore by a member state to legislate on environmental issues touching and affecting that policy are incompetent and *ultra vires*. No such fundamental limitation affects general environmental law and policy: the relationship can be characterised as a complementary relationship, a position confirmed, it is suggested, by Article 174(4). This provision of the Community Treaty states that, within their respective spheres of competence, the Community and member states shall cooperate with third countries and competent international organisations.

The Commission has attempted to advise both the Council and the Parliament of its attitude to subsidiarity.[10] In so doing the Commission has confirmed the position just referred to, in relation to the Common Agricultural Policy whilst including other areas of supposed exclusive jurisdiction, such as the area of transport policy.

It may be asked, though, whether the same effect accrues elsewhere, where the Community legislates. Again, does the incidence of Community legislation have the effect of generating exclusive competence on the part of the Community and the elimination of the subsidiarity principle? There appears to be ample authority in favour from the European Court of Justice.[11]

Despite the existence of what may be called 'entrenched competence', or subsequent Community legislation, there may be justification for an argument that subsidiarity is operative if the Community has ceded to member states the competence to develop agri-environmental schemes under the Rural Development Regulation,[12] for example. If this is correct then the opening words of Article 5 appear to allow the Community considerable freedom to apply subsidiarity where (in effect) an area of apparently exclusive competence is to be open to a measure of delegation to member states.

Should Subsidiarity Apply?

Reference to Article 5 shows that there is remarkable freedom in determining whether subsidiarity should apply. Reference was made previously to a likelihood that objectives will be insufficiently achieved by member states, as well as better achievement by the Community. Clearly, cross-border pollution will tend to necessitate action at Community level. However, the formula that is represented by Article 5 is so widely drawn that it is probably quite legitimate to consider also the integrity of the single market where the possibility of member state legislation is in prospect. It is in these seemingly large areas of policy discretion that a Protocol to the Amsterdam Treaty is potentially important. That Protocol (in Article 7) stipulates that:

> While respecting Community law, care should be taken to respect well established national arrangements and the organisation and working of Member States' legal systems.

Elsewhere the Protocol sets out a variety of criteria and procedures governing the application of subsidiarity which are enforceable before the European Court of Justice. One of the very significant consequences of this regime again is that the onus is on the Commission and other Community institutions to defend decision-making by reference to principles of subsidiarity. Against this background there is no doubt that subsidiarity has contributed to the changing shape, style and emphasis of environmental law.

The Evolving Shape of Environmental Lawmaking

If there is one increasingly distinctive contribution of subsidiarity to environmental lawmaking, it is a developing awareness of the merit of shared responsibility as between the Community and member states. Drinking water quality is a prime example. Although protection of the public health is of paramount importance, nevertheless the Community has ceded to member states the prescription of aesthetic criteria. Another example is the regime for mutual recognition of pesticide product authorisations granted by member states. In turn, provision is made for a member state to opt out of such recognition where it can be established by that state that agricultural, plant health or environmental conditions are inconsistent with those in the member state responsible for the authorisation of the subject product. The development of Community law on environmental liability and various other issues has also seen the influence of subsidiarity which was often the subject of influential comment by the House of Lords Select Committee on the European Communities.

The subject of a Community-wide law on environmental liability has been discussed now for many years. In its report on *Remedying Environmental Damage*[13] the House of Lords Select Committee on the European Communities had no doubt that Community-wide action would be justified if seen to be more effective than member states' individual initiatives which could lead to distortions of competition. Accordingly the Select Committee gave its support to a framework directive, allowing an important measure of discretion to member states on matters of detail. Such an approach would no doubt tend to allow member states' own legal systems to accommodate matters of local enforcement.

In a report on *Community Environmental Law: making it work*[14] the Select Committee took a critical look at proposals for minimum criteria for national inspectorates, disposal of public complaints about breaches of Community law at member state level, and third party enforcement of Community law before the courts. In examining these proposals from the Commission, the Select Committee was very mindful of the implications of subsidiarity. At about the same time the Select Committee published a report on *Sustainable Landfill*[15] where (in relation to the then draft Landfill Directive) the Select Committee reported that many witnesses considered that the draft Directive was too prescriptive, leaving insufficient opportunity for member states to determine appropriate measures for the achievement of reductions in methane emissions. Nevertheless, the Select Committee concluded that most matters covered by the draft Directive were consistent with the Treaty of Amsterdam Protocols (referred to previously), such as the transnational implications of global warming, for example. In the same general context of waste management there are also occasions when the European Court of Justice may be in a position to consider the influence of subsidiarity, particularly after the matter was opened up to judicial scrutiny by the Treaty of Amsterdam. In one recent case, for example, the Court of Justice confirmed that the term 'waste' cannot be interpreted restrictively, and that it is a matter for member states to choose an appropriate mode of proof.[16]

Subsidiarity and EPI

Reference was made to environmental policy integration in Chapter One while, at the start of the present chapter, reference was made to the vertical, hierarchical line that runs downwards from the centre of the Community. Also in the first chapter it was seen that EPI is difficult to realise, for a variety of structural and jurisdictional reasons within the Community. In this context the question is whether EPI is only susceptible to action at the centre. Arguably, such an assumption fails to appreciate the nature of policy integration and might even tend to focus attention on subsidiarity as a principle that distributes competence to legislate on 'one or the other': either the centre, or member states. It has been seen already, however, that the creation, implementation and enforcement of environmental law and policy is likely to be rather more subtle in nature, hence the recognition of the merit of shared, segmented competence in certain areas. Accordingly, such an approach may well have attractions as there is a growing realisation of a need to develop EPI through effective interrelationships which affect both vertical and horizontal structures extending all the way down the vertical hierarchy linking the centre to member states. However, at the end of that vertical line in the member state there are other, structural issues to address in the shape of devolution. This matter is now addressed as it affects the position in the United Kingdom.

Devolution

Recent constitutional reform has seen varying degrees of devolved powers being distributed to Scotland, Wales and Northern Ireland although Scottish devolution is characterised by the power to enact primary legislation, albeit in relation to those areas of responsibility expressly devolved by virtue of the Scotland Act 1998. Wales and Northern Ireland differ quite significantly in having relatively limited legislative competence following devolution. Devolution in Wales, for example, is governed by the Government of Wales Act 1998 and, unlike the Scotland Act 1998 providing for devolution in that country, is not based on an exercise of functions referable to subject areas. Instead, the Government of Wales Act 'shadows' prescribed functions previously exercisable by the Secretary of State for Wales under existing legislation. As such the Welsh Assembly enjoys rather limited functions in relation to the environment, for example. The Scotland Act empowers the Scottish parliament to legislate 'Acts of the Scottish Parliament' across prescribed subject areas, including the environment.

Where the implementation of Community legislation in areas such as the environment is concerned, this is within the competence of these countries now enjoying devolved powers, albeit subject to the foregoing limits on their legislative jurisdiction. Reserve powers permit any responsible United Kingdom minister to secure compliance with Community legal obligations in these countries, which may also apply to the government of the United Kingdom to seek extension of legislation to any of these obligations.

Cooperative arrangements exist between the United Kingdom government and the countries exercising devolved powers for the purpose of coordinating issues arising from Community policy, managing information exchange, monitoring the operation of devolution arrangements and dealing with disputed matters between the countries.[17] These arrangements are central to matters of implementation and enforcement of environmental law and policy across the new constitutional structures of the United Kingdom. Rationalisation across the countries is clearly a matter of considerable moment: in essence the expectation is that timely consultation will occur in order to facilitate well coordinated legislation which can take account of particular requirements. The likely operation of these arrangements can be reflected partially in the following questions. Should there be different legislative styles and techniques in a particular country? Is there a justifiable need to secure a derogation given identifiable difficulties in a part of the United Kingdom such that a directive cannot be exploited to its full extent? How and to what extent can there be an equitable sharing of legally binding commitments arising from the terms of a directive which looks to member states to contribute to reductions in pollutants reaching the environment? Where one of the countries has agreed its contribution for present purposes and fails to comply, whereupon infraction proceedings are instigated, what are the expectations in connection with the liability? This latter question of enforcement depends on the assumption of liability (which may include a compensation order by the European Court of Justice) by the responsible country whose initial responsibility is to respond to the Commission, through the government of the United Kingdom.

Environmental Standard and Target-setting

In each member state there is a measure of freedom and discretion under the terms of certain environmental laws in relation to standards and targets. That discretion and its scope is manifested in a complex matrix characterised by the dynamics of the structural relationships between the vertical and horizontal elements within and between the centre of the Community and the member states. Although the essential characteristic of the main legislative vehicle – the directive – can be represented as the fulcrum of this complex structure there are many other variables ranging from (say) mandatory limit values carried by a directive or directly applicable requirements carried by the occasional environmental regulation, to an area of law generated by a member state which, like the law on contaminated land in the United Kingdom, resides outside any existing Community jurisdiction.

The dynamics of this structure are dominated by the operation of the directive and the means adopted by any member state for the purpose of realising the prescribed objective through transposition. In turn, the characteristics of the prescribed objectives and the means adopted for the purpose of lawful transposition in a member state represent an important cross-section of the evolution of Community environmental law and policy. The common denominator though is often the use of standards.

The Royal Commission on Environmental Pollution in its 21st Report on 'Setting Environmental Standards' considered that:

> Standards backed by legal enforcement machinery are an appropriate way of dealing with some of the worst forms and sources of pollution; they can embody moral concerns; and in circumstances in which non-statutory measures might otherwise be preferred, they can be held in reserve, for use if agreement is not forthcoming.[18]

In turn, the Royal Commission considered that an 'environmental standard' is:

> ... any judgement about the acceptability of environmental modifications resulting from human activities which fulfil the following conditions: *a.* it is formally stated after some consideration and intended to apply generally to a defined class of cases; *b.* because of its relationship to certain sanctions, rewards or values, it can be expected to exert an influence, direct or indirect, on activities that affect the environment.[19]

The influence of any such standard (whatever the scale of the influence) may depend on the vehicle chosen for its application, be that through the law or voluntary devices. It has been seen already, in Chapter One, how environmental law and policy from the Community is subject to evolutionary forces. It will be seen later in this chapter and in other chapters that traditional, regulatory 'command and control' techniques are being superseded by other techniques for the implementation and enforcement of environmental standards. Some attention was given in Chapter One to the development of standards against the background of environmental policy. That process has been deeply influenced over recent years by the World Health Organisation (WHO). The WHO's work in the field of air quality and drinking water quality has had an enormous influence on the Commission and its standard-setting task. The integrity of WHO standards is best characterised by the fact that peer review and a full justification of values accompany the work carried out in this field. In turn, those values are usually seen as sufficiently robust for the purpose of taking account of local variables. At member state level expert research for the purpose of standard-setting is well established. That standard-setting at member state level may have the potential to deal with those areas of discretion left with the member state, as indicated at the beginning of this section of the chapter. In the United Kingdom, the Expert Panel on Air Quality Standards is one body that has been particularly influential.

The generation of standards by WHO, the Commission and other environmental regulators is a necessarily dynamic process, for the reason set out, above and below: the necessary evolution of regulatory techniques in the environment. Of course it has been recognised also that those techniques do not always rely on the force of law where implementation and enforcement are concerned. It was seen earlier in this chapter that the Royal Commission on Environmental Pollution has referred to the merit of standards being subject to the force of law. Traditionally, regulatory structures have tended to be characterised by a 'command and control' style where, in the case of atmospheric pollution control, for example, the concern has been with legally prescribed limit values whose rigidity and lack of incentive in some cases has been addressed by the prescription of statutory guide limits tied to a broadly defined duty requiring a member state to seek to achieve these more ambitious standards. The development of law and policy in this area in recent years can be seen in the proliferation of regulatory structures which rest on rather more ambitious devices. Those devices extend across a number of techniques, as where atmospheric pollutants are subject to integrated regulation with other pollutants, where substances are subject to so-called 'product standards' taking account of their combustion properties, where total emissions provide a ceiling or 'bubble', where the manufacture of products known or likely to have polluting properties is proscribed, and where ambient air quality is subject to standard-setting.

These devices and techniques call for a large range of regulatory and other arrangements if they are be subject to effective implementation and enforcement. One important regulatory approach which recognises the need for a rather more dynamic approach to changing circumstances is 'best available techniques not entailing excessive cost' (BATNEEC). Despite the prescription of discharge and emission limits in an authorisation for Integrated Pollution Control under Part I of the Environmental Protection Act 1990, there is a clear statutory obligation on the plant operator to keep abreast of the best available techniques. Accordingly, there is a presumption in favour of the need to remain efficient, albeit there are limits (such as costs) which may tend to mitigate any environmental benefits. The axis between technical requirements and costs is undoubtedly dynamic as a result of which it is likely that more sophisticated technical standards will tend to operate against smaller or undercapitalised companies.

The regulatory and other structures which allow implementation and enforcement of standards and targets may on occasions provide for derogations, at least if the subject directive contains the necessary authority. One such directive is Directive 88/609:[20] the so-called 'Large Combustion Plants' Directive which contains a derogation in favour of those plants burning indigenous coal, high in sulphur, where compliance with prescribed emission limits is impossible in the absence of considerable financial investment. Despite the protection of this derogation, the subject plants are obliged to comply with a desulphurisation programme prescribed by the Directive.

While derogations appear to accept that imposition of standards through a directive may be beyond achievement where political negotiation has perhaps failed to lower that threshold, there are possibilities that a directive may provide enough room for a member state to implement a more ambitious scheme or more stringent standards. It was seen earlier that the Treaty of Amsterdam has provided a rather more coherent regime should a member state wish to adopt more stringent environmental standards. It may be the case however, that a member state wishes to extend the scheme of the directive without necessarily wishing to impose any more stringent standards. The United Kingdom's Integrated Pollution Control regime under the Environmental Protection Act, just referred to, arose from Directive 84/360[21] on Air Pollution from Industrial Plants. This Directive dealing with a single medium was used by the United Kingdom to develop an integrated regulatory regime extending beyond the one medium. In turn, the experience of this multimedia approach appears to have influenced the Community's development of the Pollution Prevention and Control (IPPC) regime examined in Chapter One and elsewhere in other chapters.

There may be room within the terms of a directive to 'force' more stringent standards. This was certainly the case in relation to certain of the earlier directives dealing with air quality standards which prescribed so-called 'guide values' in addition to the mandatory limit values for atmospheric pollutants.

More recently, Directive 98/70[22] which deals with the quality of petrol and diesel provides an interesting example of the forcing of standards in the United Kingdom, in two respects. First, fiscal adjustments have been made in order to reduce the rate of duty payable in respect of low sulphur diesel as well as regulatory adjustments to improve the 'environmental' standard of the diesel that will attract that lower rate of duty, even beyond the standard prescribed for the Directive's target date. Secondly, the Directive permits a member state to apply to the Commission for permission to prescribe fuels with an improved 'environmental' standard for use in designated areas where there is adverse air quality.

The Development and Implementation of Regulatory Measures

The development and implementation of regulatory measures depends on structural arrangements both at the centre of the Community and in the member states. Many of the formal structures were examined in Chapter One.

This part of the present chapter is concerned again with structures, but on this occasion, outlining and illustrating the structures which inform regulatory development affecting the environment. For this purpose the present section of the chapter is divided into four parts: Community structural approaches in general, Community policy development, complementary mechanisms applied both at the centre and in member states, and (finally) specific approaches to implementation in member states.

Those structures again display some of the dynamics already referred to. Accordingly a good deal of this section of the chapter is concerned with the shaping of regulatory structures (and any complementary devices) as a result of policy creation at the centre and, in turn, the exposure of such regulatory structures to transposition in the member state. At member state level it is a matter of interest to see how these structures emerge from transposition, given the inherent characteristics of the directive, as well as the changing face of environmental regulation.

Community Structural Approaches

Instances of Community approaches to regulatory development have been seen already, particularly in Chapter One. The present concern is with the structures (and their dynamics) which the centre commends to member states. A straightforward example is one that was mentioned above where reference was made to statutory limit values, supported by guide values, by virtue of Directive 80/779[23] on air quality values for sulphur dioxide. This Directive is an important example of a generation of directives on the environment which is being phased out as newer ideas on regulation emerge. In this case a framework Directive – 96/62[24] – on ambient air quality assessment and management and its daughter directives governing sulphur dioxide and other atmospheric pollutants are superseding the earlier directive. The new generation of directives shows very clearly how regulatory structures and environmental control generally, are changing. Indeed, the adoption of framework directives indicates a desire at the centre to create a regulatory template within which broad principles and objectives are set for the purpose of developing more detailed prescriptions in the so-called 'daughter' directives. This trend in certain areas of Community environmental lawmaking permits a rather clearer exposition of the law in areas that are appropriate to this treatment. At the same time it appears that the principle of subsidiarity is given some recognition, albeit subject to the prescriptive objects (and detail) to be found in the daughter directives.

Community Policy Development

There is no doubt that one of the most radical developments in Community environmental policy in recent years is the continuing move away from the regulation of specific environmental pollutants. Nowhere is this better illustrated than in the Directive on Integrated Pollution Prevention and Control (IPPC).[25] Here the requirement is that environmental impacts in general are fed into the regulatory equation when an authorisation is being considered for the subject installation. However, while the IPPC Directive applies to a number of industries including chemicals, waste management and intensive pig and poultry rearing there are certain activities which fall outside the IPPC Directive so that certain activities will continue to be subject to existing regulatory requirements prescribed by (say) Directive 76/464[26] on the discharge of dangerous substances to the aquatic environment. Otherwise, IPPC will in due course supersede Directive 84/360,[27] the Framework Directive whose concern has been with the regulation of air pollution from industrial plants, implemented in the United Kingdom through Integrated Pollution Control (IPC) and Local Authority Air Pollution Control (LAAPC) in Part I of the Environmental Protection Act 1990.

Integrated Environmental Regulation The advent of IPC in Part I of the Act of 1990 provides in many ways a very significant illustration of the potential dynamism of structural development across the Community and its member states. The United Kingdom undoubtedly travelled further than was strictly necessary in implementing Directive 84/360 with its preference for an integrated, multimedia approach. As a result there is no doubt that the Community was heavily influenced by the experience in one member state of integrated control in developing a very similar regime from the centre. Although it might be assumed that the United Kingdom would experience few challenges in seeking to implement the IPPC Directive, this is not necessarily the case. For example, the consultation processes (which ran to publication of no fewer than four Consultation Papers[28]) included concerns about the distribution of regulatory functions as between the Environment Agency and local authorities, as well as the matter of subsuming landfills into the IPPC regime despite the arrival in force of the Landfill Directive.[29]

The IPPC Directive looks to regulate those pollutants which are likely to be significant emissions from the subject installation. Limit values are part of the regime, by reference those priority pollutants which are prescribed although additionally, regulatory requirements will extend to soil protection, groundwater protection and waste management. Where soil protection is concerned, regulatory requirements will not necessarily be constrained by municipal law (to be found in Part IIA of the Environmental Protection Act 1990) which operates on the basis of 'fitness for purpose' in the United Kingdom. In the case of waste management, the IPPC Directive looks for an integrated management process related to other relevant processes within the subject installation.

The foregoing regulatory structures may necessitate rather less radical transposition than might occur in those member states without similar experience of integrated environmental regulation. Nevertheless, the new IPPC regime does extend beyond those processes and activities prescribed by the previous regime: intensive poultry and pig breeding is a prime example. Sustainable operation of installations is another development of significance: energy resource management will be a feature of regulation in IPPC authorisations. In the same vein, 'best available techniques' (the essential core of the regulatory evaluation) draws into the equation rather more variables with overtones of sustainability than was the case with 'BATNEEC' as it has applied previously. Transparency of information associated with most aspects of the IPPC regulatory process is another outstanding characteristic, as is the insistence on mandatory submission of material information including information generated by other processes such as environmental assessment.

Total Pollution Loads One of the daughter directives of Directive 84/360 is the so-called 'Large Combustion Plants' Directive which introduced over a decade ago emission limits which are referable to each member state and, more particularly, the totality of emissions from existing plants.[30] The central question is how best to transpose the Directive for present purposes. In the United Kingdom, the Environment Agency has shown the likely shape of a future approach to total pollution loads in its Consultation Paper *Controlling Pollution from Existing Coal and Oil-fired Power Stations*.[31] The approach mooted appears to be heavily dependent on FGD: flue gas desulphurisation, and a preference for flexibility in dealing with sulphur dioxide emissions. Proposed limits would be allocated to generators on a company-wide basis with incentives linked to FGD. Consequently, any generator looking to increase market share might increase company-wide emissions, but only proportionately through commitment to and investment in, FGD. Such arrangements though have to be effective and enforceable. Accordingly the Consultation Paper addresses two critical issues. In the first place, the Agency would look to generators to agree the transmission of emission limits at sale, in order to facilitate maximum control of emissions regulation. Secondly, the Agency looks for the greatest possible efficiency in FGD technology through the removal of the pollutants at the earliest possible moment in any subject process. Presently about 80 per cent of the pollutant is removed, but only when the plant reaches 50 per cent load. A not dissimilar approach in relation to total pollution loads is one of the routes to compliance with the 'Solvents' Directive which is dealt with below, under the heading of *Flexible, complementary compliance.*

Ambient air quality standards Reference has been made to the transition from the limit and guide value approach found in Directive 80/779 to ambient air quality standards in Directive 96/62.[32] The former directive will be superseded by the latter and in so doing substitute a rather different regulatory regime for that which hitherto has been concerned with mandatory limit values for concentrations of sulphur dioxide at ground level, the duty of a member state to use its best efforts to achieve the more demanding guide values, and a presumption against significant deterioration of air quality. This earlier regime was notable at the time of its entry into force for its introduction of mandatory quality standards. However, one of its notable weaknesses was the relatively rigid prescription of limit values whose enforcement was difficult in relation to matters of causation and overall proof in particular. By way of contrast, the more recent directive is a framework directive: prescribed limit and so-called 'alert' values will be built up through the programme of daughter directives (including a directive on sulphur dioxide). This limit-fixing is rather more targeted than hitherto since it proceeds by reference to a number of variables including the vulnerability of different sections of the population, the effects on flora and habitats, and the feasibility economically and otherwise of prescribed limits, among others. In the meantime, the framework directive sets out standards and objectives for air quality, as well as criteria for its assessment, machinery for air quality maintenance and restoration, and the transparent management of information about air quality. Assessment criteria (as well as the machinery for assessment) are crucial elements of the Directive: member states are obliged to monitor, measure and assess air quality and respond, as necessary, with action plans to address adverse air quality according to the standards found in the relevant daughter directives. This element is intimately linked with obligations to advise the population of adverse air quality through the alert values also found in those directives. The approach to air and atmospheric pollution just described may not be appropriate in all cases and regulatory structures have had to respond to new challenges. This is particularly true where ozone pollution is concerned: in this case the Community's reaction has been through what may be called 'advisory' measures.

Advisory measures Tropospheric ozone is rather different to the atmospheric pollutants covered by the daughter directives just referred to: in practice there are clearly frequent breaches of the limits found in World Health Organisation guidelines. This alone suggests the unsuitability of disciplined regulatory approaches based on limit values or the like. Accordingly, Directive 92/72[33] adopts an approach which relies on member states monitoring the incidence of ozone pollution and, as necessary, providing public warnings where 'alert' thresholds are exceeded. Additionally, member states are required to provide the Commission and other member states with monitoring information. While this sharing of information seems to serve the purpose of future strategies to address the problem of ozone pollution, information sharing has a rather more concrete contribution to make to the development of regulatory structures, through a process which is referred to as 'mutual recognition'.

Mutual recognition Mutual recognition lies at the heart of two directives, Directive 91/414[34] on the authorisation and marketing of plant protection products ('pesticides') and Directive 98/8[35] on the authorisation and marketing of biocidal products ('biocides'). The essence of mutual recognition is that a member state is obliged to give authorisation in respect of any such product where that product has already been authorised in another member state in compliance with Community legal requirements. In these circumstances it is unlawful for a member state to insist on testing unless, having satisfied the Commission on requisite evidence, it can be established that there are cogent agricultural, plant health or environmental reasons for an exemption from these statutory requirements where (for example) ambient environmental conditions between the two member states are materially different. The 'Biocides' Directive is notable also for its inclusion of what is referred to as 'comparative evaluation'.

Comparative evaluation At the heart of the Biocides Directive is a requirement that lists of so-called 'active' ingredients are established and approved by the Community, indicative of those substances that may contribute to the manufacture of biocides. In turn, common authorisation processes operate across the Community which processes include mutual recognition. Comparative evaluation informs the approvals process and will block entry of a substance to that list where another active substance will have no significant economic or practical disadvantages and no increased impact on human health and the environment, according to scientific or technical evidence. This regime is relatively uncomplicated, given its concern for one generic product and an authorisation process which determines which prescribed substances may be used in it. However, there is no doubt that the earlier reference to *advisory measures* in relation to ozone pollution points to the potential limits of regulatory structures. Where policy suggests a need to address environmental pollution it may be clear that thoroughgoing regulation is feasible, albeit the nature of the pollutants and their status in manufacturing and other regulated activity is such that regulation should be complementary to other existing measures, and that large measures of discretion should be ceded to member states in recognition of powerful local variables. This is the case with the 'Solvents' Directive referred to briefly above and dealt with now in rather more detail.

Flexible, complementary compliance It has been seen already that the nature of environmental pollution may be such that a subtle approach is required in relation to regulatory style and emphasis. The member state may be accorded considerable extra discretion in addressing its response to a regime which seeks to complement another area of regulatory control. In many respects this approach represents a measure of sophistication in regulatory style. The one directive which presently characterises this approach is the so-called Solvents

Directive: Directive 1999/13.[36] However, this legislation has to be seen in the context of other Community legislation which, directly or indirectly, addresses the incidence of volatile organic compounds in the environment. The Solvents Directive is aimed at regulating emissions of these compounds from the use of solvents in industries such as dry-cleaning and printing. As such it operates in the midst of several other directives. Directive 94/63[37] deals with emissions of volatile organic compounds from petrol; Directive 92/72[38] deals with ozone pollution; Directive 96/62[39] deals with ambient air quality control as a Framework Directive; and Directive 96/61[40] deals with Integrated Pollution Prevention and Control (IPPC). This latter area of regulation is not so much a matter of complementary regulation as overlapping regulation given that it is not inconceivable that an installation subject to authorisation under Directive 96/61 will be subject to regulation under Directive 99/13 also. The particular interest though is in the operation of Directive 99/13.

The Directive sets out what appears to be a very flexible regime for the purpose addressing the need to reduce emissions. Accordingly, the Directive was developed by reference to member state choice on approaches to emission reduction. That choice refers to the adoption of standardised threshold and emission limit values, emission planning in respect of existing, single installations tied to the foregoing threshold and emission limit values, or national emission plans. Standardised emission limits referable to specific industrial sectors, such as the printing industry, operate either by reference to the conditions to which authorisations are subject or through so-called 'general binding rules' which are standardised conditions applicable on registration. Whichever option is chosen any installation must comply with the Directive's limits or the emission planning requirements prescribed by the Directive in respect of existing, single installations. National emission plans may allow exemptions from the foregoing regulatory arrangements just described although emissions must not exceed the ceiling defined by those foregoing limits. Such exemptions typically might be allowed in a sector with modest emissions, allied to high costs of compliance with appropriate limits imposed on other sectors chosen with particular reference (say) to their low abatement costs.

The apparent merits of the approach in Directive 1999/13 demand caution in transposition. It is quite possible that a member state could (say) choose economic instruments as a means by which some or all of the Directive might be implemented. There may for example be some attraction in resorting to a tax on solvents or arrangements for tradable 'solvents permits'. Indeed, the complexity of subject industries is such that this approach undoubtedly has attractions. Ultimately though such approaches may be expensive and difficult to administer, apart from being difficult to predict in terms of their impact on emissions: probably reasons why the United Kingdom has decided instead to rely on rather more conventional regulation. The detailed approach to implementation here is returned to in Chapter Seven. In the meantime the detailed problems of transposition in the United Kingdom are not untypically characterised by the rationalisation of the choices allowed by the Directive with the existing regulatory arrangements.

At the time of writing three sectors subject to the Directive are outside regulatory control in the United Kingdom. In bringing these areas into regulatory control the likelihood is that the Secretary of State will use the statutory power to issue directions to the principal regulators, the Environment Agency and local authorities, in order to require that the emission and threshold limit values prescribed by the Directive are incorporated in relevant authorisations. Another matter is whether the three sectors just referred to should be subject to authorisation under the Pollution Prevention and Control Act 1999 (implementing the IPPC regime of Directive 96/61) or the registration process referable to 'general binding rules'. One very big variable here is whether the onerous requirements of 'best available techniques' required in the case of the IPPC regime should apply to these sectors. Another big variable relates to the issue of emissions planning, one of the options for member state transposition.

The first variable may operate to exclude some sectors both in respect of full-blown authorisation and registration allied to 'general binding rules' (and the requirements of 'best available techniques') under the Act of 1999. Nevertheless, those sectors will need to comply with the Directive, albeit through registration and 'general binding rules' outside the Act of 1999. It will be appreciated that Directive 96/61 and the IPPC regime permits a member state to impose regulatory requirements through 'general binding rules'. Nevertheless this approach, based on registration, may not be appropriate where (as anticipated by the second variable just mentioned) the priority is to address reductions through emissions planning. The detailed monitoring and enforcement accompanying this Directive option is incompatible with the standardised conditions which apply through 'general binding rules'. This fact stresses that, as a matter of policy, there are compliance requirements emanating from the centre. Of course compliance may be so strict that legislation by directive is seen to be inadequate for the purpose, in which case there may have to be resort to a directly applicable regulation, an exceptional legislative device where environmental protection is concerned.

Strict compliance There are various reasons why the regulation may be the appropriate vehicle for the implementation and enforcement of Community environmental policy. Because a regulation is directly applicable, transposition is not part of the equation. Although there are exceptions, as where stipulations and requirements emerge from the regulation, a member state is not necessarily obliged to generate its own legislation in support of the regulation. Nevertheless, the detailed mandatory requirements of the regulation may demand attention to specific matters, if only to convert the law into a framework that is consistent with the member state's own legal system providing for enforcement for example. Accordingly, enforcement of requirements against an individual or company is rationalised, if only for the purpose of administrative efficiency.

Complementary Mechanisms

Complementary mechanisms may emerge from the centre, and from member states. Although the emphasis here is very much on formal, statutory devices this is not to suggest that informal devices might not be resorted to on occasions. These devices facilitate environmental law and policy in some material respect through structural arrangements which will vary from formal statutory provision through to other non-statutory arrangements such as contractual agreements. Categorising these complementary mechanisms is difficult so, as a result, some significant illustrations are offered against the common denominator which provides the heading for this section of the chapter. The three illustrations offered extend across Community legislation relating to voluntary measures in relation to eco-management and audit; fiscal measures, represented by the Landfill tax introduced in the United Kingdom; and the voluntary agreements on additional environmental protection from the effects of ozone arising in the United Kingdom through the operation of Regulation 3094/94.[41]

Voluntary measures in relation to eco-management and audit The European Community's eco-management and audit scheme was introduced by Regulation 1836/93[42] and came into force in April 1995. The EMAS scheme is a classic example of a complementary mechanism provided by the centre. Despite its voluntary status EMAS has an important potential in relation to future regulation of environmental protection in member states, for reasons which will be referred to, below. In the meantime, this voluntary scheme is aimed at encouraging the development and continuing improvement of environmental management standards. Although the primary participants are companies in the private sector, it will be seen later in this section of the chapter that public sector agencies may be encouraged to participate also. Whoever participates there is no doubt that there are two primary benefits. In the first place, there is the potential for a future streamlining of regulatory processes affecting the environment based on audited participation in EMAS or, indeed, any similar certified management scheme, such as ISO 140001. Secondly, participation appears to allow for development of sustainable development strategies, which have the potential to put the participating company 'ahead of the game' where future development and application of environmental law and policy are concerned. In addition to the main participants, it appears that public agencies may be encouraged to participate in EMAS. Local authorities in the United Kingdom certainly fall into this category.

Local authorities' participation in EMAS in the United Kingdom is subject to guidance in the form of a Circular issued by the Department of the Environment.[43] Interestingly, the Circular indicates that local authority participation is intended to encourage and assist local authorities in the preparation of local strategies for sustainable development. Importantly, local authorities' participation can be setting a good example bearing in mind their role as environmental regulators. Among other things, the Circular observes that EMAS:

> ... offers local authorities not only the prospect of greater efficiency and effectiveness but the opportunity to provide the public with independently verified statements of progress on meeting environmental targets ... The scheme takes account of the particular circumstances of local authorities. For example, discrete parts of a local authority ... may apply for registration rather than the whole authority, provided the authority is prepared to commit itself to seek corporate registration ... The scheme also takes into account not only the direct effects a local authority has on the environment ... but also the environmental effects arising from the delivery of services ...[44]

Fiscal measures The Landfill tax in the United Kingdom came into effect in 1996. The tax rate depends essentially on the nature of the waste with a lower rate applicable to 'inactive' waste: all other waste is taxed at a higher rate. This member state measure is to be seen as complementary since one important objective is to encourage waste to be managed other than by landfilling, a central plank of Community policy in relation to waste.

Voluntary agreements Chapter Seven will take up the matter of voluntary agreements and their role in environmental protection. Of course, such agreements may be used as part of a formal, regulatory framework or as mere *ad hoc* instruments. It is this latter use which is stressed here. Regulation 3093/94 sets the mandatory requirements which are regarded as crucial if there is to be directly applicable enforcement of standards affecting substances that deplete ozone. Perhaps the best known ozone depleters are chlorofluorocarbons (CFCs) and, as such, one of the prime targets of the Regulation. However, a widely recognised substitute – hydrofluorocarbons – were quickly recognised as greenhouse gases, whereupon (as was seen in Chapter One) the government of the United Kingdom was persuaded to conclude agreements with a number of users in order to facilitate use of feasible alternatives, as well as to facilitate minimisation of emissions if those alternatives are not available.

Specific Approaches to Implementation in Member States

Legislation by directive gives what is often considerable freedom to a member state in the process of transposition, as has been seen. That freedom normally assumes that member state measures can be identified with the essential framework of the directive in question even though it has been seen already that the Community may permit more stringent standards, limits and thresholds to be applied. Beyond this, member states may choose other complementary measures, as seen in the description of fiscal measures and voluntary agreements. A critical legal question here involves a judgement as to whether such complementary measures fall within Article 95 affecting any proposed application of more stringent measures. Accordingly, the structures in place may be regulated from the centre, or not, as the case may be. Member state proposals may fall on either side of the line, suggesting varying degrees of control according to the law from the centre. Emerging structures here may be vulnerable to challenge by reference to failure to comply with Article 95 requirements or to failure of lawful transposition. Otherwise, complementary structures created by a member state exclusively within the framework of municipal law remain vulnerable to challenge by reference to that national law alone. All of this though is not to suggest that the categories are plainly and clearly defined. Derogations provide a useful example. Many directives affecting the environment allow derogations. The Large Combustion Plants Directive[45] permits the burning of high sulphur coal in certain member states such as Spain and the United Kingdom who had cause to claim reliance. On the other hand, the Solvents Directive[46] prohibits derogations in respect of certain types of volatile organic compounds which have to be managed very strictly, given their adverse impact if allowed to escape into the environment. Whether a member state's transposition amounts to a lawful derogation (if permitted) is clearly a matter of fact and law. Where regulatory structures are implemented in the member state the areas of apparent discretionary freedom have to be read subject to restrictions on derogations. For example, a member state could not justify a proposal to use a fuel for combustion in power stations which is non-sulphurous on the alleged ground that it is to found in plentiful supplies close to the point of combustion, and can be exploited with minimal environmental impact. In other words, the generality of the discretion allowed in the directive cannot override the specific limits of a derogation.

Member State Structures for Implementation and Enforcement

Having looked at the variables which determine the synergy which affects regulatory developments along the vertical line linking the centre and member states, it is necessary to look at the formal structures developed for the purpose of accommodating the foregoing regulatory structures. Those formal structures are represented by the statutory agencies created at member state level in order to secure implementation and enforcement. In the United Kingdom and (in particular), England and Wales, the essential emphasis is on the Secretary of State for Environment, the Environment Agency and local authorities. One commentator sees these environmental agencies as follows:

> Statutory agencies have traditionally played a distinctive role in the devolved management and administration of the environment in the UK. They have combined a broad range of functions including specialist policy advice to government, and regulatory and management responsibilities in implementing policies, as well as a more general advocacy and promotional role encouraging environmental activity and awareness.[47]

The distinctive role referred to here has to be seen in the context of an evolution of structural style and emphasis. In recent years commentators have observed an increasing centralisation of much implementation and enforcement of the law in the United Kingdom, particularly where the Community is the source of that law. Two essential reasons are advanced for this increased centralisation. In the first place it is the United Kingdom government which has ultimate responsibility for enforcement of the law, despite the arrangements which now apply since the advent of devolution. Although primary lawmaking jurisdiction affecting the environment was devolved to Scotland under the Scotland Act 1998 nevertheless the United Kingdom remains the subject member state bound by the Community's legislation. Secondly, centralisation is perceived as being better able to cope with the demands of law and policy integration. Devolution is but one of the dynamics determining the structure and operation of regulatory structures in the United Kingdom. Much of the remainder of this section of the chapter is taken up with an examination of other dynamics, as well as the status and general functions of two of the most significant environmental agencies in England and Wales: the Environment Agency and local authorities, interspersed with a general reference to enforcement structures.

The Constitutional Fundamental

The European Community is empowered to bind member states by legislation and, in turn, the Commission is required by Article 211 of the Treaty to secure that the law is implemented and enforced. The constitutional responsibility of the member state necessitates the creation of appropriate regulatory and related structures. Ultimately though it is the government of the member state that carries responsibility for compliance with Community legal requirements. Some of the material in this chapter and in Chapter One has been concerned with the shades of emphasis in that legislation. Targets prescribed by that legislation provide a straightforward example of a government's legal and constitutional responsibility to secure compliance. The assumptions about data reliability for this purpose are perhaps less problematic than hitherto as a result of the creation and functioning of the European Environment Agency, whose role has been examined already. Of greater difficulty is the monitoring of other targets, such as a government's self-imposed target in relation to sustainable development, for example. In this context the member state government may be able to drag its feet rather more, as long as it knows that there are no constitutional responsibilities (directly at least) to the Community. This is a matter that has been the subject of critical comment from the House of Commons Environmental Audit Committee.[48] Accordingly, audit undoubtedly requires a certain discipline where compliance with Community legal requirements is concerned.

The Evolutionary Dynamic

It was seen at the beginning of Chapter One that both at the centre and in member states there has been considerable evolution in the nature of regulatory control of the environment. Indeed, in the United Kingdom some of the changes can certainly be characterised as dramatic when compared with the regime that predated membership of the Community. Since the appearance of the 5th Environmental Action Programme[49] there has been a trend towards rather more open regulatory arrangements, a growth of interest in subsidiarity and in more effective, objective data management. Beyond the 5th Action Programme there are other developments that will again demand movement in the structures available in many member states, not least of which is the policy preference for greater access to judicial processes as a means of challenging decisions affecting the environment. The structures in England and Wales relating to judicial review will undoubtedly require liberalising for this purpose. However, this likely need for change is not necessarily indicative of the need for radical structural change according to changing Community law and policy. Indeed, it can be argued that the trend in the United Kingdom towards centralisation in recent years has produced structures that are sufficiently streamlined to accommodate what might be quite detailed regulatory changes. This is well illustrated in the processes under discussion for England and Wales in connection with implementation of Directive 99/31: the Landfill Directive.[50]

Regulatory efficiencies The Landfill Directive, as transposed by Part II of the Environmental Protection Act, applies to all landfills. However, approximately 1,000 landfills are subject to regulation under the IPPC regime also.[51] It was seen earlier in the chapter that IPPC overlaps elsewhere also. The question then is how best member states can manage this overlap. The Environment Agency is largely responsible for the ultimate realisation of the government's preferred approach here, which is that operational landfills will transfer progressively to IPPC regulation by 2005. In the meantime there is considerable complexity involved in the existence of the two regimes, each of which displays characteristics and requirements that those affected will be well aware of. For example, the Landfill Directive imposes considerable post-closure obligations including adequate financial or similar provision, as well as requiring that landfill sites are operated by those certified as being technically competent except where 'deemed technical competence' applies if there is no significant change in the scale of the operation. On the other hand, IPPC requires publicity in respect of applications for new authorisations, that representations from the public are taken account of in decision-making, that a considerable range of statutory consultees is prescribed, and that an application be refused where the Environment Agency considers that the applicant will not comply with conditions attached to an authorisation.

Evaluating regulatory efficiencies The intention to bring all subject landfills under IPPC regulation is seen as aiding consistency and clarity. It seems clear also that the regulatory experience of the Environment Agency to date brings added efficiencies. Overall, it appears that there are advantages and disadvantages to the operators affected by these proposed arrangements. The question though is how those advantages and disadvantages can be rationalised for the purpose of claiming regulatory efficiency. Are there efficiencies for the regulator or the regulated, or both? In the first place, IPPC will not permit 'deemed technical competence' among site operators. On the other hand, the technical requirements of the IPPC regime are fulfilled where a landfill operation complies with the Landfill Directive although it is not clear how the energy efficiency criteria of the former directive will apply. The deemed compliance seems to suggest that the potentially stringent requirements of 'best available techniques' at the centre of the IPPC regime will not need to be established by an applicant.

The Environment Agency

The Environment Act 1995 stipulates that the principal aim of the Agency in its discharge of functions is to so protect or enhance the environment, taken as a whole, as to make the contribution that Ministers consider appropriate towards attaining the objective of sustainable development.[52] The nature of the relationship – based essentially on control – with central government indicates the importance of the Environment Agency's role in matters of implementation and enforcement. In turn, the relationship is close enough to enable central government to retain effective control of the essential constitutional responsibilities referred to above while at the same time seeking to push forward policy preferences in relation to matters such as sustainable development and the closely linked matter of integrating environmental policy into other sectors of activity. This corpus of activity displays the growing policy concerns of the European Community. However, there remain here, at member state level, grave concerns about the effectiveness of the Environment Agency, at least as long as the government's record on these matters appears to be less than satisfactory, a situation well documented in the House of Commons Environment Committee Report on *The Environment Agency*.[53] In part the inherent difficulty in creating structures for implementation and enforcement in member states is that there is an inevitable need to rationalise existing structures based on a variety of historical legislative provision. Even before a centralised body like the Environment Agency can address its ambitious new jurisdiction, it has to rationalise the disparate, historical elements that have now come together. Even then there will be the formidable task of creating, implementing and enforcing an ambitious jurisdiction of the sort given to the Environment Agency.

The Agency has an hierarchical structure within the limits of its jurisdiction. This structure is manifested not only in its regional organisation but also in its Local Environment Agency Plans. These Plans operate throughout England and Wales and take account of local topography, land uses and various environmental pressure points. In addition the Plans provide an important vehicle for target-setting.

Within the foregoing structures there exist arrangements which facilitate central government control of the Agency. This control is to be found in a variety of forms. There are, for example, decisions of the Agency which are subject to appeal to the Secretary of State. One of a number of examples here is the appeal provided under section 43 of the Water Resources Act 1991 in respect of the Agency's decision on an application for water abstraction. The Secretary of State of State has the power to issue directions to the Agency under section 40 of the Environment Act 1995, in addition to general guidance, and guidance as to the achievement of sustainable development under section 4 of the same Act. Accordingly, central government has considerable influence in relation to a number of Agency functions, such as enforcement, as manifested in the Environment Agency's Code of Practice on Enforcement. Enforcement structures are now examined before the position of local authorities is examined.

Enforcement Structures

The centrality of enforcement necessitates an appreciation of the broadest overview of the structures as they are found along the vertical hierarchical line linking the centre of the Community and the member states. Reduced to their essential components, the structures here provide for action by an enforcing agency in a member state which may contemplate action before the court, such as prosecution; for action before the court by a third party; for third party complaint to the Commission by a third party under Article 226 of the EC Treaty; and enforcement action against a member state by the Commission. There are undoubtedly differences between member states in the development of the second component here: it has been seen already that Community policy preferences point in the direction of an opening up of access to challenges to environmental decision-making by third parties. The limited *locus standi* thresholds in relation to judicial review in England and

Wales indicate a need for changes in the law if the foregoing policy preferences are to be realised. Beyond such matters relating to the extension of enforcement structures there is one fundamental characteristic which requires emphasis. That characteristic relates to the simple fact that these structures are referable to enforcement of the foregoing regulatory requirements. Accordingly, resort to enforcement structures and facilities will be effective in law only where it can be established (according to the prevailing standard of proof) that there has been breach or noncompliance with subject regulatory requirements. This process is one that is left to member states within the framework of any relevant Community law, for example. In the same way it was seen earlier in this chapter that the mode of proof of what may amount to 'waste' (for example) is a matter for the individual member state.[54] Nevertheless there are some matters of enforcement which are prescribed by directive.

Prescribed enforcement requirements The Directive on Integrated Pollution Prevention and Control[55] refers to the need for each member state to facilitate regulatory compliance so that conditions in particular are adhered to. In turn, the Directive requires that those responsible under the terms of an authorisation should furnish the competent authority with monitoring information. Such a requirement is of course administratively difficult where the enforcing authority is not the designated competent authority. While certain enforcement requirements may be centrally prescribed by directive, there may be occasions where member states have a choice of regulatory approaches. The major example of such an approach addressed earlier in this chapter is Directive 1999/13: the Solvents Directive.[56] Where regulatory choice is available there appear to be potential difficulties in prescribing enforcement requirements.

Regulatory choice The potential difficulties just referred to arise from the member state choices in transposition. Those choices may be seen to throw up numerous enforcement approaches which (arguably) demand matching prescriptions in a directive like the Solvents Directive. Wisely the Community has steered away from such complexity. The result is that the Directive stipulates merely that the controls are achieved through relevant conditions or, alternatively, through the adoption of general, binding rules for the purpose of realising the prescribed aims of the legislation. Beyond this provision, the Directive goes on to oblige a member state to identify effective, proportionate and dissuasive sanctions which will apply in the event of an infraction. Whether the sanctions deployed by a member state in these circumstances meet these criteria may be difficult to determine. Ultimately though it is the European

Court of Justice that will be required to determine such a matter, no doubt taking account of the aims and objectives of the directive as well as the legal system and culture of the member state in question. A decision of the Court here is of course critical in relation to member state enforcement, which may be constrained as a result.

Constraints on member state enforcement There are clearly potential problems of enforcement in a member state in the absence of transposition which accords with the subject directive or (in the same vein) enforcement requirements are seen not to be consistent with legislative intentions. In these circumstances it is possible that a defendant in criminal or other enforcement proceedings might be able to challenge the legality of any purported application of a particular sanction. A powerful example of such a challenge occurred before the European Court of Justice in *Criminal Proceedings against Arcaro*.[57] Although the proceedings related to a specific directive, the Court held that, in the absence of full transposition within the time limit a public authority in a member state cannot enforce regulatory requirements against an individual. Accordingly, so-called 'horizontal effects' cannot be deployed against an individual in these circumstances.

Local Authorities

Local government is usually a central element of the structures available in member states for the implementation and enforcement of environmental law. Any differences between member states are really matters of degree. Something has been said already about the trend towards centralisation of process in the United Kingdom. When local government in the United Kingdom was rather more involved in implementation and enforcement of law and policy prior to accession to membership of the Community, the pattern of local authority environmental jurisdiction contrasted quite sharply with contemporary reality. Broad environmental objectives tended to be the norm, accompanied by equally broad criteria such as 'best practicable means' which were often enforced by informal means in an atmosphere which undoubtedly lacked transparency. Among other things, the arrangements then existing certainly discouraged any third party enforcement. Subsequent developments show local authorities constrained in a number of important respects.

Local authorities constrained The constraints on local authorities can be appreciated from various perspectives. The environmental functions and responsibilities that fall to local authorities tend to be more heavily constrained in transposition compared with those affecting similar authorities in most other member states. Local authority statutory responsibilities are defined in considerable detail also for the purpose of manifesting the heavy control and influence exercised by central government and the Environment Agency through appeals and other arrangements which serves a number of purposes, not least of which is to secure appropriate consistency of standards and targets. Of course this picture of the role and status of local authorities is again influenced very much by the reality and consequences of Community law and policy. It has been said that local authorities generally have a much better idea of national implementing legislation and, although they may be aware of very basic directives they do not know enough about them in detail to be able to distinguish where municipal legislation is failing to implement fully the spirit or even the letter of a Community directive. These observations emerge from a report of the House of Lords Select Committee on the European Communities entitled *Implementation and Enforcement of Environmental Legislation.*[58] There is some justification for the belief that the picture has improved in the decade since that report was published: certain local authorities are certainly pro-active in the corridors of the Community. Nevertheless if there is any substance in the suspicion that consultation with local government about anything other than the detail which exists behind the main framework of Community legislation on the environment is the exception rather than the rule, there may be cause for the belief that Community legislation is seen as inhabiting a twilight world in local government. Despite this rather gloomy view of local government and the environment there may be justification for thinking that structural thinking is starting to evolve in quite significant directions.

Evolutionary development? The need to comply with targets and standards in many areas of environmental control poses a challenge to the member state to find structures which will facilitate their satisfaction. The apparent complications of devolution in this respect were touched on earlier. Arguably, the regulatory and other responsibilities of local authorities pose a rather greater challenge. It is for this reason that the foregoing consideration of strategies in Chapter One assumes considerable importance, initially as a clear indication to local authorities of their part in the realisation of Community-generated targets and standards. Indeed, the apparent uniformity of local authority participation in environmental control and regulation is increasingly under question. This is graphically illustrated in the *Waste Strategy for England and*

Wales 2000.[59] Here the government proposed, *inter alia*, different standards for different groups of authorities in relation to waste recycling, in recognition of differing local circumstances. Where such an approach is relevant and appropriate in environmental control it is capable of being carried forward by recent legislation governing local authorities which is outlined in the following section.

Local Government Acts 1999 and 2000   The Local Government Act 1999 introduces what is described as a 'Best Value' regime. Part of this regime is built on performance indicators and standards provided for by section 4 of the Act. Taking local authorities' pivotal role in relation to recycling as a convenient example from the reference above to this function, it will be remembered that there is a close relationship between waste recycling and the government's *Waste Strategy*. In turn, performance standards are prescribed in respect of this and other functions many of which affect matters of environmental control and regulation vested in local authorities. Such performance standards are intended to enable closer and more sensitive monitoring of achievement in such areas. Although it is perhaps too early to know how the new regime will operate, it may be that any perceived failure in performance is attributable to what are seen as the adverse effects of certain parts of the law. In those circumstances it may be seen to be necessary to re-caste that law and even to raise questions about any 'parent' Community law or member state transposition. Overall the approach in the Local Government Act 1999 may herald a radical new 'bottom-up' approach which might necessarily be extended to the other agencies with environmental responsibilities. The Local Government Act 2000 enables local authorities to do anything which they consider to be likely to achieve any one or more of a number of objects, including the promotion or improvement of the environmental well-being of their respective areas. Accompanying this apparent liberalisation is a statutory requirement that each local authority should prepare what is referred to as a 'community strategy' for this and other purposes, such as one contributing to sustainable development in the United Kingdom. This later Act may well evolve as a complementary provision in the present context if Community strategies are deployed for the purpose of contributing to the foregoing targets and standards.

Standardised and Sectoral Reporting

The section of Chapter One dealing with information management addressed the so-called Standardised Reporting Directive.[60] This Directive as well as other legislation is again relevant in the present context where the concern is with the structures that apply for the purpose of monitoring and measuring transposition in member states. Primarily such structures seek to underpin the accountability of the centre. However, this section of the chapter is concerned also with sectoral reporting where, in addition, there is a concern to ensure that environmental policy integration is achieved, at least within the constraints evident from what is clearly a difficult political process, touched on in Chapter One.

Standardised Reporting

The background to and status of Directive 91/692 was addressed in Chapter One, as already indicated. By way of background to reporting in member states it is useful again to recall some of the observations made in the early 1990s by the House of Lords Select Committee on the European Communities in its report on *Implementation and Enforcement of Environmental Legislation.*[61] The Select Committee considered that in so far as any reliable data is available in member states, that data is often difficult to access and analyse. On the occasion of this investigation, the Select Committee considered that lack of information was the most pervasive theme in its deliberations. The quality of reports from member states to the Commission was often considered to be variable and dependent on the range and technical parameters of monitoring adopted by the relevant national authorities. The Select Committee noted *inter alia* considerable variation in sampling techniques. One way round these constraints was the then anticipated European Environment Agency.

Operation of the Standardised Reporting Directive A decade after the report of the House of Lords Select Committee the Commission reported on the first application of standardised reports from member states under Directive 91/692, spanning the years from 1993 to 1995.[62] The Commission rehearses the essential object of the Directive, which is to facilitate individual reports from member states covering developments in relation to individual directives. Through the harmonisation and improvement of reporting requirements the intention is to generate effective, uniform information where that is an obligation under existing directives as well as where reporting obligations were incorporated subsequently in other directives. The Commission's conclusion is that there was 'significant failure' in the first application of the Directive in the period between 1993 and 1995. In arriving at this conclusion, the Commission points to various reasons for the failure.

Reasons for the Directive's failure Six reasons are advanced for the failure. In the first place the Commission is concerned about concealment of default where a member states appears to be ready to omit incriminating data. The Commission adds that it is such suspicion that would provide the motivation to prosecute for failure to report, bearing in mind that such failure could be concealing infringements of more serious legal obligations. The second reason refers to inadequacies in sampling or measurement. Incompatible measurements and units form the basis of a third reason for failure, taking account of the Directive's requirements in these respects. Inappropriate reporting areas are the fourth reason, where sampling points may have changed from year to year. Here the Commission also points to the Directive's reference to regional totals or averages and member states' submission of disaggregated data. A fifth reason points to what is described as 'muddle' where member states may be omitting a report on transposition having already carried out a similar exercise for the Commission. Finally, the Commission points to a lack of interdepartmental cooperation. Against this background, the Commission goes on to propose new structures in respect of the reporting obligations. What the Report does not point out is that some member states, although they may appear to have a better reporting record than others, may be perpetuating a flawed set of structures by virtue of equally flawed information.

Sectoral Reporting

If the reporting requirements just examined are considered to be challenging and accompanied by a high degree of failure, sectoral reporting in pursuit of environmental policy integration in particular represents an arguably greater challenge. The structural and policy challenges of this integration were addressed in Chapter One. However, at this stage it is important to point out that the reporting (and monitoring) just referred to is inherently limited in its concern for compliance with environmental standards and targets, primarily through Community directives and their transposition. The Community as well as a number of member states have recognised the limitations of this exercise in considering the future merit of so-called 'sector' reporting for areas such as transport and agriculture. It is here that structures are now being considered for the purpose of achieving, perhaps rather more efficiently, the environmental policy integration referred to in Chapter One. Arguably, these new directions raise a question mark over the style and emphasis of any changes to the reporting requirements in respect of the Community directives concerning the environment. A fresher emphasis now appears in the development of various so-called 'indicators'.

The indicators Within the Community Eurostat – the Statistical Office of the Community – has been instrumental in developing future structures based on various indicators. One set of indicators are referred to as Sectoral Integration Indicators covering areas such as agriculture and are being developed within a framework of Environmental Pressure Indicators which identify the most significant pressures on the environment as a result of human activity. Sixty of these latter indicators in 10 areas are to be further developed in order to include an indication of the contribution of policy areas such as agriculture. In addition, work has been proceeding to develop Sustainable Development Indicators and Headline Indicators. These latter indicators will assist in showing sectoral trends. Almost inevitably there is likely to be considerable overlap between these various indicators. Furthermore, the development, testing and application of sectoral and sustainability indicators is more likely to be centred in the member states. All of these developments therefore beg potentially difficult questions about the structures that may be necessary to accommodate them as between the centre and member states. Fundamentally, sectoral initiatives appear to demand an effective set of horizontal structures if relevant environmental impacts are to be both recognised and calculated. Any member state, such as the United Kingdom, which tends to approach monitoring and reporting of environmental standards and targets on an interdepartmental basis may be best placed to anticipate such structural priorities. This of course is but one of many structural questions that will have to be addressed along the vertical line between the centre of the Community and its member states. For the moment it is instructive to illustrate one area of potential progress in relation to sectoral matters, in the area of agriculture.

The agricultural sector This important sector throws up a number of important examples. The way in which this sector is regarded is represented by the treatment of two issues, emissions of nitrous oxide and the loss of nitrogen from agriculture. These issues are addressed by the European Commission in the first edition of its publication *Towards Environmental Pressure Indicators for the EU*[63] and by the Ministry of Agriculture in its publication *Towards Sustainable Agriculture: A pilot set of Indicators.*[64]

The main source of anthropogenic nitrous oxide is intensive agriculture which is dependent on high fertiliser input. The main purpose of the indicator published by the Commission is to monitor total anthropogenic emissions against a background of global and other agreements in relation to greenhouse gas emission reductions. However, it is recognised that there is great uncertainty about total emissions of nitrous oxide. This matter is dealt with by the Ministry of Agriculture under the heading of 'Input use' in relation to greenhouse gas emissions as well as in relation to manure management. In this latter context it is recognised that nitrogen can be lost from manure as nitrous oxide if there is bad manure management on farms. It is recognised further that management approaches will tend to differ according to locality, in which case targets are most appropriately based on specific farms or even fields. One possible target is the number of farmers sampling land and manure prior to land application.

Nitrogen loss from fertiliser application has to be seen in the context of total inputs. Accordingly the Commission's indicator is intended to measure the intensity of manure and fertiliser use and the attendant pressure on water resources, bearing in mind that between 10 and 60 per cent of fertiliser is not taken up by target plants. The consequence is potential damage to human health and ecosystems. Community legislation seeks to set target concentrations in the aquatic environment. Again under the heading of 'Input use' the Ministry of Agriculture refers here to nutrients and the variables which again determine the loss and rate of loss of nitrates from agricultural land. Additionally there are difficulties in discriminating between agricultural and non-agricultural targets. One possible target suggested is the decline in the loss of nitrates where a nitrate sensitive zone has been established in conformity with Community legislation.

Sectoral reporting in agriculture The foregoing examples illustrate how, at the start of the twenty-first century, a great deal of progress is required if sectoral reporting is to become effective, apart from other constraints such as the apparent 'sovereignty' of the Common Agricultural Policy. Almost inevitably there is a two-stage process which appears to characterise sectoral reporting and environmental policy integration. In the first place, the pressure indicators themselves require identification and definition, ideally by reference to a set of robust variables. Thereafter those indicators need to be exposed to those sectors where they are perceived to be relevant. It seems clear, at least from the examples provided, that development of indicators in relation to the environment is but a slow process. That process is being undertaken both at Community and member state level where the apparent difference of perception is clear to see, albeit there is the admission that some indicators are still in their infancy. Of course some indicators, in so far as there is an expectation of objectivity, are inherently difficult to define: landscape is probably a classic example here. Overall therefore, sectoral reporting in aid of environmental policy integration appears a long way off at the time of writing.

The evolution of sectoral reporting It is not unreasonable to speculate that the development of indicators at Community and member state level will tend to blur matters of sovereignty and competence as they impact on sectoral reporting which, by definition, must be regarded as a Community responsibility. Taking the United Kingdom as an example it seems likely that subsidiarity will be extremely significant in facilitating (perhaps) a template under the superintendence of the Commission, within which any member state can determine its own indicators as well as their sectoral application. That model would extend to devolved parts of a member state. In turn, any member state would be encouraged by Community policy and law to maximise related performance standards of the sort found in the Local Government legislation referred to previously. Ultimately it is of course a matter for the Commission to determine sectoral impacts, a critical element of which must be the variables legitimately manifested at member state level.

Structures for Policy Implementation and Enforcement in the United States

The fundamental constitutional structure in the United States links federal and state competence with environmental law and policy which is essentially a federal responsibility and largely justified by the transboundary impact of pollution, the need to concentrate science and technology at the centre where better resources are found, the danger that primary state responsibility here would tend to encourage standards based on the lowest common denominator, and the need to ensure harmonisation of standards across the States in aid of priorities such as certainty about environmental requirements to be met by companies operating across the country. Against this background, Congress usually legislates in broad terms under a widely-defined commerce clause of the Constitution, with the courts being called upon to add detail as the occasion requires. Legislative competence in the present context is subject to an important limitation whereby state legislation cannot be less strict than federal regulation where concurrent jurisdiction exists as between the two levels of government. Where state environmental law is in conflict with federal provision because it is less strict, for example, that state provision is vulnerable to challenge on the ground that it is null and void: so-called 'federal pre-emption'. Where the legality of federal legislation is in issue there is presumption that Congress proceeded rationally and for good cause. Interstate commerce is an area of controversy for present purposes, as will be seen in Chapter Four, usually in the context of attempts by states to legislate regulation of what may be described as 'waste tourism'. Again the presumption is in favour of federal competence here. Beyond the constitutional restrictions just referred to, other restrictions from the same source represent important constraints on the exercise of jurisdiction over the environment. These other restrictions are now outlined, after which the main legislative cornerstones of the environment are outlined.

Further Constitutional Restriction

Constitutional restrictions of particular note for present purposes extend across the Fourth, Fifth and Fourteenth Amendments of the United States Constitution. Each is outlined in turn.

The Fourth Amendment In essence Fourth Amendment seeks to protect the individual against unlawful search and seizure. Accordingly, the overwhelming constitutional requirement relates to the matter of personal security. In practice therefore the law and practice of environmental protection has to be approached with caution. Anything other than what may be described as 'evenhanded' enforcement practices in compliance with the law cannot expect to be upheld before the court.

The Fifth Amendment The Fifth Amendment to the Constitution of the United States stipulates that there should be no 'taking' without payment of due compensation. Of course the fundamental question is whether (say) regulatory action by an environmental agency is so intrusive as to amount to such a 'taking'. Typically, such regulatory action may be seen to so restrict the legitimate use of private property that it can only be regarded as a nullity by reference to this element of the constitution. On the other hand, the regulatory action may be justified by reference to what is described as a 'police power' where, for example, it can be established that action affecting an individual's land is taken for the purpose of preventing toxic pollution of a community's water supplies.

The Fourteenth Amendment This part of the Constitution seeks to guarantee equality before the law. Such protection before the law seeks to avoid unlawful discrimination in whatever form it might arise. Arguably, this constitutional guarantee provides a strong argument for linking primary constitutional competence on the environment to the federal level of government, at the centre. This constitutional cornerstone provides a good example of anticipatory protection, as well as *ex post facto* protection. In practice therefore, equality before the law will no doubt be one of the crucial factors which shapes the provisions which are ultimately legislated.

The Main Legislative Cornerstones

Although there are a number of other fundamentally important federal environmental statutes (which are examined as appropriate elsewhere in other chapters) this section of Chapter Two deals with two cornerstone provisions, the National Environmental Policy Act 1970 and the Pollution Prevention Act 1990. Each statute is dealt with in turn.

The National Environmental Policy Act The Council on Environmental Quality was created under this statute as an advisory body assisting the President on policy development affecting the environment whether nationally or internationally. Additionally there are various other functions assigned by statute, some of the more interesting being the coordination and encouragement of relations between federal, state and local government affecting the environment, reporting (to the President) on the state of the environment, facilitating further development of regulatory and other techniques, and the superintendence of federal Environmental Impact Assessment which is also provided for under the Act of 1970. Environmental Impact Assessment processes are triggered where there is a material federal legislative or other initiative or involvement in a qualifying project which has a significant impact on the human environment. Environmental Impact Assessment procedures may not apply however where an Environmental Assessment is completed and shows an absence of any of these significant impacts. Additionally, the Act obliges federal agencies to take account of the environmental consequences of their actions.

The Pollution Prevention Act This is an interesting statute which anticipates the arguments in favour of graduating beyond more traditional 'command and control' regulatory techniques in order to address pollution prevention and reduction at source. Underpinning the statutory provisions here are funding opportunities directed at the states and their relations with industry. Furthermore, the policy of the Act is very much in favour of the need for the Environmental Protection Agency to address the shortcomings of the traditional regulatory approaches to the environment.

The Environmental Protection Agency

The Agency came into existence in 1970 and has grown to be a major federal agency whose task is to integrate and coordinate measures addressing environmental pollution in cooperation with state and local government. One of the Agency's major functions relates to those few states that do not wish to operate under a federal delegation of authority in the implementation and enforcement of certain mainstream environmental legislation. In these states, the Agency undertakes the task of administering implementation and enforcement programs. In the states that have agreed to participate, usually with the benefit of a measure of federal grant-aid, the Agency nevertheless has responsibility for superintendence of state programs through its regional offices. Those programs operate on the assumption that the state will facilitate implementation and enforcement which is at least as strict as that operated by the Agency. There are powers whereby the Agency can act in default by withdrawing the delegated powers although there are less extreme powers whereby the Agency may resort to enforcement powers where the state in question has refused or failed to act. The practical difficulty in this latter case is that the Agency's action in default breaks an important relationship with the state which will have acted as the Agency's observer on the ground. The subject programs are amenable to Agency review, even as a result of petitions from third party members of the public.

The relationship between the Agency and the states is characterised by considerable tension, not least because federal programs implemented and enforced at state level depend on effective funding. Often that funding appears not to have been available. As a result of this funding shortfall the states have campaigned for greater autonomy from federal influence on the environment. One of the most significant developments in recent times has been the creation of ECOS: the Environmental Council of the States.

ECOS comprises the heads of state environmental agencies. Somewhat surprisingly perhaps, ECOS is funded by the Environmental Protection Agency. The fundamental concern of ECOS is that there should be the greater autonomy just referred to. To a certain extent that autonomy appears to be marginally larger as a result of agreements being made available by the Agency. These agreements are referred to as Performance Partnership Agreements, and Performance Partnership Grants whose parties are the Agency and individual states. The essential difficulty confronting the operation of these agreements is that there is considerable variation in the ability of states to deliver efficient implementation and enforcement of environmental programs.

Canada

Responsibility for control and regulation of the environment is shared between the federal and provincial levels of government. However, the Constitution Act 1867 contains no direct reference to the environment in terms of legislative competence as between the two upper levels of government. The consequence is a rather blurred definition of responsibilities. Nevertheless, a necessary starting point is the Constitution Act.

The Constitution Act 1867

Section 91 of the Act confers on federal government competence in 29 areas, exclusive of certain areas of residual jurisdiction which are not obviously allocated to either level of government and involving matters of peace, order and good government. Areas where the federal government has express competence extend to include jurisdiction over shipping, fisheries, criminal law and interprovincial and international transport and communications. Sections 92 and 93 of the Act confer 17 areas of provincial jurisdiction including the following: municipalities, local works and undertakings, property and civil rights, and the management and sale of public lands in the ownership of a province. In some areas there is a concurrent competence, as in the case of agriculture, by virtue of section 95 of the Act. If a conflict between federal and provincial jurisdiction arises, federal jurisdiction is paramount. Indeed, despite the considerable width of provincial jurisdiction over the environment, there is a considerable residual jurisdiction left with the federal government. That residual jurisdiction will be relied on where the federal government can establish that a subject transaction would frustrate its pre-eminence under the

Constitution of Canada. This legislative framework has not always proved to be totally robust, as a consequence of which the court has sometimes been called upon to determine what may be difficult jurisdictional questions in relation to matters of constitutional competence in the environment. Two critical issues here relate to federal power to deploy the criminal law power in aid of environmental protection and to impose requirements on provincial projects.

Federal Pre-eminence?

The Supreme Court of Canada has in recent years been concerned with the federal power to make criminal law, which is found in section 91(27) of the Constitution Act.[65] By a narrow majority the Supreme Court has found in favour of the criminal enforcement of the Canadian Environmental Protection Act 1985 relating to the regulation of toxic substances. In upholding the validity of certain provisions the Supreme Court stressed that parliament is empowered to legislate only in so far as it does not trespass on areas of exclusive provincial competence. The legislation in issue before the court was not seen as an encroachment on provincial jurisdiction, despite the fact that it might affect matters falling within that competence. Indeed, it was pointed out that the federal power here does not preclude an exercise of provincial powers either independently or in collaboration with the federal power. Five years earlier the Supreme Court had considered whether the federal parliament had power to order an environmental assessment of a 'local work or undertaking', such as a project for the building of a dam in a province.[66] Here the Supreme Court rejected the argument from the province that there was no competence to deal with the environmental effects of provincial project. Stress was placed on the sharing of environmental competence. One member of the Supreme Court rejected any attempt to classify projects as 'federal' or 'provincial' so as to be subject to the exclusive jurisdiction of a particular level of government. The justification for this view is that there is a need to avoid a general doctrine of interjurisdictional immunity to shield provincial works and undertakings from otherwise valid federal legislation.

The Realities of Jurisdictional Distribution

The court has a particularly important function in the present context where, unlike the United States, environmental jurisdiction appears to have fewer clearly drawn constitutional lines. It is not unreasonable to start from a presumption that environmental legislation from either level of government is unlikely to be struck down as a nullity. Ultimately the court seems concerned that there should be no sterilisation of federal or provincial jurisdiction. In many instances legislation emanating from both levels of government may be seen as different responses to the same matter. The fact that more cases do not reach the court on the present issue of jurisdiction is probably explained by a pragmatic desire of the parties to overcome the lack of constitutional clarity affecting competence in the area of the environment.

The Canadian Council of Ministers of the Environment

The Council (CCME) was created for the purpose of promoting cooperation and the coordination of interjurisdictional issues affecting the environment and environmental protection. The Council comprises 14 environment ministers from the federal, provincial and territorial governments who work to propose nationally consistent standards, targets and objectives against a background of federal and provincial government legislative sovereignty. Critically therefore, each constituent government retains competence in relation to matters of implementation and enforcement, including of course competence in deciding whether to adopt proposals emanating from CCME.

Environment Canada

Environment Canada (created in 1971) is the principal federal environment ministry although other federal ministries have environmental responsibilities: Heritage Canada, for example. Environment Canada operates through five regional offices and enforces about 15 federal statutes which are binding on the provinces. This federal legislation contains many provisions which seek to encourage cooperation with the provinces, usually through the environment ministries of those provinces.

The National Round Table on the Environment and Economy

This body dates from 1994. As an agency independent of the federal government the Round Table undertakes the generation of objective, accurate information for the benefit of agencies concerned with the environment. In addition the Round Table has responsibility for the formulation of policy and recommendations for action in connection with sustainable development. Soon after creation of the Round Table the federal government established a Commissioner of the Environment and Sustainable Development reporting to the Auditor-General on his monitoring of ministries' compliance with strategies for sustainable development. At provincial level, in Ontario, there exists the Ontario Bill of Rights allowing public participation where proposals for legislation and other measures affecting the environment are placed in the public domain. The Bill of Rights is subject to the superintendence of the Environmental Commissioner who reports to the provincial Parliament, which is responsible for his appointment.

Notes

1   Buller, H. (1998), 'Reflections across the Channel', in P. Lowe and S. Ward (eds), *British Environmental Policy and Europe*, Routledge, London, p. 68.
2   OJ L87, 27.3.85.
3   OJ L365, 31.12.94. *Cf.* Chapter One, nn. 23 and 95.
4   Unreported: Case C–473/98, ECJ 11.7.2000.
5   Cases C–418/97 and 419/97, 15.6.2000. ARCO is reported at [2001] Env.L.R. DG6.
6   OJ L35, 5.2.97.
7   2nd Report (Session 1997–98).
8   9th Report (Session 1991–92).
9   EC Bulletin, Vol.26, Part 10, at p. 118.
10 EC Bulletin, Vol.10, Part 8, at p. 121.
11 See, for example, *Officier van Justice v. van den Hazel* [1977] ECR901, at p. 909.
12 OJ L160, 26.6.99.
13 3rd Report (Session 1993–94).
14 2nd Report (Session 1997–98).
15 17th Report (Session 1997–98).
16 *ARCO Chemie Nederland* and *Epon* (Joined Cases C–418/97 and 419/97), *supra*, n. 5.
17 Memorandum of Understanding and Supplementary Agreements between the United Kingdom Government, Scottish Ministers, the Cabinet of the National Assembly for Wales and the Northern Ireland Executive, Cm 4806, July 2000.
18 Cm 4053 (1998), The Stationery Office, London, para. 8.76.
19 *Ibid.*, para. 1.16.
20 OJ L336, 7.12.88.
21 OJ L188, 16.7.84.
22 OJ L 350, 28.12.98.
23 OJ L229, 30.8.80.
24 OJ L296, 21.11.96.
25 OJ L257, 10.10.96.
26 OJ L129, 18.5.76.
27 *Supra*, n. 21.
28 DETR, Scottish Office, Welsh Office (July 1997 and January 1998) (1st and 2nd Consultation Papers); DETR (December 1998) (3rd Consultation Paper); DETR (August, 1999) (4th Consultation Paper).
29 OJ L182, 16.7.99.

30 *Supra*, n. 20.
31 Environment Agency (1999). *Cf.* Chapter One, nn. 53 and 54.
32 *Supra*, nn. 23 and 24.
33 OJ L297, 13.10.92.
34 OJ L230, 19.8.91.
35 OJ L123, 24.4.98.
36 OJ L 85, 29.3.99.
37 *Supra*, n. 3.
38 *Supra*, n. 33.
39 *Supra*, n. 24.
40 *Supra*, n. 25.
41 Chapter One, n. 20.
42 OJ L168, 10.7.93.
43 Circular 2/95, Department of the Environment.
44 *Ibid.*, paras 6 and 7.
45 *Supra*, n. 20.
46 *Supra*, n. 36.
47 Lowe, P. and Ward, S. (1998), 'Domestic Winners and Losers', in P. Lowe and S. Ward
    (eds), *British Environmental Policy and Europe*, Routledge, London, p. 96.
48 1st Report (Session 2000–01).
49 OJ C485, 18.3.92.
50 OJ L182, 16.7.99.
51 *Supra*, n. 40.
52 Environment Act 1995, s.4(1) to (3).
53 6th Report (Session 1999–2000).
54 *Supra*, n. 5.
55 *Supra*, n. 25.
56 *Supra*, n. 36.
57 [1998] Env.L.R.39.
58 9th Report (Session 1991–92).
59 Chapter One, n. 51.
60 Chapter One, n. 88.
61 *Supra*, n. 58.
62 European Commission (2000), 'The Standardised Reporting Directive', Luxembourg.
63 European Commission, 1999.
64 Ministry of Agriculture, 1999.
65 *R. v. Hydro-Quebec* [1997] 3 SCR213; (1997) 118 CCC(3d) 97.
66 *Friends of the Oldman River Society v. Canada* (Minister of Transport) [1992] 1 S.C.R.3.

Chapter Three

Policy, Principle and Law

The Background

This chapter builds on the first two chapters in considering the status of the Community principles referred to in the first chapter and listed below, in relation to the process of implementing and enforcing Community law and policy on the environment. Additionally and in the first part of the chapter consideration is given to what is capable of implementation and enforcement by way of standards and targets. As such this first part of the chapter not only builds on elements of the first two chapters but also anticipates much of what appears in the remaining chapters. The principles are widely defined and include proportionality, the precautionary principle, the preventative principle, the polluter pays principle and the proximity principle. As well as the principles just listed, reference must be made also to environmental policy integration (EPI) referred to in Chapter One, and subsidiarity, referred to in Chapter Two. Towards to end of the chapter attention turns to the way in which the foregoing principles have influenced the shape, content and evolution of 'best available techniques not entailing excessive cost' (BATNEEC), 'best available techniques' (BAT) and 'best practical environmental option' (BPEO) as the drivers of several important regulatory regimes.

The Realisation of Standards and Targets

European Community policy on the environment seeks to set standards and targets by reference to numerous impacts. Whether such policy is crystallised in law, typically through the terms of a directive, will depend on many variables not least of which will relate to the question whether any standards and targets are legally enforceable. Where a standard is the potential subject of a legally-enforceable limit, it may be assumed that there is some justification, albeit a 'precautionary' justification for crystallisation in law. However, it must be asked whether, if that standard is implemented through the law, there is justification for (say) regulatory control. That justification is manifested by some assumption or assurance that the law will be effective and, in turn, credible. In practice it is often the case that thresholds represent an important variable for these purposes: prescribed standards may be qualified for good reason if it is not practicable to pursue enforcement against a large number of smaller industrial polluters, for example. This is not to suggest that other varieties of threshold are not available in relation to the substance for which a standard may be prescribed by law. Of course there is the possibility that no threshold operates in respect of the substance concerned. However, whether effective enforcement is available in such circumstances may be open to debate. Accordingly the need for practicability if implementation and enforcement is to be effective necessarily directs attention to other approaches, such as averaging emissions or discharges or ensuring that the subject standard is achieved (say) in 95 per cent of all samples taken. In turn, such sampling for the purposes of monitoring depends on there being an effective definition of that standard. Given the nature of Community law and policy development on the environment involving political compromises on occasions for example, it might be rather ambitious to claim that all Community standard-setting here is 'effective'. Indeed, there may be occasions where developments in environmental regulation are perceived as being desirable in a member state but progress is thwarted by uncertainties about the position as it is affected both by Community and municipal law. This appears to be the case in relation to the development of toxicity-based consents in the United Kingdom.

Toxicity-based Consents

The control of complex chemical discharges presents a particular problem since not all of the constituents can be monitored and regulated. It is against this background that toxicity-based consents appear to have advantages compared with more traditional approaches. Those advantages arise from the ability to measure the overall effects of all the pollutants in a discharge. Some of those pollutants may not be easily identifiable while the toxicology of others will be difficult or even impossible to define with certainty. Adoption of toxicity-based consenting has an interesting potential also because toxicity criteria affecting wildlife can be developed, for example. Otherwise the general merit of such an approach is that it allows attention to focus on the impact of industrial discharges on the receiving medium. However, there has been long-term controversy in the Community on the merits of 'end of pipe' approaches to control of the aquatic environment, compared with regulatory approaches which focus on the capacity of the receiving medium. For many years member states have had the freedom to adopt either approach in their transposition of water legislation. Apart from this background of political controversy and likely objection to toxicity-based consents within the Community, there appear to be barriers to such a change of approach in United Kingdom legislation. This is to be seen in the Water Industry Act 1991, which (in its provisions governing trade effluent discharges to the public sewer) refers to the limits to be set for the 'constituents of a trade effluent' rather than broader matters of toxicity. Similarly, in the Water Resources Act 1991 there are prescribed criteria for the setting of discharge conditions. Here, conditions may include a specification about the nature, origin, composition, temperature, volume and rate of discharge of an effluent, as well as periods when discharges may occur. Away from the uncertainties just described how can Community standard and target-setting be characterised?

Community Standard and Target-setting

Although there some are examples of Community environmental legislation which lacks specificity in relation to standards and targets, the overall legislative style seeks generally to avoid discretion. The merit of an approach which avoids undue discretion lies of course in the facility for more efficient control of member state transposition of environmental legislation including the enforcement of standards and targets at member state level. That control is of course ultimately in the hands of the Commission and, finally, the European Court of Justice. The nature of that control goes beyond matters of strict legality of the sort that characterises judicial review under English law, for example. The scope of control here is a necessary consequence of the fact that standard and target-setting may be less than specific. A lack of specificity may be seen most clearly in relation to the means of implementation as well as in relation to matters of enforcement where there is a clearer assumption that member states will have discretion. Each of these situations will now be examined in turn. These situations can be contrasted with other areas of Community legislation where the member state is given discretion to disapply standards and targets.

Means of implementation Directive 94/62[1] on Packaging and Packaging Waste sets a range of mandatory targets for member states. However, the Directive goes on to give member states discretion in relation to implementation of their own return and management systems. Elsewhere, the Bathing Waters Directive[2] requires that member states take all 'necessary' measures to comply with prescribed limit values.

Matters of enforcement The extent of member state discretion here is seen in the Solvents Directive[3] (Directive 1999/13) which allows a member state to prescribe sanctions in the event of an infraction. Such sanctions must be '... effective, proportionate and dissuasive'. By contrast, the Bathing Waters Directive just referred to contains no express reference to requirements following noncompliance which could be seen to keep member state options open: for example there would be no necessary obligation on that member state to prohibit swimming.

Discretion to disapply targets and standards The Waste Framework Directive[4] (75/442) seeks to encourage waste recovery. In so doing the Directive provides member states with discretion to provide exemptions in respect of recovery projects, albeit subject to conditions. A notable example here is the '... spreading of waste on land resulting in benefit to agriculture or ecological improvement', as described by the municipal regulations applying to England and Wales. Other exemptions under the same municipal regulations and from the same Directive relate to land reclamation projects. The Environment Agency is subject to a statutory duty to undertake periodic inspections of such projects. However, there are necessary concerns arising from such discretionary arrangements. For example it may be asked, how much waste is being consigned to these exempt sites, do the exemptions protect the environment and human health, and is there any suggestion that 'sham' recovery is occurring here? Reference will be made later to the matter of enforcement at member state level. In the meantime it is necessary to recognise that member states are obliged to report their transposition measures to the Commission.

Monitoring Transposition

Enough has been said above to indicate that transposition is a multifaceted process which depends essentially on the terms of the subject Community legislation. It appears that the major problem relates to the time taken by member states to report their actions for this purpose. This emerges from a report published by the Community and entitled *Monitoring the Application of Community Law.*[5] Here reference is made to particular problems with two directives: those dealing with Environmental Assessment (85/337)[6] and Freedom of Access to Environmental Information (90/313).[7] The first of these directives has attracted consistent criticism of member state transposition, for a variety of reasons including the coverage of environmental assessment requirements in municipal law and the need for effective interstitial application within the existing framework of planning, pollution and amenity regulation. The second of these directives has attracted criticism by reference to noncompliance with the requirement that suitable procedures are provided for the purpose of challenges to wrong decisions in respect of applications for access to information. These examples provide suitable illustrations of the more difficult areas of implementation and enforcement where there is no question whether an objective standard or target has been achieved. Nevertheless, even here implementation and enforcement by member states is certainly not without difficulty where the legality of transposition is in issue. This of course is one major reason why attention was given earlier in this work to Community initiatives for the purpose of improving the integrity and accuracy of environmental data. Although such initiatives may give the impression that it is the Community alone that has a concern for such matters, member state institutions such as the courts (the subject of Chapter 4Four), environmental agencies and parliamentary bodies may also contribute to the matter of compliance through accurate transposition. The sections of the chapter that follow look at transposition monitoring by parliamentary bodies and environmental agencies in member states, followed by some additional reflections on transposition processes affecting standards and targets as a result of such experience.

Parliamentary monitoring Frequent reference has been made already to the work of Select and other committees of the United Kingdom parliament in addressing the adequacy – and quality – of transposition in the United Kingdom. The process and adequacy of transposition is an important matter in many of the deliberations of the Joint (House of Commons and House of Lords) Committee on Statutory Instruments. By way of example, the Joint Committee pointed out in one of its reports[8] that an item of subordinate legislation, the Batteries and Accumulators (Containing Dangerous Substances) Regulations 1994,[9] had not fully implemented Directive 91/157 on Batteries and Accumulators.[10] The Directive requires the manufacturer of an appliance to ensure that a battery or accumulator which is, or is to be, incorporated into that appliance can be readily removed, when spent, by the consumer. Against this background, the Committee considered that limiting the time during which a blind eye is turned to further breaches of statutory requirements cannot be described as remedying a breach that has occurred. Furthermore, if compliance with the Directive is to be 'ensured' the need for redesign (for example) is time-limited to before the occurrence of any breach of the municipal regulations. Those regulations in failing to provide any sanction for breach of particular

Directive requirements for present purposes, had failed fully to implement its terms according to the Committee's report. That report appends the response of the Department of the Environment and shows graphically the difficulty of transposition as a practical exercise in some cases. The Department of the Environment considered it reasonable that a manufacturer should be given an opportunity to remedy a breach before enforcement measures via a criminal prosecution are applied. Ensuring that a battery can be readily removed by the consumer involves redesign and consequential retooling, all of which takes time. The Department of the Environment went on to stress that the length of the prescribed period of notice should take account of these matters, and that the intention of this part of the Directive is more effectively achieved by these means, rather than through immediate application of criminal sanctions.

Monitoring by environmental agencies The enforcement process in member states may provide critical evidence of the effectiveness of transposition. A reading of annual reports of bodies such as the Environment Agency in the United Kingdom will identify assumptions and expectations in relation to the essential requirements of Community law. It may be, for example, that enforcement policies and indicators do not marry up with directive requirements for the important purposes of specific sampling, general monitoring and overall enforcement. It is in this latter area where the adequacy of transposition has to be regarded with some caution in the light of the discretion accorded to member states in the matter of enforcement. It will be recalled that reference was made above to the Solvents Directive[11] where sanctions must be '... effective, proportionate and dissuasive'. If the Commission and, ultimately, the European Court of Justice are to intervene there will be a need for cogent evidence of failure in respect of adequacy of the statutory enforcement provisions or their application, or both. In this latter respect, statutory and political control of enforcing agencies is clearly a matter of importance where member state accountability before the law of the Community is concerned.

Transposition processes The foregoing reference to transposition of the Batteries and Accumulators Directive serves to emphasise the difficulties of transposition through municipal legislation, despite the extent of available discretion to reflect cultural and other member state characteristics. A far less complicated approach is based on the use of statutory directions to the enforcing agencies where such directions directly incorporate Community standards and targets in relation to environmental authorisations and consents. Direct application of such standards and targets have the apparent advantage of avoiding many of the procedural requirements which attend the making of subordinate legislation through statutory instruments. Delay in this latter respect may for example compromise member state attempts to secure timely implementation where (for example) consultation processes have occupied a considerable amount of time. Statutory directions are ostensibly less potentially controversial than subordinate legislation since their essential purpose is to implement legislated Community targets and standards. Clearly though, statutory directions have only a limited utility. Where there is significant discretion left to the member state, there will no doubt be a wish to adopt its own approach to enforcement, for example. Where (say) an area of environmental regulation has been enforced hitherto by criminal sanctions it may be seen that such a limited approach is not necessarily '... effective, proportionate and dissuasive', to use the words of the Solvents Directive, previously referred to. In these circumstances there may be a wish to transpose the subject directive by means of rather more positive measures which do not (initially at least) rely on the application of criminal sanctions. Much of what has been written here assumes that Community law as manifested through a directive requires transposition within a discrete regulatory or similar framework. However, transposition may have added complications of a considerable magnitude beyond the directive in question. This is certainly the case where the Habitats Directive[12] (Directive 92/43) is concerned. Where Special Areas of Conservation are designated, all discharge consents, abstraction licences, integrated pollution control authorisations, flood defence arrangements and planning consents have to be subjected to review to ensure habitat and species protection. In this case regulatory and other arrangements, not all of which will have emanated from Community law, will demand reconsideration.

Community Environmental Principles

The EC Treaty refers at the outset to a rather disparate set of so-called 'principles' although not limited to matters of the Community environmental competence. This section of the chapter deals with those principles as they affect the environment. The exceptions are subsidiarity and environmental policy integration (EPI) which have been dealt with earlier. The remaining principles are recognised, to a greater or lesser extent, by the Treaty.[13] The general characteristic of the principles is that they must be presumed not to be legally enforceable, but serve essentially as a guide to the formation of policy generally and (for present purposes) the formation of environmental policy.

In practice the principles, or some of them, are used by member states either for purposes connected with implementation of their own policy beyond the jurisdiction of the Community, or for purposes connected with their own transposition of Community-generated standards and targets. The presumption that the principles are not legally enforceable is tested in Chapter Four. Suffice it say here that the principles may have the potential, exceptionally, for enforcement in relation to decision-making which is vulnerable to judicial review. With the exception of subsidiarity and EPI, each of these principles is now dealt with, in turn.

Proportionality

Simply stated this principle requires that the costs of complying with legal requirements should be proportionate to the assumed beneficial outcome of such compliance. Excessive requirements therefore will be presumed not to apply. In order to determine whether the principle might apply to negate a policy initiative on the environment, a balancing of economic and other inputs is required in order to appreciate the net benefit where protection or enhancement of the environment is concerned. As such, it will be seen below that this principle complements the precautionary principle in the development of Community environmental and other policies. In a communication adopted by the Commission on *The Precautionary Principle*[14] it is stated that any measure (not necessarily a legal measure) emerging from the Community where scientific risk assessment is not complete should be proportionate in the level of protection provided, nondiscriminatory in application, consistent with other comparable measures, subject to cost-benefit analysis and reviewed by reference to scientific data.

In a wider context, proportionality has been a general principle of Community law for some time and has been relied on where the legality of Community action has been contested or where the legality of a member state measure seeking to implement a Community requirement has been open to challenge before the court. Even where it is not a Community requirement which is in issue, proportionality may have an important bearing on the enforceability of environmental standards and targets. This was seen in Chapter One in relation to the matter of overlapping policy concerns.[15] In *Commission v. Denmark*[16] the European Court of Justice held that Denmark's deposit and return scheme was not disproportionate to environmental objectives: in some circumstances environmental protection can be accorded the status of a mandatory legal requirement that may justify a restriction on the free trade in goods throughout the Community. Any such member state scheme will therefore be expected to comply with the principle of proportionality as well as being nondiscriminatory. The same approach can be seen in *Aher-Waggon Gmbh v. Germany*[17] where the directive in question set noise standards in respect of aircraft. Transposition in Germany was on the basis of higher standards. However, these higher standards applied to aircraft previously registered in another member state of the Community: aircraft previously registered in Germany were not subject to these more stringent requirements. The question for the European Court of Justice was whether this approach was contrary to Article 30 of the Treaty in hindering intra-Community trade. It was held that despite hindrance to such trade, the approach could be justified by reference to considerations of public health and protection of the environment. Furthermore, the approach adopted in this case was not seen as being disproportionate to the objectives of the legislation. The courts' attitude to proportionality will be taken up again in the following chapter.

To return to the matter of environmental policy and proportionality, it is essential that the present principle is adhered to in policy development at the centre as well as at member state level. The final consultation on implementation of Integrated Pollution Prevention and Control[18] illustrates the point well. Here the government took the view that, in the absence of express textual support in the Directive an implied triviality threshold for those installations posing only a minimal environmental impact could not be justified by reference to the principle of proportionality. Interestingly though, awareness of the principle pushed the consultation in the direction of a proposal to treat such installations with a rather lighter regulatory touch by subjecting them to a simplified 'permitting' regime.

The Precautionary Principle

Defining the precautionary principle contrasts with the relative certainty of defining a principle which is encapsulated in statute law, such is the rather elastic, political nature of this principle. Equally elastic (and uncertain) is the relationship between the precautionary principle and the next principle to be examined, the preventative principle. Nevertheless, one useful starting point is the definition of the precautionary principle found in the Rio Declaration on Environment and Development. The Rio Declaration saw the principle in these terms:

... where there are threats of serious or irreversible damage, lack of full scientific certainty shall not be used as a reason for postponing cost-effective measures to prevent environmental degredation.[19]

This and other closely related views of the principle are not without difficulty, as will be seen below. However, before these difficulties are addressed it is necessary to recognise also the extent to which the principle is already part of the grain of environmental law and policy in many corners of the world, largely as a result of the influence of the Rio Declaration. Indeed, Principle 15 (from which the extract above is taken) starts by declaring that:

In order to protect the environment, the precautionary approach shall be widely applied by States according to their capabilities.[20]

However, even before the Rio Declaration, global and other initiatives on the environment were cognisant of the principle, as can be seen in the first global initiative on atmospheric quality, the Vienna Convention on the Protection of the Ozone Layer, a Convention to which the Community is a party. Here the text shows that the framers of and parties to, the Convention were:

... mindful ... of the precautionary measures for the protection of the ozone layer which have already been taken at national and international levels.

Two years later, the Montreal Protocol was notable for its development of the Vienna Convention and, more particularly, a precautionary approach referable to the restriction of production of ozone-depleting substances. The Montreal Protocol demonstrated an awareness of the need for regulation based on what was described as 'relevant scientific knowledge'. Nevertheless, the Protocol goes on to stipulate that the parties are determined to address protection of the ozone layer through precautionary measures for the purpose of equitable control of total global emissions. Despite the clear importance of these ambitions there remain real problems associated with the meaning that might be given to the precautionary principle. These problems, which are debated later in the chapter, are worthy of emphasis since, as will be seen, the precautionary principle has been actively applied – and recognised – by the Community (including the European Court of Justice) as well as member states. In the meantime, attention must turn to the essential characteristics of the principle before consideration is given to problems of meaning, the status of the principle in policy formation and in the enforcement process.

Characteristics of the Precautionary Principle

The principle has been described frequently as one that necessitates a change in the burden of proof on environmental issues. These were the terms in which the Royal Commission on Environmental Pollution approached the principle in its 21st Report on 'Setting Environmental Standards'.[21] The Royal Commission goes on to view the principle as a rational response to the uncertainties of science as they affect the environment, as well as the uncertainties surrounding the consequences of action or inaction.[22] Against this background the principle operates as a political variable, initially in the policy-making process. The inherent flexibility of the principle, as well as its important relationship with some or all of the other principles to be examined later in the chapter can be illustrated in several sets of circumstances as the policy-making process develops into implementation and enforcement. In the first place, there is important flexibility in the uncertainty surrounding some of the words and phrases, allowing deployment of a very fluid political discretion in policy formation and beyond. Secondly, a notional, vertical scale of scientific certainty may allow maximum flexibility in determining whether the principle will apply to particular policy transactions. For example, it may be determined that there is 'sufficient' scientific certainty such that the principle need not apply, or that such certainty can be achieved within an effective limit of time. Thirdly, there appears to be a larger measure of flexibility in the initial policy-making process at the centre of the Community unlike the situation where others may subsequently be called upon to apply or determine the 'proper' application of the principle, albeit defined in marginally more objective terms. In other words the greater the politically-charged policy-making process the more likely it is that the principle will be seen as having fewer hard edges constraining action. Nevertheless, against this background, the Commission has published guidelines relating to the precautionary principle.[23]

Commission guidelines The Commission notes that one particular area of concern relates to those occasions when science is unable to give a full evaluation of critical risks. Against this background the Commission recognises that the principle is an element in risk management where the environment, human and animal health are concerned. Importantly, the Commission goes on to stress that the principle should be resorted to where there is *potential* risk rather than to disguise arbitrary decision-making of the sort that might tend to arise where there appears to be a large measure of political discretion available in the policy-making arena. That discretion may also be influenced by pressures exerted by the need to recognise individual rights as well as trade implications, both of which may be compromised by a perceived need for regulatory or other legislation. The Commission's guidance seeks to focus attention on those circumstances where science identifies potentially negative effects in the absence of a quantification of the certainty of that risk. It is here that the Commission counsels adoption of the precautionary principle. However, a scientific audit of a failure to act is seen as being necessary: such an audit would need to be communicated to interested parties for the purpose of determining possible risk management options. In turn, and beyond this perceived need for transparency and public participation, any resulting action (which may not necessarily be statutory measures) needs to be proportionate to the level of protection to be applied, nondiscriminatory in application, consistent with other comparable measures, subject to cost-benefit analysis, and reviewed against the background of scientific data. Once again there is recognition by the Commission of the likely need to reverse the burden of proof in pursuit of the precautionary principle. There is no better illustration of this reversal of the burden of proof than in Community legislation governing dangerous, toxic substances. The regulatory measures dealing with dangerous, toxic substances shows that precautionary approaches may be justified, because sufficient scientific evidence is as yet unavailable or that available evidence is, as yet, insufficiently robust. This is but one example of several that are set out in this section of the chapter.

Regulatory control of dangerous, toxic substances The Community generated legislation towards the end of the 1960s in order to deal with the classification, packaging and labelling of dangerous substances. Directive 67/548[24] operates essentially by requiring testing and assessment prior to any marketing of a subject dangerous substance. The harmonised arrangements necessitate reporting of test results and risk assessment by the manufacturer or importer. This regulatory regime emphasises the formidable challenge presented by the need to assess and approve huge numbers of new substances by reference to the underlying assumptions carried by the precautionary principle. Community legislation was seen as necessary also for the purpose of dealing with risk assessment affecting existing substances. This was achieved through Regulation 793/93[25] which again addresses the regulatory obligations of manufacturers and importers of substances covered by statute here. This area of regulatory action is addressed in rather more detail, along with the development of US law, in Chapter Eight. Before this matter is left, it is important to stress that the express terms of the legislation set out the regulatory framework and the control factors which will restrict marketing pending examination and approval of substances by reference to their impact (or likely impact) on the environment, human and animal health. The implicit basis of such legislation is the foregoing precautionary principle. While the explicit regulatory framework is legally enforceable, the same cannot be said of the precautionary policy base from which that framework was implemented by the force of law.

The precautionary principle and legal enforceability There is ample authority for the conclusion that the precautionary principle is not of itself legally enforceable. This matter was before the English High Court in *R. v. Secretary of State for Trade and Industry, ex p. Duddridge*[26] where it had been alleged that the Secretary of State should have taken precautionary action to prevent the risk of childhood leukaemia arising from exposure to the electromagnetic fields created by overhead power cables. The applicants proceeded (in part) on the argument that the precautionary principle is a binding legal principle in the law of the United Kingdom and the European Community. Failure by the Secretary of State to legislate by regulation in the present context was argued to be in breach of this principle. Smith, J. confirmed the absence of any comprehensive and authoritative definition of the precautionary principle. Accordingly, the judge rejected argument that precautionary measures will be required where evidence exists of a possible risk, despite the fact that that evidence is presently unclear and there is no proof of a causal connection. The judge therefore held that the principle had no binding legal authority, having been adopted voluntarily by the government of the United Kingdom as a policy principle only. The court in *Duddridge* was referred to authority in the European Court of Justice, in the case of *Peralta,* adopting essentially the same approach.[27]

Problems of Meaning

Given the nature of the precautionary principle it is hardly surprising that there is a lack of clarity in its meaning. The Royal Commission on Environmental Pollution has observed[28] that the interpretation and application of the principle inevitably raises questions about values where (for example) terms such as 'serious and irreversible', 'full scientific certainty' and 'cost-effective' are concerned. These uncertainties are in addition to the broader question whether, in policy-making, the principle is to apply as a matter of political or other discretion. Equally there is no doubt that uncertainties about meaning lead to the concerns expressed by the Commission in its guidelines on the application of the principle. One example is found in a report of the House of Lords Select Committee on the European Communities on *Waste Incineration*.[29] The Select Committee observes that there was no evidence presented of any scientific proof of a direct causal link between any incinerators in the United Kingdom and local mortality or morbidity. In turn the Committee considered it to be wrong that, when the precautionary principle is applied, public concern about health implications is discounted (particularly in relation to dioxins) on the ground that it is derived from experience of an older generation of municipal incinerator which has been effectively been outlawed under terms of Community legislation on the subject.

The Status of the Principle in Policy Formation

It has been seen already that the principle is open for application both at the centre of the Community, and in member states. At member state level, the principle is in evidence not only in connection with policy formation but also in anticipation of policy formation.

In England and Wales the *Waste Strategy 2000* deals with matters such as sewage sludge management and gives explicit recognition to an informal agreement between the water industry and major food retailers, as a result of which various precautionary changes will apply to the application of sludge to agricultural land. In particular, the strategy points to a phasing out of all use of untreated sewage sludge on agricultural land by the end of 2001; more stringent requirements applying to the performance of sludge treatment processes; and the reduction of maximum lead concentrations in soil. The strategy also anticipates necessary amendments to statute, as well as changes in accompanying codes of practice referable to the spreading of sewage sludge on agricultural land.

Wherever the principle is in evidence at member state level its influence must be regarded with some caution according to the emphasis chosen by the government of that state. In 1990, the United Kingdom government's approach to the precautionary principle was seen in an attitude that allowed resort to it only in the event of a *significant* risk of environmental damage, and where there is justification based on cost/benefit analysis.[30]

At the centre of the Community it has been seen already how the principle has influenced the core of policy on dangerous substances. Another significant example of the precautionary principle in action is to be found in Directive 91/271 on Urban Waste Water Treatment.[31] This Directive is based squarely on the principle: as such it does not identify the water quality to be achieved but defines the means by which its environmental objectives can be achieved. More specifically there are in the law here requirements for further treatment of sewage prior to discharge through prescription of treatment standards, as opposed to a concern for water quality standards that characterise many other directives in the aquatic environment. Accordingly, Article 4 of the Directive identifies so-called 'secondary' treatment as the norm for receiving water which are not defined as being 'sensitive' waters. Those sensitive waters demand more stringent treatment of waste water.

The Status of the Principle in the Enforcement Process

Although the precautionary principle receives no definition in the EC Treaty it is well recognised (following the Maastricht Treaty) in the terms of Article 174 which insists that policy on the environment shall be based on precaution, prevention and proximity. It is clear though that the principle works on a wider scale, particularly at member state level, where it can play a part both in policy formation as well as in the enforcement process. The only caution here is that a member state attitude (such as that of the United Kingdom) might be regarded as qualified attitude to the principle. This is the case in the United Kingdom where it has been seen already that precaution tends to be hedged around with conditions relating to its application. Apart from this the principle has what can only be described as (at least) an implicit recognition among those who may have a part to play in the implementation and enforcement of law and policy on the environment. The House of Commons Environment Committee in a report on *Water Conservation and Supply*[32] was concerned about the incidence of drought orders: at the time of the Committee's deliberations on the subject drought orders had been implemented in 11 of the 20 years since 1976:

> This represents a considerable erosion of environmental safeguards and indicates that drought orders may be becoming a routine aspect of water management ... the precautionary principle is not being applied in practice ... We do not consider that drought orders are an environmentally and economically viable way of managing water supplies ...[33]

This and other aspects environmental management may of course benefit from the precautionary anticipation of problems.

Such an approach can be found in the development plans which are provided for under the Town and Country Planning Act 1990. Where development control decision-making is concerned precautionary policies in planning terms may directly benefit matters of environmental and pollution control.

The enforcement process necessarily includes the courts who should be aware of the essential objectives of Community law and policy manifested in Article 174. In *ARCO Chemie Nederland and Epon*[34] the European Court of Justice was concerned with the meaning of 'waste' for the purposes of the Community's Waste Framework Directive. The Court had no doubt that the term had to be interpreted by reference to the aims of the Directive whose essential objectives are the protection of human health and the environment at a high level of protection based on precautionary and preventative action.

Previously the Court had been concerned with the legality of a regulation introduced by the Danish government prohibiting the keeping of bees, except the Laeso brown bee. The proceedings arose when a local beekeeper was convicted after acting in breach of the regulation, whereupon he sought to raise the legality of the regulation by reference to the applicability of national restrictions extending to, *inter alia*, the protection of health and life of animals. Because the restriction was regarded by the Court as being proportionate it was upheld. However, the Court also upheld the legality of the statutory restriction by reference to the fact that there is no requirement for an immediate threat to the life of animals since the precautionary principle allows for anticipatory measures.

Nevertheless, there may be a difficult line to draw between precaution and proportionality, as was seen in a decision of the English High Court in *R. v. Environment Agency, ex p. Dockgrange Ltd. and Mayer Parry Ltd.*[35] In this case the applicants undertook recycling in the United Kingdom and were importers of fragmentiser waste from the Netherlands and Germany. The relevant Community regulations categorise waste as 'green', 'amber' and 'red' for the purpose of identifying (respectively) wastes which are least environmentally hazardous, wastes requiring prior notification to the competent authorities in the countries of dispatch and destination, so allowing objections, and (finally) wastes which are most environmentally hazardous, again requiring prior notification but with no limit of time in relation to the giving of consent. Fragmentiser waste was not expressly listed as such. The Agency took the view that this waste remained unassigned under the terms of the subject regulations and therefore was to be treated as 'red' waste, despite the fact that the 'green' list contained categories of waste contained in fragmentiser waste. The decision of the Agency, which caused the applicant companies considerable hardship, was argued to be consistent with the precautionary principle. However, it was held that the Agency's approach could not be justified where (as here) the components all were found to be in the 'green' category. The judge was aided in his conclusion by what were described as ordinary principles of purposive construction and proportionality which avoid companies being put out of business where a solution is available, consistent with the scheme of Community law. Accordingly, the order of the court was that the Agency should desist from enforcement action against the companies.

The Preventative Principle

This principle is of course intimately connected with the precautionary principle for the purpose of the fundamental terms of the Treaty as manifested in Article 174, already referred to. Explicit recognition was accorded originally by the Single European Act but not before, in 1983, preventative action was announced as a cornerstone of the 3rd Environmental Action Programme. Against this background it is perhaps easy to conclude that prevention adds very little, if anything, to precaution. Before any effective conclusion can be drawn about the status of preventative action for present purposes it is necessary to see where such action features in the implementation and enforcement processes which characterise environmental law and policy.

Preventative Action in Practice

A number of examples drawn from the law will serve to establish a pattern which may help to identify a specific role for the preventative principle. In the first place, Directive 84/360 on air pollution from industrial plants stipulates that authorisation granted by competent authorities in member states should be subject, *inter alia*, to a condition that:

> ... all appropriate preventative measures against air pollution must be taken (this includes applying the best available technology provided this does not entail excessive costs); emissions, particularly those listed in [Annex 2], must not cause significant air pollution; emission limit values must not be exceeded [and] air quality limit values must be taken into account.

Directive 94/67[36] on the incineration of hazardous waste stipulates that an authorisation here depends on the matters of design, equipment and operation being linked with all appropriate pollution prevention measures. In similar terms, the IPPC Directive (96/61[37]) carries the requirement that any subject installation is operated by reference (again) to appropriate pollution prevention measures. Here the law is attempting to force the technology surrounding the process towards an engineered solution which either minimises or avoids generation of offending pollutants in the first place. Finally, the Environmental Assessment Directive (85/337[38]) is characterised by a concern for prevention where (for example) it is considered that a subject project will have 'significant effects' on the environment, if implemented. However, resort to a preventative principle here is qualified in the absence of any prescribed standard or target, either in Community legislation or in member state legislation seeking to achieve transposition.

The Status of the Preventative Principle

The foregoing examples from the mainstream of Community environmental law show that the principle may have a rather more immediate task in the implementation and enforcement of law and policy compared with the precautionary principle which (arguably) resides in the policy-formation arena. With this arguable distinction in mind, it must of course be remembered that the precautionary principle operates where (for whatever reason) scientific evidence is lacking while the preventative principle operates where there is relative certainty about the likely adverse impacts of particular processes, so justifying regulatory control by reference to a number of devices, not least of which may be the preventative principle. Whether this distinction is robust, clear and sustainable in practice may be doubtful. At the centre is not unlikely that political negotiation may see the two principles linked according to member states' attitudes to scientific and other evidence. As a result it is again arguable that any resulting directive may be muddled in terms of its aims: any member state may be in a position to disagree that legislative action is justified by reference to the preventative principle given its uncertainty about the existence of credible scientific evidence. The reality is that any axis linking the principles may tend to be blurred in practice. A tentative example of this tendency to 'muddle the axis' may be seen in the development of Directive 91/676[39] on the protection of water from pollution by nitrates. During the evolution of the proposal behind this Directive there were objections from some member states, including the United Kingdom, to its reliance on the preventative principle. The political negotiation surrounding the proposal led eventually to legislation allowing an important measure of discretion to member states through facilities for derogation from certain prescribed concentrations of nitrates, for example. In crude terms it is arguable, on this evidence at least, that political movement and negotiation can tend to qualify and compromise resort to the preventative principle. As such it is the case that the principle, like the precautionary principle, can be seen as a 'soft' principle. If the preventative principle is indeed 'soft' how might a 'hard' version of the principle be recognised?

A 'Hard' Preventative Principle

At federal level in the United States, the late 1980s saw considerable debate about the efficiencies – or lack of them – in relation to the operation of traditional regulatory regimes characterised as 'command and control' regimes. In essence the debate can be summarised in terms of the realisation that disproportionate regulatory input was seen as achieving ever more marginal reductions in environmental pollution. The outcome of the debate was the Pollution Prevention and Control Act of 1990 and its concern for what Congress described as 'source reduction' of offending pollutants. Source reduction was described as something fundamentally different and more desirable than waste management and pollution control. The Act stipulates that the Environmental Protection Agency shall identify specific organisational responsibilities for preventative action within its hierarchy. Additionally, grant-aid is provided for under the Act in order to facilitate state initiatives through programmes with industry.

The Polluter Pays Principle

As with the other principles now under consideration, the polluter pays principle shares all of the uncertainties which arise what is essentially a political principle operating in the area of policy formation. Any attempt to crystallise the principle as a legally enforceable principle would be confronted by insurmountable difficulties, even if a range of exceptions were drafted into the formulation. Who, for example, is the 'polluter' where non-point pollution sources are concerned? How might Community requirements in connection with state aids be reconciled with a legally-defined polluter pays principle? These and many more objections show that the principle can only be a loosely-bound objective behind Community (and member state) legislation governing the environment. Pursuit of that objective is though a matter of undoubted importance as far as the Community is concerned. Against that background it will be seen that pursuit of the principle and its increasing realisation depends on developing policy in areas such as the need for greater reliance on devices such as economic instruments for the purpose of encouraging the internalisation of costs on the part of polluters. In essence therefore the principle assumes that policy and law on the environment will drive in the direction of a decreasing subsidisation of environmental damage and degradation by the state.

Community Origins of the Principle

The first Environmental Action Programme in 1973 recognised the necessity of the principle as an element in Community policy-making on the environment. Recognition in EC Treaty terms occurred with the legislation of the Single European Act in 1987. Subsequently, two exceptions to the principle were incorporated into Recommendation 75/436.[40] In the first place, an application of stringent standards is likely to result in serious economic problems by reference to greater social costs. In this case, polluters should be given time to adapt. Secondly, financial assistance should be available for the purpose of solving problems arising in other policy sectors. The Recommendation defines the principle, as follows:

> ... persons ... responsible for pollution must pay the costs of such measures as are necessary to eliminate that pollution or to reduce it to comply with the standards or equivalent measures which enable quality objectives to be met or, where there are no such objectives ... with the standards or equivalent measures laid down by public authorities.

Beyond Community recognition of the principle, customary international law has applied the principle (again subject to all its uncertainties and lack of definition). The *Trail Smelter Arbitration*[41] between the United States and Canada is a famous example. Smelter emissions from Canada were established as a material cause of crop damage in the United States, whereupon the government of Canada was obliged to abate the polluting emissions, to act to avoid future damaging emissions, and to pay compensation for the crop damage. The proceedings here again stressed some of the uncertainties inherent in the principle, not least of which is the matter of identifying appropriate remedial measures required of the person found to be the polluter for present purposes.

Limitations and Prospects

The definition of appropriate remedial measures has just been referred to. There is no doubt that any statutory formulation of legal obligations in relation to the environment which are said to be dependent on the polluter pays principle will be the more credible and effective if based on efficient machinery for the identification of the polluter. This though is not the only requirement. Credibility and effectiveness also depend on an efficient quantification of damage as well as a facility for determining causation where that damage can be identified with the polluter. In practice though it is unlikely that many cases will be straightforward cases since there may be a number of polluters associated with relevant activities which have caused environmental damage. A strong example of the principle in legislation, which appears to satisfy these characteristics is the contaminated legislation found in Part IIA of the Environmental Protection Act 1990. What follows is a thumbnail sketch of that legislation, followed by a brief consideration of the common law of nuisance, the development of Community law and policy on environmental liability, and the relevance of so-called 'joint compensation funds' using the International Convention on the Establishment of an International Fund for Oil Pollution Damage as an example but not before the operation of the closely related Civil Liability Convention (which seeks to harmonise requirements for strict liability in respect of maritime oil pollution occurrences) is considered, as another example of attempts to realise the polluter pays principle in the broader international context.

Contaminated land legislation Achievement of effective identification for the purpose of law enforcement is unlikely to be straightforward, as was the case with the development of new statutory provisions on contaminated land under Part IIA of the Environmental Protection Act 1990, in England and Wales. Essentially this legislation, based very much on the polluter pays principle, operates by reference to the identification of so-called 'Class A' and 'Class B' persons. The general rule here is that either Class of person (or company) may be liable for remediation of contaminated land: there may be several of each Class in some cases. Exceptionally the public purse (in this case the local authority as the main regulatory agency) will have to take the financial or other responsibilities because of some prescribed failure associated with Class 'A' or 'B' persons. However, the assumption is that a Class 'A' person will be legally responsible for remediation by virtue of proof that that person 'caused or knowingly permitted' the subject contamination of the land. Where it is impossible to establish the existence of a Class 'A' person or that such a person did not 'cause or knowingly permit' the land contamination then attention shifts to attempt to identify any Class 'B' person unless (say) there are other Class 'A' persons who may be liable. A Class 'B' person is any owner or occupier of the land or some material part of it although again (as with Class 'A') there are exemptions and exclusions.

The common law of nuisance The polluter pays principle can be recognised in the common law of nuisance where a plaintiff has to establish that the defendant interfered unreasonably with the use and enjoyment of his land. Whether the common law is enforced is of course dependent on so-called 'accidents of litigation'. However, assuming that plaintiff's claim relates to some adverse environmental intrusion affecting the use and enjoyment of his land, that claim will be sustainable only where the type of damage, loss or injury is foreseeable.[42] Furthermore, the law will enforce its requirements where there is what is often referred to as 'sensible' damage, loss or injury which is not merely contingent, prospective or remote.[43] There may be doubt therefore as to whether the court would be willing to find an actionable nuisance where (say) mere trace elements of a pollutant are found to have affected the plaintiff's land although the court has been willing to sustain claims based on damage to amenity, such as smells emanating from pig farms. Equally, it may be doubtful whether the court would require full reinstatement of major environmental features that have suffered as a result of an actionable nuisance. This common law position does raise a question as to whether there may be circumstances in which Community law might be enforceable in respect of its prescribed limits while a claim at common law for nuisance might be unsuccessful according to this principle.[44] Overall therefore, recognition of the polluter pays principle is heavily qualified in the common law of nuisance. However, there exists a body of law in the United Kingdom known as 'statutory nuisance' where, in relation to a detailed categorisation of nuisances for this purpose, local authorities have powers under Part III of the Environmental Protection Act 1990 to act in the public, local interest against polluters. Additionally, Part III of the Act empowers individuals who are 'aggrieved' by a statutory nuisance to initiate proceedings, even though the bulk of cases here relate to local authority tenants acting against their public landlord in respect of adverse housing conditions. Whatever the form of statutory nuisance proceedings, Part III of the Act assumes that the essential test to be satisfied is that which applies to common law nuisance.

Community law and policy on environmental liability There is little doubt that one of the most significant developments in achieving a rather more effective recognition and enforcement of the polluter pays principle is the evolution of a European Community policy on environmental liability. At the time of writing the most recent position is set out in a Commission Communication adopted in February 2000.[45] It is recognised here that the essential purpose of any environmental liability regime is to ensure that those who cause damage, loss or injury pay for it: the polluter pays principle. In turn, the objective must be that of prevention and precaution.

The twin objectives of Community policy here are the need to provide uniformity across the Community, as well as providing a measure of certainty for the benefit of insurers. The policy proposal is that a framework directive should carry the law forward. Hitherto liability matters have been noticeably absent: for example, Directive 90/220[46] on the environmental release of genetically modified organisms contains no reference to determination of liability where an escape causes damage in the environment at large. The core of the proposed framework directive will be strict liability for environmental damage, including land contamination, biodiversity damage as well as other forms of loss, damage or injury suffered by person or property, all arising from dangerous activities regulated within the Community. The policy proposal is that liability will extend to fault-based liability for damage to biodiversity as a result of dangerous activities. The proposal is that the liable party will be the 'operator' of the subject activity but liability will not be retrospective. Member states will be obliged to secure remediation: failure will trigger challenge through judicial review by public interest groups. Such groups might even have *locus standi* to sue the party seen to be liable. In turn, such groups might have the power to seek injunctive relief to prevent the occurrence of damage, the power to take preventative action in an emergency, as well as an entitlement to recover costs from the liable party. For some member states, the United Kingdom in particular, there are considerable implications arising from future transposition, should the framework directive reach the statute book.

In the municipal law of the United Kingdom a transposed framework directive would involve a radical extension of rights available in law to public interest groups. There seems little doubt that a combination of the proposed directive along with recent reform of civil justice through the Civil Procedure Rules 1998 will encourage consideration of legislation facilitating representative actions by public interest groups. Whether the law might be developed even further in order to facilitate injunctive relief and the right to sue any liable party in favour of such groups may though be open to doubt although such developments are rather more likely to be realised through the application of the European Convention on Human Rights in the United Kingdom. Despite such a likely limitation, nevertheless, public interest groups may well be conferred with sufficient standing to pursue judicial review proceedings. Of course there is a need also to recognise and deal with the possibility of vexatious litigation by public interest groups, in which case there would be a necessity for there to be a cross-undertaking in damages for the protection of any successful defendant. Anticipation of Community legislation is often a matter of difficulty in a member state given the frequent complexity of transposition. That difficulty is compounded by uncertainties which, at the time of writing, still pervade the proposed framework directive and its attempt to carry forward the polluter pays principle.

At the time of writing the Community's proposals are devoid of any indication of a likely approach to the burden of proof. The essential challenge in legislation relating to environmental liability is the need to facilitate proof of facts by a plaintiff where those facts are essentially within the knowledge of a defendant. Again though English law, for example, is seemingly well-equipped with approaches to the burden of proof which could be open to adaptation in transposition. The principle of *res ipsa loquitur* in the civil law of negligence, and the reversal of the burden of proof in the criminal enforcement of strict liability both point to a tradition well capable of adaptation for present purposes.

Further uncertainty is manifested in the absence from the Community's proposals of an indication of the defences which might be available in proceedings under a new liability regime. At no point is there an awareness of thresholds beyond which liability will be triggered, in terms of the need for what was described earlier as 'sensible' damage, or through prescription of the mandatory limit values in Community legislation, for example. Furthermore, and as a reminder of what was said earlier about the need for credible, enforceable law for the purpose of the polluter pays principle, the Community's proposals are silent on important matters such as appropriate standards of remediation, and the means by which those attracting liability might be identified. Nevertheless, the policy debate over many years has stressed the difficulty of enforcement of any liability regime where members of an identifiable class might be liable for damage to the environment. It is here that the debate has often focused on the efficiency and effectiveness of so-called 'joint compensation funds' in realising the essential objectives of the polluter pays principle. One such scheme operates under the Brussels Civil Liability Convention – the Convention on Civil Liability for Oil Pollution Damage of 1969 – through which strict liability compensation arrangements for maritime oil spills are operated by a central fund contributed to by the oil transport industry in signatory countries.

The Civil Liability Convention

The Convention seeks to ensure that adequate compensation is available to persons who suffer pollution damage arising from spills of persistent oil from laden tankers through discharge or escape. In turn, the intention is that there should be a harmonisation of international rules and procedures in relation to the determination of liability. The Convention (which came into force in 1975) extends to pollution damage caused on the territory or the territorial sea of any party to the Convention and extends further to include measures following a spill, for the purpose of preventing or minimising the subject damage. The Convention provides also for the limitation of liability where the tanker owner is not at fault in respect of the oil spill.

The United Kingdom and Canada are parties, the United States is not. The consequence of this state of affairs in the law of the United States is that the determination of liability on facts falling within the Convention remain unconstrained by the terms of the Convention and, in particular, the limitation of liability. As a result there may be continuing reliance on traditional common law litigation of liabilities where it is possible to pursue proceedings in the courts of the United States, or indeed any other State which is not a party to the Civil Liability Convention. This was the case in *The Amoco Cadiz*[47] where, even though the disastrous oil spill occurred off the coast of France, nevertheless those French interests that suffered oil pollution damage sought damages without being subject to the fetter of liability limitation under the Convention. However, whereas the machinery of the Convention facilitates expedited compensation payments to victims from the joint compensation fund, resort to traditional common law litigation usually means that although the polluter may be liable to pay for all reasonably foreseeable damage without limitation, nevertheless any result of such litigation may take many years to emerge. In *The Amoco Cadiz* litigation in the United States, the plaintiffs sought to persuade the US court that it had jurisdiction by virtue of the fact that the tanker was owned by a subsidiary of a United States holding company, Standard Oil.

As an example of harmonisation of rules and procedures, the United Kingdom legislation implementing the Convention again illustrates the need for clear, precise statutory rules if the polluter pays principle is to be realised in suitably efficient terms. Nevertheless, it is necessary to question what is meant by 'the polluter pays' here. Clearly, international agreement may (as here) involve something less than total and absolute polluter liability. Merchant Shipping legislation has been the traditional vehicle for implementation of the Civil Liability Convention in the United Kingdom. This legislation shows that where, as a result of any occurrence taking place while a vessel is carrying bunker or other oil, or a cargo of persistent oil in bulk, such oil is discharged or escapes, the owner is liable for any contamination damage in the United Kingdom, the cost of any measures reasonably taken to prevent or reduce damage after escape, and any damage caused in the United Kingdom by measures taken after discharge or escape. No liability is incurred where it is proved that discharge or escape resulted from an act of war, hostilities, civil war, insurrection or an exceptional, inevitable and irresistible natural phenomenon, or was due wholly to the negligence or wrongful act of a government or other authority in exercising its functions of maintaining lights or other navigational aids, for the maintenance of which it is responsible. Although the legislation imposes strict liability in aid of the polluter pays principle, it goes on to exempt the owner, his servants or agents from other types of legal liability (in negligence, for example) as a result of any discharge or escape and even though there is a defence provided elsewhere in the legislation. As has been seen already, the court can impose a limit on the amount for which an owner is liable, if a request is made for this purpose, and assuming that the owner is not at fault. Importantly for the purposes of the polluter pays principle, compulsory insurance is required and shipping movements may be restricted in those sea areas controlled by the United Kingdom, unless such insurance is in force.

Joint compensation schemes: the International Convention on the Establishment of an International Fund for Compensation for Oil Pollution Damage There has been considerable criticism of the strict rather than fault-based liability regime of the Civil Liability Convention. On the other hand there was a feeling also that the limits prescribed by the Convention were increasingly inadequate, given the rapidly increasing capacities in ever larger tankers. Accordingly, it was proposed that the cargo undertakings involved in the worldwide tanker industry should contribute to an international fund which would have two benefits. In the first place, shipowners would be relieved of the immediate financial liability triggered by an application of the Civil Liability Convention. Secondly, additional compensation would be available to the victim of an oil pollution occurrence where, under the Civil Liability Convention, compensation is not payable, or is otherwise inadequate. Additionally, shipowners would be relieved of additional financial burdens arising under the Civil Liability Convention unless damage was caused by wilful misconduct or failure of a vessel to comply with international conventions. The result was the so-called Fund Convention of 1971 which adopted these proposals. Additionally the Fund is obliged to pay compensation to states and persons suffering pollution damage where such compensation cannot be obtained from liable shipowners, or that compensation is inadequate. Subject to prescribed limits under the Fund Convention victims of oil pollution damage may receive compensation beyond the extent of the shipowner's liability. On the other hand, the Fund may have to contribute all the compensation due where no shipowner is liable or a shipowner is unable to meet the liability. In the case of the United Kingdom, Merchant Shipping legislation again implements the Fund Convention. Disputed claims under this and the Civil Liability Convention are litigated before the courts of the United Kingdom.

The Polluter Pays Principle in Existing Community Law

The influence of the principle can be seen very plainly in a number of items of Community legislation affecting the environment. For example, Directive 75/439 on waste oil disposal[48] is built on the provision of indemnities to those undertakings which process waste oils covered by the Directive. Those indemnities may be realised through charges on waste oil or products which, after utilisation, are regarded as waste oil. A similar approach is found in the Waste Framework Directive[49] where it is stipulated *inter alia* that the cost of waste disposal is the responsibility of a waste holder whose waste is collected by a collector or disposer. Interestingly, the Directive on packaging waste[50] recognises that in the absence of Community provision for economic instruments, a member state is empowered to develop its own measures along these lines for the purpose of realising the objectives of the law by reference to the polluter pays principle. There are however areas of application of the principle which are not without controversy. This is the case with Directive 91/676[51] on the protection of water from pollution by nitrates.

In a reference to the European Court of Justice in *R. v. Secretary of State for the Environment, ex p. Standley*[52] the issue was the designation of vulnerable waters for the purpose of this Directive. The Court stressed that a member state in identifying waters affected by pollution in accordance with Article 3(1) is obliged to apply the criteria in Annex 1. It does not follow that there is a need to determine precisely what proportion of pollution in the waters is attributable to nitrates of agricultural origin or that the cause of such pollution is exclusively agricultural. It was held to be incompatible with the Directive to restrict identification of affected waters to cases of agricultural pollution alone: the Directive requires that the nitrogen contribution of agricultural and other sources be taken into account. Essentially, the Directive applies where nitrogenous discharges of agricultural origin make a significant contribution to the pollution. Against the background of this decision of the Court of Justice, it is instructive to examine some of the arguments addressed in these proceedings and focusing on the contention that the Directive is invalid.

The first of these arguments was that the requirements of the Directive give rise to disproportionate obligations on the part of farmers, thus offending the principle of proportionality. The Court responded here by concluding that the Directive contains flexible provision enabling member states to appreciate and comply with matters of proportionality. The second argument was that the Directive offends the polluter pays principle since farmers alone bear the cost of reducing nitrate concentrations, to the exclusion of others. Here the European Court of Justice observed that member states are obliged to take account of other sources of pollution while implementing the Directive. Accordingly, and having regard to the circumstances, member states are not to impose unnecessary costs of pollution elimination on farmers. The polluter pays principle therefore reflects proportionality in this case. This conclusion affected the third of the arguments here, that environmental damage should be rectified at source, as a priority, taking account of atmospheric deposition emanating principally from industry and transport. The final argument was that the right to property was infringed through the imposition on farmers of the entire responsibility for, and economic cost of reducing, nitrate pollution where others were the major or substantial producers of such concentrations. The Court considered that the right to property in Community law is not absolute right, and has to be seen in the context of its social function. The restrictions on land-spreading of fertilisers and manure are referable to the protection of human health, an objective of general interest which is capable of being rationalised with the right to property.

The Polluter Pays Principle and Environmental Taxes

Although environmental taxes are examined in rather greater detail in Chapter Six, it is necessary to recognise at this point the importance of the relationship between these taxes and the polluter pays principle. Taxes are an increasingly important part of policy-making on the environment. Fundamentally such taxes may enable the polluter's liability to be brought into a disciplined, statutory framework where, once again, the necessary assumptions about credible, effective and efficient lawmaking still obtain. The framework just referred to in turn facilitates an arrangement whereby the cost of polluting activity, including all the relevant externalities, can be reflected in the cost of goods and services generated by the companies affected. Valuing those externalities is a matter of some difficulty although some costs are more easily quantified than others. Cost recovery charges covering the regulatory costs tend to be more easily identified. However, so-called 'incentive' charging seeks to modify polluters' behaviour and it is this charging which poses the greatest difficulty, for a variety of reasons. In the first place, how extensive is an incentive to be and how effective can a charging regime be? In part this question is a political question, to be addressed at the policy-making stage. Secondly, how can the impact of such an incentive charge be assessed, taking account of the fact that other variables may be at work. If the polluter pays principle is to be a credible principle then it must be sustainable and effective, for a variety of purposes, not least of which is the need to develop further and improve such charges as environmental policy evolves.

The Proximity Principle

The essence of the proximity principle is that waste should be disposed of as near to the point of generation as possible. In broad terms, any policy based on the principle tends to aim at measures which will minimise or eliminate the export of waste to regions or even countries beyond that point of generation, sometimes referred to as 'waste tourism'. In turn, the policy appears to be aimed at encouraging the development of waste management installations close to or at the points of waste generation. It will be seen below that Community policy is undoubtedly instrumental in encouraging such developments. It will also be seen that the principle provides an important linkage between the so-called waste hierarchy and the principle of 'best practicable environmental option', again for strategic purposes in relation to waste management. It is here that one of the more controversial issues in relation to proximity is seen, to the extent that the cost of transporting waste for reprocessing at a distance may (perhaps exceptionally) be regarded as the best practicable environmental option when compared (say) with reprocessing close to the point of generation. The issues are highlighted to an even greater extent if the subject waste happens to be hazardous waste where specialist treatment installations are few in number. In these circumstances therefore it is hardly surprising that another important variable is the availability of appropriate, environmentally-friendly treatment.

Development of the Proximity Principle in Community Policy

The Commission's Strategy for Waste Management in 1989[53] declared

> ... that provision must be made to ensure that as far as possible waste is disposed of in the nearest suitable centres, making use of the most appropriate technologies to guarantee a high level of protection for the environment and public health ... Here the 'nearest' does not necessarily mean, in every case, close-by. To achieve the best possible distribution of installations, account must be taken of requirements and capacities for treatment. The distribution of plants for the reception of domestic refuse, for example, cannot be the same as for installations for disposing of ...

hazardous chemical waste. Subsequently a Council Resolution[54] dealing with waste policy stressed the environmental importance of measures to deal with waste close to the point of waste generation, thus minimising waste transportation. Additionally, the Resolution points to the need to reduce the amount and toxicity of waste consigned to landfill as well as the need for a network of adequate, integrated disposal installations. Very soon after the appearance of this Resolution, Directive 91/156[55] set about implementing these policies in Community law.

Article 5 of the Directive is particularly important for present purposes in providing for the network of disposal installations:

> This network must enable the Community to become self-sufficient in waste disposal and the member states to move towards that aim individually, taking into account geographical circumstances or the need for specialised installations for certain types of waste. The network must also enable waste to be disposed of in one of the nearest appropriate installations, by means of the most appropriate methods and technologies in order to ensure a high level of protection for the environment and public health.

In considering Directive 91/156 it is necessary to recognise that Community law draws an important line, dividing disposal from waste recovery. Accordingly, the proximity principle operates in relation to waste disposal rather than waste recovery: a reference particularly to the need for a network of waste disposal installations just referred to. Nevertheless, as will be seen below, there seems no bar to a member state extending waste treatment installations to recovery as well as disposal processes.

The European Court of Justice appears not to have recognised this distinction until recently, in *Chemische Afvalstoffen Dusseldorp BV and Others v. Minister van Volkshuisvesting, Ruimtelijke Ordening en Milieubeheer*[56] where the Court was concerned with a ban on the export of used oil filters where processing outside the Netherlands was considered to be inferior to domestic processing. As a result there was protection of what was primarily a state-owned recovery enterprise. The questions for the Court were whether the principles of proximity and self-sufficiency were applicable to the shipments of waste, and whether there was here an unjustified restriction on the free movement of goods. It was held that the Waste Framework Directive (75/442[57]) and Regulation 259/93[58] on the regulation of waste shipments within, into and out of the Community cannot be interpreted as meaning that the principles of self-sufficiency and proximity are applicable to waste shipments which are destined for recovery. Member states can adopt rules and requirements pursuant to Article 176 allowing more stringent measures only where they are compatible with Articles 28–30. The prohibition on exports was a measure equivalent to quantitative restrictions proscribed under Article 29. Even if it could be justified by reference to environmental protection requirements, the Netherlands' economic arguments relating to the profitability of its domestic recovery operation did not justify barriers to the free movement of goods. There was no evidence before the Court that shipments of filters to Germany posed any threat to the environment or to the life and health of humans. Accordingly, the action could not be justified under Article 30. The Court also held that Article 86, in conjunction with Article 30, prohibited rules such as those in the Netherlands' waste management plan where a member state required undertakings to deliver waste for recovery to a national undertaking with exclusive rights to incinerate dangerous waste, unless processing in another member state was of better quality. However, such a prohibition depends on an absence of any objective justification and necessity where the rules operate in favour of the national undertaking, and for the purpose of increasing its dominant position.

More recently, Community law and policy on landfill have again stressed the importance of the proximity principle. The Landfill Directive[59] seeks to harmonise disposal costs and it is against this background that the policy of avoiding unnecessary waste transportation represents a significant variable. However, the proximity principle has received significant recognition beyond the Community in the development and implementation of the Basel Convention on the Control of Transboundary Movement of Hazardous Wastes and their Disposal.

The Basel Convention

The essential concern of the 1989 Basel Convention is to ensure that environmentally-adverse transportation of hazardous waste intended for final disposal between developed and developing countries is avoided or minimised. That objective has been realised through a regulation of trade, based on control exercisable by the countries of important and export. The main onus and responsibility here lies on the exporting country. The Convention requires that trade in hazardous waste shall occur internationally only where there is prior notification of a subject transaction to a competent authority in the exporting state and, as the case may be, in a transit state, accompanied by the written consent of the importing state. Each consignment moved under these arrangements must be accompanied by a consignment note from the commencement of export through to final recovery or disposal. The consignment note is required to provide timely, accurate and comprehensive information about the hazardous waste.

The objectives of the Convention The Convention seeks to ensure that there is minimisation of hazardous waste as close to the point of generation as is practicable, to promote environmentally sound management and disposal of such waste, to prevent the generation of pollution from such waste, and to minimise transboundary movement hazardous waste.

Further development of the Convention In 1995 an amendment to the Convention provided for an export ban in respect of hazardous waste for final *disposal* from OECD countries, Community member states and Liechtenstein, to any other states not included in that list. Furthermore, a ban was concluded (subject to ratification) also on transboundary movements of hazardous waste intended for *recovery* as between OECD countries, Community member states and Liechtenstein. It has been observed in one commentary on the Convention by the United Nations Environment Programme: *Policy Effectiveness and Multilateral Environmental Agreements*[60] that

> ... the majority of intra-OECD hazardous waste trade is intended for final disposal ... Several important industrial sectors which depend on the import of re-cycled wastes as intermediate inputs in downstream industries – that is, which have insufficient domestic supplies – may be particularly and adversely affected commercially by the ban. Moreover, an adverse secondary environmental consequence of the ban is that economically useful recyclable materials cannot

be used as inputs in many countries, leading to an increase in primary production of such materials ... This could encourage a shift towards more pollution-intensive production processes, depending on the waste, as opposed to relying on relatively more environmentally benign recycling materials as production inputs, thereby leading to a deterioration in other environmental indicators.[61]

More generally, the same commentary stresses that Convention implementation is largely procedural, that specific technologies are not mandated and that there are no prescribed thresholds for environmental impacts.[62] These limitations are undoubtedly evidence of pragmatism, given the difficulty of political negotiation and agreement. However, within these limits it is clearly important that there is recognition of the need to avoid an inflexible application of the proximity principle which ignores the clear merits of good environmental practice. Companies may for example have developed their own self-contained waste management strategies which necessitate transportation over considerable distances.

The Convention and the Community The Convention has been ratified by the Community and the United Kingdom. The primary Community legislation here is Regulation 259/93[63] which seeks to rationalise Community law with the Basel Convention. There is little doubt that the perceptions of proximity among the member states involved in the development of the Regulation resulted in a conditional prohibition only in respect of transboundary movements by reference to various considerations, including proximity. Furthermore, there is a so-called 'triviality threshold' in operation so that the prohibition will not apply in respect of small consignments if the development of specialised disposal facilities is uneconomic. The operation of the law and policy behind the Regulation can be seen in member state approaches to the issue of waste management.

Proximity and Member State Implementation

The proximity principle has percolated into the law and policy on waste management in the United Kingdom in a variety of different ways. *Waste Strategy 2000*[64] declares that by virtue of the principle waste should in general be disposed of as near to its place of origin as possible. In that way there can be an avoidance of export of wastes to other areas or regions: waste tourism, it is observed, brings its own environmental problems. On the matter of hazardous wastes, the policy document goes on to say that the government is committed to a network of high-temperature incinerators where such incineration is the best practicable environmental option. These facilities must, the government insists, be subject to high standards for the protection of human health and the environment. Closely allied to this policy document is planning policy guidance which seeks to focus on the location of waste management facilities by reference to proximity principles, including disposal and recovery facilities, as well as the development control function which goes hand in hand with waste management licensing under Part II of the Environmental Protection Act 1990. That policy guidance is presently found in Planning Policy Guidance on *Planning and Waste Management*[65] which has to be read in conjunction with the foregoing *Waste Strategy 2000*.

There is no doubt that PPG 10 and related policy instruments exert a very important influence on the implementation and enforcement of principles like the proximity principle. PPG 10 in particular looks to provide advice on the way in which the system of development control can contribute to the government's policy objectives for sustainable development through the provision of waste management facilities. That advice focuses particularly on the general policy context as well as the criteria for the siting of facilities and the increasing importance of regional provision. Accordingly, waste planning authorities will be assisted in policy-formation and in the determination of applications for planning permission for the siting of waste management facilities.

Among the objectives to be achieved by the planning system here, PPG 10 lists the need to minimise adverse environmental impacts arising from factors such as the transport and disposal of waste. As a result, the government's policy ambition in PPG 10 is framed by a declared desire to see waste management decisions based on consideration of the best practicable environmental option for each waste stream, regional self-sufficiency, the proximity principle, and a waste hierarchy. In the case of regional self-sufficiency, PPG 10 stipulates that most waste should be treated or disposed of within the region in which it is disposed of while the proximity principle is realised in terms of the priority for waste generally to be managed as near as possible to its place of production by virtue of the adverse environmental impact of waste transportation.

The Application of Principle

The point of reference for this final section of the chapter is the reflection of some or all of the foregoing principles in three devices which are central to the regulatory process: 'best available technology not entailing excessive cost'; 'best practicable environmental option'; and 'best available techniques'. Each is examined in turn.

Best Available Technology not Entailing Excessive Cost

This concept (BATNEEC) has been seen already, in Chapter Two. It was seen there that the concept is a central part of the regulatory variables which affect emissions to the atmosphere from industrial installations, by virtue of Directive 84/360.[66] As implemented in the United Kingdom the reference to 'technology' becomes the rather wider 'techniques' covering the operating elements of a process, and their interrelationship. The 'best' techniques are those regarded as being the most effective for the purpose of preventing or minimising polluting activity. Whether such techniques are 'available' assumes that the plant or equipment in question is available from one source at least. These elements of the formula are of course qualified by matters of cost. Among other things the cost variable will be seen in the light of the scale of any adverse impact that the installation's operation has, or will have on the environment, as well as factors such as the capacity of a similar but typical operation in the same industry to absorb the cost of additional abatement measures.

One of the critical regulatory factors to be considered here has to be seen against the essential characteristic of BATNEEC as a 'technology forcing' requirement. Accordingly, where abatement measures are required to be installed, what time limit may be imposed for this purpose, bearing in mind that it may also be assumed that, in the absence of those measures, the installation may have to cease operation? The answer to such a question depends again on a number of variables set out in guidance. An installation in need of abatement measures which does not operate at full capacity and which therefore does not have a particularly serious polluting impact may be allowed a rather longer life than an installation that is operating at full capacity with a significant adverse impact on the environment. The longer term effect of such a regulatory approach will no doubt be a rationalisation of subject installations in favour of those operating companies with greater efficiency borne no doubt of better investment.

It may be asked whether BATNEEC contains any effective recognition of the preventative and precautionary principle. It can be argued that BATNEEC involves a qualified recognition of the former principle. Regulatory authorisation by reference to BATNEEC may indeed prevent polluting emissions, particularly in the case of a new installation. However, whatever the status of the installation, it has been seen that BATNEEC is qualified by cost variables which may tarnish any preventative credentials. Fundamentally, there is no certainty that where an authorisation is in place, environmental impacts will be limited or eliminated by reference to specific, stringent values or limits. As such it appears that BATNEEC is again difficult to rationalise with the preventative principle. Furthermore, BATNEEC is not based on any statutory requirement to act, ahead of scientific uncertainty. As such it is difficult to rationalise BATNEEC with precautionary action, given the concern to balance environmental goals with financial variables. Although those financial variables may be seen to dilute the obligations of the operator of an installation subject to regulatory control, the other side of the coin sees a very qualified recognition of the polluter pays principle. That qualified recognition arises from the fact that it is of course unlikely that anything like the full cost of adverse environmental impact will fall on the operator beyond the cost of necessary abatement measures.

Best Practicable Environmental Option

Perhaps the best perspective on the status and operation of 'best practicable environmental option' (BPEO) is to examine its relationship with BATNEEC. Under section 7 of the Environmental Protection Act 1990 the regulatory agency may be concerned with releases, discharges or emissions to more than one environmental medium. In this case the task of minimising pollution of the environment as a whole is addressed by BATNEEC but by reference to BPEO also.

Having identified a particular substance it will be necessary to define the best practicable environmental option for management of the waste stream in question before defining the best available techniques not entailing excessive cost in respect of the process at large. In essence therefore, BPEO is really concerned, after due enquiry, with that option which maximises environmental benefits or minimises adverse environmental impacts, taking account of cost as well as the long and short-term effects. For any option to be 'practicable' there is an expectation that it will be consistent with contemporary technical knowledge as well as being financially feasible. In turn, there is an expectation that BPEO will not be compromised through the influence on decision-making of irrelevant considerations outside local social, economic and environmental factors.

Two serious limitations of BPEO are pointed out by the Royal Commission on Environmental Pollution:[67]

> ... it applies only to authorisation of those projects subject to integrated pollution control [and] even in that context, BPEO is given a narrower meaning than the [Royal] Commission advocated in its Twelfth Report. In particular, differences in the energy requirements between different options are not taken into account: achieving the lowest possible emissions from a process may not in reality represent BPEO if that requires large amounts of energy and will result in a large increase in emissions from a generating plant. And, although solid waste arising is taken into account, the regulator is not entitled to take into account how it is dealt with if it is disposed of at another site.

Against this background it can be seen that BPEO, with its limited statutory status, operates across a narrow horizon, at least compared with the waste management policy background of its operation mentioned above. At best in both contexts however, it can be said that BPEO is again a heavily qualified manifestation of the preventative principle.

Best Available Techniques

Best available techniques (BAT) lies at the core of the IPPC Directive.[68] Ostensibly this concept appears to be rather more stringent than BATNEEC. However, the Directive stipulates that the reference to 'available' techniques demands consideration of what is economically and technically viable. Nevertheless, the Directive goes further in requiring consideration of a range of other factors such as energy efficiency, decommissioning, overall emissions from the installation, and so on. Overall, it is difficult to see that the principles addressed previously in relation to BATNEEC are significantly advanced by this new regime, although it may be argued that this rather more comprehensive regulatory regime does represent a rather more stringent representation of the preventative principle. As such it is perhaps worth stressing that the preventative principle operating at grass roots level is potentially a useful indicator or measure of the general scale of the effectiveness of a regulatory regime, at least where emissions are controlled without reference to specific limits at the factory boundary.

Notes

1   OJ L365, 31.12.94.
2   OJ L31, 5.2.76.
3   OJ L85, 23.9.99.
4   OJ L194, 25.7.75.
5   OJ C254, 24.9.95.
6   OJ L175, 5.7.85.
7   OJ L158, 23.6.90.
8   10th Report (Session 1993–94).
9   SI 1994, No.232.
10   OJ L78, 26.3.91.
11   *Supra*, n. 3.
12   OJ L206, 22.7.92.
13   Kramer, L. (2000), *E.C. Environmental Law*, Sweet and Maxwell, London, pp. 9–20.
14   COM 2000/1, January 2, 2000.
15   Chapter One, nn. 17–19.
16   [1988] ECR4607.
17   [1998] ECR I–4473.
18   Department of the Environment, August 1999.
19   Rio Declaration on Environment and Development, 1992.
20   *Ibid.*
21   Cm 4053 (1998), The Stationery Office, London, para. 4.41. *Cf.* Chapter One, n. 8.
22   *Ibid.*, para. 4.44.
23   COM 2000/1, February 2, 2000.
24   OJ L196, 16.8.67.
25   OJ L84, 5.4.93.
26   [1994] EnvLR1.
27   [1994] ECR I–3453.
28   *Supra*, n. 21, at para. 4.46.
29   11th Report (Session 1998–99).
30   'This Common Inheritance, Britain's Environmental Strategy', Cm 1200 (1990), HMSO, London.
31   OJ L135, 30.5.91.
32   1st Report (Session 1996–97).
33   *Ibid.*, para. 187.
34   Cases C–418/97 and 419/97, 15.6.2000. ARCO is reported at [2001] EnvLR DG6.
35   *The Times*, June 21, 1997; [1998] JEL146.
36   OJ L194, 25.7.75.
37   OJ L257, 10.10.96.
38   *Supra*, n. 6.
39   OJ L375, 31.12.91.
40   OJ L194, 25.7.75.
41   (1939) 33 AJIL182; (1941) 35 AJIL684.
42   *Cambridge Water Co. v. Eastern Counties Leather Co.* [1994] 2 AC264 (HL).
43   *Salvin v. North Brancepeth Coal Co.* (1874) 9 ChApp705, *per* James, LJ, at p. 708.

44   Hawke, N. (1997), 'Toxic Torts and Regulatory Standards in the Law of the United Kingdom and the European Union', 10 *Tulane Environmental Law Journal*, No. 2.
45   EU Document 6055/00.
46   OJ L117, 8.5.90.
47   [1984] 2 LlRep304.
48   *Supra*, n. 4.
49   OJ L194, 25.7.75.
50   OJ L365, 31.12.94.
51   *Supra*, n. 39.
52   [1999] QB1279; [1999] All ER (EC) 412.
53   SEC (89) 934.
54   OJ C122, 18.5.90.
55   *Supra*, n. 10.
56   [1999] EnvLR360.
57   *Supra*, n. 4.
58   OJ L30, 6.2.93.
59   OJ L182, 16.7.99.
60   Environment and Trade Series, No. 17, Geneva, 1998.
61   *Ibid.*, at pp. 80–81.
62   *Ibid.*, at p. 81.
63   *Supra*, n. 58.
64   Cm 4693 (2000), Department of the Environment.
65   PPG 10, Department of the Environment, October 1999.
66   OJ L188, 16.7.84.
67   *Supra*, n. 21, para. 3.20. *Cf.* the 12th Report of the Royal Commission, Cm 310 (1988), The Stationery Office, London.
68   *Supra*, n. 37.

Chapter Four

The Role of the Courts

National Courts and the European Court of Justice

Given that much of the environmental law in force in member states such as the United Kingdom emanates from the European Community, it is necessary to appreciate the role of the courts, both at the centre – the European Court of Justice – and in the member states. Towards the end of this chapter some consideration is given to one of the critical consequences of the role of the European Court of Justice: the further development of legislation as a result of its decisions. Clearly, in the case of a member state like the United Kingdom there are categories of municipal law to be applied and enforced which have no connection with the law of the European Community: the law governing statutory nuisance in Part III of the Environmental Protection Act 1990, for example. However, the weight and status of European Community law on the environment necessarily focuses much of the attention of this chapter on the status of and interplay between national courts and the European Court of Justice in the interpretation, application and enforcement of the law. Those processes of interpretation, application and enforcement direct attention in turn to the essential character of Community environmental law, as seen already in earlier chapters. Above all, Community law here is not directly applicable normally, given the overwhelming emphasis on directives and decisions as the vehicles which carry policy into law. It is against this background that the courts can often address their task without necessary and direct reference to certain primary and directly applicable Treaty provisions such as those which seek (through Article 28 of the Treaty) to proscribe trade barriers for example. Accordingly the concern of the courts dealing with matters of environmental law extends from questions of the legality of the subject legislation, through the interpretation of that legislation, to the legality of its transposition and enforcement in member states. This though is a fairly crude representation of the courts' role in relation to environmental law, not least because there are other factors which shape the operation of the judicial function. In the first place, it will be seen that in some instances there is a formally prescribed distribution of functions, usually where the European Court of Justice enjoys jurisdiction (or ultimate jurisdiction) in respect of a legally defined function.

Even here though, there are circumstances where there is a certain discretion given to a national court in determining whether a reference is made to the European Court of Justice on a matter of Community law. Secondly there are fundamental Treaty provisions of general application which drive a court's jurisdiction whether the matter before it is environmental or otherwise.

Fundamental Treaty Provision

Article 10 of the Treaty stipulates that member states are obliged to take all appropriate measures to ensure fulfilment of Treaty obligations or of actions undertaken by the institutions of the Community. Member states are obliged in turn to facilitate achievement of the tasks of the Community and to avoid any measure that would jeopardise attainment of Community Treaty objectives. Not surprisingly therefore, member state legislation which has the effect of constraining the jurisdiction of its courts in relation to Community law (whatever its subject-matter within the limits of Community competence) will be seen as being contrary to Article 10. Another part of the Treaty – Article 175(4) – is perhaps a surprising accompaniment to Article 10. Article 175(4) obliges member states to secure implementation of those measures generated by Community environmental policy. Nevertheless, this provision of the Treaty does provide a useful reminder of the twin obligations of any member state here: to secure transposition of directives according to law (in accordance with Article 249 of the Treaty), and to enforce compliance. Compliance extends very widely of course and the courts' role may be seen as limited, even though they have the ultimate responsibility of ensuring that that compliance is achieved according to law. Where the European Court of Justice is concerned, Article 220 requires the Court to ensure that in the interpretation and application of the Treaty, the law is observed. The ultimate authority of the Court in relation to matters of Community law means that national courts also are necessarily and fundamentally bound by this requirement.

The Interpretation and Application of Directives

The interpretation and application of directives is the central concern of much of this chapter, which concludes with an examination of the judicial interpretation of environmental legislation in the United States. Essentially, this theme divides into four parts. In the first part elements of judicial interpretation are addressed. These elements cover five matters, all of which affect Community law on the environment in critical respects. The elements are those relating to so-called 'sympathetic interpretation'; proportionality; direct effect; member state liability for damages; and (finally), the courts' approach to the legal status of the Community environmental principles addressed towards the end of the previous chapter. The second part of this section of the chapter moves on to look at certain specific issues relating to the jurisdiction of the European Court of Justice. Those issues are three in number and concern proceedings under Articles 226 and 230 of the Treaty; interim relief pending decisions of the European Court of Justice; and noncompliance with judgments of the Court and the impact of Article 228 of the Treaty. The third section of the chapter seeks to determine whether regulatory requirements prescribed by statute – such as Community environmental directives – might be seen to aid and support common law claims affecting the environment. Before the final section of this chapter there is an examination of the courts' attitude to that fundamental characteristic of transposition by directive: the scope of member state discretion and freedom in realising the essential objectives of any such directive. For this purpose there will be particular interest in the judicial control of administrative discretion wielded through the powers of relevant environmental agencies. Again specific areas of environmental law, such as nature conservation law, will be examined against the background of the central question here: how far does Community law on the environment allow a member state to determine the application of regulatory and other requirements according to law.

Elements of Judicial Interpretation

Sympathetic Interpretation

In *Von Colson and Kamann v. Land Nordrhein-Westfalen*[1] the European Court of Justice held that a member state's obligation arising from a directive, to achieve the objective set out there, as well as the fundamental obligation arising from Article 10 of the Treaty, is binding on all member state authorities including (for matters within their jurisdiction), the courts. Accordingly, in applying national, municipal law, member state courts are required to interpret that law in the light of the wording and purpose of the directive, by reference to their fundamental obligation under Article 249. Subsequently, in *Marleasing v. la Comercial Internacional de Alimentacion*[2] the European Court of Justice held that any national court is obliged to interpret municipal law in compliance with Community law, even though that national, municipal law is clear and unambiguous. Accordingly, and in the absence of a relevant provision of Community law, the Spanish court involved in these proceedings was disabled from applying a provision of Spanish law. Even beyond this principle of Community law the European Court of Justice has further insisted in *ASBL v. Region Wallonie*[3] that prior to the coming into force of a directive, any member state is prohibited from acting in a way which will seriously prejudice the realisation of the objectives of that law. It seems clear and logical that such a prohibition will necessarily bind the court and restrict its jurisdiction accordingly. The court will be obliged for example to proscribe any attempt by a member state to implement measures contrary to any directive during its period of transposition. Essentially, the purpose of this principle is that there is a fundamental need for each member state to achieve those measures necessary to fulfil the objectives of the directive, as a binding legal obligation. The critical point of reference here is the date of notification of the subject directive: from this date the directive has binding legal effect in the member state. Nevertheless, application of this principle is not without its difficulties, as where it is contended by a member state that legislative measures are introduced on a transitional basis and that while those measures prejudice the objectives of the directive there is no serious prejudice in the period leading to final transposition by the due date.

Otherwise, the doctrine of sympathetic interpretation may give rise to problems where, for example, it is suggested that an obligation in law is binding on an individual even where the relevant Community law has not been transposed according to law. Such a suggestion will be particularly controversial if the obligation in question is enforceable through the categories of the criminal law. This was debated before the European Court of Justice in the case of *Criminal Proceedings against Arcaro*.[4]

In *Arcaro* the facts indicated that criminal proceedings had been brought against Arcaro in respect of the unlawful and unauthorised discharge of cadmium into surface waters. The defendant argued here that, because the subject plant was an existing plant, it remained unregulated under Italian law. The matter was referred to the European Court of Justice under Article 234 of the Treaty, the Italian court seeking a preliminary ruling on several matters. The Court first concluded that Directive 76/464[5] on the pollution of water by dangerous substances requires prior authorisation for the discharge of cadmium, no matter when it occurs. The Court went on to refer to the Cadmium Directive (83/513[6]) in concluding, secondly, that in the absence of full transposition within the prescribed time limit, a public authority in a member state may not enforce the relevant regulatory requirements against an individual. In other words, there can be no so-called 'horizontal' effect against a private individual where the enforcement of Community law is concerned. Finally, the Court confirmed the absence of any provision in Community law whereby a national court can ignore provisions of national, municipal law contrary to the terms of a directive which has not been transposed, particularly (as here) where the criminal law would be applied to a person such as Arcaro failing to comply with that directive.

Proportionality

Reference to proportionality was made in Chapter Three. The concern in this chapter is with the way in which the court addresses the matter. Where the common law is concerned there is no doubt that proportionality brings with it a certain novelty, bearing in mind its origins in the civil law jurisdictions of continental Europe.

The status and application of the principle The essence of the principle has been expressed thus by the European Court of Justice, in *R. v. Ministry of Agriculture, Fisheries and Food, ex p. Fedesa*[7] where it is said to apply when:

> ... the lawfulness of the prohibition of an economic activity is subject to the condition that the prohibitory measures are appropriate and necessary in order to achieve the objectives legitimately pursued by the legislation in question; when there is a choice between several appropriate measures recourse must be had to the least onerous, and the disadvantages caused must not be disproportionate to the aims pursued.

Against this background, how might the court approach an enquiry into proportionality? It has been suggested, by the Advocate-General of the European Court of Justice, in *SPUC v. Grogan*[8] that a three stage process is necessary. In the first place it must be asked, does the prohibition pursue a legitimate aim of the public interest fulfilling an imperative social need? Secondly, is such an aim being realised by reference to means which can be regarded as necessary and acceptable in a democracy, for the purpose of that aim? Finally, are those means employed proportionately in relation to the aim without infringement of any attendant fundamental right as a result? The difficulty facing a court whose task is characterised as one of judicial review in a common law jurisdiction is that it may be suggested that an enquiry into proportionality may be seen to go beyond the legality of decision-making. The European Court of Justice appears to be alive to this problem. In *Upjohn v. Licensing Authority*[9] for example, the Court said that:

> ... in such cases, the community judicature must restrict itself to examining the accuracy of the findings of fact and law made by the authority concerned and to verifying, in particular, that the action taken by that authority is not vitiated by a manifest error or a misuse of powers and that it did not clearly exceed the bounds of its discretion.

Through the jurisprudence of the European Court of Justice there is a clear appreciation of the difficulty of application of proportionality. One of the most important means of overcoming that difficulty is through the application of what is referred to as the 'margin of appreciation'.

The margin of appreciation The 'margin of appreciation' was explained in clear terms by the Court of Appeal in *R. v. Secretary of State for Health, ex p. Eastside Cheese Co. and R.A. Duckett & Co.*[10] In these proceedings, one of the main issues for the Court of Appeal was whether the Secretary of State had acted disproportionately in choosing to act under section 13 of the Food Safety Act 1990 which empowers the making of emergency control orders but which generally excludes compensation entitlement in favour of those subject to such regulatory intervention. An alternative would have been to act under the more limited terms of section 9. It was held that the Secretary of State's action in choosing to make an emergency control order under section 13 fell within the margin of appreciation. According to the Lord Chief Justice, Lord Bingham, the margin of appreciation may be broad or narrow:

> The margin is broadest when the national court is concerned with primary legislation enacted by its own legislature in an area where a general policy of the community must be given effect in the particular economic and social circumstances of the Member State in question. The margin narrows gradually, rather than abruptly, with changes in the character of the decision-maker and the scope of what has to be decided ...[11]

The nature of the dispute in this litigation is succinctly described by the judge at first instance, Moses, J.[12] Moses, J., considered that the Department of Health:

... should not resort to the exercise of section 13 powers unless it considers that the protection offered by section 9 would be inadequate. In my view, the scheme of the 1990 Act discloses an hierarchy of powers which should inhibit the Department from taking those powers which remove the right of compensation save when it considers that only by the exercise of those draconian powers can protection be effective. If section 9 powers are considered to be equally effective then it is those powers which should be exercised. Any other approach offends the principle of proportionality ...[13]

Before the judge at first instance it was accepted by all parties that the exercise of section 13 powers interfered with the operation of Article 29 of the Treaty prohibiting all export restrictions and measures of equivalent effect, unless there is a justification based on Article 30 where restrictions can be justified on grounds relating to the protection of health and the life of humans. In determining the margin of appreciation here, against the background of E-coli 0157 poisoning following the consumption of cheese manufactured by one of the applicants, the Lord Chief Justice in the Court of Appeal had no doubt that in the application of the foregoing Article 30, the maintenance of public health must be regarded as a very important objective such that it carries 'great weight' in the balancing exercise.

Proportionality, trade and the environment It has been seen already, in Chapter Three, that in *Commission v. Denmark*[14] the European Court of Justice has held that Denmark's deposit and return scheme was not disproportionate to environmental objectives. Accordingly, in some circumstances environmental protection can be accorded the status of a mandatory legal requirement that may justify a restriction on the free trade of goods throughout the Community. In these proceedings (the first before the Court where proportionality and the environment had been raised) the Commission had argued in its submissions before the Court that the requirements of the Danish scheme were contrary to the principle of proportionality to the extent that the aim of achieving environmental protection could be realised by less restrictive trade measures. The Court accepted in principle at the outset that environmental protection, as one of the essential objectives of the Community, may justify limitations on the free movement of goods. However, the Court recognised that such limitations cannot go beyond the inevitable restrictions justified by the environmental protection objective. The Court was concerned essentially with two issues in these proceedings initiated by the Commission.

In the first place there was concern with the status of the deposit-and-return scheme for empty drinks containers. Here the Court concluded that the requirements of this scheme represent an indispensable element of a scheme intended to ensure the re-use of drinks containers and therefore was necessary to achieve the aims of the government of Denmark. Any restrictions on the free movement of goods were not therefore regarded as being disproportionate.

The second issue addressed the matter of non-approved drinks containers. In this case the law permitted a producer to market up to 3,000 hectolitres of beer and soft drinks per year in such containers, provided that a deposit-and-return scheme was established. In this case the Commission's contention was that such a scheme was unnecessary to achieve the desired aims and was therefore disproportionate. Here the Court held that the restrictive effect of such a scheme on imports rendered it disproportionate.

The Commission had argued that environmental protection can be achieved through the recycling of containers, among other approaches. It is unclear from the decision of the Court which approved the Danish deposit-and-return scheme why other schemes might not have merit and, indeed, be less restrictive. Furthermore, it may suggested that the decision can be seen as bringing proportionality into disrepute: why for example is there no reference in the judgment to factors and variables which should determine whether a particular scheme has overriding merit for the purposes of environmental protection? Despite the fact that the decision of the Court begs these important questions, the decision does nevertheless highlight an essential fundamental where there is a tension between trade and the environment. The Court's decision was founded on the recognition of environmental requirements as mandatory requirements for the purpose of the Treaty.

Mandatory environmental requirements Prior to the decision in *Commission v. Denmark*, the Court had held in *Rewe v. Bundesmonopolverwaltung*[15] that where Community statutory provision was absent, municipal legal restriction on the free movement of goods in a member state can be presumed to be lawful, at least to the extent that such provision could be shown to be necessary (say) for the purposes of consumer protection, without being discriminatory or disproportionate. To the extent that this and other purposes can be regarded as 'mandatory requirements', the Court considered that other such requirements might emerge. It was in *Commission v. Denmark* that the Court added the environment to the list of so-called 'mandatory requirements', arguably because the exceptions to what are now Articles 28 and 29 on the freedom of trade in the Community are clearly difficult, if not impossible, to rationalise with the facts of a case of this sort.

Article 30 exceptions The Article 30 exceptions referred to above were not raised before the Court. Those exceptions are defined as follows, indicating that Articles 28 and 29:

> ... shall not preclude prohibitions on imports, exports ... justified on grounds of ... the protection of health and the life of humans, animals or plants ... Such prohibitions or restrictions shall not, however, constitute a means of arbitrary discrimination or a disguised restriction on trade between Member States.

It is clear that environmental protection is not always capable of rationalisation with (say) the protection of human life or health except where the issue relates to the regulation of pesticides or other toxic substances, for example. This is not to suggest that the exceptions are without utility. Those exceptions were before the Court in *Criminal Proceedings against Ditlev Bluhme*.[16] Here the Danish Ministry of Agriculture introduced a regulation prohibiting beekeeping on the island of Laesco except where the Laesco brown bee was being kept. The purpose of the regulation was to conserve a geographically and morphologically distinct population of bees. A local beekeeper was prosecuted for acting in breach of the regulation. The question for the Court was whether the regulatory restriction was contrary to Article 28. At the outset the Court considered that the regulation was concerned essentially with the intrinsic characteristics of the 'Laesco Brown'. The question was whether the restriction could be justified under Article 30. In particular, are those exceptions capable of extending to justify the maintenance of biodiversity? It was held that Article 30 could extend to justify the restrictions imposed: measures to preserve an indigenous animal population with distinct characteristics contribute to the maintenance of biodiversity by ensuring the survival of the subject population through an avoidance of interbreeding. Accordingly, the regulatory measures were seen by the Court as protecting the life of the bees. Furthermore, the regulations could be justified by reference to the precautionary principle, in anticipation of the threat to the bee population in question.

Direct Effect

Judicial interpretation by the European Court of Justice and the courts of member states may raise the question of an individual's status in the environmental law of the Community. Where Community law in general is concerned there has for some time been an acceptance that certain Treaty provisions are for example capable of enforcement by individuals, as a result of judicial interpretation. Where directives are concerned, the position is rather more difficult, given the essential character and status of these legislative instruments. Article 249 of the Treaty in particular is very specific in indicating that regulations are directly applicable and binding in member states without more. Directives on the other hand enjoy the force of law only when transposition has occurred in a member state at the date prescribed. Nevertheless, the European Court of Justice has adopted a very positive policy on this matter, pointing to the mischief that occurs where a member state might point to irregular or even nonexistent transposition as a means of escaping liability here. The approach to direct effect was explained by the Court in *Comitato di Coordinamento per la Difesa della Cava v. Regione Lombardia*[17] according to the characteristics of the directive in question where that directive is subject to irregular or nonexistent transposition. In these proceedings the directive in question was found to be insufficiently precise and unconditional. If on the other hand the subject-matter of the directive is unconditional and sufficiently precise, a finding of direct effect applies in favour of the individual concerned and against the member state in question. These essentially are the tightly constrained terms of the direct effect doctrine so that any application against an individual or as between individuals in dispute lies beyond its terms. In the same way it has been seen already, in *Arcaro*,[18] that direct effect cannot facilitate enforcement of the law against an individual. In this case the Court avoided any conclusion on the matter of direct effect. The Advocate-General on the other hand concluded that the subject directive was again insufficiently precise and unconditional for present purposes. The reasons for this conclusion were twofold: in the first place, it is open to a member state to prescribe emission limits which are more stringent than those prescribed by the directive. Secondly, the Advocate-General observed that member state discretion was substantial, to the extent that more extensive discharges might be permitted, at least as long as water quality objectives in general were complied with.

Vertical operation It has been seen above that direct effect operates vertically, against the state (or an emanation of that state) rather than horizontally, against an individual. If an individual is to sustain a claim based on direct effect, it is necessary therefore to ensure that that claim is against a body, organisation or other agency which is sufficiently well identified with the state, as well as being referable to a directive affecting the environment which is sufficiently precise and unconditional. In *Foster v. British Gas*[19] the European Court of Justice has held that for a body to be sufficiently well identified with the state that body must provide a public service, it must be under state control, and it must have 'special' legal powers beyond those possessed by individuals under the general law. Interestingly, these three prerequisites were found to exist in relation to a privatised water company in *Griffin v. South West Water Services Ltd.*[20] Although the English High Court found no direct effect in relation to an employment directive, the decision is of interest in at least one respect, in relation to the potential enforcement of directives on the environment, by individuals. As a matter of the substance, the court concluded that the public service rendered by the company must be subject to control, as was the case here where regulatory control of water companies is facilitated under the terms of the Water Industry Act 1991. The impact of direct effect in relation to the enforcement of directives on the environment can best be described as cautious in the United Kingdom. The two areas of greatest actual or potential development to date appear to be in relation to enforcement of directives on environmental assessment and shellfisheries.

Direct effect and environmental assessment Two seminal decisions, of the English High Court and House of Lords respectively, show the extent of enforceable personal rights under Directive 85/337[21] relating to environmental assessment. In the first case, *R. v. St Edmundsbury Borough Council, ex p. Walton*[22] an application for judicial review was before the court in respect of a decision not to require the production of an environmental assessment, and to grant a brewing company planning permission to build an access road to its depot, across a water meadow of historic and local amenity importance. The development fell within the terms of Directive 85/337 and the insufficiency of environmental information before the decision-making committee of the local authority led the court to decide in favour of quashing the decision at the instance of the applicant, a local resident. The facts before the House of Lords in *Berkeley v. Secretary of State for the Environment*[23] showed that an environmental statement did not accompany an application for planning permission, and that the local planning authority was not asked to express an opinion on the question whether one was required. Again a local resident applied to the court to have the decision granting planning permission quashed as being *ultra vires* in the absence of the environmental statement.

The essential question for the House of Lords in *Berkeley* was whether the objectives of Directive 85/337, as transposed into municipal law, had been substantially satisfied. Giving the opinion of the court, Lord Hoffmann referred to the decision of the European Court of Justice in *World Wildlife Fund v. Autonome Provinz Bozen*[24] where it was observed that the Directive confers directly enforceable rights on the citizens of member states. Accordingly, where the Directive's discretion on the necessity for and categorisation of, a project has been exceeded, it was held that individuals may rely on the Directive before the court of a member state in order to secure a setting-aside of national measures which are incompatible with its provisions. Applying this statement of principle, Lord Hoffmann concluded that individuals affected by development have a directly enforceable right to have the need for an environmental assessment considered before a grant of planning permission rather than after the event, by a judge. However, there was one further problem for the House of Lords: the absence from the municipal regulations transposing the Directive of any general obligation to consider whether an application for planning permission falls within the defined requirement for an environmental assessment by virtue of its allegedly 'significant effects' on the environment.

The municipal regulations, it was observed, require an expression of opinion on this matter by the local authority only if requested to do so by the applicant for planning permission. Where the Secretary of State is concerned there is no express requirement that the matter be considered: the only obligation is to notify the applicant where the application 'appears' to fall within the prescribed categories set out in the Directive. Lord Hoffmann's approach to this apparent gap in municipal law was to imply into the regulations an obligation to consider the need for an environmental assessment, in accordance with the need for sympathetic interpretation, examined earlier in this chapter.

Direct effect and shellfisheries legislation Late in 1997 an application was made in the case of *Bowden v. South West Water, the Environment Agency, the Secretary of State for the Environment and the Director-General of Water Services*[25] to strike out certain causes of action brought by a Devon shell fisherman. One of the issues before the court was whether damages might be available to such a fisherman as a result of the failure of the defendant bodies and agencies to comply with and enforce Community legislation. As a result, it was alleged, shellfish stocks were damaged through failure of the statutory duty to treat sewage in accordance with prescribed Community standards. The judge, Carnwath, J., doubted whether the Shellfish Directive[26] was sufficiently specific to justify a personal claim, in respect of duties which the judge considered to be in favour of the public at large. Early in 1998 an application for leave to appeal against the striking out of the various claims by Carnwath, J., was made to the Court of Appeal.[27] Before the Court of Appeal, the core of the applicant's argument was that the foregoing and other related directives confer an enforceable right to compensation. The Court of

Appeal decided in favour of restoration of that part of the claim relating to the Shellfish Directive, influenced probably by the proprietorial character of shell fisheries, as recognised by the terms of municipal legislation as well as by other factors emerging from the Community legislation. This litigation will be examined again in rather greater detail in the following section of the chapter which deals with the liability for damages of a member state.

Liability of a Member State for Damages

The directly effective rights of an individual just discussed relate directly to the question whether a member state might be liable for damages in certain circumstances. Such liability was an issue in *Bowden* and that case is returned to, below. In the meantime, the essential principle underlying member state liability for damages is to be seen in *Francovich v. Italy*,[28] a case on enforcement of Community law governing employee protection but equally applicable to matters affecting the enforcement of environmental law.

The decision in Francovich The decision of the European Court of Justice in *Francovich* indicates that in certain circumstances a member state may be liable for damages for loss caused to an individual as a result of an infringement of Community law committed by that state. Typically it appears that the principle here will apply where a member state is found to have failed to take all necessary measures to achieve the result identified by a subject directive even though the facts of the case involved total failure to implement the directive by the due date. However, liability arises only where certain conditions are satisfied: that the objective identified by the directive involves a right conferred on the individual in question; that the content of that right may be identified on the basis of the directive's provisions; and there is some causal link between the failure of the member state to fulfil its obligations, and the damage suffered by the individual affected. Subsequently, the European Court of Justice has proceeded to deal with the matter of liability for damage caused by breaches of Community law attributable to a member state where a national legislature is responsible for such breaches. This development of the *Francovich* principle in Community law will be examined following a return to the *Bowden* litigation.

The Bowden litigation The previous section of this chapter made reference to this litigation. The present section of the chapter provides an opportunity to expand on several of the issues surrounding this litigation, divorced from the merits of the facts involved which, at the time of writing, remain to be tried. The case arose from designation by the Ministry of Agriculture of shellfish waters where the plaintiff mollusc fisherman harvests shellfish but where it was alleged that income had reduced significantly. The Court of Appeal held that it is arguable that such fishermen have directly effective rights under Community legislation. The Court was influenced in its conclusion by an acknowledgement that such fishermen play a significant part in securing compliance with, and enforcement of, directives such that directly effective rights might accrue.

Any immediate cause of the plaintiff's inability to harvest shellfish for human consumption was seen by the Court of Appeal as being referable to Directive 91/492[29] relating to the protection of the consumers of shellfish. Otherwise, the Court saw Directive 79/923[30] prescribing quality standards for shellfish waters as intended to safeguard shellfish populations from various harmful consequences. A failure of protection could give rise to unequal conditions of competition: in those circumstances the Court of Appeal suggested that it may have been intended that those who harvest and market shellfish should have a right of reparation through failure to implement the Directive's requirements. The reference here to unequal conditions of competition directs attention to the fact that the Directive was adopted, in part, under Article 100 (now Article 94) of the Treaty by reference to the establishment and functioning of the common, internal market. If this specific basis for adoption of Community legislation is ultimately recognised, perhaps in proceedings before the European Court of Justice, this alone may be a tenuous basis for determining the existence of directly effective rights in respect of legislation affecting the environment. However, this is not the only issue which was considered by the Court of Appeal for this purpose. Attention was given also to a contention based on an alleged breach of section 7 of the Sea Fisheries (Shellfish) Act 1967: the Court of Appeal upheld the decision of Carnwath, J., at first instance that this contention should be allowed to proceed.

Section 7 of the Act of 1967 is an interesting provision, dealing as it does with fisheries protection. The section is concerned with proprietorial issues affecting fisheries owned independently of the Act, as well as those granted under the terms of the Act. Unlawful interference with such fisheries is enforced through the imposition of criminal sanctions. However, much of the Court of Appeal's deliberations were taken up with arguments relating to the above Directive 79/923, Directive 76/160[31] (the Bathing Water Directive), and Directive 91/271.[32] The core of the plaintiff's argument here was that these directives confer an enforceable right to compensation by virtue of the

Francovich principle. At first instance, Carnwath, J., was not prepared to recognise such a right, although he did recognise the closer connection between Directive 79/923 and the plaintiff's livelihood. Indeed, the plaintiff's counsel in the Court of Appeal brought the Court's attention to the decision of the European Court of Justice in *Commission v. Germany,*[33] a case relating to Directive 80/68[34] on the protection of groundwater, where it was stated that the procedural provisions prescribe precise and detailed rules intended to create rights and obligations for individuals for the purpose of securing effective protection of groundwaters.

Against the foregoing background, the Court of Appeal was prepared to give leave to restore that part of the statement of claim concerning Directive 79/923. The Court was also willing to allow the plaintiff to take forward the argument that any legal obligations in Community legislation here are relevant to the lawfulness and reasonableness of the alleged failure by the water company (South West Water) to incur expenditure which would have prevented damage to public fisheries which, in turn, allegedly damaged the plaintiff's fisheries in a manner that amounted to an actionable nuisance in the law of tort.

Development of the Francovich principle The European Court of Justice has decided two important cases in developing the *Francovich* principle, albeit in areas unconnected with the environment. Nevertheless, the principles emerging from these two decisions may be referable to the environment, assuming of course that relevant Community law can be construed consistently with the extended principle, on the facts of the individual case. The two cases in question are *Brasserie du Pecheur SA v. Germany*[35] and *R. v. H.M. Treasury.*[36]

In *Brasserie du Pecheur* the European Court of Justice stressed that state liability in the present context is an inherent part of the Treaty and applies whatever organ of the state is responsible for the breach which attracts application of the law in this case. Above all the Court underlined the fundamental assumption that every state authority – including the legislature – is bound to comply with Community law affecting the position of individuals in the discharge of its functions. It was against this background that the Court set out the prerequisites for state liability: the rule of law whose infringement is in issue must be intended to confer rights on individuals; the breach must be sufficiently serious; and (finally) there should be a direct causal link (to be determined by a national court) between the state's obligation and the damage, loss or injury suffered by the individual claimant. Perhaps the most difficult matter for the Court takes it beyond the narrower categories of judicial interpretation in order to determine in relation to the second of the above requirements whether the breach is sufficiently 'serious'. In this case the Court indicates that what is needed is evidence to suggest that a state or Community institution has manifestly and gravely disregarded the limits of its discretion. The Court suggested that certain factors will be taken into account for the purpose of determining such an issue: the clarity and precision of the rule or requirement whose breach is in issue, the extent of the discretion available, whether the infringement causing loss, damage or injury was or was not intentional, whether any error of law was excusable, and (finally) any contribution to the infringement by a Community institution. An infringement will be regarded as being sufficiently serious according to the Court where it persists after a judgment finding it established, or where a preliminary ruling or settled case law of the Court makes it clear that there is an infringement. In determining reparation for present purposes, the Court stressed that fault is not a determining factor. However, it is necessary that reparation should be commensurate with the loss, damage or injury suffered. It may be asked, for example, whether the claimant used reasonable diligence to avoid loss and whether all available legal remedies had been exhausted.

The second of the decisions of the Court, *R. v. H.M. Treasury, ex p. British Telecommunications Plc*, relates to the question whether there was a sufficiently serious infringement of Community law in the United Kingdom's transposition of the Telecommunications Directive. In its decision the Court was concerned as a matter of policy to avoid too wide a view of the consequences arising from an infringement, in this case a matter of incorrect transposition. Essentially, the concern of the Court was to avoid undue hindrance of the legislative process through resort to actions for damages where legislation impacts on individuals. For this reason there is a sufficiently serious infringement of Community law where a Community institution or member state manifestly and gravely disregards limits to the exercise of its powers. In approaching the question whether there was clarity and precision in the rule under scrutiny the Court concluded that there was some ambiguity in the subject directive. As a result, the exclusion of certain services by the government of the United Kingdom in the course of transposition was not considered to be a sufficiently serious infringement of Community law.

The nature of environmental directives is such that it must be presumed that application of the *Francovich* principle and its extension will be exceptional. The decision in *Bowden* appears to suggest that the identification of 'rights' sufficient to trigger an application of the principle will be unusual. Again, it may be suggested that any rights crystallised in Community environmental legislation will tend to be interpreted by the court as rights to be enjoyed by the public at large rather than individually. All of this suggests that total or partial failure of transposition will not usually result in damages for the infringement of rights within the foregoing principle.

The Courts' Approach to the Community Environmental Principles

Some consideration was given in Chapter Three to the status of Community environmental principles in two areas: policy-formation and in the courts' approach to judicial interpretation of Community legislation. In order to gain an insight into the actual and potential problems associated with the relevance of the principles and their application to, specific problems, attention is now given to the treatment of one of the principles – the precautionary principle – by the courts. The judicial interpretation of the precautionary principle has attracted attention in jurisdictions well beyond the European Community and its member states. As a result there is an increasingly clear view of the critical issues which attend the precautionary principle, and its application. At the outset though it must be appreciated that the principle attracts controversy by virtue of uncertainties of meaning. One reason for such uncertainty may be found in the deployment of the principle across policy-formation and in judicial proceedings. As will be seen below, those judicial proceedings may take the form of judicial review of administrative decision-making affecting the environment as well as proceedings by way of appeal where the court is looking at and deciding a case *de novo* on the merits. In both instances it may be arguable that the precautionary principle is a legally relevant consideration.

Precaution as a legally relevant consideration A not untypical issue in judicial review is that the principle is a legally relevant, material consideration for the decision-maker. This was the case in *R. v. Leicestershire County Council, ex p. Blackfordby and Boothcorpe Action Group Ltd*[37] where it was contended that the local authority had failed to take account of and apply the health implications of further landfilling on a particular site. The further contention was that lawful application of the principle here would have resulted in a rejection of the development application pending resolution of the impact of such operations. The court however noted that the principle was incorporated as part of government policy and had correctly been taken into account. This was a case of judicial review where the legality of the decision-making process was in issue. It is a fundamental feature of judicial review that the weight and emphasis to be given to a material consideration is for the decision-maker, not the court. This means that there are certain matters of discretion that are assumed to reside exclusively within the decision-making jurisdiction. Not surprisingly there are some matters that depend on the judgement of the decision-maker, such as the extent of existing scientific knowledge and the likely extent of any adverse effects on the environment if (say) certain development is allowed to proceed. Plainly though, a failure to give consideration to the principle, if it is legally relevant, material consideration may have the effect of rendering the decision *ultra vires* on review or of permitting an appeal court to substitute a decision in which the principle plays a part. This latter situation occurred in the Land and Environment Court of New South Wales, Australia, in *Leatch v. Director-General of the National Parks and Wildlife Service.*[38] In *Leatch* the question was whether a licence to take or kill endangered fauna should be granted on appeal following approval for the construction of a new road. One of the main contentions before the Court was that a licence should not be issued if, *inter alia*, there was scientific uncertainty about the effect of the development on the species said to be endangered. The judge, Stein, J., considered the principle to be:

> ... a statement of common sense. It is directed towards the prevention of serious or irreversible harm to the environment in situations of scientific uncertainty. Its premise is that where uncertainty or ignorance exists concerning the nature or scope of environmental harm (whether this follows from policies, decisions or activities), decision makers should be cautious.[39]

The judge concluded from the terms of the relevant legislation that the precautionary principle was not extraneous: although there was no express provision requiring consideration of the principle, consideration of the state of knowledge or uncertainty regarding a species, the potential for serious or irreversible harm to endangered fauna and the adoption of a cautious approach were found to be consistent with the subject-matter, scope and purpose of the Act. Stein J., refers, variously, to 'scientific uncertainty' and the 'scarcity of scientific knowledge': assumptions underlying the precautionary principle which give rise to real problems. Before returning to the judicial mechanics associated with the principle, it is necessary to look at these problems, at least in terms of the way that they have been dealt with by the courts in a variety of contexts.

Scientific uncertainty In the United States, the Supreme Court has established important criteria by which the court can determine whether it should admit expert scientific evidence. In *Daubert v. Merrill Dow Pharmaceuticals Inc.*[40]

the Supreme Court was confronted by the Federal Rules of Evidence and their interpretation for present purposes. The critical part of these Rules stipulates that all 'relevant' evidence is admissible: 'relevant' evidence is that which has any tendency to make the existence of any fact that is of consequence to the determination of the action more or less probable than it would be without the subject evidence. The principle enunciated by the Supreme Court is that any scientific evidence has to be both relevant and reliable, that 'scientific' evidence is evidence that implies a grounding in the methods, procedure and discipline of science, and that 'knowledge' extends beyond mere subjective belief or unsupported speculation. There is however no expectation that the subject-matter here should be 'known' to a certainty although there needs to be support through appropriate validation by reference to 'good grounds' based on what is known. The essential question therefore is whether scientific evidence is reliable. In turn it has to be asked whether there is scientific validity in the underlying reasoning or methodology which is properly applicable to the facts in hand having been tested through peer review and publication. Although not regarded as being decisive, peer review will be regarded as a relevant consideration in the assessment of scientific validity. Additional factors identified by the Supreme Court related to the need for judicial assessment of any known or potential rate of error and evidence of general acceptance by any appropriate scientific community.

Expectations and decision-making In any challenge before the court it may be argued, for example, that there is in law an expectation that decision-making should be based on conclusions to be validly drawn from available scientific information. This of course assumes that the foregoing criteria generated by cases such as *Daubert* are appreciated and applied by the court. The assumption in turn is that these conclusions obviate the need to rely on the precautionary principle. Nevertheless, recognition of the principle in law has the potential to give rise to impossible forensic complication, whether the court is concerned with judicial review or appeal. This was certainly evident in *Leatch*, a decision which may suggest an 'all or nothing' approach where a court is minded to enforce the precautionary principle. If the impossible forensic complication is in the forefront of the court's mind there may be an argument in favour of regulatory consent for the otherwise controversial development with conditions attached for the purpose of varying or even revoking that consent where necessary, in the light of evolving scientific evidence.

In another Australia case, again before the Land and Environment Court of New South Wales, *Greenpeace Australia Ltd v. Redbank Power Co. Pty*,[41] the issue before the Court was the impact of carbon dioxide emissions from the operation of a power station whose development Greenpeace wished to prevent. It was recognised that there is continuing uncertainty about the impact of such a greenhouse gas on the environment. Greenpeace argued that that uncertainty should not be used as a reason for ignoring that impact and that the precautionary principle should be taken account of. The Court stressed that there were instances of scientific uncertainty on both sides of the case and that precaution requires caution, not that the greenhouse gas issue should outweigh all other issues in the case.

The decision of the English High Court in *R. v. Secretary of State for Trade and Industry, ex p. Duddridge* has been seen already.[42] The relevant statute law here required the Secretary of State to determine whether there existed any dangers or risks arising from exposure to electromagnetic fields: it was found that there was no scientific evidence to sustain such a link. Nevertheless it was argued by the applicants that the Secretary of State was obliged to apply the precautionary principle by reference to a possibility of an increased risk of leukaemia as found by the National Radiological Protection Board. The Court held that there was no duty to apply the principle here. Smith, J. observed that in *Leatch* the statute in question gave a power to take account of the principle whereas no such position applied according to the judge's interpretation of the present statutory background. Overall, therefore, the approach seems to depend on judicial interpretation of the statutory vehicle for decision-making. If there is room for a duty or a discretion in respect of the principle then the court has to determine whether the threshold of scientific evidence is reached. If not and there is what the court might characterise as scientific uncertainty, taking account of the fact that there is no absolute scientific certainty, then the principle is applicable. Where the court is concerned with judicial review it will need to ask the question whether the principle was considered. If not, any resulting decision will be held to be *ultra vires*. If the principle has been taken account of, the weight and emphasis to be accorded to it will be a matter for the decision-maker.

Aspects of European Court of Justice Jurisdiction

Matters of interpretation and application of the Treaty are ultimately the responsibility of the European Court of Justice under Article 220. With this fundamental responsibility for ensuring application of the law comes a number of other responsibilities, some of which are examined in this section of the chapter. One which is not, given its limited application to environmental law in the Community, is Article 234 whereby a national court may request a preliminary determination on the validity and application of Community law. In some cases the national court will be bound to make the reference. Rather more needs to be said about the operation of Articles 226 and 230 of the Treaty.

Article 226

Where the Commission considers that a member state has failed to fulfil an obligation under the Treaty, Article 226 justifies a reasoned opinion on the issue, but only after allowing that member state the right to make observations. If thereafter the member state fails to comply with the reasoned opinion within a period prescribed by the Commission, the Commission is empowered to bring the issue before the Court. Before the Court the fundamental starting point is the Article 174 obligation of a member state to implement legislation adopted by the Community. Thereafter the matter usually relates to member state failure to transpose correctly, or at all, some aspect of a subject directive. Arguably, one of the most difficult issues calling for careful, comparative analysis arises from the contention of a member state that existing provision and practice shows consistency with the Community legislation. Equally difficult though is the case where it is alleged by the Commission that a member state has failed in its application of Community legislative requirements. This was the case in *Commission v. Italy*[43] for example. Member state adoption of Community requirements through transposition is one thing, but (as is seen in this waste management case) there is additionally the obligation under Article 249 to achieve the result prescribed by the directive in question. This case showed a failure to draw up and execute plans relating to different types and quantities of waste as well as sites for its disposal. The case also showed the other major difficulty confronting the Commission in obtaining accurate, timely information for the purpose of these enforcement proceedings, an issue which will be returned to later in this section of the chapter. When the Court arrives at a judgment on the Article 226 reference it is clear that the onus is on the member state to comply: the Court will not intervene to declare member state provision a nullity, or to prescribe measures necessary to secure lawful compliance with Community law as interpreted.

Article 230

This provision of the Treaty gives the Court jurisdiction to annul Community legislation on an application by a member state, a Community institution or a person directly affected. Member states and Community institutions have certain advantages over individuals in activating Article 230. These advantages are seen in the need to establish that the measure complained of is of 'direct and individual concern' to an individual.

This was the issue before the Court in *Stichting Greenpeace v. Commission*.[44] Here the Court was concerned with the grant of structural funds to Spain to construct two power stations in the Canary Islands. The relevant Community regulation stipulated that such funds shall be in keeping with the requirements of environmental protection. It was claimed that local authority authorisation was not supported by an environmental assessment. As a consequence, Greenpeace, two local environmental groups and 16 residents sought annulment of the funding order. In addressing *locus standi* requirements the Court proceeded on the basis of authority that had addressed this matter only in connection with economic transactions. The Court held that there was no justification for a conclusion that the applicants were affected in a sufficiently distinctive manner from others living and working in the area, despite the fact that some of the applicants had previously lodged complaints with the Commission. Furthermore, it was held that Greenpeace and the two environmental groups were not sufficiently distinctive from the individual applicants. In practice, rather more cases arise under Article 230 in relation to the Treaty basis on which Community legislation has been adopted. This is seen in two important cases affecting the environment.

The first of these cases is *Parliament v. Council*[45] where the Court is again concerned with the familiar tension between trade and the environment. On this occasion the Court was invited to annul Regulation 259/93[46] on the supervision and control of waste shipments within, into and out of the Community. It was held that the regulation fell within the framework of environmental policy and, as such, could not be seen as an instrument facilitating the free movement of waste within the Community. Accordingly, the Council was held to have validly based the regulation on what is now Article 175 (formerly Article 130s) despite the fact that, by harmonising the conditions on which movements of waste take place, regulated movements of waste had a resultant bearing on the internal market. Perhaps significantly, Article 175 provided at the time of the adoption of the regulation that the Parliament was to be consulted, whereas the provision argued for by the Parliament – Article 95 (formerly Article 100a) – required cooperation with the Parliament.

In the second of these cases – *Parliament v. Council*[47] – the challenge was aimed at seeking the annulment of regulations on forest protection which had been adopted by the Council under a Community scheme for atmospheric pollution protection, thereby safeguarding the productive potential of agriculture. It was argued by the Council that adoption should have been by virtue of Article 175 rather than under Treaty powers relating to the Common Agricultural Policy. It has been seen above that Article 175 provides for consultation with the Parliament. It was held that the regulations should be annulled, albeit subject to a delay in order to allow the situation to be regularised. Essentially the regulations were 'environmental': trees (for example) could not be regarded as 'agricultural products'.

Interim Relief Pending Decisions of the Court

The matter of interim relief occurs not only in relation to the proceedings of the European Court of Justice but also in relation to proceedings in anticipation where they occur in the courts of member states. The present section of the chapter address both possibilities, given their inter-connectedness. Article 243 of the Treaty gives the Court a considerable discretion to prescribe interim relief, whether or not the Commission applies to the Court for such relief, typically in a case which is pending. If the Court is willing to entertain interim proceedings it seems quite possible that national measures might be subject to temporary suspension. Perhaps one of the best known cases of an application (albeit unsuccessful) for interim relief was in *Commission v. Germany*[48] (the 'Leybucht Dykes' case). In the context of proceedings relating to dyke construction which was alleged to be contrary to Directive 79/409[49] the Commission sought interim relief from the Court. The relief sought would have required the government of Germany to suspend dyke construction and to delay commencement of a new stage of the construction work. The Court refused the application for interim relief, indicating that it was made when the construction project was well under way and a large part of the work completed. Clearly therefore, time is of the essence here, as it would tend to be in any other similar proceedings. However, as has been noted already, interim proceedings may be material in a member state court, in anticipation of an eventual decision of the European Court of Justice.

In another case concerning the foregoing Birds Directive, *R. v. Secretary of State for the Environment, ex p. RSPB*,[50] the House of Lords has held that, pending a decision of the European Court of Justice, it was inappropriate for the United Kingdom court to make an interim declaration that it would be contrary to law for the Secretary of State to fail to act to avoid deterioration of habitats and the disturbance of species in an area whose status as a special protection area is under consideration. Pending the decision of the Court the Secretary of State could not know the proper basis of an assessment. It was conceded by counsel for the Royal Society that the real objective was to delay further development of the site subject to controversy: Lappel Bank on the River Medway. However, it was recognised by the House of Lords that the extant planning permission would permit the controversial land reclamation works to continue. Only an interim injunction would have been capable of requiring positive action to stop such works but the court would be unlikely to grant such a remedy pending a definitive decision of the European Court of Justice and in circumstances where the Royal Society was unwilling even to give a cross-undertaking in damages in respect of the application for the interim declaration.

Subsequently the Divisional Court of the English High Court dismissed an application for interim relief to suspend the operation of a pesticides approval where it was alleged by the manufacturer that it had been granted to a third party in breach of Community law: *R. v. Ministry of Agriculture, ex p. Monsanto Plc.*[51] The question for the Divisional Court was whether interim relief was available in the form of a stay on the operation of the approval, pending the decision of the European Court of Justice on the status of the provision of Community law concerned. In a wide-ranging decision, the Divisional Court stressed the importance of presuming in favour of the licensing decision of a public authority and the need to avoid undue advantages to competitors who might be able to prevent successful licence applicants realising a return on their investment perhaps over a long period before the European Court arrived at a decision in the proceedings.

Noncompliance with Decisions of the Court

Failure of compliance here triggers Article 228 of the Treaty and empowers the Commission to renew its application to the Court. As originally drafted, the Article simply refers to the requirement for the member state in question to take 'the necessary measures' to comply. The Article – now extended by the Maastricht Treaty – stipulates that if the Commission concludes that the member state has not taken compliance measures it shall issue a reasoned opinion identifying the points of noncompliance, but only after giving the member state an opportunity to make observations. Repeated failure of compliance thereafter allows the renewed application referred to at the outset, whereupon the Commission is able to specify an appropriate payment to be made by the member state. Only where the Court confirms that its judgment has not been complied with will there be imposition of a lump sum or penalty payment. This procedure however appears not to prevent Commission reliance on a political solution to the problem of noncompliance. Although the Commission has prescribed an approach to penalty payment calculation, the European Court of Justice in its first case where payments have been enforced, in *Commission v. Hellenic Republic*,[52] has set out criteria to be applied in determining the amount of any penalty to be levied on a member state. In the first place, the penalty has to be appropriate to the circumstances and proportionate both to the breach and the member state's ability to pay. Secondly, the degree of urgency for the fulfilment of obligations will vary in accordance with the noncompliance. To ensure a coercive effect, and a uniform, effective application of Community law the following matters will be taken into account: the duration of the infringement, its degree of seriousness, and the ability of the member state to pay.

The Common Law and Statutory, Regulatory Requirements

The emphasis in this section of the chapter is towards the common law jurisdiction in England and the question whether regulatory requirements and standards prescribed by statute might have some influence on common law claims affecting the environment. Nuisance liability is addressed first, followed by liability in negligence and a general note about tortious liability generally.

Nuisance liability   The starting point is the Court of Appeal decision in *Cambridge Water Co. v. Eastern Counties Leatherwork Co.*[53] where the court was confronted by facts indicating that a statutory water company had purchased a site containing a bore hole from which water could be pumped from a chalk aquifer. Initially the water from the bore hole was declared to be wholesome, by reference to water quality standards then extant. However, following entry into force of Directive 80/778 the water was tested and showed concentrations of organochlorines including tetrachloroethane, a dry-cleaning solvent, much used in the tanning industry for degreasing sheepskin. The concentrations discovered were well in excess of the limits permitted by the Directive and the regulations transposing them. Although the decision was reversed by the House of Lords on strict liability principles, the Court of Appeal held that in so far as the interference with a public water supply was an actionable nuisance, the liability was strict so that there could be liability for 'any' damage. In so holding, the Court of Appeal refused to attach any importance to the fact that the appellant suffered loss only when quality standards were raised under the influence of Community law three years after abstraction commenced, and many years after the respondent had ceased to spill organochlorines. The Court of Appeal had no doubt that, *prima facie*, wholesomeness of water depends on compliance with Community water quality standards, even though there may be other factors which influence such judgments.

Negligence liability It seems clear that the common law may accept liability in negligence, whether or not relevant statutory requirements have been complied with. It appears that what overrides either situation is satisfaction of the prerequisites relating to negligence liability. Examples of each are now set out, below.

The failure to comply with regulatory requirements prescribed by statute as a result of which third party neighbours suffer asbestosis has been held by the Court of Appeal to attract liability in negligence, in *Margereson and Hancock v. J.W. Roberts Ltd.*[54] This is but one example of the way in which negligence liability might attach: at first instance it was said that the subject regulations must have raised awareness of the dangers arising from the process being carried out in the defendant's factory such that it was reasonably foreseeable that injury might accrue through noncompliance with the statutory requirements. It was not necessary here that the defendant company should be aware of the *precise* effects of noncompliance. The only requirement was that there should be reasonable foreseeability of damage to human health. Accordingly, the company was liable to third parties in respect of historic contamination.

Even where regulatory requirements prescribed by statute have been met, there may be room on the facts for the enforcement of a duty of care. For example, a statutory water undertaker is arguably bound by a duty of care to ensure that wholesome water is provided at common law. That undertaker's liability at common law may be manifested by a failure to warn consumers that water supplied is contaminated as a result of its passage through lead pipes. The point is well made in the Court of Appeal decision in *Barnes v. Irwell Valley Water Board*[55] where it was said that:

> ... the plaintiffs ... [are] entirely dependent upon the supplier of the water to see that it [is] water which [is] not in its nature poisonous.

Tortious Liability Generally

For the purpose of considering other areas of relevance a further example of common law treatment of tortious liability is to be found in the English High Court decision in *Losinjska Plovidba v. Transco Overseas Ltd (The Orjula).*[56] Here a charterer leased containers to a third party for use in the transportation of drums of acid being shipped to Libya, via Rotterdam. On arrival in Rotterdam the containers were found to be defective, whereupon the charterer was required by the port authority to unload and decontaminate the containers. It was held by the High Court that the charterer of the vessel had an independent cause of action in tort. Given the increasingly strict statutory controls over dangerous and environmentally intrusive substances, this decision of the High Court appears to provide the person in possession of defective or dangerous substances with an action against the supplier or transferor. This has interesting possibilities and raises the prospect of actions in tort against, say, the producer of waste at the instance of a transporter where, through a misdescription, a landfiller refuses to accept the consignment. Another example relates to agricultural sludge where the sludge supplied by one farmer to another is found (contrary to the recorded characteristics) to contain traces of heavy metals beyond the prescribed statutory limit. In both these examples civil liability would be in addition to any criminal liability.

The European Court of Justice and Legislative Change

Given the centrality of the Court's essential role, there are occasions when decisions may impact on legislative developments affecting the environment throughout the Community. It has been seen already that proceedings which reach the Court may arise in a variety of different ways. A particularly significant illustration arose from proceedings against the United Kingdom in respect of methods which were regarded as being contrary to law for the purpose of complying with Directive 80/778.[57] An examination of the full chronology of events is useful for present purposes, taking account of the fact that these proceedings were not the only proceedings taken by the Commission against erring member states in relation to the Directive. Indeed, various shortcomings and irregularities were alleged by the Commission here, not just the specific irregularity alleged against the Government of the United Kingdom. A second illustration arises from the original proceedings before the European Court of Justice in *Commission v. Germany* [1989] (proceedings interim relief in this 'Leybucht Dykes' case were dealt with earlier in this chapter) where significant changes in Community law occurred.

Commission v. United Kingdom[58]

Prior to these proceedings before the European Court of Justice the Court of Appeal had upheld an earlier decision of the High Court dismissing applications for judicial review of decisions of the Secretary of State for the Environment whereby he accepted undertakings from water companies to take such steps which appeared to him to be appropriate to ensure compliance with the duties in respect of water quality prescribed by section 68 of the Water Industry Act 1991.[59] The Court of Appeal did not consider that the undertakings represented an unlawful approach to the need to remedy breaches of the Directive comprising an alleged failure in respect of the quality of water intended for human consumption. The Court of Appeal considered also that consideration of practicality formed part of the decision as to how a breach might be remedied 'as soon as possible', especially since there is no principle of Community or domestic law that requires the court to ignore practicalities. Subsequently, the European Court of Justice held that this approach to undertakings was unlawful as a means of complying with the Directive. Apart from anything else, the Water Industry Act did not specify the matters to be covered by undertakings: in particular, derogations, programmes of work to be completed, the time-scale for such work and (where appropriate) the information to be given to the public for these purposes. As a consequence the position has been regularised when secondary legislation – the Drinking Water (Undertakings) (England and Wales) Regulations 2000[60] – came into force. As a result, an undertaking in respect of a breach of section 68 can be accepted only in very specific circumstances, as prescribed by the Regulations.

Commission v. Germany[61]

The decision of the Court here related to the Birds Directive[62] and imposed on member states an obligation to protect sites frequented by birds which was regarded by many member states as being overly strict. The consequence was that the later Habitats Directive[63] contained what may be described as a softening of the Court's view of the essential principles governing the designation of protection areas for birds. The Court had indicated that the economic and recreational considerations referred to in Article 2 of the Birds Directive cannot override the general system of protection established by the

Directive. The so-called 'softening' provision just referred to now indicates that where a project affecting a habitat must be undertaken for imperative reasons of public interest (including social and economic matters) a member state is obliged to take all compensatory measures necessary to ensure that the overall coherence of Community nature conservation measures is protected. The obligation of a member state here is to advise the Commission of the compensatory measures adopted.

Judicial Attitudes to Transposition

Reference has been made earlier in the book to the inherent nature of transposition where Community directives are concerned. The extent of any member state freedom is of course subject to the court's interpretation of the limits of transposition and that is the concern of this penultimate section of the present chapter. Of particular interest here is the control of administrative discretion affecting the environment as well as the limits of member state discretion in areas such as nature conservation. Apart from nature conservation, the particular concerns are with the way that the courts have approached certain aspects of Community law relating to water quality and environmental assessment.

Community Water Quality Law

The scope of member state freedom in transposition has occurred as an issue in relation to almost all of the critical directives. These directives have been subject to detailed scrutiny by the courts and the European Court of Justice in particular. The first of these is the Nitrates Directive.

The Nitrates Directive: 91/676 [64] The European Court of Justice was invited to make a preliminary ruling relating to the designation of vulnerable waters for the purpose of the Directive, in *R. v. Secretary of State for the Environment, ex p. Standley.* [65] Among the matters before the Court was the perhaps difficult line that has to be drawn between member state designation of waters affected by pollution here, and the determination of the proportion of pollution attributable to pollution by nitrates. Essentially in this part of the decision the Court emphasised that a member state cannot escape the criteria for designation found in the Directive, although Community law does not give rise to a need to determine precisely what proportion of water-borne pollution is attributable to nitrates of agricultural origin or, indeed, that the cause of such pollution is exclusively agricultural. It was against this background that the Court held that it is incompatible with the Directive to restrict identification of affected waters to cases of agricultural pollution alone. The Directive requires that the nitrogen contribution of agricultural and other sources is taken into account.

The Directive on Dangerous Substances in Water[66] Two very significant decisions of the Court have dwelt on the meaning of that centrally important term 'discharge' as it appears in the Directive: *AML van Rooij v. Dagelijksbestuur van het waterschap de Dommel*[67] and *Nederhoff & Zoon v. Dijkgraaf en Hoogeemraden van het Hoogheemraadschap Rijnland.*[68] This section will look at these two decisions before going on to consider rather broader issues arising from lack of clarity that can arise in the drafting of Community directives on the environment. In the first of the cases above the issue related to steam generated from a wood treatment plant where that steam contained toxic and even poisonous substances. It was claimed that through precipitation in particular these substances reached the aquatic environment, necessitating the appropriate regulatory consent according to law. The Court held that the term 'discharge' in the Directive refers to any act attributable to a person by which one of the prescribed dangerous substances is directly or indirectly introduced into a relevant body of water. Accordingly, the Directive applies in these circumstances, no matter what the physical state of the substance happens to be. The second case was concerned with the use of wooden posts to shore up river banks, where those posts had been treated with the preservative, creosote. A regulatory consent had been refused on the ground that creosote is responsible for introducing toxic substances to the aquatic environment. It was argued that the sinking of the treated posts was not a 'discharge' for the purpose of the Directive. The Court held that a regulatory consent was required since there had been a 'discharge' within the meaning of the Directive. Again the term was seen to include the sinking of the posts into the water by a specific, identifiable person.

Both decisions stress the necessity for a purposive approach to judicial interpretation if much Community legislation is to be effective when matters of uncertainty suggest a need for the assistance of the courts. Compared with municipal legislation in the United Kingdom and its tradition of precisely drafted statutes, Community directives by comparison are characterised by a far more general approach, although considerable stress is placed on introductory statements of legislative objectives which may aid judicial interpretation.

Nevertheless, there can be difficulties with uncertain drafting in directives, an uncertainty that may of course affect the court's deliberations on matters of interpretation. Equally, failings in the primary legislation are likely to have knock-on effects in relation to member state transposition. These difficulties are the subject of a perceptive study by one commentator[69] who looked at a number of problems surrounding Directive 90/313[70] on Access to Environmental Information. Recent decisions of the European Court of Justice provide some insight into the problems which follow on from inadequate drafting as it affects directives. Two cases in particular are worthy of special attention, both affecting Germany: *Commission v. Germany*[71] and *Mecklenburg v. Kreis Pinneberg-Der Landrat.*[72]

In *Commission v. Germany* the case before the Court was based on a failure of transposition, on various grounds advanced by the Commission, many of which indicate crucial uncertainties and ambiguities of meaning affecting both the Commission and the member state in question. Even where a directive can be regarded as a model of clarity there are likely to be difficult matters of emphasis and degree where transposition is concerned. Those matters become rather more difficult if the language of the directive itself is unclear and ambiguous. In the present case one of the grounds relates to the matter of 'reasonable cost' for information access, one of the areas of the Directive which lacks clarity. The present ground raised the question whether the subject German law was incompatible with Article 5 of the Directive, to the extent that it did not restrict the imposition of a charge to a reasonable amount and did not exclude a charge where a request for access was refused. It was held by the Court that the Commission had not proved the absence of a restriction to a reasonable amount, although it was incompatible to impose a charge where a request for information access was refused.

In *Mecklenburg* the Court was concerned with another area of the Directive which lacks clarity: what constitutes information relating to the environment. Here it was held by the Court that, in order to constitute 'information relating to the environment', it is sufficient for there to be a statement of views (in this case by an agency responsible for countryside protection) capable of adversely affecting or protecting the state of the environment, as where those views relate to an application for planning consent, for example. The Court pointed to the absence of any definition of 'information relating to the environment' in the Directive: the inadequacy of the legislation here is perhaps reflected in the conclusion that the views expressed were able 'materially' to influence the decision affecting relevant environmental interests. The Court's approach here suggests attempts beyond interpretation to redraft the legislation.

The Drinking Water Directive[73] The need for the Court to undertake what may appear to be a redrafting of directives appears also in a case that arose under Article 10 of the Drinking Water Directive which permits a member state to authorise values in excess of maximum permitted concentrations in 'emergencies'. In *Pretura Unificata Di Torino v. Persons Unknown*[74] the Court construed the term 'emergencies' as meaning urgent situations in which the competent authorities are required to cope suddenly with difficulties in the supply of water for human consumption. Supplies exceeding the maximum permitted concentrations are allowed only for a limited period, corresponding to the time usually required to restore normal supplies. The Court went on to stress in this case that it is for a national court of a member state to decide whether municipal legislation contains appropriate provisions restricting the circumstances in which derogation is permitted under the terms of the Directive.

The Bathing Water Directive[75] It has been argued before the European Court of Justice that the definition of 'bathing water' in this Directive is so imprecise as to require a member state to resort to its own prescribed thresholds, numerically defined. This was the argument advanced by the Government of the United Kingdom in *Commission v. United Kingdom.*[76] The Commission's proceedings before the Court arose from what it saw as a failure to take all necessary measures to ensure that the quality of bathing waters in the bathing areas of Blackpool and adjacent to Formby and Southport conformed to the limit values in Article 3 of the Directive. The government's argument on this occasion was rejected by reference to the Directive's definition of 'bathing water' as well as the underlying objectives of the statute, including environmental protection, public health and the improvement of living conditions. The Court concluded that the government's reliance on a threshold determined by the number of bathers was insufficient: various facilities such as changing huts and the presence of lifeguards provided evidence that a bathing area is frequented by a large number of bathers, whose health had to be protected. Arguably, this decision again illustrates the *lacunae* that occur in broadly drafted Community directives. The definition of 'bathing water' refers to explicit authorisation of bathing or that bathing is not prohibited 'and is traditionally practised by a large number of bathers'. This level of generality might be seen as an invitation to member states to set their own criteria in circumstances where the Commission remains free, *ex post facto*, to intervene to seek the aid of the Court in attempting to prescribe standards which (arguably) should have been found in the Directive as originally legislated. Interestingly, the Directive is deficient also in its failure to prescribe measures where there is noncompliance: for example, competent authorities are not obliged to prohibit bathing.

The Urban Waste Water Directive[77] The Directive distinguishes between 'sensitive' and other receiving waters for the purpose of determining the level of prescribed treatment for urban waste water. In the United Kingdom the approach to transposition and implementation was based on the avoidance of secondary treatment facilities in areas draining into 'less sensitive' waters. The basis of this governmental approach was the priority of ensuring that implementation costs were minimised. The Department of the Environment sought to draw the necessary limits for these purposes but was met with challenges through judicial review instigated by local authorities who saw their areas being adversely affected as a result. In these cases – *R. v. Secretary of State for the Environment, ex p. Kingston upon Hull City Council* and *R. v. Secretary of State for the Environment, ex p. Bristol City Council*[78] – the essential core of the challenge related to the legality of the establishment of the outer-estuarine limits of the Humber and Severn estuaries. In the absence of criteria in the Directive, the Secretary of State argued that he had a wide discretion in arriving at his decision. It was argued by the applicant local authorities that certain objective criteria were appropriate to the decision: the salinity of the receiving waters or their topographical features, for example. Cost, it was argued, was not a relevant consideration. The judge, Harrison, J., pointed to criteria which are relevant to the decision-making process for the purpose of identifying the true limits of the estuaries in question. In each case it was held that there must be a genuine and rational assessment of what constitutes 'the estuary', bearing in mind the characteristics of the area of water and the purpose of the Directive in addressing adverse environmental effects. Against this background, cost is legally irrelevant: an area of water is either an estuary or not, regardless of cost. The fact that cost had played a part in the Secretary of State's decision-making vitiated the decision under review: the cost of secondary treatment in certain areas was entirely a pragmatic decision.

Community Environmental Assessment Law

Directive 85/337[79] has been dealt with previously, at various points. Earlier in the present chapter the Directive's interpretation as a directly effective provision was examined. For present purposes, one critical question is whether any discretion is ceded to a member state. The European Court of Justice in *World Wildlife Fund v. Autonome Provinz Bozen*[80] has held that although there is a certain measure of discretion available to the member state in determining whether there are significant environmental effects necessitating an environmental assessment (a matter for determination by a national court) this does not exempt large classes of development. Nevertheless, a member state is able to adopt its own approach which may not necessarily depend on the criteria and thresholds prescribed by the Directive for this purpose. The essential core of the Court's approach to the Directive is of course the need for compliance with the core of Community law, a fundamental starting point for the deliberations of national courts. In *R. v. Rochdale Metropolitan Borough Council, ex p. Tew*[81] for example, the English High Court saw no way round the need for an environmental assessment even though the proposed development was subject to an application for outline planning permission and would proceed over a period of 15 years. The same local planning authority nevertheless has responsibility for determining whether an assessment is required, subject to scrutiny by a national court and, ultimately, the European Court of Justice: *R. v. North Yorkshire County Council, ex p. Brown.*[82] Equally, the local planning authority will be in breach of the Directive where it purports to decide an application for planning permission without a requisite assessment. Equally, if that authority purports to arrive at a decision in the absence of an assessment as prescribed by the Directive, its decision will be *ultra vires*: *R. v. Oldham Metropolitan Borough Council, ex p. Foster.*[83] This is not to suggest that a national court will be ignorant of other illegalities emanating from decision-making here. The English High Court has observed that the terms of the Directive would be frustrated if the requirement for an environmental assessment could be avoided simply by virtue of a municipal law deeming a decision to have been made after the expiration of a prescribed period.

Community Nature Conservation Law

Although much of the controversy that has generated litigation in this context relates to the lawful basis for the designation of habitats and areas of protection, one critical issue is the territorial extent of the relevant Community law. This is a matter that is not necessarily exclusively within the jurisdiction of the European Court of Justice although it retains ultimate jurisdiction to overrule a national court on such matters within its competence. The potential for a national court to determine what may be described as a fundamental issue of Community law is seen in *R. v. Secretary of State for Trade and Industry, ex p. Greenpeace Ltd.*[84] In granting permission for and allowing in part, an application for judicial review the High Court held that the presence of a particular reef-forming coral in a list contained in Directive 92/43[85] – the Habitats Directive – necessitated a purposive construction of the legislation if it is to have effect, in this case beyond territorial waters where oil exploration licences were being distributed. Accordingly, a member state is obliged to be aware of judicial interpretation emerging both from the European Court of Justice as well as its own, national courts. However, as already indicated, much of the controversy surrounds the process of designating conservation areas in member states. That controversy has often arisen in relation to the court's interpretation of restrictions on member state freedom to take account of economic factors in the designation of conservation areas.

Restriction of member state powers by reference to economic factors The European Court of Justice has held in *R. v. Secretary of State for the Environment, ex p. RSPB.*[86] that a member state is not empowered to take account of economic requirements in designating and defining the boundaries of an area for present purposes. In other words, economic requirements cannot be regarded as being superior to the Directive's ecological objective. This was a decision under the Birds Directive, as was the decision of the Court in *Commission v. Germany*[87] (the 'Leybucht Dykes' case) which has been dealt with already,[88] in connection with matters of interim relief before the European Court of Justice. In present proceedings, it is interesting to see that the Court took the view that the desire to see the survival of a fishing port could be taken into account in deciding on the location of a newly constructed dyke because there were 'offsetting' ecological benefits. Such rationalisations are clearly important in determining member state strategies, usually where significant commercial or similar developments are in prospect. Subject to such rationalisation by reference to the essential ecological objectives of relevant Community law there seems little doubt about the judicial interpretation of those objectives. In *R. v. Secretary of State for the Environment, ex p. First Corporate Shipping*[89] the Secretary of State for the Environment indicated that he proposed to identify to the Commission the whole of the Severn estuary for possible designation under the Habitats Directive,[90] whereupon the applicant, the Bristol Port Authority, sought judicial review on the ground that Article 2(3) of the Directive obliged the Secretary of State to have regard to economic, social and cultural requirements. The European Court of Justice held that a member state cannot take account of these considerations when selecting and defining a site for proposal to the Commission as a site of Community importance. The margin of discretion is clearly very limited.

The margin of discretion Arguably the most telling decision of the European Court of Justice in the present context occurred in *Commission v. Netherlands.*[91] The government of the Netherlands argued here that designation of a Special Protection Area under the Birds Directive was only one of the measures which could be undertaken by a member state for the purpose of fulfilling its obligations under Article 4(1) of that Directive. Accordingly, infringement proceedings are appropriate only where no special conservation measures have been taken. The Court rejected this argument, holding also that the economic factors set out in Article 2 of the Directive may not be taken into account when selecting a Special Protection Area (SPA) and defining its boundaries. Member states are required to approach the classification process by designating SPAs by reference to those sites 'appearing' to be suitable for the conservation of the prescribed species. It can be seen from this approach that within the mandatory framework of Community law there is an apparent measure of member state discretion, to the extent that national judgement can operate in determining whether it appears that any particular site appears to be suitable for conservation. However, that member state discretion is of course limited as Community law becomes more prescriptive in relation to the designation process.

Of course Community law may change under the influence of judicial interpretation, as occurred following the decision on substantive issues in the *Leybucht Dykes* case.[92] A member state may attempt to restrict the dimensions of a designated SPA and to plead in turn that such a decision is entirely consistent with provisions and practice in its municipal legal system. Such an argument has been roundly rejected by the European Court of Justice in *Commission v. France.*[93] Such an attitude on the part of Community law is undoubtedly a powerful example of the limitation of member state discretion. Another case involving the government of France – *Commission v. France*[94] – arose from an allegation that that government had failed to comply with the Birds Directive and the Habitats Directive, on the ground that certain areas designated as SPAs within marshland were insufficient to meet statutory requirements. Granting the declaration sought, the European Court of Justice held that an insufficient area had been designated. On the facts it was clear to the Court that, in order to avoid deterioration, requisite measures had to be deployed and that those measures need not necessarily be undertaken on SPA land.

Interestingly, such an argument had been mirrored by the court in Scotland, in *World Wildlife Fund UK Ltd v. Secretary of State for Scotland*[95] where it had been argued that designated boundaries should be drawn by reference to scientific criteria alone, so that all contiguous or linked qualifying habitats or species had to be included. Effectively the argument here was that member states have no discretion in boundary delineation. Lord Nimmo Smith, giving judgment, accepted that ornithological factors alone governed the creation of SPA boundaries and accordingly rejected the foregoing argument of the petitioners. In turn the court rejected an argument that, under the Birds Directive and the Habitats Directive, the identification of sites and the delineation of boundaries are distinct steps, only the former involving an exercise of discretion. The court had no hesitation in stressing that the two are integrated processes: a discretion has to be exercised throughout as much in the determination of boundaries as in other matters of site selection. Accordingly, the court concluded that the exercise does not require that all contiguous or linked qualifying habitats or species populations have to be included. Overall, the impression is of considerable difficulty in defining with any certainty the point at which Community legal requirements are superseded by discretion in member state. Again, the weakness of Community law may be seen in the absence of detailed statutory criteria for decision-making in some cases by member states where (in turn) the omission tends to be supplied by judicial interpretation. The picture emerging from the two decisions of the European Court of Justice just examined is that there may be justification in law for factors and variables outside the SPA to be taken account of, probably by reference to member state impressions of the scientific evidence. Ostensibly, such a matter is within the discretion of the member state although judicial interpretation through some of the cases examined leaves a measure of doubt about this.

Judicial Interpretation in the United States

At federal level, Congress tends to legislate on the environment in very broad terms. As a consequence, and subject to state provision, there a tendency for reliance on judicial interpretation in the absence of detailed statutory prescription. As between federal and state courts there may be exclusive jurisdiction in cases affecting the environment conferred on federal courts or concurrent jurisdiction conferred on courts at both levels.

The Commerce Clause of the Constitution

Federal legislative competence in relation to the environment comes from the Commerce clause of the United States Constitution which, among other things, enables legislation regulating commerce between the constituent states.

Whether the Commerce clause can be relied on for present purposes is largely a matter of degree, albeit it can be assumed that legality really depends on any matter subject to legislation being substantially connected to interstate commerce, even where that connection is no more than an indirect connection. The fundamental need here is to establish a rational basis for the claim that any matter subject to legislation here touches and affects interstate commerce. There are numerous dimensions to this difficult question, as will be seen below, where contrasts are drawn between the United States, the European Community, and Canada.

Contrasts with the European Community The contrast with the European Community is considerable: initially the Treaty of Rome contained no provision in respect of legislative competence on the environment. Although that omission has now been repaired and reinforced with the specific environmental objectives found in Article 174 of the Treaty, there is no definition of what the 'environment' might comprise. In so far as there may be any controversy (which may result in litigation) on the constitutional basis for Community legislation, that controversy often relates to the extent and scope of the involvement of Community institutions in the legislative process. Nevertheless, the courts of the Community maintain a cautious watch on what might be described as a frequent tension between the environment and trade within the internal market. As a consequence it may be the case that most, if not all, levels of legislative (and administrative) activity within the Community may be vulnerable to challenge where it is suggested that environmental regulation is in fact a disguised restriction on trade in the internal market, for example.

Constitutional competence and questions of harmonisation If in the case of Community law harmonisation is a fundamental objective, albeit extending now beyond the original framework of the European Community as an economic union of member states, it is arguable that the Commerce clause in the United States Constitution serves a broadly similar purpose. The Supreme Court was invited to consider whether strip mining affects interstate commerce in *Hodel v. Virginia Surface Mining and Reclamation Association Inc.*,[96] against a background of concern in Congress about the adverse environmental effects of water pollution generated by this form of mining. This issue of water pollution and the perceived need for harmonised standards across the United States persuaded the Supreme Court that resort to the Commerce clause was legitimate even if (as the Mining Association claimed) statutory regulation here was an interference with private land use which falls within the competence of states, in the exercise of their so-called 'police' powers.

Federal jurisdiction and state and provincial police power The foregoing example of litigation on matters of legislative competence is doubly significant since it also shows the limit of state jurisdiction. A simple example from what has gone before relates to an attempt by a state to legislate in order to regulate interstate commerce, where it must be presumed that the resulting legislation is unconstitutional. The constitutional structures in Canada, which were outlined towards the end of Chapter Two, show that there is rather less sharp distinction between federal and provincial legislative competence in relation to the environment. Whether this suggests a rather less well-defined block on provincial legislation in Canada is difficult to say since both jurisdictions will tend to proceed by reference to the question whether state or provincial legislation poses something less than substantial regulation of interstate commerce, which also lies within Canadian federal jurisdiction. It may be, for example, that the major concern is the imposition and enforcement of provincial or state police powers. Thus the Supreme Court of Canada in *Ontario v. Canadian Pacific Ltd.*[97] was concerned with federal competence in relation to the regulation of railways. Nevertheless it was held that Canadian Pacific had been lawfully subject to criminal enforcement powers under the Ontario Environmental Protection Act when smoke pollution occurred in the course of controlled burns on track in that province. The Supreme Court stressed the lack of constitutional justification for there being (as it were) federal 'enclaves' artificially immune from provincial legislation of general application. There are of course other constitutional restrictions on the use and application of environmental protection powers. One crucial example is examined next: the so-called 'takings' doctrine.

Fifth Amendment and Other 'Takings', and Environmental Protection

Reference to the Fifth Amendment and its constitutional limitation on 'takings' without compensation was referred to towards the end of Chapter Two. Judicial interpretation of this so-called 'takings' clause is of considerable moment where environmental protection is concerned. Equally, there are increasingly significant parallels in relation to Community law and the European Convention on Human Rights, now a part of the law of the United Kingdom.

Operation of the Fifth Amendment In the United States though, the not uncommon argument is that environmental protection powers – state 'police' powers for example – negate reliance on the 'takings' clause. The opposing argument, typically, is that the deployment of those powers represents a 'taking' without due compensation, despite an essentially public purpose. Whether the court will intervene in support of the latter argument appears to depend on whether there is such an extreme deployment of the powers in question that it can be regarded as resulting in an equally extreme diminution in the value of the plaintiff's property. However, the threshold seems to be represented by evidence which the court regards as indicating that state intervention is justified by a concern to prevent serious public harm. This is the essence of the decision of the United States Supreme Court in *Keystone Bituminous Coal Association v. De Benedictus.*[98] Subsequently, in *Lucas v. South Carolina*[99] the Supreme Court considered that a 'taking' had occurred, attracting compensation, where environmental protection regulations were aimed at preventing what were described as 'harmful or noxious uses'. This represents a considerable constraint on regulatory action compared with the approach in *Keystone.* Beyond such general constitutional constraints on environmental protection powers, it is possible that specific states will nevertheless stipulate that certain action amounts to a 'taking', thus imposing restrictions which may for example bind those who would otherwise wish to develop land in a particular manner.

Adaptation of the 'takings' doctrine   Specific statutory adaptation of the 'takings' doctrine is well illustrated by the terms of the Endangered Species Act 1973. A central issue in this federal legislation is the definition of the term 'harm'. The federal government's approach to this term tended to restrict the range of development affecting land, particularly where there is what is described as significant habitat modification or degradation. Certain interests sought to challenge this approach, pointing to the fact that habitat modification did not appear in the prescribed list of unlawful 'takings' under the Act. The decision of a Federal Court of Appeal in *Sweet Home Chapter of Communities for a Greater Oregon v. Babbit*[100] was subsequently upheld by the Supreme Court: both courts held that the government's approach was reasonable with the consequence that much development is circumscribed as a result of this powerful regulatory restriction, as interpreted by the court. This federal legislation represents one of several important protective measures: another significant example is manifested through the so-called 'public trust' doctrine.

The Public Trust Doctrine

The public interest in environmental protection may be realised through the operation of this doctrine. The Supreme Court enunciated the essential characteristics of this doctrine in the late nineteenth century, in *Illinois Central Railroad Co. v. Illinois*[101] where it was stated that there is a title in land which is held in trust for the people of the state, and that state control for the purposes of the trust can never be lost. This suggests that the public trust can cut both ways. On the one hand the state has a protective role, which may of course include environmental protection responsibilities arising from or otherwise affecting the subject land. On the other hand, the state itself may be constrained in law, as where a state government or one of its agencies may seek to undertake polluting activity on the land or adjacent land, for example. Whether an individual or group of individuals has *locus standi* – standing – in order to persuade the court to enforce these or any other rights according to law is always likely to be controversial.

Standing

The leading authority on standing in the United States is *Sierra Club v. Morton*[102] where the Supreme Court indicated a need to establish adverse effects of noncompliance with environmental laws which impact on the members of a particular organisation, even though they are not the only persons to suffer from the infraction. Later developments have served to qualify this arguably generous view of standing. The Supreme Court in *Lujan v. Defenders of Wildlife*[103] tightened the requirements by deciding that an organisation has standing only where one or more of its members were directly affected by virtue of their special interest. Arguably it is difficult to generate any general principle of standing, given the range of applicants and the range of alleged failures to comply with a variety of different environmental legislation. Certainly, the factual background to *Lujan* was unusual, involving as it did an argument that the Endangered Species Act 1973 should apply in respect of US funded activity out of the jurisdiction. In *Bennett v. Spear*[104] the facts were arguably more conventional, involving proposed action by the Fish and Wildlife Service whereby water to irrigation facilities would be reduced in order to protect endangered fish species. The Supreme Court here was confronted again by the Endangered Species Act which allows proceedings by 'any person', a term interpreted to include the applicant ranchers and irrigation regulators where one of the arguments was that the proposed restriction would have adverse economic impacts. More recently still, in *Steel Co. v. Citizens for a Better Environment*[105] the Supreme Court was concerned with alleged failures by the company to file, contrary to law, reports in connection with hazardous chemicals in use. In holding against a claim of standing by the Citizens, the Supreme Court stressed, not for the first time, the need for some 'redressable' loss or injury. Again, the nature of the infraction and its failure to impact on the Citizens were clearly critical factors. No doubt a legal obligation to report allied to a legal duty to advise citizens in the immediate locality of the industrial operation would suggest the existence of sufficient standing.

Notes

1   [1984] ECR1891.
2   [1990] I ECR I–4135.
3   [1998] 1 CMLR1057, at p. 1085.
4   [1998] EnvLR39.
5   OJ L129, 18.5.76.
6   OJ L291, 24.10.83.
7   [1990] ECR I–4023, at p. 4063.
8   [1991] ECR I–4685, at p. 4726.
9   [1999] 1 WLR927, at p. 945.
10   [2000] EHLR52.
11   *Ibid.*, at p. 75.
12   [1999] EHLR313.
13   *Ibid.*, at p. 334.
14   [1988] ECR 4607.
15   [1979] ECR 649.
16   [1999] CMLR612.
17   [1994] ECR I–483.
18   *Supra*, n. 4.
19   [1990] ECR I–331.
20   [1995] IRLR15.
21   OJ L175, 5.7.85.
22   [1999] EnvLR51.
23   [2000] 3 All ER897.
24   [2000] 1 CMLR149.
25   [1999] 3 CMLR897.
26   OJ L281, 10.11.79.
27   [1999] EnvLR438.
28   [1991] ECR I–5357.
29   OJ L268, 24.9.91.
30   *Supra*, n. 26.

31 OJ L31, 5.2.76.
32 OJ L135, 30.5.91.
33 [1991] ECR I–825.
34 OJ L20, 26.1.80.
35 [1985] ECR 1981.
36 Unreported, High Court, 14 November 1996.
37 [2000] EHLR215.
38 (1993) 81 LGERA270.
39 *Ibid.*, at p. 282.
40 125 L Ed2d 469; 113 S Crt2786 (1993).
41 (1994) 86 LGERA143.
42 Chapter Three, n. 26.
43 [1991] ECR I–5987.
44 [1998] 3 CMLR1.
45 [1995] EnvLR195.
46 OJ L30, 6.2.93.
47 [1999] EnvLR604.
48 [1989] ECR2849.
49 OJ L103, 25.4.79.
50 [1997] EnvLR431.
51 *The Times*, 12 October 1998.
52 *The Times*, 7 July 2000.
53 [1993] EnvLR287.
54 [1996] EnvLR304.
55 [1938] 2 All ER650, at p. 659.
56 [1995] 2 LlRep395.
57 OJ L229, 30.8.80.
58 [1999] ECR I–2023.
59 [1996] EnvLR198, affirming [1994] 2 CMLR760.
60 SI2000, No. 1297.
61 [1991] ECR I–883.
62 *Supra*, n. 49.
63 OJ L206, 22.7.92.
64 OJ L375, 31.12.91.
65 [1999] QB1279.
66 *Supra*, n. 5.
67 [2000] EnvLRD16.
68 [1999] ECR I–6385.
69 Kimber, C. (2000), 'Implementing European Environmental Policy and the Directive on Access to Environmental Information', in C. Knill and A. Lenschow (eds), *Implementing EU Environmental Policy*, Manchester University Press, ch. 8.
70 OJ L158, 23.6.90.
71 [2000] EnvLR141.
72 [1999] EnvLRD6.
73 *Supra*, n. 57.
74 [1990] 1 CMLR716.
75 *Supra*, n. 31.

76 [1993] ECR I–4109.
77 *Supra*, n. 32.
78 [1996] EnvLR248.
79 *Supra*, n. 21.
80 [2000] ICMLR149.
81 [2000] EnvLR1.
82 [2000] 1 A.C. 397.
83 [2000] EnvLR395. *Cf. Berkeley, supra*, n. 23.
84 [2000] EnvLR221.
85 *Supra*, n. 63.
86 [1997] EnvLR442.
87 [1991] ECR I–883.
88 *Supra*, n. 48.
89 [2001] EnvLR34.
90 *Supra*, n. 63.
91 [1999] EnvLR147.
92 *Supra*, n. 87.
93 [1999] 2 CMLR723.
94 [2000] 2 CMLR681.
95 [1999] EnvLR632.
96 452 US264 (1981).
97 [1995] 2 SCR1031.
98 480 US572 (1987).
99 112 US286 (1992).
100 1 F3d 1 (DC Cir. 1993).
101 146 US387 (1892).
102 405 US727 (1972).
103 504 US555 (1992).
104 520 US154 (1997).
105 118 S Crt1003 (1998).

Chapter Five

Policy Priorities and the Law

Introduction

This chapter seeks to build on the first four through an analysis of the question whether and to what extent law is an appropriate vehicle for the implementation and enforcement of environmental policy across the member states of the European Community. Chapter Three referred to the question whether any law for present purposes can be regarded as 'effective' and 'credible': two important variables in determining whether law might be used as the vehicle for implementation and enforcement. Of course the process of policy-formation will often be affected by political complications and compromises such that there is always the possibility of what may be described as an irrational decision to use the law, despite doubts about its efficiency and credibility.

The Law, Credibility and Efficiency

Previous references to environmental management systems provide a good example of the law's operation as a mere facilitator. It is not difficult here to assume that Community policy development was seen in terms of the need for essentially voluntary action where the need for the law as a vehicle would be very limited. Matters of practicability were no doubt very marginal here, at least as long as the policy priority was not in favour of wholesale regulation of environmental management by law. Had this been the favoured priority the practicability of the law as a vehicle for implementation and enforcement would have been a contentious issue where, among other arguments, it might have been considered that the law might not be credible, given the range of businesses affected and the resulting bureaucracy. Of course there are numerous areas of Community policy which clearly demand enforcement by the law. However, the same problems of credibility and practicability arise. Indeed, it has been seen already that the law governing volatile organic compounds is based, in part, on 'thresholds' below which regulatory and other requirements enforced by the law will not operate, given in particular the large number of very small businesses, whose activities would be very difficult to monitor and enforce. On occasions these thresholds are referred to as 'triviality thresholds' although they may be characterised in all sorts of different ways. For example, prescribed limit values may be set at a level where emissions are regarded as scientifically significant for various reasons, such as the practicability of monitoring and enforcement in addition to what is perceived as being beneficial to the environment. How such thresholds are implemented and enforced in member states is of course aided considerably by the nature of the directive, its essential objectives and the freedom of transposition conferred on the member state.

Assumptions about Law

Previous chapters have largely assumed the merit of the law as the vehicle for implementation and enforcement where the environment is concerned. This is seen very clearly in Chapter Two where structural matters were examined. Indeed, the evolution of policy on the environment within Community structures as they extend to member states may suggest the strength of this assumption, apart from the need to ensure that standards and requirements are properly enforceable *per se*. The development of subsidiarity and devolution represent two reasons why there is an arguable need for the certainty of the law, both from the point of the Community at the centre and the member states affected. In other words, the law is capable of defining arrangements through which accountability can be recognised which, in turn, gives the potential for relevant enforcement processes to be deployed. Nevertheless, these other factors such as subsidiarity and devolution must represent so-called secondary structural incidents since they are not really capable of standing alone as a justification for deployment of the force of law. Again, the essential justifications for resort to the law in implementation and enforcement of environmental policy are those adverted to, above. Traditionally and typically therefore the law has been used, via the directive, for the purpose of 'command and control' regulatory arrangements. Even beyond this relatively well-defined arrangement it must be assumed that the law will be necessary for other, related purposes. For example, economic instruments (the subject of the following chapter) will on occasions require the force of law where, for example, a taxation regime is required as part of a process whereby environmentally-adverse behaviour is to be modified other than by the more traditional regulatory methods. In this case though the purposes served by the statutory regime may differ materially. An obvious example is that an economic instrument backed by law is unlikely to be concerned (say) with whether prescribed limit values have been adhered to. In turn, criminal enforcement of such a failure will be otiose. On the other hand there will no doubt be a clear statutory prescription linked to enforceable liability to pay a tax or other charge, according to compliance with what may be described as 'qualifying conduct'.

Hard law versus soft law From the foregoing it can be seen that the law serves usually well-defined purposes against a background of value judgements about matters such as credibility and practicability. Traditional regulatory models will tend to be preoccupied with adherence to limit values, for example. These and similar examples can be characterised as 'hard' law. By way of contrast, reference has been made in Chapter Three to the principles of Community environmental policy, such as the 'polluter pays' principle. On occasions it was seen also that such principles may be seen to graduate to considerations of law in certain decision-making contexts. Thus, the precautionary principle, for example, may emerge from operative environmental policies and priorities to be so elevated, as a legally material consideration. As an item of so-called 'soft' law, nevertheless a finding from the court that the decision-maker has failed to take account of that consideration is always capable of condemning the subject decision as an *ultra vires* decision. Such an item of soft law is therefore likely to be relatively discreet compared with the hard law which is set out in a directive or municipal law through which transposition is achieved.

Developing law There seems little doubt that the style and emphasis of that law will change in coming years. Areas of change can be seen in the preceding chapters. These areas of change are partially a function of the perceived need to regulate environmentally-adverse processes and products in a different manner as well as a need to refine the machinery available for this purpose. This though is not only a matter of initiative at the centre since member states' municipal law may be reshaped within the freedom allowed by the directive. As such these developments may be justified by a quest to raise the efficiency levels of the law. For example, it may be seen that the monitoring and enforcement of emission limits for individual pollutants are increasingly open to criticism on grounds of practicability. Accordingly, the law may (and is) encouraged to look at the overall efficiency of industrial installations in relation to all polluting emissions and discharges. Although it is difficult to generalise here, one possible label for such a development refers to environmental performance standards. Only through such an evolution is it possible for law and policy-makers to claim continuing credibility for the law in relation to environmental control. This issue is one that will be returned to in Chapter Seven.

Law as a Vehicle for Environmental Policy

At the outset the question was posed, whether and to what extent the law is an appropriate vehicle for the implementation and enforcement of policies affecting the environment. Clearly the answer is in the affirmative, given that the law can bring (among other things) coercive force to bear, if necessary. Admittedly, not all products of policy formation are suitable subjects for enforcement through the law although it has been seen already that soft law principles may creep into law enforcement where they are accepted by the courts as legally material considerations. Against this background, the significant question is just how policy priorities can be crystallised through the law. That is the central theme of the present chapter which, in turn, builds on the previous chapters. To begin with, there will be a concern for those occasions where (for whatever reason) the law is actually excluded from the arena. Assuming though that the law is regarded as appropriate to the realisation of policy priorities, it is necessary next to look at the law's capacity for adjustment, taking account of uncertainties in Community law as well as member state priorities in approaching transposition. Within that framework the law may be required to deliver structural or substantive change or (more commonly), both. Nevertheless such requirements are often distorted as a result of various factors, not least of which may be the available science or matters of political compromise, or both. Where the law emerging from the Community is subject to transposition there may be efficiencies by virtue of the need (or the desire) to effect changes or improvements in other interlinking areas of the municipal law which may itself be the product of other, earlier Community law. Whatever the shape and consequences of the transposition, derogations may be permitted in line with Community law. Ultimately though noncompliance with Community law (say) because there has been irregular transposition may invite enforcement by the Community. How that noncompliance is dealt with under the terms of particular directives may be a difficult matter, as will be seen in this penultimate section of the chapter. These are the issues to be explored in the remainder of the chapter, culminating with one further matter concerning fundamental rights. In looking at fundamental rights there is a direct link to the previous chapter. For present purposes though, the question is whether fundamental human rights are recognisable where environmental law is concerned and whether such rights (as interpreted by the court) can be regarded as constituent part of Community policy priorities.

The Exclusion of Law

Environmental policy will of course remain as such without further development through the law. In these circumstances, policy will continue to perform its essential function as an indication of the essential preferences and priorities where action on the environment is concerned. However, there are many incidents of policy which will be developed through the law. Typically such policy will relate to what may be described as 'substantive issues' affecting the need for regulatory or similar action which in turn is likely to demand enforceability. Problems of definition here make any generalisations difficult, a point well illustrated by previous references to the status of Community environmental principles. It has been seen that these policy-like principles are capable of elevation to the status of law. However, legal status here is severely qualified, for two reasons. In the first place, the principles may gain legal status only on an *ad hoc* basis. Secondly, the principles have no formal legal status and enforceability as such: this appears to be entirely a matter for the court where the issue arises and is argued on the facts of the case. Consequently, there may be occasions where the Community environmental principles are not excluded and may indeed be positively enforced. Arguably, those occasions where the principles are not excluded as legally enforceable principles are exceptional: for the most part therefore the principles operate in the policy context alone. This though is not the only area where there is an exclusion of the law. The remainder of this section of the chapter is devoted to a number of situations where the law, be it Community or municipal law, may be (or has been) excluded in certain circumstances. Those situations can be categorised as follows: constitutionally-excluded law; member state noncompliance with Community law, whether or nor proceedings for infringement have been taken; the operation of deregulation legislation; and the operation of human rights legislation in order to activate a declaration of incompatibility.

Constitutionally-excluded Law

The inherent treaty limits of the Community necessarily mean that municipal lawmaking by member states is not necessarily constrained by Community law enforcement. Clearly, the Commission would have justification for infringement proceedings against a member state where that state sought (for example) to legislate by way of transposition in such a way that less stringent requirements would be applied. Equally, it would be possible to resist as unlawful, Community legislation seeking to regulate matters lying outside

the limits of treaty competence. For example, despite the existence of
Community competence in relation to fisheries, that competence does not
extend to private law rights to exploit fisheries. Federal systems such as those
of the United States and Canada also operate to exclude law on the ground of
jurisdiction and competence, as seen already. Thus in the United States it has
been seen that federal legislative jurisdiction on the environment, via the
commerce clause of the Constitution, operates effectively to exclude state
jurisdiction in this area. However, not all issues arising in this context are
necessarily clear-cut. A Canadian case decided by the Supreme Court of New
Brunswick serves as a good illustration. In *New Brunswick (Minister of the
Environment) v. Canadian Pacific Ltd*[1] the court refused to restrain proceedings
for the commencement of the abandonment of a railway in the province. The
court recognised that an intrusion into the management and operation of a
railway (as a federal matter) could not be justified where it had been claimed
that application to the federal authority for abandonment amounted to the
'commencement' of an undertaking, thus triggering requirements under
provincial environmental assessment legislation. Whether physical
abandonment of railway property would trigger provincial environmental
assessment requirements was not before the court although it is arguable that,
had it been, such a transaction might well have fallen within provincial statutory
requirements.

Member State Noncompliance with Community Law

Where the Commission has successfully completed proceedings before the
European Court of Justice in respect of a member state's noncompliance there
is a secure base on which it can be declared that inconsistent municipal law
and reliance thereon has no status in law. Among other things it may be possible
in these circumstances that any penalty previously enforced against a defendant
may then be open to challenge. Of course a lot depends on the nature and
extent of member state noncompliance as well as the offence or other sanction
sought to be enforced. In practice a member state will usually comply with
the decision of the court although, strictly, any inconsistent law which the
member state purports to implement and enforce is *ultra vires*. Pending any
decision on noncompliance there is little, if anything, that the Community
can do in order to enforce the precise terms of any directive which the member
state has not transposed, or has failed to transpose correctly. There exists
therefore a period of time during which Community law may be excluded as
a result of this noncompliance, although towards the end of this chapter

reference is made to the jurisdiction of the European Court of Justice in respect of fines and penalties against member states found to be in breach of that law. It was seen in the previous chapter that Article 243 of the EC Treaty confers on the European Court of Justice jurisdiction to grant interim relief. Whether such relief may extend beyond cases pending to present circumstances is not without difficulty, particularly in view of the Court's jurisdiction to make various orders consequent on its decisions.

The United Kingdom and other member states have been found to be in breach of the Groundwater Directive: Directive 80/68.[2] At the core of Community law here is the prescription of 'List I' substances which are toxic, persistent or bio-accumulative, and 'List II' substances, which could have adverse effects on groundwater. The discharge of List I substances directly to groundwater is prohibited while any indirect discharge is subject to investigation and authorisation requirements. The discharge of List II substances is also subject to investigation and authorisation. One interesting characteristic of the Directive here is that there is no prescription of discharge limits or quality standards. The finding of acts in breach of the Directive centred on failures by the member states in question to apply the foregoing regulatory requirements to all the categories prescribed, as well as a failure to apply regulatory requirements in respect of spent sheep-dip. One of the clearest expositions of Community law here occurred before the European Court of Justice in *Commission v. Germany*[3] where it was held unequivocally that the prohibition in respect of List I substances is absolute. Otherwise, in relation to indirect discharges of List I substances the Court found that German law did not cover every type of discharge while the requirements relating to the discharge of List II substances were also found to be in breach of the Directive by virtue of a failure to require mandatory and specific prior investigation. More generally though it was clear to the Court that the full extent of Community law had been excluded through failure to appreciate one particular provision in the Directive: Article 2(b). That provision allows a member state to implement exceptions to the prohibitions where discharges are found to contain only *de minimus* quantities of substances which will not be prejudicial to groundwater: a 'triviality threshold'. This provision was regarded by the government of Germany as conferring a discretion for the purposes of implementation.

The problem of member state transposition has been adverted to previously. The present example serves to re-emphasise the difficulty of interpretation and application of Community law in certain cases. As a result of controversies such as the present relating to groundwater pollution and the absence of any facility for direct intervention by the Commission in a member state where, in the circumstances set out above, Community law is effectively excluded pending lawful transposition. Essentially in the present case, member states undoubtedly considered that more discretion was available in implementation than the law apparently allowed. In the United Kingdom a significant part of the response to the Court's findings against it was the legislation of the Groundwater Regulations 1998.[4] These Regulations now operate in order to increase considerably regulatory control in a number of crucial areas. Where wastes containing traces of pesticides are to be disposed of, special areas will have to be designated for the purpose of dealing with washings from tank cleaning, the exterior of sprayers and personal protective equipment. Regulatory requirements here involve three crucial conditions: any area designated for discharge will need to be of low environmental value, isolated from a watercourse, and offer no threat to groundwater resources. In this latter respect, land in nitrate vulnerable zones will be further protected by the introduction of new technology such as bio-beds which are sealed containers filled with a mixture of straw, peat and topsoil wherein bacteria will break down pesticides.

The Operation of Deregulation Legislation

Policy preferences in favour of deregulation may lead to legislation which seeks to realise the removal or reduction of what may be described as statutory burdens. This is the case with the Deregulation and Contracting Out Act 1994 in the United Kingdom. The Act contains a range of provisions which seek to remove or reduce these burdens, in favour of those carrying on trades, businesses or professions. The impact of this legislation in relation to matters affecting the environment is minimal. However, the Act has an interesting potential through its facility whereby a Minister of the Crown is also empowered to act to improve enforcement procedures by reference to matters of fairness, transparency and consistency.

Declarations of Incompatibility in the Human Rights Act 1998

The Human Rights Act 1998 came into force in the United Kingdom in October 2000 and incorporates certain of the rights and freedoms guaranteed under the European Convention on Human Rights, allowing the enforcement of such rights before national courts. The question of fundamental rights is addressed towards the end of this chapter, with particular reference to such rights as they affect the environment, its exploitation and enjoyment, as well as their impact on Community and the municipal law of member states. For the moment though and matters of exclusion of the law, attention turns, briefly, to so-called declarations of incompatibility under the Act, largely for the purpose of clarification since a declaration here does not in fact lead to an exclusion of the relevant law. The Act of 1998 impose on the court an obligation to interpret legislation in order to achieve compatibility with the rights found in the European Convention. In practice, such judicial interpretation may be seen to test the semantic limits of legislation. If such rationalisation proves to be beyond any such limits of judicial interpretation the court is empowered to make a declaration of incompatibility. There is for this purpose no distinction between primary or secondary (delegated) legislation although the power is conferred only on the superior courts. A declaration does not operate to invalidate the subject legislation so there is no question of an exclusion of the law. The essential intention of the Act here is that the responsible Minister of the Crown should initiate remedial legislation in order to secure rationalisation with Convention rights. Interestingly though any such Minister is not bound by any legal duty to secure remedial measures here.

The Law's Capacity for Adjustment

There have been several references so far (including one in the present chapter) to member state misinterpretation of Community law such that infringement proceedings are pursued by the Commission. As a result, adjustment will be required in order to secure compliance according to the law as interpreted by the European Court of Justice: an issue covered in the previous chapter. This process of adjustment may arise from infringement or, indeed, it may arise from initial transposition. Whatever the case the municipal law of the member state will require careful design and implementation, perhaps the more so where more sophisticated modes of environmental control are demanded by Community law or member state policy appears to move in the same direction for the purpose of transposition. Equally, Community law may be lacking in prescription or may demand extremely ambitious requirements in terms of limits or standards or indeed, in relation to their monitoring for enforcement purposes. Essentially therefore the question is how robust the law is in attending to the foregoing policy priorities emanating both from the Community and a member state like the United Kingdom. There is little doubt for example that one not uncommon reason for delay in transposition arises from difficulties in the framing and phrasing of municipal legislation. This was seen for example in the delays experienced in implementing Part II of the Environmental Protection Act on waste management in the United Kingdom, and controversies arising during debates about the (then) draft Directive on the incineration of waste which was destined for transposition through Part I of the same Act.

Transposition Difficulties Affecting Waste Regulation

Part II of the Environmental Protection Act seeks to reconcile Community legal requirements in respect of waste management. One significant reason for what was a considerable delay in bringing Part II into force was the difficulty in reconciling the requirements of Directive 91/156.[5] One major difficulty was in addressing the requirements of Article 4 of the Directive by which regulatory licensing requirements might not apply where the disposal of waste occurs at the point of production, or where specific waste recovery and disposal processes operate. To take advantage of licence exemption, the Directive requires precise definition of waste type and quantity, as well as precise definition of waste recovery and disposal processes. In turn, each member state is obliged to ensure no adverse environmental impact. This was a matter of some difficulty for the Department of the Environment which had responsibility for sponsoring the municipal legislation. The Department seemed to rely on the provisions of section 33(1)(c) of the Act which stipulates that a person shall not 'treat, keep or dispose of ... waste in a manner likely to cause pollution of the environment or harm to human health'. Failure to comply with this requirement is an offence. However, this provision is essentially reactive or retrospective rather than anticipatory. In the case of the (then) draft Directive on the incineration of waste, one proposal was to ensure uniform monitoring standards throughout the Community. However, the draft in its reference to regulatory requirements for dioxins and furans, sought to impose what were regarded as impossibly small values in connection with emission requirements. Indeed, many of the values were so small as to be beyond continuous measurement. As such, transposition would represent a considerable challenge to the law as the vehicle for implementation. In some cases Community law may appear to be silent on certain issues, in which case it will be up to the member state to fill the gap if regulatory arrangements are to be effective. For example, under the Part I arrangements in the Environmental Protection Act relating to Integrated Pollution Control just referred to, there is no explicit obligation of the Environment Agency, as regulator, to carry out an exhaustive examination of all practical options and techniques relating to a process as a whole regardless of circumstances where an application for the variation of an authorisation is submitted. In these circumstances, the court may intervene to determine the position. This was the case in *R. v. Environment Agency, ex p. Gibson*[6] where the English High Court, although not ruling out such an exhaustive examination, considered that such an examination would be unnecessarily burdensome for the Agency and would tend to discourage plant operators from bringing forward applications for variation. Community law may be found to be silent on other matters of even greater importance, again posing a challenge to municipal law and processes in order to adjust to regulatory and other realities. One such area relates to monitoring requirements.

Monitoring Requirements

Directive 80/778[7] on drinking water quality lacks prescription on the water quality monitoring process. The Directive is silent on the sampling and storage processes which, in terms of Community-wide water quality analysis, is a significant omission. Clearly, the room for adjustment of municipal law in member states is, as a result, considerable. A powerful example occurs in the Water Supply (Water Quality) Regulations 1989[8] which extend to England and Wales. These Regulations were added to in 1999 in order to address a specific public health problem that arose through outbreaks of cryptosporidium, an organism occurring in water that is capable of causing severe gastrointestinal illness. The 1999 additions to the Regulations made provision for risk assessment and continuous monitoring. Furthermore, monitoring and analysis are subject to very detailed requirements which enable these processes to be conducted under high security conditions. As a result there exists for the first time an objective standard in respect of the organism. Apart from the anxiety surrounding the outbreaks of illness there appeared to be concern about the evidential failure which led to the acquittal of one water company which had been charged in the present context with supplying water unfit for human consumption, contrary to section 70 of the Water Industry Act 1991. Essentially, the epidemiological evidence was ruled to be inadmissible since the defence did not have access to the data which was used to compile the report submitted by the outbreak control team. The new and very onerous requirements are criminally enforceable by reference to any failure to comply with the new, prescribed standard, subject only to a defence of due diligence. The new requirements have directed attention at performance and it appears that no further outbreaks of crypotosporidium have been reported. It is the relationship between performance criteria and monitoring which appears to be a particularly important element of effective implementation, as was seen in Chapter Two where the Local Government Act 1999 was referred to. Effective implementation through the law's capacity for adjustment may also be seen in broader issues involving structural and substantive change.

Structural and Substantive Change

The influence of Community law is such that a member state may be confronted by the need to develop policy priorities in favour of what are seen as necessary structural or substantives changes or, more likely both. Such changes, again under the influence of Community law (particularly as interpreted by the European Court of Justice), will almost inevitably necessitate intervention of the law rather than the administrative circular, for example.[9] However, there may be some structural changes which will not require implementation exclusively through the law. For example, Directive 75/442[10] (the Waste Framework Directive) brought about structural changes in waste management in the United Kingdom through a move away from regulatory and similar responsibilities being devolved to local authorities, to national arrangements which focus very much more on strategic priorities in relation to matters of planning in particular. But for membership of the Community there is very little doubt that many such structural and substantive developments would not have been implemented in the United Kingdom. Indeed, there is no doubt that the coming into force of Community law in many areas has effected what can often be regarded as a fundamental reappraisal of environmental control. This was certainly the case in the United Kingdom's implementation of two crucial water directives: Directive 76/160[11] (the Bathing Water Directive), and Directive 78/659[12] (the Freshwater Fish Directive).

The Bathing Water Directive

Structurally, the Bathing Water (Classification) Regulations 1991[13] prescribe a system of classifying the quality of relevant territorial waters, coastal waters and inland waters, which are bathing waters. The classification here reflects the mandatory standards found in the Annex to the Directive. In turn, the classification set down in the Regulations is intended to be used for the purpose of establishing quality objectives under section 83 of the Water Resources Act 1991, in respect of bathing waters.

The Freshwater Fish Directive

The Directive is concerned with the protection and improvement of fresh waters for the benefit of fish life. Water quality standards are set for the protection of coarse and game fisheries. The Directive also provides for the monitoring of standards. According to the then National Rivers Authority in 1994,[14] since the Directive came into force in 1978, the United Kingdom had designated 56,000 kilometres of rivers and lakes. The principal mode of enforcement is through the Salmon and Freshwater Fisheries Act 1975. The Water Resources Act, referred to above, provides an important framework through which schemes for classification can be formulated. The classification system here is set out in the Surface Waters (Fishlife) (Classification) Regulations 1997.[15] Water quality objectives under the Act are based on the uses to which waters may be put. Such objectives are to be based on current uses, but will take account of improvements to support additional uses by reference to Community legal requirements. The Surface Waters (River Ecosystems) (Classification) Regulations 1994[16] is made up of five tier classes. Every stretch of river will be given an associated target class, to be maintained or achieved after improvement. Classes RE1 and RE2 equate to salmonid waters, classes RE3 and RE4 to cyprinid waters, and RE5 equates to poorer quality water. This system of classification applies to all fresh waters, giving a wider coverage than that provided by the Directive. Furthermore, a rather more sensitive system of compliance calculation applies compared with that provided for under the Directive, where a 95 percentile approach marks a simple 'pass or fail' regime. This then is a good example of transposition which extends beyond the threshold of compliance with a directive. In other situations where a directive has been adopted by the Community, its terms may be seen to be affected or even flawed by uncertainty and even ambiguity. Such limitations may be explained by various problems, not least of which may be negotiations driven by political compromise and a lack of clarity about any supporting science.

Law, Science and Compromise

Typically, the political compromise just referred to will tend to be manifested in a directive whose text is characterised by undue generality, as was seen previously in Chapter Four where reference was made to Directive 90/313 on Access to Environmental Information.[17] While it may be possible to describe this Directive as flawed at least in relation to the difficulties encountered in transposition, such a description does not necessarily fit Directive 76/464[18] which deals with dangerous substances in the aquatic environment.

Limit Values versus Quality Objectives

The opposition of the United Kingdom government to an approach based on limit values for discharges led to an agreement whereby two approaches are incorporated in Community law, the other being the application of criteria relating to quality objectives in respect of the waters to which discharges are made. Significantly though, any adoption of these criteria relating to quality objectives favoured at the time by the United Kingdom government necessitates proof, to the satisfaction of the Commission, that those prescribed objectives have been satisfied. Whatever the merit of a two-pronged approach in the case of this Directive, it will not necessarily be appropriate elsewhere. Indeed, many other directives will not necessarily be affected by the political difficulties that characterised Directive 76/464, particularly given the progress towards institutional arrangements such as majority voting. An interesting contrast for present purposes is to be seen in Directive 91/271[19] which does not as such identify the water quality to be achieved although it does prescribe the means by which environmental objectives are to be achieved. Nevertheless, the survival of Community environmental law based on discharge or emission limits and quality objectives is to be seen in Directive 96/61[20] on Integrated Pollution Prevention and Control (IPPC). Initially, Directive 76/464 will continue to apply to certain installations until IPPC is fully in force. On the other hand, Directive 76/464 will remain the applicable Community law where particular installations are not included in the categories of IPPC regulation. Interestingly though the language of the Directive, although it stresses emission limits, refers also to the importance of environmental quality standards.

Limit Values, Quality Objectives and Best Technical Means

Directive 76/464 is worthy of closer examination in relation to what may be described as the competition between limit values and quality objectives. This Framework Directive has given rise to a number of daughter directives which incorporate this twin track approach, albeit reliance on quality objectives is perhaps demanding given the general stringency of the objectives prescribed in the directives concerned. This approach is linked to the necessity that such objectives must be realised by what are described as 'best technical means' for the purpose of minimising environmental impacts, although failure to adhere to this standard may be permitted where the Commission can be persuaded on the merits of the case.

Interlinking Municipal Law

Transposition of Community law will on occasions demand amendment or revocation of other, inconsistent areas of municipal law. Equally, transposition of new Community law may encourage member state initiative in revisiting other areas of environmental regulation and control. For example, the Surface Waters (Shellfish) (Classification) Regulations 1997[21] which implemented Directive 79/923[22] on Shellfish Water Quality provided an important opportunity for a governmental review of the designation of shellfish waters, particularly against the background of the need to identify so-called 'sensitive waters' for the purpose of the Urban Waste Water Directive.[23] This though is not the limit of interlinking issues concerning water quality. The Regulations have the effect of modifying section 83 of the Water Resources Act 1991, previously referred to, through the imposition of a duty on the Secretary of State to exercise the powers existing there to classify and designate waters which will realise the objectives of the respective directives. Also of considerable relevance here in relation to water quality is the United Kingdom's experience in the implementation of the Freshwater Fish Directive.[24] Pollution control priorities here have been aimed principally at agricultural pollution sources. In turn, some ammonia pollution problems have been addressed through a review of sewage discharge consent limits.

Derogations

Whether Community law provides for a derogation is of course a matter of detailed interpretation of the individual directive. In turn, the directive will specify the terms on which a derogation may be sought. Essentially there may be automatic derogation or derogation dependent on the consent of the Commission. Where a member state is able to rely on a derogation there are likely to be complications in framing the relevant municipal legislation. Unless that legislation is carefully framed there may be difficulty in comprehending the extent of any exemption or indeed, the limit of time within it may operate if it is not an open-ended derogation. Two examples of derogation focus on the Freshwater Fish Directive, and the Directive on Volatile Organic Compounds from Petrol. The Freshwater Fish Directive just referred to contains a facility for derogation in Article 11. More specifically, a member state is permitted to derogate from certain parameters prescribed by the directive either by virtue of exceptional weather or special geographical conditions, or where designated waters undergo natural enrichment in certain circumstances so that certain prescribed values cannot be adhered to. The United Kingdom sought derogations for zinc in areas of high mineralisation where levels were naturally high, and for pH in upland waters which are susceptible to acidification. Directive 94/63[25] on Volatile Organic Compounds from Petrol introduced requirements in respect of a petrol distribution system by which petrol vapours are recovered and regenerated instead of being vented into the air. When the draft Directive was under debate in the Community there was considerable consensus in favour of a concession to small petrol stations in rural areas. The United Kingdom government in particular voiced concerns about the likely closure of such rural facilities with adverse environmental consequences so that travelling distances were increased by those in rural areas driving greater distances to seek petrol. In these circumstances a member state is permitted to grant a derogation to certain petrol stations whose throughput is below a prescribed limit and if emissions will not contribute significantly to adverse environmental or health problems.

Enforcement Issues: Fines and Penalties

Noncompliance processes under Article 228 of the Treaty were dealt with in Chapter Four, along with the criteria by which financial penalties are calculated by the European Court of Justice. This section of the present chapter looks at the nature of noncompliance with Community legal requirements and some inherent difficulties in the way of their enforcement. In so doing, the assumptions about the law enunciated towards the beginning of the chapter will be very much in mind. The particular focus is the Bathing Waters Directive.[26]

The Bathing Waters Directive

It has been observed that there is a tendency for bathing waters to move in and out of compliance.[27] As many as 30 per cent of bathing waters fail the standards prescribed by the Directive for one, two or three years. Furthermore, it is not possible to determine whether these bathing waters fail as a result of changed water quality or because of the volatility of the assessment methods set out in the Directive.[28] It can be seen therefore that there are considerable controversies affecting this Directive. It has been seen already that the United Kingdom has had considerable difficulty with matters of implementation and enforcement. Proceedings under Article 228 of the Treaty may lead to continuing fines against the member state responsible: as much as £70,000 per day. In the case of the Bathing Water Directive the fundamental problem is that compliance is reported on, annually, an arrangement which is not unique to this area of Community law. A finding of noncompliance in this case will no doubt involve major works, suggesting ultimate fines of enormous magnitude. This though is not the only problem confronting the law's enforcement of the Community's policy on bathing waters. Since 1994 the Commission has been attempting to develop acceptable proposals for a new, revised directive.

A Revised Directive?

One of the substantial problems affecting Commission proposals to date[29] is the criticism that standards, such as that for enterovirus, are not capable of practical implementation and enforcement. As a result the credibility of Community law is threatened if such standards are legislated. Equally, the Commission has proposed rationalisation of the directive provisions with the principle of subsidiarity. Again, such an exercise demands great accuracy in the law. The difficulties facing the Commission's proposals were well described by the House of Lords Select Committee on the European Communities in its Report *Bathing Water Revisited:*[30]

> ... we believe the enterovirus standard as formulated in the Commission's proposal could not be achieved unless all discharges of sewage were subjected to primary and secondary treatment followed by filtration and disinfection by chemical or ultraviolet radiation treatment. These levels of treatment are exceptional in the Member States and could not be introduced without major new engineering work ... The Commission's claim that the proposed new bathing water directive would be broadly cost neutral ... does not survive scrutiny ...[31]

The Select Committee concluded that there is no justification for imposing on the general public significantly greater costs in order to reduce somewhat the present risks of self-limiting illness associated with bathing. Accordingly, the view was that the Commission's proposals remained unjustified on the evidence then available. The Committee was supportive of a regime which is not mandatory but (in the spirit of subsidiarity) allows full consultation locally with the public on the question of appropriate standards to be applied. In broader terms, the Select Committee had a preference for a strategic approach to the improvement of urban waste water and bathing water which takes account of economic, public health and environmental considerations. Precisely what new policy proposal on bathing water quality will emerge from the Commission is not presently clear. However, the Commission will be obliged to take account of comment about the need for the law developed from such policy to be both credible and practicable both in implementation and enforcement.

The Environment, Law and Fundamental Human Rights

That fundamental, human rights are a policy priority in the jurisdictions under examination hardly needs emphasis. However, what is of particular interest is the scope and enforceability in law of such rights. These issues are of particular interest as between the European Community and member states like the United Kingdom. Indeed, one critical question is whether fundamental human rights as recognised and enforced across these jurisdictions include fundamental environmental rights, such as the right to a clean environment. In order to develop a picture of the status of the law as the foundation for the realisation and enforcement of fundamental rights in the environment it is necessary to look at the various sources of law and approaches to interpretation. A necessary starting point is the Human Rights Act 1998 in the United Kingdom through which certain rights and freedoms are guaranteed by virtue of the European Convention on Human Rights. In turn the various relevant rights which affect the environment will be examined, together with relevant case law under the Convention. Thereafter the relationship between fundamental, human rights in member states and the Community will be analysed, taking account of issues such as the supremacy of Community law. Interstitially there will be references made to experience with fundamental rights under the United States constitutional Bill of Rights.

The Human Rights Act 1998

At the core of the Act is a prohibition on public authorities acting incompatibly with the terms of the Convention. To that extent the Act like the Convention operates vertically rather than horizontally so excluding litigation between private individuals, for example. The Act in fact extends to cover a large number of bodies which, despite their status otherwise, exercise public functions. However, it is the essentially 'public' functions of these bodies which are caught.

Qualifications

Certain of the Convention Articles, such as Article 8 guaranteeing a right to private and family life are subject to express qualification, so enabling the right in question to be balanced against the public interest. If the qualification accords with the law of the United Kingdom and is necessary for the purposes of a democratic society (say) in order to protect the public health then it will be operative. However, it is also necessary for any operative restriction or qualification to be proportionate in relation to the objectives, so minimising the impact on an individual's rights.

Judicial functions The Act requires a court to interpret legislation compatibly with Convention rights. Fulfilment of this obligation may of course result in what may be described as something approaching a distortion of that legislation. Indeed, where there is distortion and it is clearly impossible to rationalise subject legislation with Convention rights any superior court is empowered to make a declaration of incompatibility, whether the legislation is primary or secondary legislation. However, the declaration does not affect the status of the legislation in question. The declaration is intended to facilitate remedial action by any responsible Minister of the Crown, although the Act does not prescribe a specific duty to act here.

Breach of Convention rights If it is found that a public authority or other body exercising public functions has acted in violation of a right guaranteed under the Convention the court has quite widely drawn powers to grant a range of remedies, including an award of damages where judicial review proceedings are before the court.

Rights Affecting the Environment

Two Convention rights are of particular significance. Article 8, just referred to, guarantees a right to respect for private and family life while Article 1 of the First Protocol secures peaceful enjoyment for an individual in respect of his possessions. The case law under these heads is now summarised.

Claims under both heads   In *Baggs v. United Kingdom*[32] the European Commission of Human Rights deemed the applicant's claim to be admissible under both heads when it was claimed that noise from Heathrow Airport adversely affected enjoyment of his home. Both heads were again cited in *S. v. France*[33] in connection with a claim based on the adverse effects of a nuclear power station adjacent to the claimant's home. In the case of Article 1 of the First Protocol the Commission held that property values may be seriously affected by noise nuisance, thus amounting to a partial expropriation or 'taking'. In the case of Article 8 the Commission considered that the Convention right here extends not only to direct measures by a public authority but to indirect measures also which may unavoidably cause noise and other environmental intrusions. Such intrusions were regarded by the Commission as being capable of adversely affecting physical well-being and therefore interfering with a claimant's private life. In a third case, *Marcic v. Thames Water Utilities Ltd,*[34] the claimant's cause of action was in respect of a nuisance caused by frequent flooding over a period of nine years which the water company had known about, or at least had the means of knowing about. Under the water company's system of priorities there was no prospect of the problem being remedied. As an infringement of the claimant's human rights the judge stressed the need for proof of justification, the onus of proof being on the water company. The judge considered that there would be justification if the company's system of priorities could be proved to be necessary in order to strike a balance between the competing interests of the claimant and other customers, allowing the company a margin of discretion. It was held that the company had failed to prove justification: the fact that the existing system of priorities did not obviously fail to strike a fair balance was insufficient. The nuisance giving rise to the Article 8 infringement was held to be a continuing nuisance. The inactivity of the water company was held to be unlawful so that the cause of action arose when the Human Rights Act came into force on 2 October 2000: that cause of action was also held to be a continuing cause of action. Additionally it was held that the claimant had a cause of action under Article 1 of the First Protocol. There was held to be no defence by virtue of the defendant's inability to remedy the situation.

Claims under Article 1 of the First Protocol   The peaceful enjoyment of possessions was in issue in two cases of relevance to the environment. In the first of these cases – *Matos E. Silva LDA v. Portugal*[35] – the European Court of Human Rights was concerned with the case of a private company which owned land where it extracted salt and bred fish. The government of

Portugal expropriated the land for the purpose of establishing a nature reserve. Following an unsuccessful challenge to the expropriation the company pursued a challenge on various grounds, including Article 1 of the First Protocol, arguing that there had been violation of the right to peaceful enjoyment of its possessions. The Court's decision fell into three sections.

In the first place it was held that the term 'possessions' under Article 1 of the First Protocol has an autonomous meaning. The company's unchallenged rights over the subject land for 25 years and the revenue derived therefrom in working it might qualify under the term 'possessions'.

Secondly, although the disputed measures by the government had, as a matter of law, left the company's right to deal with and use its possessions, they had greatly reduced its ability to do so in practice. Governmental intervention since 1981 meant that the company's rights over their possessions had become precarious. There had been an interference with the company's right to peaceful enjoyment of its possessions, aggravated by resort to the combined use of so-called 'public interest declarations' and the creation of a nature reserve over a long period.

Thirdly, it was held that the effects of the measures were not such that they could be equated with deprivation of possessions. The measures in question could be identified with public interest aims: because they had serious and harmful effects that had hindered the company's ordinary enjoyment of its rights, it had to bear an individual and excessive burden which had upset the fair balance which should be struck between the requirements of the greater public interest and the right to peaceful enjoyment of an individual's possessions.

This latter point featured significantly in another leading case of relevance in the present context, *Sporrong and Lonnroth v. Sweden.*[36] Here the European Court of Human Rights concluded that, to decide whether a justification is established, the Court must determine whether a fair balance was struck between the demands of the so-called 'general' interest of the community and the requirements relating to protection of the individual's fundamental rights. This of course was a central issue in *Marcic*, dealt with previously. It was also an issue examined by Lightman, J. in the English High Court, in *R. v. North Lincolnshire Council, ex p. Horticultural and Garden Products Sales (Humberside) Ltd,*[37] where it was pointed out that a planning consent is a property right which may fall to be protected under Article 1 of the First Protocol. Furthermore:

Withdrawal of planning permission is not a formal expropriation of property, but is an interference with a property right and requires justification. Justification may be found in the second sentence of Article 1, for withdrawal may constitute the exercise by a State of the right to control the use of property in accordance with general interest … If the State establishes that such justification exists, there can be no breach … The requisite proportionality between the interference with the individual's rights and the public interest will not be found if the person concerned is required to bear 'an individual and excessive burden' … and there must be a degree of protection from arbitrariness…[38]

It was held here by Lightman, J. that the balance had been properly established and that the public interest was a material influence in the decision-making. In *Matos Silva* also, the public interest was found to be a significant justification for governmental action, albeit against the background of a conclusion that there had been interference but not deprivation in circumstances where the 'fair balance' had not been established. Against this background, nature conservation and other statutory designations required by Community law will be increasingly vulnerable by reference to the provisions of Article 1 to the First Protocol. The possibility of tension between Convention rights and the assumed superiority of Community law is taken up later in this chapter. More immediately it is necessary to look at relevant case law arising in relation to Article 8 of the Convention.

Claims under Article 8 Two very significant cases to be considered here are *Guerra v. Italy*[39] and *Lopez Ostra v. Spain*,[40] both decided by the European Court of Human Rights. In the first of these cases it was held that the effect of toxic emissions from a factory polluting the indoor atmosphere in the claimant's home fell within Article 8. The Court stressed that:

> … although the object of Article 8 is essentially that of protecting the individual against arbitrary interference by the public authorities, it does not merely compel the State to abstain from such interference: in addition to this primary negative undertaking, there may be positive obligations inherent in effective respect for private or family life.[41]

In *Lopez Ostra* the Court found that Article 8 had been violated following severe pollution which adversely affected the claimant's home with offensive fumes from an adjacent waste treatment plant. For such a claim to be successful it is necessary to establish a clear and serious risk to health or severe environmental pollution as well as an omission by the state in question to remedy the situation. The treatment plant had been operating without the necessary regulatory approval. However, this plant was the only such plant operating in the town where other environmental problems would be generated if it was subject to closure. Nevertheless, the Court struck the balance in favour of the claimant. It is not difficult to speculate about even more difficult situations. If, for example, a waste treatment facility is the preferred waste management option in a locality but attracts a claim under Article 8 would the court be obliged to strike the balance just referred to in *Lopez Ostra* in the same way?

The significance of Convention rights In so far as the foregoing provisions of the Convention may be applied to adverse environmental intrusions affecting a claimant, who is now able to proceed before the courts of the United Kingdom, there are interesting and significant advantages where environmental law is concerned. In the first place enforcement of Convention rights represent a potentially powerful addition to common law rights, in the tort of nuisance, for example. Although there are still sometimes difficult qualifications to satisfy before violation of Convention rights can be enforced, nevertheless, this route to a challenge may be seen as less constrained by detailed restrictions on rights which might otherwise be enforceable through the common law. However, like the common law of nuisance, the Human Rights Act does allow the court to examine matters of balance and reasonableness through concepts such as 'justification' and the 'margin of discretion', both of which may be seen to allow rather greater exposure of governmental and other public authority decision-making affecting the environment. Whether a claim is pursued (say) in tort, at common law, or through the Convention under the Human Rights Act may be influenced by many variables, one of which may be the perceived effectiveness of the particular remedies available. However, there is one outstanding issue. That issue is the relationship between Convention rights as they affect the environment, and Community law and its assumed superiority among member states, all of whom accept that Convention rights are legally enforceable within their respective jurisdictions.

Convention Rights and Community Law

No Community treaty presently provides power to enact provision for human rights. Given that gap in Community provision, and the fact that all member states accept Convention rights as being legally binding within their jurisdictions, what status do those rights have if they are potentially or actually in conflict with supposedly superior Community law? An important starting point in addressing such a question is the approach of the European Court of Justice to the judicial interpretation and enforcement of human rights.

The European Court and human rights There is little doubt that if (and when) there is Community accession to the European Convention on Human Rights a very significant re-configuration of constitutional structures will be necessary if human rights are to be effectively protected within the terms of the Convention, whose terms would require acceptance into the Community legal order. Those constitutional structures refer to Community treaty amendment although it is by no means clear where treaty competence exists in the Community for this purpose. No matter how, if at all, such a change could be justified here, the likely stumbling block would be the need for recognition of superiority of Convention rights by the European Court of Justice. This essentially political difficulty might of course be overcome through interstitial acceptance of the Convention into Community law without any suggestion that the Court might be legally accountable to the European Court of Human Rights. This is the approach taken by the United Kingdom and many other member states of the Community. Thus, in the United Kingdom, it has been seen already that the Human Rights Act 1998 operates to incorporate the Convention and its attendant rights into municipal law. However, progress at the centre of the Community can be assessed only by reference to the continuing attitude of the European Court of Justice to human rights.

European Court of Justice attitudes to human rights The Court's jurisprudence shows a concern for the assumption that a fundamental prerequisite of any lawful Community act is that it respects human rights, the source of which are the common, traditional constitutional practices of member states as well as the relevant international treaties of which they are signatories and in whose development they have collaborated. As such, it is not difficult to see how the Court's approach here merely reflects other developments in Community law following an apparent synthesis of the municipal law of member states: direct effect as described in Chapter Four is a good example.[42] Where human rights in Community law are concerned, there is a considerable potential to require more than mere adherence to fundamental, human rights. There is the potential in the case of the environment and other areas that may be affected to require recognition of a legally enforceable duty to comply with such rights, as defined. As ever though derogations may play their part in cutting down any such duty on occasions. In this and other areas of judicial activity there is again an important normative function for the European Court of Justice and national courts to perform. That normative function will in turn affect the scope of Community legislative competence on occasions.

The application of human rights Case law from the European Court of Justice show the bases from which the jurisprudence is likely to develop further. In the first place, the Court has sought to impose human rights principles where member state activity subject to challenge has arisen from agency functions on behalf of the Community. The same applies in the second area where litigation relates to member state reliance on derogations from Treaty provision relating to trade barriers. However, such an approach begs the question; *which* fundamental, human rights are to apply? Of course in strictly logical terms, the answer to this question is that Community law alone is relevant. However, it has been seen that the European Court of Justice appears to draw on member states' common, traditional constitutional practices for these purposes. The suspicion though is that the Court can be extremely selective in drawing on such sources, if only because of the formidable nature of any task involving the rationalisation of so many differing sources and their emphases. Equally problematic here is the scope of the Court's jurisdiction, given that there is (arguably) an axis whose extremes are represented by a review process and, on the other hand, an intervention based on the full merits of the case: effectively an appeal. It may be suggested that the typical complexity of many cases will tend to blur these two extremes. Accordingly, in any case relating to environmental regulation by a member state the possibility that the predominant reason for member state intervention is in fact to create trade barriers may necessitate consideration of the merits. Matters of proportionality may also force the Court in the same direction. In so far as Convention rights may be pleaded before the Court for any of these purposes, what position should the Court take?

Community versus Convention rights It is possible to suggest that the Court, seeking to avoid conflict, actively addresses its jurisdiction here with an approach which seeks maximum accommodation as between Community law, the municipal law of member states and the law of Convention rights. Such 'maximum accommodation' probably depends on the facts of the individual case which may indicate a concern with matters which fall squarely within Community competence, as well as matters which fall within the law of the Convention. Given the status of Convention rights in member states and the Court's attitude to the source of Community human rights, there seems little objection to a decision which seeks to rationalise both sources of law for application to the facts. Even a new Charter of Fundamental Rights in the Community is unlikely to change such rationalisation before the European Court of Justice.

The Community Charter of Fundamental Rights The Charter,[43] which at the time of writing, has no legally binding status in the Community addresses the environment only very briefly:

> ... a high level of environmental protection and the improvement of the quality of the environment must be integrated into the policies of the Union and ensured in accordance with the principle of sustainable development.

Elsewhere in the Charter the tension between Community law and Convention rights appears to be reconciled through the following provision in Article 53:

> Nothing in this Charter shall be interpreted as restricting or adversely affecting human rights and fundamental freedoms as recognised, in their fundamental fields of application, by Union law and international law and by international agreements to which the Union, the Community or all the Member States are party, including the European Convention for the Protection of Human Rights, and by the Member States' constitutions.

Equally, Article 53 of the European Convention is in these terms:

> Nothing in this Convention shall be construed as limiting or derogating from any of the human rights and fundamental freedoms which may be ensured under the laws of any High Contracting Party or under any other agreement to which it is a Party.

Article 53 of the Charter appears to raise the level of tension affecting the normal expectation that Community law is superior: *Costa v. ENEL*.[44] This is particularly the case in relation to the Charter's reference to 'Member States' constitutions'. For example, might it be the case that in litigation before a national court where the member state provides more extensive human rights than those prescribed by what would be a legally binding Charter, such a court could ignore an application of Community law? In practice it is probably unlikely that there would be any great difference between Community and municipal law for present purposes. Indeed, with certain exceptions, such as that relating to the environment, the Charter (if it attained legally binding status in its present form, at the time of writing) appears to crystallise Convention rights as a threshold for Community human rights provision. Furthermore, it seems unlikely that such a fundamental as the superiority of Community law within its area of competence might be sacrificed without consideration of the enormous constitutional implications. Nevertheless, there are *dicta* in the superior national court of at least one member state – the Supreme Court of Denmark in the case of *Carlsen v. Denmark* – suggesting reservation of a right to nullify an act recognised by the law of the Community where that act is in conflict with national constitutional provision.[45] The supremacy of Community law is the creature of case law whereas, in the United States, under the Ninth Amendment enshrining the Bill of Rights, federal supremacy is effectively entrenched in the Constitution. In addition, that Ninth Amendment also contains a provision similar to Article 53:

> The enumeration in the Constitution, of certain rights, shall not be construed to deny or disparage others retained by the people.

The Supreme Court of the United States also approaches the matter of human rights by reference to the experience of the constituent states. However, in the process the Supreme Court has refused to interpret the right to privacy in such a way that there is recognition of any right to a clean environment. In part such a reluctance is based on the absence of any historical constitutional reference to the environment, as well as the pragmatic issue of just how far such a constitutional right might extend.

Notes

1   Unreported, 5 August 1993.
2   OJ L20, 26.1.80.
3   [1991] ECR I–825.
4   SI 1998, No. 2746.
5   OJ L78, 26.3.91.
6   [1999] EnvLR73.
7   OJ L229, 30.8.80.
8   SI 1989, No. 1147.
9   *Supra*, n. 3.
10   OJ L194, 25.7.75.
11   OJ L31, 5.2.76.
12   OJ L222, 14.8.78.
13   SI 1991, No. 1597.

14 National Rivers Authority (1994), 'EC Freshwater Fish Directive: UK Implementation', Water Quality Series, No. 20.
15 SI 1997, No. 1331.
16 SI 1994, No. 1057.
17 Chapter Four, nn. 69–72.
18 OJ L129, 18.5.76.
19 OJ L135, 30.5.91. *Cf.* Chapter Three, n. 31.
20 OJ L257, 10.10.96.
21 SI 1997, No. 1332.
22 OJ L281, 10.11.79. *Cf.* Chapter Four, n. 26.
23 *Supra*, n. 19.
24 *Supra*, n. 12.
25 OJ L365, 31.12.94.
26 *Supra*, n. 11.
27 National Rivers Authority (1994), 'Bathing Water Quality 1994', Water Quality Series, No.22.
28 *Ibid.*
29 COM(94)36: OJ L112, 22.4.94.
30 7th Report (Session 1994–95).
31 *Ibid.*, at paras 14 and 16.
32 (1985) 9 EHRR235.
33 (1990) 65 D&R250.
34 [2001] EHLRDG6.
35 (1997) 24 EHRR 573.
36 (1983) 5 EHRR 35.
37 [1998] EnvLR295.
38 *Ibid.*, at p. 304.
39 (1998) 26 EHRR 357.
40 (1994) 20 EHRR 277.
41 *Supra*, n. 39, at pp. 382–3.
42 Chapter Four, nn. 17–27 in particular.
43 [2000] OJ C–364/01.
44 [1964] ECR 585.
45 [1999] 3 CMLR854.

Chapter Six

Economic Instruments, Law and Policy

The Role and Status of Economic Instruments

Although variously described as 'fiscal' or 'market-based' instruments, for present purposes reference throughout will be to 'economic instruments'. These instruments represent a significant development beyond the traditional assumptions about the implementation and enforcement of policy affecting the environment. Those assumptions, which rest very largely on the adoption of regulatory models, tend to be characterised as 'command and control' approaches to environmental regulation. As such, they have necessarily relied on the law as an essential vehicle for their implementation and enforcement. It will be seen below that such traditional approaches display certain limitations, particularly when compared with economic instruments which, among other things, tend to influence behaviour affecting the environment rather more sensitively and effectively. However, it is necessary to arrive at any evaluation through a careful appreciation of the respective merits of both types of environmental control. Any such appreciation is made that much more difficult by virtue of the different features of economic instruments in particular. Before those features are examined in rather more detail through the remainder of this chapter it is instructive to look at the claims made for economic instruments although, again, it has to be borne in mind that there are numerous types of instrument, each with their own peculiar characteristics. Nevertheless, it is claimed that they generate incentives to develop and apply clean technology and other innovation in environmental management, that they limit the cost of environmental protection in resource and transaction cost terms, and that they facilitate more effect control of pollution from diffuse sources. In some cases of course tax revenues will benefit. Nevertheless, whatever their nature, these instruments still depend on the law for the most part in order to enable monitoring and measurement as well as enforcement. Indeed, the law plays a part both for these purposes and by virtue of the general acceptance that economic instruments are generally complementary to traditional regulatory arrangements.

A Categorisation of Economic Instruments

In order to see the scale and variety of instruments that are available to the policy formation process, it is instructive to attempt a general categorisation. That categorisation covers ten types of instrument, as follows: taxation, tradable permits, deposit and return or refund systems, cost recovery and incentive charges, product charges, input charges, legal liability, subsidies, loans and grants. Some of these economic instruments will be examined elsewhere in the chapter. Whether any one or more of these instruments is chosen in the course of policy formation will of course depend on many variables. Such variables might include the relationship with any regulatory regime founded on statute. Otherwise a choice of economic instrument appropriate to the circumstances will demand attention to criteria allowing evaluation of that choice.

Criteria for Evaluation

Environmental effectiveness and economic efficiency are regarded as the major criteria for the evaluation of economic instruments, while the social and legal objectives of government policy demand that these instruments satisfy a need for acceptability based on an equitable distribution of effects, transparency and concordance with institutional frameworks.[1] These latter demands are of course capable of refinement in the course of the processes adverted to in Chapter 1: consultation with interested parties, for example. More specifically, charges in respect of emissions to the atmosphere may be appropriate in cases of a restricted number of stationary sources where monitoring is feasible. Such charges can be 'efficient' when marginal abatement costs vary across polluters, provided that they are able to react to financial incentives. Product charges, on the other hand, are potentially applicable to products that pollute in the consumption phase: such products should be identifiable, consumed in large quantities and in diffuse patterns. Deposit and return or refund systems can be considered for products that can be re-used, recycled or that must be returned for destruction after use. Finally, tradable permits relating to atmospheric emissions offer advantages in situations where marginal abatement costs differ among polluters and in which maximum ceilings to total pollution are urgently required.[2] There may be circumstances where economic instruments can play only a minor role, supplementing regulatory control. This is the case with hazardous air pollutants. Subsidies have been used in some countries for the development of control technology and measuring devices, in addition to tax differentials to encourage the combustion of cleaner fuels. Whatever the relationship between regulatory regimes and economic instruments it is necessary to appreciate the synergy between them, particularly where policy formation is concerned.

Regulatory Regimes and Economic Instruments

The justification for environmental regulation lies in widespread market failures which give rise to external costs which are not always internalised in decision-making in perfectly competitive markets. On occasions such market failures may be the concern of international conventions. CITES, for example, may operate where prices are sensitive even to enhanced threats to species, resulting in increased demand. Accordingly, environmental regulation is concerned essentially with changing market behaviour using feasible, cost-effective measures which display acceptable distributional effects. Nevertheless, this objective is often achieved only imperfectly so that there is regulatory failure on occasions.[3] There seems little doubt that environmental regulation is experiencing considerable development and reform,[4] as a result of which complementary economic instruments may be seen to be better integrated into regulatory regimes. Such developments have the potential to weld the strengths of these respective approaches to environmental control. For example, the likely freedom to respond to stimuli where economic instruments are concerned will tend to be characterised as a cost-effective reaction whereas traditional regulatory structures will tend to ignore the cost impacts on companies subject to that regulation. Nevertheless, the critical question in the case of many economic instruments is whether any stimuli are strong enough to generate an effective signal to those whose behaviour otherwise might have an adverse environmental effect. With this in mind what follows is a perceptive view of the overall differences between these two increasingly complementary approaches:

> The most obvious advantage of direct regulations is the grip authorities have on the behaviour of actors, with a more or less certain outcome in terms of environmental effectiveness. Therefore, economic instruments rarely act as a substitute for direct regulations. Instead, the choice is among various combinations of direct regulations and economic instruments ... In such combinations economic instruments (i) raise revenues for financing environmental measures, (ii) sometimes provide incentives to better implement the associated regulation and (iii) have a possible impact on technical innovation. Direct regulations are

maintained because of their grip on actors. Economic instruments and negotiations might add more flexibility to mixed systems.[5]

Although economic instruments may be put to work as a tax or as a subsidy of some sort, there is (as will be seen later in the chapter) growing interest in the creation of quite sophisticated artificial markets.

Artificial Markets and Environmental Control

Artificial markets may be created in order to facilitate the buying of 'rights' to pollute which may in turn be sold on in certain circumstances. This is but one example of such an artificial market. Nevertheless, several types of artificial market exist: emissions trading where, within prescribed pollution limits, permits to pollute within that limit can be traded; price support systems allowing the payment of subsidies for a specific environmental purpose; and insurance markets, where premiums reflect risks with the possibility of incentives to encourage better environmental performance.[6] Allied to the operation of insurance markets is the possible need to establish liability in law. Such liability itself may be counted as a form of economic instrument, at least where the risks are accepted by such markets. Nevertheless, the status of legal liability as an economic instrument is open to doubt, as will be seen below.

Liability in Law

Any evaluation of legal liability for present purposes has two elements. The first of these flows from the response of markets, and insurance markets in particular. The second is a more general evaluation. Each is addressed in turn.

Where the court has determined liability in law according to the facts, any compensation awarded may be paid through any relevant and applicable insurance cover. That cover may be offered on terms which attempt to induce better environmental compliance. Alternatively, determination of liability by the court may relate to a novel process or activity which may be open to evaluation by the insurance market, with a possibility that cover (again on terms) might be offered. If some or all of such risks will not be so covered government may have to step in order to ensure that the risks – and the consequences of those risks – are effectively managed and distributed. That state of affairs may of course persuade the government to legislate in order to require (say) compulsory insurance or to require the creation of a joint compensation fund. Indeed, international conventions may operate in exactly this way, with signatory nations agreeing to legislate in these terms. Whether the full cost of the environmental externalities affected will be reflected in any of these events may of course be open to doubt. If so, then such a qualified response to the economic distribution of loss or damage casts doubt on the optimum efficiency of legal or insurance liability as an economic instrument.

In more general terms companies and other business associations will usually be conscious of costs arising from a liability in law, although it seems likely that that awareness will often be an awareness of the cost of insurance cover. Away from the insurance regime it may never be precisely clear what the impact of potential or actual liability in law may be. There may be an element of deterrence although it is difficult to be confident about such an impact. On the other hand it can be asserted with some confidence that the primary motive behind litigation here is compensation rather than any attempt to restore the environment, unless of course there is an attempt to enforce liability through a statutory framework which makes provision for environmental restoration through an order of the court. The efficiency of liability in law as an economic instrument is arguably low on the scale, primarily because the actors in question will often be unclear about the basis of such liability or even its costs and benefits. Indeed, it can be argued with some confidence that the actors' perceptions are only marginally improved through information available in the insurance markets and in the regulatory process, if it applies in the area of activity concerned. In this latter area of regulatory activity, compliance with such requirements does not necessarily suggest immunity from liability at common law, for example.[7] Furthermore, it is by no means clear whether litigation to establish such liability will occur. Whether through the common law or by statute, it is by no means certain that action to establish or test liability in law will occur. Some of the general uncertainties here are shared by another form of economic instrument, the subsidy.

The Subsidy

Again it is unclear what efficiencies may flow from the presence of subsidies as they affect the environment. Before there can be any clarity on such a matter it is necessary to identify the scope of the term 'subsidy' for present purposes.

For example, a policy preference may be in favour of a subsidy which attracts companies and other business associations on terms which effectively marginalise any environmental efficiency. Even where there is such inward movement encouraged by the availability of subsidies, any linked subsidy may be characterised by wasteful or even excessive spending on, and application of, environmental control technology at an ill-considered point of impact, for example. This of course is apart from any concerns about impact on public finances or accusations from the Community that subsidy represents unlawful and uncompetitive 'state aid'. Nevertheless, subsidy which is perceived to be efficient is likely to be so regarded by virtue of the level and quality of innovation in relation to activity such as the development and application of environmental control technology. More generally therefore, subsidy may be regarded as a potentially efficient economic instrument where the resulting financial assistance (which may have to be administered under the law at considerable expense) is seen to provide incentives towards effective action as it impacts on the environment. That efficiency may accrue from an acceleration of investment processes or (where longer-term subsidy is made available) from adoption of processes or technologies on a carefully planned basis. As such the term 'subsidy' can be seen to include grant-aid, preferential loans where interest is fixed below prevailing market rates, tax allowances referable to income and profit management, and market price support. What though are the likely effects on the environment of removal of subsidy?

In the first place, there is the likelihood that subsidy removal will visit hardship on the companies and business associations to whom it has been payable. In a 1998 Report, the OECD indicated that, despite pressure to reduce subsidy, levels of support in OECD countries remains high:[8]

> Given the volumes of pollution and waste associated with many of the supported activities, a reduction in support levels could lead to environmental benefits in addition to the economic gains from reduced government outlays and improved economic efficiency ... [t]he non-internalisation of the full environmental and social costs of economic activities ... is sometimes referred to as an 'implicit subsidy' ... support removal ... is viewed as one step towards the full cost pricing of environmentally harmful activities. As such, it is not a substitute for but a complement to policies which internalise the social and environmental costs of these activities. It is the combination of support removal and the introduction of economic instruments to internalise the external costs of economic activities that will result in 'getting the price right', and thus optimising the economic system.[9]

The avoidance of subsidy will sometimes be found in much wider contexts, such as international conventions. The Montreal Protocol on the Control of Substances that deplete the Ozone layer requires that parties discourage to 'the fullest practicable extent' various inconsistent activities, such as the provision of new subsidies in respect of the manufacture of proscribed substances.

The second consequence of subsidy removal is that policy, and any attendant legislation, is seen to move towards the 'polluter pays' principle which has been examined earlier in this book. Fundamentally, that principle is necessarily opposed to subsidy in its concern to ensure that relevant costs are properly internalised and that the polluter is fully accountable for what may be presumed to be environmentally-adverse activities. However, such a generalisation may of course be misleading by reference to what has been said already about the rather positive environmental traits that may be seen to emerge from policy priorities in relation to subsidy. What may be useful in any analysis of relevant policy and law here is an approach whereby it may be possible to analyse subsidy by reference to its function as an economic instrument whose substantial aims and objectives are to achieve positive environmental impacts. Community policy in relation to the Common Agricultural Policy is a clear example of this approach where the domination of subsidy may be offset by initiatives to develop agri-environmental law and policy. Scrutiny of Community law and policy as well as the response of member states to the available schemes here may enable a future estimate of the point at which subsidy becomes something other than the dominant force, to be replaced by measures which allow more sustainable environmental priorities to be substituted. The process of estimate and analysis here is one which, increasingly, is linked to the question of sustainable development and the deployment of indicators of environmental impact. These issues will be addressed after a general description of the charge as an economic instrument.

The Charge

The charge can be characterised in three ways, as a cost recovery instrument, as an instrument to encourage incentive, and as a tax-raising instrument. It is not inconceivable that any one charge may be seen to display all three character-istics. However, it has been observed that there is widespread acceptance of so-called 'cost recovery charging' where the administrative costs of regulatory control are intended to be recovered, in whole or in part.[10] Typically, charging schemes will be linked, directly or indirectly, to regulatory systems which provide the necessary statutory and institutional framework for implementation and enforcement. In turn, there is seen to be a need for schemes to be equitable, fair and transparent.[11] However, experience of charges as applied in Germany through a water effluent charge, and in the Netherlands through a water pollution charge demonstrate that there are other factors which may reinforce the merit of the charge as a potentially effective economic instrument.

The essential objective of the German charge is that it is tied to compliance with standards prescribed by statute. Indeed, the rate of charge is reduced by 75 per cent where it can be shown that there is source compliance. The prescribed standards are subject to regular review and updating. However, where updating leads to a change in the prescribed standard, the law provides a transition period. It is only after expiration of that period of transition that compliance with the new prescription becomes legally binding. Where there is source compliance with a new standard before the date when it becomes legally binding, that source becomes entitled to a 75 per cent reduction in the charge. Evidence suggests that there is a considerable increase in investment in water treatment in anticipation of the announcement of new prescribed standards.[12]

The water pollution charge in the Netherlands is aimed at providing finance for sewage treatment and the improvement of water quality. That charge operates against both direct and indirect discharges to the aquatic environment. It has been suggested that reductions in industrial pollution are attributable to the charge, rather than to traditional, direct regulation by statute. For a majority of the companies affected, it appears that the charge has been the decisive factor in decisions to invest in abatement and treatment facilities. Among the factors which seek to explain the impact of the water pollution charge, it has been suggested also that the high level of charging and the role of positive negotiation between the water boards and industry have contributed significantly to the success and impact of the charge.[13]

Sustainable Development

Realisation of policies on sustainable development both at Community and member state level is seen to depend, increasingly, on the development and use of economic instruments. However, it has been seen already that only the effective and efficient use of instruments is likely to achieve such an objective. At the front end of this policy formation process therefore it is necessary to ensure reliance on a variety of indicators which, *inter alia*, identify pressure points on environmental media. Thereafter policy formation depends, in theory at least, on conclusions about the effective realisation of sustainable development objectives through rationalisation of the messages received from the indicators, and the role which may be played by economic and other instruments. Superimposed on this process is the question how best to secure implementation and enforcement, whether (as is likely) by law, or otherwise. In so far as this process of policy development relies on strategies for sustainable development, there is no doubt that economic instruments represent an important approach. However, it will be seen later in this chapter, in the section on environmental taxes, for example, that the Community has been, and continues to be, hamstrung by a seeming lack of constitutional competence in seeking to develop these crucial economic instruments. As a result it will be seen that the initiative has very largely been ceded to member states who have developed their own measures – and expertise – in the development and application of these instruments. Arguably, this development represents what may be described as 'implied subsidiarity'. Should the Community in future wish to harmonise in this area, it may prove very difficult to achieve any such standardisation among so many different approaches. However, it is equally arguable that approaches to economic instruments in member states do not vary fundamentally as was seen for example in the case of water charges in Germany and the Netherlands; that many such charges will have been adopted only after verification was obtained that Community legal restrictions on matters such as trade and competition were not infringed; and that some instruments will have been adopted as elements complementary to the transposition of existing Community law on or affecting the environment. However, at the core of this discussion is the assumption that effective and efficient economic instruments increasingly provide the necessary foundation for sustainable development.

The Community Sustainable Development Strategy   In October 1999 the Environment Council of the Community determined that consideration should be given to the need for a comprehensive Community strategy for sustainable development, with a view to providing a framework within which development of all sectoral policies and measures can occur.[14] Such a strategy has considerable merit in view of the three main obstacles to the environmental policy integration process where often strict functional divisions characterise treaty provision, the organisation of the Council and the organisation of the Directorates-General. Achieving an effective strategy however is likely to be difficult, for three main reasons. In the first place there are the functional divisions at the centre, just referred to. Secondly, there is substance in the assertion that member states' policies and strategies on sustainable development take little account of any Community dimension. A prime example is the sustainable development strategy for the United Kingdom, set out in a document entitled *A Better Quality of Life*.[15] Finally, there is the constraint (already referred to) on Community competence in relation to the generation of law and policy on environmental taxation which is always likely to be a central plank of sustainable development. Despite these constraints and difficulties the Commission has published the product of a pilot study of sustainable development methodology appropriately entitled *Indicators of Sustainable Development.*[16] This is one of several publications dealing with sustainable development and is particularly significant in setting out a methodology stretching across several categories of indicator, including environmental indicators. Most recently, in 2001, the Commission has published *Environmental Pressure Indicators for the EU.*[17] This publication (now seen in its second edition) serves a number of policy purposes in dealing with so-called 'integration indicators' as well as sustainable development indicators. Among the many indicators is an indicator relating to the agricultural consumption of pesticides.[18] What follows is an outline appraisal of the difficulty of developing robust indicators as evidenced in the findings of the Community, the OECD and the United Kingdom, taking account of difficulties of measurement and definition. However, it must be borne in mind that one of the essential purposes behind this exercise is to develop law and policy which will promote and maximise the environmentally sustainable use of pesticides in agriculture. Such an exercise has necessarily to recognise the environmental impact of pesticides on water and soil quality, for example.

The development of indicators for pesticide use in agriculture One of the first attempts to develop a specific indicator emerges from the OECD.[19] OECD recognise the difficulties here. Those difficulties extend from variations in pesticides' toxicity, persistent and mobility, through quantities capable of leaching into soil and water, a lack of comparability of data between countries, to the fact that a pesticide risk classification system is not yet complete in many of them. Nevertheless, OECD indicates that the approach under consideration involves classification of pesticide use data into different environmental risk categories, in quantity terms. Such an approach, it is claimed, combines information on pesticide use with that relating to the chemistry of pesticides influencing environmental risk. Elsewhere the approach appears to be rather more cautious. Generally that approach is to suggest factors and variables which might be used to construct an indicator. In its 1997 publication *Indicators of Sustainable Development* the Commission points to the addition of persistent, organic chemicals to ecosystems, other agricultural intensification practices and the new generation of pesticides which are more powerful biologically and can be applied in more modest amounts, as important factors.[20] Beyond this earlier methodology the Commission in its *Environmental Pressure Indicators for the EU* points to the quantity of active ingredients per hectare but stresses the real risks associated with the type of product, toxicity, persistence, climate and soil conditions, type of cultivation and application practices, all of which would be taken into account in what is described as a 'proper' pesticide risk indicator.[21] In the United Kingdom, the former Ministry of Agriculture published *Towards Sustainable Agriculture: A Pilot Set of Indicators*.[22] This set of indicators – again rather tentative – refers to the significance of the amount of pesticide applied whilst recognising that this may not be a good indicator, before going on to acknowledge that risk is markedly influenced both by toxicity of active ingredients as well as the way in which the pesticide is applied. This category is described as a set of 'Driving Force Indicators', pointing to the cause of changing environmental and other conditions. There is no attempt to prescribe quantities of active ingredients used although, usefully, there is reference to relevant cross-linkages to other indicator areas, such as that referring to agricultural land subject to environmental conservation measures. All of the foregoing is, in one way or another, relevant to the basis on which a pesticides tax might operate as a potentially important part of the sustainability equation.

Pesticides taxes Four member states of the Community – Belgium, Denmark, Finland and Sweden – apply pesticide taxes. It is pointed out by the European Environment Agency[23] that there should be a more general approach than is in evidence presently in these member states where the tax applies. The Agency stresses the need for more adequate account to be taken of hazards to the public health and the environment while at the same time acknowledging taxation rules in the internal market. This is against the background of somewhat disparate approaches to the tax adopted by the four member states in question. Two of the member states, Sweden and Denmark rely, respectively, on concepts referable to quantitative active ingredients and retail price.[24] Effective experience of the operation of a pesticide tax in the Community is lacking although the essential character of the tax appears to be that of an incentive charge.

The pesticide tax in Denmark and Sweden The Danish tax operates variably by reference to the retail sale of a product, according to the size of the container. Where the product is imported the rate of tax rises. By contrast, the Swedish tax operates by fixing a fiscal rate referable to the quantity of active substance present. In both jurisdictions some fairly dramatic reductions in pesticide use were reported. In Denmark, the tax came into force in 1995. In the following two years it was reported that pesticide use fell by 10–13 per cent although there may have been contributions from newer formulations which are effective at lower application rates. In Sweden, the tax has been in force since 1984. Compared with the average figure applicable to the years from 1981 to 1985, pesticide use had declined by 35 per cent in 1995.[25] Interestingly it is suggested that while the tax may well have discouraged pesticide usage to an extent, it is the indirect effect of the tax and its financing of advisory, research and development services which has had the principal impact.[26]

Environmental Taxes

Environmental taxes can be assumed to be intended to modify the behaviour of those to which they apply. Such taxes generally operate against products and processes. Accordingly, as has just been seen in connection with a pesticide tax, the intention is that levels of use will be reduced with attendant benefits for the environment. However, before some specific characteristics are examined, it is useful to consider the general characteristics of environmental taxes. The European Environment Agency has identified those general characteristics, as follows:

> Environmental taxes are supposed to improve integration of environmental protection requirements, to internalise external effects, to promote eco-efficiency, to provide incentives for pollution abatement at minimum cost (static efficiency), to encourage innovation (dynamic efficiency), to raise revenue for financing environmental activities or, if taxes are unrequited, to finance reductions in other (distortionary) taxes ('double dividend'). Finally, environmental taxes are intended to broaden the range of policy instruments and to reinforce other environmental policy instruments. Not all environmental taxes necessarily have to serve all these functions.[27]

The term 'environmental tax' is, *per se*, very broad. As such a tax can be seen to include so-called 'charges'. For the purposes of this chapter, charges (characterised here as 'cost recovery' and 'incentive' charges) are dealt with separately, in the following two main sections. Nevertheless, both categories of charge are effectively a tax on operations that impact on the environment. However, the primary purpose of a tax is the raising of funds while a secondary purpose may be to influence behaviour. Where environmental taxes are concerned it is difficult to generalise about approaches to the primary purpose, mainly because activity touching and affecting the environment may attract tax liability as part of the general system of taxation or as the central feature of a specific environmental tax arrangement. Even this picture is capable of confusion if there is inclusion of charges in the generic definition of environmental taxes since they are usually levied, not as part of a tax system, but as a separate arrangement where, for example, an environmental regulator administers and enforces a charging scheme prescribed by statute. As will be seen later in the chapter, the income from such charges will often be applied to cover some or all of the costs of regulation. It is only as the scale of a charge increases that it may be characterised as an incentive charge, at which point it becomes rather more difficult to distinguish from a tax. If this is seen as a problem from a policy point of view there is of course an option to remove matters of administration and enforcement from the environmental regulator responsible and absorb what may now be labelled a tax, into the formal system of taxation. Such a change though might be more readily explained by a policy preference in favour of regarding such transactions as 'unrequited' payments. Nevertheless, such a move may have adverse effects on the implementation and enforcement of environmental law and policy. The reason for such adverse effects lies in the possible reduction in 'environmental tuning' of the liability as well as the possibility that the environmental regulator may be forced to replace these fiscal arrangements with rather more traditional regulatory approaches, which may be regarded in policy terms as a retrograde step. There is, though, one qualification to such a view. That qualification arises from the fact that most such charging schemes administered by environmental regulators are likely to be heavily prescribed by government, in which case any change from 'charge' to 'tax' may in reality be very marginal in effect.

Taxes and Charges Contrasted

Reference has just been made to tax as an 'unrequited' payment, indicating that the income is consigned to general taxation without reference to the purpose represented by the label given. By contrast, charges are 'requited' since they are presumed to be referable to the prescribed purpose behind the administration and enforcement of the charge. For the purposes of this chapter taxes and charges will normally be treated separately although, as has been seen already, it may not always be easy to distinguish between unrequited tax payments and requited incentive charges. Indeed, it may also be the case that cost recovery charging operates at such a level that there is an incentive effect which, but for the prescribed destination of revenues, would beg comparison with an environmental or other tax.

Taxes and Tradable Permits Contrasted

A system which relies on tradable permits is concerned fundamentally with the task of setting targets for the reduction of discharges or emissions in respect of prescribed pollutants. Such a system may also be location-specific for these purposes. Initially, the permits issued are referable to the targets set and those to whom they are issued are able to trade them. However, a dynamic market may not function where there are few participants or few permits issued. Indeed, even where these limitations do not apply it may be difficult to anticipate the strategic attitude of companies affected.

All of these potential problems may arise singly or in combination to frustrate what otherwise might have been assumed to be an efficient market. Essentially therefore, tradable permit systems depend essentially on the quantities of pollutant whereas systems based on taxes and charges depend essentially on price-based considerations. However, according to OECD in its publication *Taxation and the Environment*:

> The principal theoretical consideration relates to the impact of uncertainty ... If well monitored and enforced, a system of tradable permits guarantees the quantitative reduction in pollution, but at uncertain cost, whilst a price-based mechanism ... has an uncertain impact on the quantity of emissions, but fixes the marginal cost to polluters of emission controls.[28]

Although it is difficult to generalise about the initiation of a system of tradable permits, such a system may have its attractions where permits are allocated to existing companies *in situ* in the areas affected if that allocation is at no charge. Whether such an arrangement is advantageous may have to be determined by considering whether there could be undue discouragement to companies wishing to locate in those areas. In turn, the ostensible attraction of a system that does not involve tax liability may be offset if market adjustment meant that all existing and newly arriving companies were to pay for their permits.

Subject to these foregoing limitations there is the potential in a system of tradable permits to move beyond mere tax liability in respect of discharges and emissions, even though such liability may have an incentive effect where it is fixed at a sufficient level. Tradable permit systems certainly have the potential to encourage pollution abatement, but whether such an efficiency is greater than that carried with tax liability at a sufficiently high pitch may be open to debate. Equally, both approaches will have merit if they are capable of simple, transparent modification and extension as circumstances dictate.

Varieties of Environmental Tax Liability

Tax liability can be modelled in a variety of different ways and numerous policy preferences and constraints will be in evidence. For example, there may no doubt be evidence in tax law and policy of attempts to avoid undue distortion of markets. Equally, concern for sustainable development, a matter to be addressed later, will tend to be manifested in tax law and policy which stresses the need to link liability with the avoidance of resource depletion and environmental pollution. Tax regimes of the latter variety will manifest liability in different ways, all of which may have merits of one sort or another. For example, the choice of model may suggest 'end of pipe' tax liability, according to the quantity of effluent or other pollutant which is discharged or emitted. Equally, tax liability may accrue in advance of that point or beyond it, or even in respect of a product and its polluting characteristics.

The respective efficiencies of these options will be affected by a multitude of variables, many if not all of which may suggest that taxation is a rather more cost-effective approach compared (say) with traditional regulatory techniques where there are fewer personal choices to invest in and apply abatement or remedial technology at lowest price. Such traditional regulatory techniques may in turn lack incentives in favour of resort to such technologies unless of course there are built-in legal obligations to maintain continuous improvement in abatement and similar measures. However, again it is unlikely that such comparisons will be clearly valid unless tax rates are high enough and (perhaps) direct rather than indirect in their operation. When they reach an optimum level of efficiency though, environmental and other taxes may be regarded as being efficient in terms of cost and otherwise by virtue of being self-regulating.

The varieties of tax liability are distributed through different modes of calculation. For example, tax liability may depend on the quantity of pollutant generated from the end of the pipe. Such an approach is arguably inefficient by virtue of its ignorance of preventative measures in order to eliminate or at least minimise the subject pollutants, and by virtue of its tendency to address single pollutants. Nevertheless, any attempt to deal with a process introduces complications of definition, and enforcement. By way of contrast, environmental taxes may be seen to operate indirectly, as where liability accrues in respect of a product, service or other prejudicial activity. Another indirect approach to tax liability may be dependent on the general system of taxation through which allowances may be available in order to create incentives. Such incentives may seek the phasing out of outdated abatement technology, for example, with an attendant allowance for its replacement with more effective equipment.

The Effectiveness of Environmental Tax Liability

Unlike regulatory techniques, the adoption of environmental taxes does not always allow a clear indication of the fulfilment of the desired effect. This, in part, is one of the consequences of the foregoing characteristic of self-regulation. Any tax introduced will require monitoring, for a variety of reasons ranging from questions of general effectiveness through questions of adjustment of tax rates. It is beyond these questions that monitoring and evaluation becomes rather more difficult. In other words, determining the effect of a tax on specific environmental targets may bring with it certain difficulties, not least of which is whether the tax – and the rate at which it is levied – represents the material reason for progress, or lack of, towards the prescribed target. In the case of traditional regulatory approaches this matter of causation is rather more straightforward in many cases, particularly where there are clearly prescribed limits and statutory regulation tied directly to them. There may though be another situation where, despite these apparent shortcomings, environmental taxes are particularly advantageous.

In both Chapter One[29] and Chapter Two[30] reference was made to the implementation and enforcement of Community legislation relating to volatile organic compounds. It was seen that Community legislation operates only at and above a prescribed threshold. One of the principal reasons for this is that numerous small businesses use solvents, in the printing industry, for example. The practicality of attempting to enforce the law against so many small businesses renders necessary the foregoing 'triviality threshold'. Nevertheless, below that threshold it remains open to a member state to apply an environmental tax where it is considered appropriate to 'mop up' the bulk of the remaining solvents emissions. At the time of writing only one European country – Switzerland – operates what is a product charge in the present context. Any product containing an organic solvent is subject to the product charge, which came into force early in 2000. The rate of the charge is due to rise in 2003. Revenue from the charge is rebated *per capita* through premiums payable in respect of medical insurance. Two questions arise from this particular model. Given that throughout Europe and the Community in particular, product charges on items such as batteries are increasingly popular, are those charges fixed at a sufficient rate to give rise to the incentives and behavioural changes which are so crucial to environmental taxation? Secondly, although the Swiss product charge allows revenues to be rebated to the population on a *per capita* basis, why should other policy options not be considered? In particular, revenues might serve a direct environmental purpose where revenues are used for the purpose of promoting research, development and use of water-based inks in the printing industry.

Matters of effectiveness are difficult to address with any confidence. The question of 'causation' focuses on whether a tax has had a substantial impact on the realisation of incentives and a change of behaviour on the part of those targeted by the tax. However, the question is even more difficult to address since environmental taxes are unlikely to stand alone. If (for example) a member state of the Community chose to complement Community law on volatile organic compounds by the introduction (as in Switzerland) of a tax below the 'triviality threshold' such a comprehensive approach might give credibility to statistics relating to any significant reduction in the use of solvents. In the absence of such provision below the threshold it becomes that much more difficult to determine the part played by Community law and policy, as well as the style and emphasis of member state transposition, in achieving that reduction. There may of course be efficiencies to be gained here through infrastructure in support of the implementation and enforcement of economic instruments. The consultative processes referred to in Chapter 1 are a good example of the way in which the support of those affected by taxes may be a considerable benefit. This is underpinned by the merit of educating those affected through demonstration of the economic and social benefits accruing from any new measure here. A good illustration of the way in which something other than hard law *per se* may produce constructive effects, is where revenues from the Swedish pesticides tax invested in training and education are suggested to have had a significant effect on reductions in pesticides use. Another consideration in the process of seeking to create an efficient and an effective environmental tax is the integration of that tax in the course of policy-formation. Before this matter of integration is looked at, some reference has to be made to Community competence in relation to legislation covering environmental taxes.

Environmental Taxes and Community Competence

In July 1997 the Commission published a Communication – *Environmental Taxes and Charges in the Single Market*[31] – which provides advice for member states on the development and implementation of environmental taxes, albeit biased towards product charges and taxes, given their closeness to internal market concerns. However, in the absence of clear Community competence it seems unlikely that environmental taxes will feature heavily in Community law and policy development beyond the limited achievement hitherto. That limited achievement is seen in the single market prescription of minimum excise rates for motor fuel in member states following legislation of Directive 92/82:[32] the so-called 'Mineral Oils' Directive.

The Nice Treaty failed to address the Community's limited competence in relation to environmental taxes. It appears therefore that any progress will have to be reference to so-called 'enhanced cooperation' whereby eight or more member states are empowered to conclude an agreement setting out rules and principles for a prescribed transaction where remaining member states decide not to participate. Arguably, such a fractured approach to the development of law and policy on environmental taxes at the centre is distinctly undesirable. Against such an argument it may be contended that if a coherent set of rules and principles were to emerge from 'enhanced cooperation' which, *inter alia*, provided a clear framework in respect of some or all of the concerns (set out below) that member states have about the Community impact of taxes, a number of politically acceptable advantages would accrue. For example, the Commission and the European Court of Justice would have rules and principles to act on, instead of dealing on an *ad hoc* basis with applications for determinations by member states.

Until the Community can escape from the restriction whereby unanimous voting is required for legislation on taxation affecting member states, it is unlikely that the centre can do more than provide the sort of guidance just referred to. In this context there are issues to be addressed by any member state seeking to develop its own environmental taxes which relate to restrictions in Community law. For example, will the operation of a tax allowance (for example) require Commission approval as 'state aid'? It has to be asked also whether a particular facet of a proposed tax is anti-competitive and, as such, inconsistent with the operation of the internal market. To that extent, the Commission – and the European Court of Justice – have important supervisory roles relating to member state activity here, albeit set against the background of general Community law and only marginally concerned with environmental considerations.

Environmental Taxes and Policy Integration

Environmental policy integration was dealt with in Chapter One. There seems little doubt that Community policies have often represented the very antithesis of policy integration which, ultimately, will carry effective policies on sustainable development. The gradual development and harmonisation of law and policy on environmental taxation may represent an effective method of policy integration. Experience to date is undoubtedly an important marker. In 2000 the European Environment Agency reported that as much as 95 per cent of environmental tax revenue in Europe came from the energy and transport sectors.[33] By contrast, the Agency reported that:

> There is no ... quantification of negative environmental externalities for agriculture as there is for transport and energy, though a preliminary estimation indicates considerable costs due to pesticides and fertiliser use, and biodiversity loss. Apart from some pesticides and fertiliser taxes there are few examples of taxes being used to internalise these costs. Similarly, positive environmental externalities from agriculture, such as carbon sequestration and maintenance of biodiversity justify their internalisation via appropriate subsidies such as the agro [*sic*] – environmental measures of the CAP.[34]

Until member states, perhaps with the encouragement of the Commission, address the valuation and quantification of the relevant externalities and thereafter set an effective rate of tax it will be difficult to make substantial progress towards policy integration. For the moment, it appears that environmental taxation is regarded as something of a novelty. That novelty brings with it a cautious attitude arising from anxieties about the impact of taxes on competitiveness and other factors such as inflation. Such anxieties would of course be reduced were the Community to be in a position to harmonise tax rates for present purposes. This though is but one part of the process of securing effectiveness. It has been suggested that there are various obstacles in the way of a wider and more consistent use of environmental taxes:

> ... uncertainty as to the precise environmental outcome and as to the economic and budgetary implications; concerns about competitiveness and/or distributional effects; lack of communication and co-ordination between environmental and fiscal authorities ...[35]

It has also been suggested that concerns about fairness and competitive capacity are often overstated. The greening of tax systems can be achieved if existing distortionary direct or indirect taxes as well as tax provisions and subsidies likely to have negative environmental impacts are identified and then removed. Overall, environmental taxes can contribute to a better integration of environmental and economic policies compared with traditional regulatory approaches.[36] The process of policy integration and the objective of promoting sustainable development were of course given important encouragement by the Amsterdam Treaty but it can be appreciated from the foregoing that realisation of integration and sustainability depends on greater sectoral integration from the centre of the Community, and development of member state perceptions of the efficiencies of environmental taxation with harmonisation and guidance from the Community within the limits of its competence. Such efficiencies will be manifested also from the environmental principles recognised by the Community and described previously, in Chapter Three.

Environmental Taxation and Policy Principles

It has been suggested, for example, that a

> ... broadening of the environmental tax base reflects a widening of the 'polluter pays' principle to the more comprehensive 'user pays' principle, where users pay for ecological services and thus contribute to reductions in material inputs and improvements in eco-efficiency.[37]

Furthermore,

> Given the uncertainty about the effects of many ... chemicals and other products on humans and the environment, any increase in eco-efficiency that environmental taxes encourage also helps to implement the 'precautionary principle', i.e. the reduction of exposure to substances before there is conclusive evidence of serious harm.[38]

These two examples are by no means the only ones which may influence policy priorities in the shaping of environmental taxes for implementation in aid of sustainable development and other similar priorities. The proximity principle further illustrates the way in which tax may operate as an incentive to encourage or avoid an activity in a particular locality according to its perceived environmental merit. A possible example of this principle and its influence on an environmental tax is seen in the United Kingdom's aggregates tax. This and another example of environmental tax in the United Kingdom – the landfill tax – are now outlined. The new Climate Change Levy is dealt with later in the chapter.

Environmental Taxes in the United Kingdom

The aggregates tax comes into force in April 2002 and applies to the extraction of sand, gravel and crushed rock in the United Kingdom or its territorial waters. The objective of the tax is to address the environmental impact of extraction on landscapes and, in turn, to encourage the use of secondary building material. The revenues will be fed back into the businesses affected through a reduction in national insurance payable, as well as being paid into a new Sustainability Fund, which will seek to realise environmental benefits for those communities affected by the extraction of aggregates. The tax recognises that regulatory controls do not take account of various incidents of quarrying and extraction: noise, dust, vibration, visual intrusion and loss of amenity, and interference with biodiversity. The identification of these externalities and their incorporation in calculations of the tax are intended to internalise the foregoing environmental and other costs of aggregate extraction. By way of contrast, the landfill tax came into force in 1996. One of the prime objectives behind the tax was to anticipate and complement Community law governing landfilling in Directive 99/31.[39] In so doing the essential purpose of the tax is to minimise the quantity of waste that is landfilled, the tax being applied to all waste disposal operations at landfill sites through an *ad valorem* levy on operators' charges. Liability is designed to apply at the earliest point in delivery of subject waste to a site: revenues are applied to the businesses affected through a reduction on national insurance thus lowering labour costs, as well as through payments to environmental trusts. As a tax it is of course open to an operator to seek to avoid liability, either by avoiding landfilling or minimising the amount of waste being disposed of along that route. Some evidence of the success of the tax is seen in the growing investment attraction of materials recovery facilities.[40]

Cost Recovery Charging

Charging for cost recovery is justified by reference to the 'polluter pays' principle for the purpose of realising the costs associated with regulatory control and management or treatment of pollutants. Whether in practice the true cost is reflected in charging schemes here is probably open to doubt. However, charging to recover these costs is the longest established fiscal instrument affecting the environment. Although the following section of the chapter shows that a distinction is claimed between this and the incentive-based charge, it is perhaps difficult to claim that the cost recovery charge is always devoid of incentive effect.

Despite this uncertainty the essential function of cost recovery is the gathering of revenues for specific environmental purposes. Careful calculation and setting of tax rates will be necessary if distortions are to be avoided. The relevant statutory background will therefore require flexibility if tax rates are to be modified from time to time. Such modification may well be required if it is found that investment in effluent treatment facilities is insufficient by reference to Community legal requirements, for example. This example represents another area of influence exerted by Community law in relation to the operation of environmental taxes and charges. Generally though the need for structural change will be minimised where the essential foundation of the charge is seen to be sufficiently robust.

Whether the cost recovery charge is sufficiently robust to serve its essential purpose will be aided by effective consultation of the sort described in Chapter 1 in relation to the policy development process. Certain principles are undoubtedly crucial in the design and development process. The charge must be equitable and proportionate in the allocation of costs to the participating companies and businesses: regulatory workloads for this purpose will require careful consideration, the more so if policy suggests a lighter touch based on perceived corporate risks in environmental management of subject processes; transparent in identifying categories clearly for the benefit of all parties concerned; practicable in terms of ease of administration and enforcement; flexible, in facilitating easy updating; and sustainable in producing revenues which will finance the purposes for which the charge is put in place.

Incentive Charging

Incentive charging will occur where there is no particular concern to cover the administrative and other costs which characterise cost recovery charging. Fundamentally though, incentive charging is concerned with influencing behaviour which, without the charge, would be characterised as being environmentally-adverse. As with cost recovery charging, careful attention will have to be given to the nature and the scale of the charge, in order to realise the purpose behind the arrangement.

The Swedish Nitrogen Oxides Charging Scheme

A good example of the incentive effect of a charging scheme is the Swedish scheme which imposes a charge on nitrogen oxide emissions which came into force in January 1992. The charging scheme applied originally to large combustion plants but was extended to smaller plants in 1996: emissions are monitored with measuring apparatus whose cost resulted in the scheme being limited originally to plants with the largest input only. Revenues generated are redistributed to the plants liable to pay the charge. It is estimated[41] that annual emissions have reduced significantly below the level that would otherwise have applied. Despite initial criticisms that the time allowed to respond to the charge was too short, it appears that industrial and district heating plants took steps to reduce emissions in anticipation of the charge coming into force. The incentive effect of the Swedish scheme has been described thus:

> The ... charge provided an incentive for monitoring and abatement measures in liable plants. Emissions per energy unit fell by about 60% between 1990 and 1996, whereas total emissions fell by approximately 50%, from about 24,500 tonnes to 12,500 tonnes. According to the Swedish [Environmental Protection Agency] [nitrogen oxide] emissions in 1995 would have been 10,000 tonnes greater if the nitrogen oxides charge had not existed ... Originally the Swedish government expected a reduction of only 5,000–7,000 tons. Emissions from boilers subject to the charge would have been 80% higher.[42]

The largest net payments are made by the Swedish waste incineration industry whose emissions have been reported to reach 40 per cent although the metal industry receives the largest rebates. A crucial part of the calculation of the charge was (and is) the relationship between the scale of the charge and the likely costs of emission reduction in the plants covered by the scheme. The ratio here is regarded as indicating that the charge provides a strong incentive for tracing and applying cost-effective solutions.[43]

The Development of Incentive Charging

It is usually the case that incentive charging schemes supplement regulatory arrangements. As such, these schemes have considerable merit where (as with the Swedish scheme above) there is a certain forcing of innovation and investment in technology which might not occur where regulation alone applied. Reference back to the description – earlier in the chapter – of the water effluent charge in Germany and the water pollution charge in the Netherlands might usefully be made in this connection. The Royal Commission on Environmental Pollution in its 16th Report on *Freshwater Quality*[44] has stressed the merit of developing incentive charging in United Kingdom water legislation, drawing on the experience of Germany and the Netherlands. However, payment of charges here might be seen as the sale of a right to indulge in environmental pollution. Where this is a serious political objection there may be merit in consideration of an arrangement based on the tradable permits already referred to.

The Swedish incentive charging scheme in respect of nitrogen oxide is a potentially good example of an arrangement where a tradable permit system might usefully be substituted, given two apparent fundamentals of such permits: the availability of a viable market based on a sufficient number of market actors and the opportunity to maximise cost-effective compliance with prescribed emissions targets set by Community law. Directive 96/61[45] – the Integrated Pollution Prevention and Control Directive – comes into force in the power and heat generation industries in 2006. The core of the Directive is seen in the need to comply with 'best available techniques', a seemingly stringent legal requirement which may not be capable of achievement where permit terms are such that they fall below this statutory threshold. The solution, which member states like Sweden may have to address, probably lies in member state legislation transposing Community law in order to achieve rationalisation. Assuming that the Directive's terms are adhered to, it appears that a member state should be able to facilitate arrangements for tradable permit schemes. In Great Britain, section 2 of the Pollution Prevention and Control Act 1999 empowers the Secretary of State to make regulations authorising plans for the setting of overall limits, the allocation of quotas or the progressive improvement of standards or objectives, and authorising the making of schemes for the trading or other transfer of any quotas so allocated.

Incentive charging and tradable permits may have a common aim in some circumstances. For example, there may be a need to rationalise problems of high demand and adverse environmental impact in relation to water abstraction, for example. It has to be assumed that traditional regulation here is incapable of achieving a sufficiently sensitive and efficient equation between the marginal cost of reducing abstraction, and the marginal benefit of such reduction. There will be numerous variables which determine any choice between the two, not least (again) is the attraction of a scheme based on tradable permits where there are sufficient actors to constitute a viable, efficient market for issued permits where cost efficiencies are maximised through a rapid trading process.

Tradable Permits and Emissions Trading

A permit scheme is based on reduction targets relating to prescribed pollutants where the permits issued are tied to those targets. The allocation process may differ and range from the distribution of permits without charge for existing operations, to distribution based on tenders or even an auction. Because tradable permits operate by reference to a binding ceiling on emissions, discharges or abstractions, with no particular concern about marginal costs of abatement, there can be some certainty about quantitative reductions in targeted pollutants. However, on top of the constraints of such schemes, some of which have just been referred to, there may be a necessity so to design them that there is an avoidance of national targets for such targeted pollutants. A permit system predicated only on national targets is unlikely to take account of environmentally sensitive areas where targets need to be rather more stringent. This is but one element to be considered in the design and implementation of a permit scheme. In this section of the chapter, reference will be made to various areas of the environment where permit trading schemes have been implemented or are the subject of policy discussion. Those areas are as follows: water abstraction, waste management and air pollution. The exception is the emerging greenhouse gas emissions trading scheme in the United Kingdom. This emerging scheme will be described in the following section of the chapter, to be followed by the closely-related Climate Change Levy. At the time of writing both the trading and climate levy schemes are due for imminent implementation.

Water Abstraction

At the time of writing there is considerable policy discussion on the adoption of permit trading schemes in relation to water abstraction. A Consultation Paper on *Economic Instruments in Relation to Water Abstraction*[46] shows the extent of the likely policy options should such a scheme be implemented through a Finance Act in the United Kingdom. At the root of the debate is the need for a more rational use of water resources, taking account of another priority, the minimisation of environmental damage. This and any other similar permit trading scheme must, as a matter of necessity, be tied closely to a regulatory framework. However, the nature of the regulator's function cannot be the subject of generalisation since all permit trading schemes will have their own distinct environmental and other badges. In the case of permit trading in relating to water abstraction, the regulator will no doubt be required to prescribe – and enforce – the environmental priorities behind the scheme and its operation in the areas of abstraction. Such prescription can be achieved through so-called 'open' trading schemes although their voluntary character removes any mandatory quality attached to environmental and other priorities. As a result attention will tend to focus on 'closed' trading schemes.

Closed trading schemes Such schemes, which are not confined to the present context, operate by reference to the aforementioned 'ceiling' with the possibility of additional abstractions being permitted through a buying in of abstraction permits from another scheme participant whose rights are in turn reduced. Where such trading occurs it can be seen that permit trading almost inevitably relies on detailed statutory definition of the regulator's function and the terms on which trading may occur. Matters of market efficiency were touched on earlier, when it was stressed that permit trading is more likely to be effective where there is a critical number of market participants. In turn, it must be assumed that the environmental assumptions of the scheme are prescribed in such a way that the regulatory process realises initial policy priorities affecting the environment.

Environmental protection A number of variables will tend to influence the environmental success of a permit trading scheme affecting water abstraction. Some of those variables are fairly obvious: the number of abstraction permits issued will have to take account of water volume extracted according to the location and its environmental pressure points. On occasions policy priorities here may even be seasonal, determining that abstraction be limited to those times in the year where water resources are more plentiful. The terms of the licence may also involve the transfer of any attendant statutory liabilities, under the Water Resources Act 1991, for example. Such liabilities will no doubt extend from personal responsibility for compliance with permit and licence conditions to compliance with other freestanding statutory liabilities. Indeed, those liabilities may well extend more widely. For example, a nature conservation designation may be such that abstraction in a prescribed area is entirely prohibited under the terms of the Wildlife and Countryside Act 1981. In these circumstances the permit cannot be exploited, suggesting the need for careful consideration of permit value in relation to water resources and their location.

Waste Management

In dealing earlier in the chapter with the United Kingdom's landfill tax, the significance of Community law was referred to. The Landfill Directive[47] requires each member state to implement a plan whereby the volume of biodegradable waste destined for landfill is reduced. In addition, the Directive prescribes reduction targets in respect of biodegradable municipal waste. The *Waste Strategy for England and Wales 2000*[48] sets out proposals to apply in England whereby tradable permits will be issued to local authorities. The intention is that those permits will be issued free to the local authorities, each permit indicating a reducing amount of biodegradable waste to be landfilled in order to comply with the targets set by the Directive. The attraction of tradable permits is stated to be seen in terms of the cost-effectiveness of achieving compliance with targets. In turn, local authorities will be in a position to decide whether there are cost and other efficiencies in purchasing unused permits from other local authorities in order to landfill additional waste, or whether there is merit in investing in alternative waste reduction and disposal techniques. The implementing legislation will contain appropriate enforcement provisions to be exercised by the regulator who, not surprisingly, will have statutory responsibility for superintending trading under the scheme. At the time of writing it is not clear what sanctions will be included in the legislation where there is noncompliance with the limits on these tradable permits.

Air Pollution

To date, the only substantial experience of tradable permit schemes occurs in the United States where they have been operative since 1976. So-called 'emissions trading' is complementary to the statutory regulation of air pollution under the Clean Air Act 1969. Air quality standards set at federal level by the Environmental Protection Agency are implemented by the states through State Implementation Plans. These plans set emission levels for existing (or modified) and new sources of emissions to the atmosphere. New sources are subject to more stringent regulatory requirements. In turn, those regulatory requirements at state level can prescribe abatement technologies to be applied by companies without regard to matters of cost-effectiveness. Trading in so-called 'offsets', where emission targets are transferred between company sites, marked the start of a more formal trading regime. Some states like California legislated for the establishment of trading registration arrangements which impose restrictions on what otherwise would be informal 'offset' trading as well as facilitating the banking of surplus emission reductions for exploitation in the future. As a result trading is subject to detailed regulation through which exacting requirements can be imposed, particularly in relation to new sources.

It appears that the stringency of the regulatory function here has often had the effect of kick-starting a dynamic market in surplus emission reductions. Whether that dynamic market depended on strong growth in the economy is difficult to say although it probably exerted more than a merely marginal effect. Even within such an apparently dynamic market there are those companies which are reticent about trading and will see the cost-effective reaction in terms of their own, private investment in pollution abatement technology. That reticence may be based on perceptions of high transaction costs as well as the fear of additional regulatory requirements if the regulated trading arena is entered.

The success of the emissions trading regime in the United States is not easily evaluated. Nevertheless, some broad features have been discerned and it has been observed that it

> ... has achieved cost savings, but the number of trades has remained limited and most trades have been intra-company. The limited effects are due to the restricted scope of the program (allowing only trading of emission reductions beyond regulatory base-lines), the trading rules (promoting mainly intra-company trading) and the uncertainty created by the joint application of command and control regulation next to the tradable permit program.[49]

Before some other aspects of emissions trading are examined it may be asked whether tradable permit schemes are capable of transposition to the international arena. Given the increased contemporary interest in worldwide controls over greenhouse gases and ozone-depleting products, are permit schemes capable of playing a part in relevant international conventions?

Tradable Permits and International Environmental Regulation

The need for enforceable schemes suggests that the necessary techniques may be difficult to implement against sovereign states. Where a scheme anticipated additional discounted permits being granted to developing states, again enforcement of regulatory requirements might be a matter of difficulty. However, there are examples of international conventional assistance to such states, to aid their compliance in a positive way in order to keep them within the convention framework of obligations. Although there are likely to be similar problems in keeping developed states on board, again positive incentives for compliance might be built into the infrastructure of the convention. In this way compliance might be seen to be politically acceptable, and desirable. Structurally, though, it has to be conceded that the regulation of trading between numerous states is a rather more complex process than most other regulatory processes provided for in international conventions.

Greenhouse Gas Emissions Trading in the United Kingdom

As explained previously, this emissions trading scheme is closely related to the United Kingdom government's Climate Change Levy, which will be addressed in the section following that which refers to the Community's proposed greenhouse gas emissions trading scheme. The emissions trading scheme (ETS) is a potentially important part of the government's climate change programme. Initially the intention is that ETS operates as a carbon trading scheme, saving up to 2m tonnes of carbon by the year 2010. Companies contracting as parties to sectoral agreements under the Climate Change Levy will not qualify for the ETS incentives described below by virtue of their qualification for 80 per cent discounts in respect of the Levy. The overall quantity of such companies' greenhouse gas emissions subject to control is relatively limited however. The need to maximise reduction explains the policy priority in favour of ETS, and its potential to maximise reductions of greenhouse gas emissions and carbon dioxide in particular, through the involvement of companies not subject to the Levy. Those companies not subject to the Levy include the electricity generators who, perhaps perversely, have access to cost-effective facilities for minimising greenhouse gas emissions. The likely explanation for the initial exclusion of the generators is an economic argument based on an inflation in natural gas prices which might ultimately affect the price to the electricity consumer.

ETS: the Main Elements

ETS is essentially a voluntary scheme which, in part, explains government investment of £30m per year in order to encourage those companies not participating in the Climate Change Levy's sectoral agreements to participate in emissions trading whereby they will limit their emissions. These incentive funds will be auctioned: companies will offer emission reductions at a set price. There is of course a possibility that the aggregate total of bids exceeds the financial ceiling offered by the government. If this is the case, the intention is that bidding continues to the point where the aggregate satisfies the ceiling set by the government. Once ETS is operative an 80 per cent Levy discount will apply and emission allowances will be allocated free of charge through a 'grandfathering' arrangement. The associated emission targets are calculated by reference to emissions averaged over three years up to and including the year 2000. A further limit refers to the need for any participating company to submit all operations in a prescribed sector to the prescribed target reduction. In other words, companies are not permitted to 'cherry pick' although there will be freedom to exclude unrelated operations. Emission performance against the target will be objectively verified.

Qualifying Participation in ETS

Three categories of participation are recognised by ETS. In the first place, direct entrant companies who will operate against absolute targets while qualifying for the financial incentive referred to previously; secondly, companies which have contracted under the Climate Change Levy in respect of sectoral agreements who will operate against 'output-weighted' targets which are flexible enough to accommodate production increases; and other companies and organisations operating outside the foregoing target obligations. These companies and organisations are to be permitted to trade by acquiring and cancelling surplus emission allowances, for example. Ultimately ETS will operate against absolute targets in order to ensure that United Kingdom arrangements are consistent with international emissions trading which is likely to be in place by 2008. Until the end of the year before – 2007 – surplus emission allowances to be drawn on in later years may be banked, without limit. A Community ETS for carbon dioxide, referred to below, is set to operate by the year 2005.

Trading Regulation

A registration function will be undertaken by an Emission Trading Authority. That function is primarily concerned with the tracking of recorded sales and transfers of surplus emission allowances. In addition, the Authority will enforce a 'gateway' function affecting those companies involved in sectoral agreements and operating against 'output-weighted' targets. This is a restrictive function limiting access by these companies to the ETS market for the purpose of ensuring that they do not sell to it surplus emission allowances in excess of credits accumulating in their own 'unit sector' for the purpose of the Levy. This market restriction is potentially very important. Where such companies in the unit sector expand production, the possibility of adverse effects on surplus allowances is very real. If those allowances are traded out of the Climate

Change Levy sector and the sector is unable to meet its target, companies face the prospect of losing their 80 per cent discount on the Levy. Equally, there is a real danger of a shortage of emission allowances available for sale outside the United Kingdom in the future when an international emissions trading regime starts by 2008.

Regulatory Flexibility

Provision is made in the ETS for a variety of situations which might be capable of compromising the trading arrangements. Those situations will arise where, for example, a company reduces production, undertakes a takeover or merger, secures a demerger or out-sources a subject operation. Taking account of the scope and nature of the scheme as described above, the critical question concerns a company's rights and entitlements to emission allowances. If that company reduces production there will no loss of entitlement to emission allowances. However, closure of an operation will necessitate a recalculation proportionately to revised values relating both to the averaging baseline and the resultant targets, albeit above a prescribed threshold. This approach, appropriately refined to take account of the nature of the corporate transaction, will apply to the other situations listed above.

The Legal Status of ETS

ETS is not a statutory scheme as such. It appears that some difficulties may arise from the decision of government not to legislate specifically for the purpose of implementing and enforcing the scheme. The absence of a statutory framework means that a company failing to comply with an ETS target will face the prospect of losing an incentive payment. Equally, it is difficult to anticipate any obvious legal basis for corporate liability if, for example, a transaction relating to the sale of a surplus emission allowance is affected by a material irregularity. Payment of the £30m per year to the voluntary participants in ETS will be undertaken through section 153 of the Environmental Protection Act 1990. This provision empowers the Secretary of State to give financial assistance to prescribed organisations although the statutory power can be extended

> ... by adding ... any description of organisation, scheme, programme or international agreement whose purposes relate to the protection, improvement or better understanding of the environment.[50]

The essential purpose of the section is the provision of financial assistance: arguably use of the powers here to facilitate incentive payments is *ultra vires*. An equally substantial objection to use of section 153 is the absence of any reference here to the giving of financial assistance to a 'person', seemingly a deliberate omission. Normally, it can be assumed in the course of statutory interpretation that the term 'person' will include a corporation, unless the contrary intention appears.[51]

Greenhouse Gas Emissions Trading in the European Community

The Community's Green Paper on greenhouse gas emissions trading was published in 2000.[52] The Community anticipates its own trading scheme which is to be operative by 2005, ahead of the international scheme in 2008. As in the United Kingdom, the preference in the Community is for a scheme which is initially referable to carbon dioxide. In turn the preference is to target large, fixed point sources. This probably suggests that power stations, accounting for about half of the Community's emissions, will be the principal targets of the scheme.

The United Kingdom Climate Change Levy

The relationship with the ETS in the United Kingdom has been seen already. This section of the chapter looks at the specific features and implications of the Climate Change Levy, as well as examining in outline the experience of other Community member states which have implemented a carbon tax. Revenue from the Levy will be recycled into the companies subject to the charge. That recycling of revenues will be aimed at cutting national insurance contributions in order to reduce labour costs, and funding developments in the area of energy efficiency. Discounts of up to 80 per cent are available to companies willing to negotiate and conclude agreements covering energy efficiency and carbon dioxide reductions. These 80 per cent discounts are available to those companies regulated under the Integrated Pollution Prevention and Control (IPPC) regime. Interestingly, certain industrial sectors outside the IPPC regime have voluntarily sought to be regulated under its terms, in order to take advantage of the discount available, surely an unforeseen benefit of the policy on climate change. The negotiated agreements do allow an important measure of discretion by which the Secretary of State can decide whether a company's realisation of the prescribed target has been 'satisfactory'. This discretion will permit any noncompliance to be ignored, at least where the Secretary of State is satisfied that a 'constraint or requirement' has had a major effect on progress. The contingencies covered by this formula appear to include frustration of energy-saving initiatives where there is an unforeseen change in energy supply arrangements.

The IPPC Base for the Levy

The IPPC regulatory regime, as transposed by the Pollution Prevention and Control Act 1999, is subject to an implementation programme which extends up to the year 2007. The statutory framework will impose regulatory control on most major energy users and will account for approximately 40 per cent of the greenhouse gases emitted in the United Kingdom. Despite its central concern with efficient energy management there is little doubt that, by itself, IPPC regulation is incapable of realising cost-effective reductions in energy consumption and greenhouse gas emissions. Not surprisingly, therefore, the Pollution Prevention and Control Act in section 2, mentioned previously in the chapter, empowers the Secretary of State to use subordinate legislation for the purpose of complementing IPPC with schemes which are more likely to achieve that cost-effectiveness.

Is IPPC the most effective basis for the operation of the Climate Change Levy? This question deserves clarification since the Climate Change Levy will depend crucially on its 'cutting edge': qualification for the discount, based on the conclusion of a negotiated agreement. It is qualification for this purpose that triggers recognition of those companies – generally the larger corporate industrial operations and installations – that will be in a position to qualify for 80 per cent discounts. The arguments advanced by government for this approach are that IPPC regime is already concerned with energy efficient operations, and that that regime offers legal certainty in defining those companies eligible to enter negotiated agreements and therefore to qualify for the discount. The government reiterated these arguments to the House of Commons Environment Committee and are set out in its Report on the *UK Climate Change Programme*.[53] Nevertheless, this basis for the operation of the Climate Change Levy has attracted considerable criticism, some of which was heard by the House of Commons Environment Committee. For example, the foregoing model adopted by the government has been described as 'illogical'. Indeed, the Committee heard of various anomalies, such as that concerning the water industry – the third most energy-intensive industry in the United Kingdom – which falls outside IPPC.[54] A further limitation of the Levy arrangements is that, generally, smaller companies and other business undertakings in the manufacturing sector will also fall outside, even though the Levy is intended to be revenue neutral.[55] The only general exception to this state of affairs is where such companies are part of an industrial association which voluntarily seeks and obtains entry to the IPPC regulatory regime.

Is the Climate Change Levy a robust environmental tax? The Climate Change Levy has to be seen against the background of the government's assumptions about the characteristics of 'good' taxation. In the present context the government has published a document entitled *Environmental Taxation Statement of Intent.*[56] The following statement appears in the Statement of Intention:

> ... environmental taxation must meet the general tests of good taxation. It must be well designed, to meet objectives without undesirable side-effects; it must keep deadweight compliance costs to a minimum; distributional impact must be acceptable; and care must be had to implications for international competitiveness.[57]

The House of Commons Environment Committee has concluded that the Levy does not meet the tests of good taxation. This conclusion is based on the exemptions available, negotiated agreements and reduced rates, all of which are considered to result in an extremely complex and cumbersome market instrument which will provide only modest emission reductions. Whether this view takes adequate account of the ETS arrangements referred to previously is open to argument. As a supplementary market-based mechanism, ETS is undoubtedly an important contributor to carbon dioxide emission reduction. Furthermore, the overall concern is with greenhouse gas reduction which (arguably) makes assessment of the effectiveness of the Climate Change Levy premature. Nevertheless, there is undoubtedly a measure of complexity in the arrangements, exacerbated it would appear by the willingness of the government to accept three industries into 'membership' of the IPPC regime. Earlier reference to this change, enabling companies comprised in the industrial sectors concerned to be subject to regulation and thus qualify for the discount via participation in the negotiated agreements on emissions, depended on criteria that may be regarded as opaque.[58] The experience of other member states in the implementation of carbon energy taxation is of interest here.

Carbon Energy Taxes in other Community Member States

Six other member states of the European Community have adopted carbon energy taxation. Among the first in the field were Finland and the Netherlands, in 1990. Other member states whose experience with implementation is worthy of consideration are Sweden and Denmark, although Italy has implemented taxation in the present context, albeit tied to Community law regulating large combustion plants. Comparisons though are difficult because carbon taxes are in many cases combined with general energy taxation.

Finland Finland in 1990 was the first of the group of countries listed above to introduce a carbon tax. The tax was a distinct carbon tax and was related to the carbon content of fuel. No concessions or exemptions in favour of energy-intensive operations were prescribed. Given the apparent merit of levying environmental taxes as close to the subject environmental impact as possible, the Finnish approach of taxing fuel inputs affecting electricity production according to carbon content of the fossil fuels appeared to be well founded. However, various problems not the least of which was incompatibility with Community law resulted in the Finnish government deciding to tax electricity directly. An additional problem referable to the modest level of the tax has been addressed by successive increases in the tax rate. Other changes have involved differentiation between the rate of tax payable as between domestic households and industry, for example. The distinctiveness of the Finnish carbon tax is such that evaluation of its impact is marginally easier compared with the taxes from other member states examined below. It has been claimed, for example, that in the absence of the tax, emissions would have been 7 per cent higher than the 57m tonnes recorded in 1998.[59] Arguably, but for differentiation and increases in the tax rate that figure would have been somewhat lower than 7 per cent.

The Netherlands Fuel charges have been in force in the Netherlands since the early 1980s but only in 1996 was there introduced the so-called 'regulatory energy tax'. The tax is structured in order to permit a measure of differentiation. One of the outstanding features of this differentiation is that large energy consumers are exempt from liability for the tax, together with certain other prescribed users. On the other hand, the horticulture industry pays a reduced tax rate. In industrial sectors like this, environmental agreements are a potentially important feature. However, although it may be premature to draw conclusions in respect of a tax that is of such recent creation, it has been suggested that agreements have exerted a positive influence on investment in cost-effective measures by industry. On the other hand what evidence there is seems to suggest that such investment has failed to offset a growth in carbon dioxide emissions which has occurred as a result of increases in production levels. A further suggestion is that environmental agreements here do not provide sufficient incentive for industry to utilise lower carbon material.[60] The tax is revenue neutral: domestic households receive income tax rebates while industrial companies receive rebates referable to lower labour costs.

Sweden The Swedish carbon tax was introduced in 1991 and covers oil, coal, natural gas, liquid petroleum gas and petrol. Two years later the tax rate for manufacturing industry and commercial agriculture was reduced to 25 per cent of the national rate. At this time the tax liability of domestic households was also increased. Sweden is one of the member states where it is difficult to identify the impact of the carbon tax, given that it takes its place in the general regime of energy taxes. The carbon tax has been raised quite substantially in recent years: in 1997 for example the rate was increased by 50 per cent of the level originally set for the tax. There is evidence that in 1994 emissions were 9 per cent lower than they would have been had the tax not been introduced.[61] It may also be speculated that the high level of the tax set will have tended to encourage companies to opt for fuels which avoid or minimise carbon dioxide emissions.

Denmark A carbon tax was introduced in Denmark in 1992 for domestic households and in 1993 for industry, based on the carbon content of fuels at the point of combustion. Rates of carbon tax were increased in 1995. However, lower tax rates apply to energy-intensive industries although liability was phased in over the years 1996 to 2000. A proportion of the tax is reimbursed to companies, subject though to certain exceptions. Subsidies and investment incentives are tied to the tax in order to promote investment in cost-effective measures to minimise or eliminate carbon dioxide emissions. There are certain exemptions from carbon tax liability. Carbon tax is imposed on electricity at the point of final consumption, again based on a calculation of the carbon content of the coal. Differentiation is a notable feature of the Danish carbon tax for the following reasons: the tax as it affects industry takes account of competitiveness; rates may vary according to industrial process; and rates may vary further where an environmental agreement exists. It has been reported that total carbon dioxide emissions by 1999 amounted to a 9 per cent reduction over a period of eleven years. It has also been suggested that the tax has been responsible for cost-effective innovation even beyond obligations in agreements that have been struck, and that investment has been rather more rapid than it would have been in the absence of the carbon tax.[62]

Evaluation The foregoing thumbnail survey shows the relative sophistication of the Danish carbon tax. Arguably though, the introduction of detailed exemptions, the conditions required for those exemptions, differing tax rates and the actions which may trigger advantageous rates introduce a large measure of complexity. However, running through all of the tax arrangements examined is the clear need for an effective rate of tax, tied where possible to positive environmental incentives through negotiated agreements. The opportunity to bolster available incentives may be important although it appears that reliance on subsidies as a means of compensating for a low level of tax is not necessarily indicative of efficiency. Furthermore, the whole process of differentiation and subsidies brings with it the need for a member state to consult the Commission to ensure that such measures are compatible with Community law. This and other related matters draw attention to Community policy on economic instruments, a subject that is taken up in the following section of the chapter.

Community Law and Policy on Economic Instruments

Already in this chapter, Community policy and its influence have been noticed. Bearing in mind the way in which Community law sets requirements and priorities and, as such, influences the evolving shape and pattern of economic instruments in member states, it is necessary at this point in the chapter to set out the essential nature of that law and policy. The critical point here is the extent to which, if at all, the design, implementation and enforcement of any member state economic instrument is contrary to Community law in particular. In the first instance this is a matter for the Commission although, as ever, the ultimate adjudication has to be that of the European Court of Justice. Typical of the emerging role of the Commission in this respect is the design of the United Kingdom's greenhouse programme, previously described in this chapter. The programme rests on three essential features: incentive payments amounting to £30m per annum, an 80 per cent discount in respect of the Climate Change Levy, and a 'grandfathering' allocation of emission allowances. Approval by the Commission here and in relation to other member states' economic instruments is referable to its Communication[63] as well as detailed consideration of the relevant Community law. Although the Communication relates to environmental taxes, it may be unwise to interpret that term too narrowly since what may appear to be a broad-based economic instrument is in fact an instrument which depends to a greater or lesser extent on an element of taxation. Unfortunately, there is a further complication. The Communication refers to taxes as they attach to products. This association of 'product' and 'environmental tax' is perhaps too artificial, even if it is the closest generically to the Community's preoccupation with trade and the internal market.[64] The foregoing Communication from the Commission is but one element of Community policy in the present context. In order to appreciate the true dynamics of Community policy on economic instruments as well as the prospects for its implementation, it is necessary to look at facilitative policy, Community strategies and the policy on Cohesion. 'Facilitative policy' is arguably a misnomer since (as will be seen) there are instances where Community law has intervened in order to guide and channel chosen policy priorities. This section of the chapter concludes with a reference to some of those areas of Community law which actively encourage member state initiative in the development, implementation and enforcement of economic instruments.

Facilitative Policy

The preferred policy dynamic in the Community is of course based on integration of economic and environmental policy through the different sectors such as agriculture, in pursuit of sustainable development. That dynamic is manifested through the activities of the Council and the Commission and, more particularly, the Economic and Finance Directorate-General and its related (ECOFIN) Council as well as through Community Cohesion Policy, which is examined below, following a section on Community Strategies. The dynamic just mentioned is tied to the Treaty which, in Article 98, stipulates that economic policy in member states shall be conducted with a view to contributing to Community objectives, one of which is sustainable development.

ECOFIN The ECOFIN Council carries this policy process forward through Policy Guidelines initiated by the Commission and which are used actively to promote sustainability through measures including economic instruments in member states. These Guidelines, and the other policy emphases to be mentioned below are particularly important in view of the limit on Community competence where environmental taxation is concerned.

The Treaty of Nice In the light of recent political failure to achieve qualified majority voting for the legislation of environmental taxation in the Community, the Treaty of Nice shows again that Community policy is severely compromised. That compromise is represented in the Nice Treaty by words which indicate that 'full use' should be made of Treaty mechanisms, including market-oriented incentives and instruments intended to promote sustainable development.

Limitations on Community legislative competence Very largely, the Community is left with the responsibility of ensuring that legal requirements at the centre are satisfied in relation to member state initiatives, and developing policy priorities and preferences, as it has done for example in its Green Paper on Emissions Trading.[65] The distinction between these examples of facilitative policies and the Community strategies, to be looked at next, is by no means plain. For example the Community, anticipating the next and sixth Environmental Action Programme refers to the preparation of a 'thematic strategy' on the sustainable use of pesticides, for example.[66] It may be assumed that such a strategy will be rather more prescriptive than a general policy. As such it has to be assumed that that prescription has clear limits, particularly in avoiding requirements which, in effect, amount to Community law with coercive impact on member states.

Community Strategies

Reference has been made earlier to the Community's quest for a strategy on sustainable development.[67] It has been recognised both within the Community and elsewhere that considerably more progress is required which may in part explain the increasing interest in thematic and other strategies. For example, the integrative process at the centre of the Community may now suggest a need for rather more sharp-edged strategies if sectoral boundaries are to be broken down. In its report on *EU Policy and the Environment: An Agenda for the Helsinki Summit*[68] the House of Commons Environmental Audit Committee observes that the Community's assessment of the fifth Environmental Action Programme

> ... acknowledge[s] that traditional environmental policy, which promotes better technology and stricter environmental controls, is insufficient in itself to reverse the negative effects of social and economic development and the resulting structural changes in society. It concludes that the main challenges are linked to

unsustainable patterns of consumption and production and that there is a need to change the way in which we define economic, social and environmental objectives so that they become complementary and jointly contribute to sustainability.[69]

In order to move policy implementation forward against what may be quite formidable obstacles both at the centre and in member states, it is at least arguable that resort to economic instruments is a necessity if the limitations of more traditional approaches are accepted. However, Commission efforts to develop 'strategies' may (again) be of limited impact without full legislative and constitutional competence. Community waste strategy, for example, may seek to 'promote' the use of economic instruments when in reality what exists is a rather pale facilitative policy which lacks the all-important force of law.

Cohesion and Related Policy

The Community's Cohesion Policy is certainly facilitative as a result of its concern to ensure that funding is available for the pursuit of policies on the environment. However, cohesion in the Community is carried forward both by law and policy. A Cohesion Fund was created under the terms of Regulation 1164/94[70] in order to facilitate projects undertaken in the four member states where *per capita* GNP is less than 90 per cent of the Community average. The projects for which financial support is available relate to environmental protection and transport infrastructure. Supplementary funding is also available to these and other member states, from Community Structural Funds. Immediate Community concerns here have related to the need to improve enforcement of environmental requirements in the application of financial assistance from the Cohesion Fund, and the need to ensure member state compliance with certain prescribed areas of Community environmental law (via 'cross-compliance) in the application of Structural Funds. By way of contrast, the Community has resorted to a statutory framework in legislating another regulation – Regulation 1973/92[71] – for the creation of 'LIFE': otherwise known as a financial instrument for the environment. The funding that LIFE provides is aimed at the development and implementation of Community policy on the environment. There are prescribed funding priorities which cover projects that seek to promote sustainability, for example. As such, LIFE appears to provide a rather better developed opportunity to promote the use of economic instruments than the foregoing Structural and Cohesion funding. The subject of Community Structural funds will be returned to, later in the chapter.

Community Law Promotion of Economic Instruments

It has been stressed already that the way in which economic instruments are developed, implemented and enforced in the Community among member states is a clear manifestation of subsidiarity. Whether it can be claimed that this is a positive policy preference on the part of the Community is at least doubtful. More likely is the conclusion that member states have, individually, recognised the merit of such instruments and the need for environmental regulation to evolve and broaden. That member state initiative has been seen to thrive in recent years is probably down to the ongoing limitation of Community legislative competence in relation to environmental taxes. Arguably, the residual functions of the Community in relation to ensuring compliance with the law here provides an important synergy, contrasting with areas of discretionary initiative by member states. As such, in the evolution of Community law and policy on the environment, this builds on member state responsibility for transposition of the many directives which have generated Community law and policy over the years. Accordingly, there is a convergence between member state initiative on economic instruments justified by municipal law, and the promotion of these instruments from the centre via particular directives.

An early example of an economic instrument is found in Directive 75/439[72] on the disposal of waste oil. The Directive provides recognition of facilities for the collection, treatment and disposal of waste oil, as well as imposing obligations related to these functions. However, taking account of the nature of these functions and the attendant risks, the legislation permits indemnities to be granted to those involved in these activities. The financing of such indemnities may be achieved through a charge levied on waste oil covered by the Directive, indicating also the close relationship between this regime and the 'polluter pays' principle. As ever, though, Community law is alive to the trade implications of environmental law and policy. Accordingly, under this Directive it is prescribed very clearly that there should be no distortion of competition as a result of a scheme governing these indemnities.

Directive 94/62[73] – the Packaging Directive – is a very clear example of Community encouragement of member state initiative in relation to economic instruments. In what is a very pragmatic provision, the Directive indicates that where the Community omits to adopt economic instruments, a member state can so act, in order to realise the legislative objectives. Once again, the 'polluter pays' principle is one of the primary justifications for this Community preference.

The 'polluter pays' principle is also very much in evidence in the Landfill Directive – Directive 99/31[74] – where the recitals refer also to the need to ensure that the price charged for landfill use accurately reflects the true lifetime cost of its operation. Essentially, the objective of Community law here is that those who operate landfills should cover all costs associated with the setting up and operation of the site, including aftercare, site closure costs and financial security to meet environmental obligations for up to 50 years. Whether such provision represents an effective internalisation of environmental costs may well be open to debate. However, as a matter of principle this element of regulatory control is important in attempting to recognise sustainability in the environment.

Valuing and Costing the Environment

One of the critical starting points in the design and implementation of any economic instrument which is referable to its essential market environment is an effective valuation of the environmental externalities which may be internalised in the costs of the operation subject to regulation or other control. The design of any such instrument in the policy formation process and beyond will be driven by the 'polluter pays' principle in particular, as well as the need to address what is usually perceived as a market failure. Overall this process is central also to the development of policies for sustainable development in the environment. However, there is undoubtedly a considerable gap between this simplified view of costing and valuing the environment, and the reality. This section of the chapter looks at some of the important issues which show how difficult it might be to close that gap in practice.

Externalities and Market Distortion

One of the prime reasons for resorting to economic instruments such as environmental taxes is to realise a policy priority which seeks to reflect the value of externalities in the price of goods or services rendered. In other words such a policy priority will seek to reflect principles such as the 'polluter pays' principle which is the antithesis of circumstances in which the environment is otherwise seen to subsidise those goods or services. Subject to the potential difficulty of defining *who* the polluter is, it is that polluter who will be legally accountable if the policy priority is translated into legislation or the court finds that liability can be imposed beyond statute, as at common law for example. Whatever the basis of such liability, there will be a rebuttable presumption in favour of that liability being passed on to the polluter's customers, for example. If the chain is not to stretch that far, it will be necessary to find either in statute or in the court's definition of legal principle, some justification for a limitation of the internalised costs to the polluter.

Valuing the externalities Market distortion is said to occur where externalities are not maximised in the price of goods or services. If this is the case the above assumption occurs, that the environment effectively subsidises the industrial or related activity. In many cases very explicit subsidies are paid: the possible implications of their removal are addressed below.

It has been seen above that where the Landfill Directive is concerned, there is real doubt whether all the costs – externalities – associated with the operation and ultimate closure of a landfill are encompassed in the regulatory requirements placed on the operator, whose task it is to provide appropriate financial security against some of the contingencies. This case emphasises three fundamental difficulties in valuing environmental externalities for policy and other purposes, many of which are now associated with the promotion and realisation of sustainable development.

The three difficulties are these. First, what *are* the externalities? Second, how can those externalities be valued? Third, what variables, such as discounts, might be applied and for what purpose? It is beyond the scope of this book to enter a detailed debate about these complicated questions. However, it can be said with some confidence that it can normally be assumed that externalities are approached conservatively. As the European Environment Agency has said:

> Estimating the economic value of externalities of economic sectors is not easy and is restricted to that part of the total that is quantifiable; it is usually an indicator of the boundary of costs that are not controversial.[75]

Furthermore,

> The 'ideal' environmental tax includes these external costs in prices ... so that both social and private costs are brought closer together. The more that prices allow the markets ... to work with full costing, the more efficiently they help to internalise these costs.[76]

Again, it is very easy in the present context to beg the question. Here for example, the obvious question is 'what is full costing'? It is easy, in theory, to see that some risks and impacts affecting the environment are uninsurable, in which case it makes (theoretical) sense to impose such costs on the operator of the industrial undertaking responsible. In practice, it can be assumed that, even for preventative purposes, full costs here are unlikely to be a policy priority for implementation by law.

Environmental costs and sustainability The foregoing view of the potential significance of fully costed externalities provides an important marker in making progress towards sustainable development. The question of sustainability will be addressed more directly, below. Ignoring for the moment the pressing question of how to value the environment, there is no doubt that as long as there is widespread ignorance of the need to put values on the environment and its many assets, apart from the need for a robust valuation process, the related costs will not be properly visible. As long as those costs are not properly visible, effective debate on the choices and decisions associated with sustainable development will not be possible.

Environmental quality targets Numerous examples of environmental quality targets have been seen in this and earlier chapters. The development of such targets has shown some of the elements characterising the evolution of environmental law and policy. The constraints on the setting of such targets have been noted also. Science has represented one constraint although it has been noted also that uncertainties here may be overcome through application of the precautionary principle. A rather greater challenge though is the impact of economic instruments as an increasingly important strand of policy on the environment. Such instruments are intimately linked with policy on sustainability and, to have credibility politically and otherwise, it is increasingly necessary to ensure that they are capable of closing the gap between an industrial operator's costs and environmental costs. The closing of that gap, and the resulting efficiencies in internalising costs are powerful engines of sustainable development. However, environmental targets will, increasingly, be driven by the need for a fully costed environment in order to realise the foregoing, sustainable efficiencies. The route to a fully or properly costed environment is undoubtedly fraught with difficulty and complication. One of the likely incidents is the removal of artificial subsidies.

Subsidy removal The fundamental policy appraisal here requires the identification of those subsidies which are probably responsible for the more significantly adverse impacts on the environment. Again there may well be very complicated variables at work here. For example, an adverse impact damaging an environmental asset will be difficult to value as long as there is no definable market against which damage to that asset can be objectively costed. Another example may occur where there is no regular pattern of impacts, which tend to be seasonal. If in pursuit of policies on sustainable development, a subsidy is removed consideration may well be given to costs which accrue by virtue of the need to compensate those losing the financial or other associated benefits. If such compensation is to be paid, there may be an important argument in favour of avoiding unsustainable strategies which might otherwise see the compensation qualification as the perpetuation of the unsustainable subsidy. Far more satisfactorily perhaps is a compensatory measure that takes the form of an allowance which provides an environmentally-friendly incentive. Of course there is the possibility that subsidies are phased out and replaced by rather more sustainable measures which are maximised through a careful appreciation both of the adverse impacts and (perhaps more importantly) the points at which those impacts occur. All of these processes again make assumptions about valuation of the environment and its assets, as well as the points at which those assets may be adversely affected.

Basic valuation markers In certain instances the existence of a market framework will permit relatively straightforward valuation, as in the case of the valuation of stocks and shares in public limited companies which are quoted on a Stock Exchange. The environment though is rather different, given the absence of a market for most, if not all, environmental assets and features. How, for example, can a particular landscape be valued? The process of valuation here necessitates monetary values being imputed to such assets and features. Admittedly, in some cases that process may be easier than in others where (say) a fisherman is unable to land a catch for two weeks while the fishing ground is closed through an imminent threat of pollution by oil. In other cases it is necessary to ascertain markers or pointers which will suggest relative preferences, in the absence of any other more objective criteria. Where, for example, an area of landscape is damaged it may be possible to collate typical expenditure on restoration. However, the attribution of a value here will assume that the damaged landscape is one that has nature conservation merit for example, such that there is a desire to see restoration. Even here though there are potentially difficult variables. For example, there may be several different methods of securing restoration, in which the question is why one method may be more cost-effective than another, and why that method should be costed into the replacement equation. Indeed, there may be compelling arguments, objectively supported, in favour of something less than full restoration. Such arguments might typically rest on evidence of the ability of certain landscapes to satisfy original purposes, such as a mix of farming and nature conservation. This issue is one that is further complicated by questions of value which are influenced by the identity of the users of the environmental asset or feature where such users attribute their own value which, again, may legitimately feature in the valuation equation.

The Maastricht Treaty and economic variables The Treaty introduced what is now Article 174(3) of the Community Treaty. This provision, whose significance in the development of Community law and policy may be marginal, requires that potential benefits and charges are taken account of by Community policy. What this amounts to is a requirement that costs and benefits are regarded in the development of Community policy on the environment. Again, this formula finds itself pitched against the formidable question of how environmental benefit, for example, is measured and valued. Beyond the specific terms of the Treaty it has been seen earlier, in Chapter Four,[77] that the European Court of Justice has taken a very distinct view of the status of economic considerations as they affect the implementation and enforcement of Community law on nature conservation.

Environment Agency functions In Chapter One it was seen that section 39 of the Environment Act 1995 requires the Agency to ensure that decision-making in pursuit of its functions takes account of costs and benefits according to whether or not its statutory powers are exercised. It was seen also that this duty will not apply if it is considered unreasonable to enter into the calculation necessary by reference to the nature or purpose of the power in question, or the circumstances overall. Elsewhere in the Environment Act – in section 4 – it is stipulated that the Agency's principal aim is to discharge its functions so as to protect and enhance the environment, taken as a whole, so contributing to the objective of achieving sustainable development.

Sustainable Development

The Treaty of Amsterdam introduced sustainable development as an explicit objective of the Community. In addition, the Treaty underpinned and strengthened other environmental dimensions of the Treaty. However, where sustainable development is concerned, there is no doubt that, for the reasons advanced in the previous section of the chapter, the Amsterdam Treaty poses a very considerable challenge to the whole ethos of Community law and policy on the environment, its implementation and enforcement. The extent of that challenge, which should render economic instruments far more visible, is seen in the following observation from a report of the House of Commons Audit Committee on *Environmental Audit: The First Parliament:*[78]

> ... we regard the environment to be the weakest leg of the sustainable development tripod. The economic impacts of policy may transpire within months; social impacts more likely within years; but environmental effects may well not be manifested for generations.[79]

This though is not the only challenge. It has been stressed already that economic instruments are crucial to the realisation of progress towards sustainable development which in turn will depend on environmental policy integration. Community and member state targets and indicators on sustainable development will give substance to progress here, although the United Kingdom's strategy has been criticised for its failure to give much recognition to Community strategies.[80] It is to the United Kingdom that the chapter again turns next, to examine the development of economic instruments in the light of those instruments already covered in this chapter.

Economic Instruments and Sustainable Development in the United Kingdom

This penultimate section of the chapter is concerned with those elements of law and policy governing economic instruments in the United Kingdom that have not been covered already, and to outline the relationship between such instruments and sustainable development. Earlier in the present chapter it will be recalled that reference was made to existing and proposed economic instruments. To date the United Kingdom's approach to economic instruments is characterised by the Climate Change Levy, the related Emissions Trading Scheme, the Landfill tax and the Aggregates tax. Under active consideration, at the time of writing, are schemes for economic instruments affecting water abstraction, and a tradable permit scheme affecting waste management. Various other fiscal measures have come into force at the time of writing. These budgetary measures seek to apply tax and price discrimination in favour of low sulphur fuels for motor vehicles, to reduce excise licence duty for fuel-efficient cars, to tax company cars by reference to their carbon dioxide emissions, to increase Landfill tax, and to reduce rates of Value Added tax in respect of energy-saving material incorporated in buildings. The first part of this section looks at the status and operation of institutional structures concerned with sustainable development. The second part looks at two areas of waste management law and policy which depend on economic instruments as part of government's waste strategy and its sustainable development priority.

Institutional Structures

Institutional structures are an important starting point here, bearing in mind that economic instruments are increasingly a central element in the development of strategies for sustainable development. Indeed, as has already been suggested, the axis between economic instruments and sustainable development will lead inexorably to changing assumptions about the nature, scope and impact of environmental control. Those changing assumptions however do not include any assumption that traditional regulatory approaches will be abandoned. Whatever their long-term prospects, regulatory approaches to the environment are likely to be complemented by an array of increasingly effective economic instruments.

Sustainable development and economic instruments Sustainable development objectives and targets will no doubt be realised in large part through regulatory provision, supplemented by economic instruments. Essentially, an evolving approach to environmental control will focus increasingly on what may be seen to be more sophisticated methods based on both these elements. Targets and objectives can be seen to be 'hard' or 'soft' depending (respectively) on the question whether they are crystallised in law or are part of a national strategy, for example. Sustainable development strategy in the United Kingdom has been open to criticism through its perceived failure to reflect Community sustainable development strategies.[81] Such a failure compares though with the consequences of failure to transpose Community law. However, failure to reflect Community sustainable development strategies in a member state is not necessarily a serious omission, as long as there is correct and timely transposition of Community law. Otherwise, it is clear that Community environmental law and policy exercises a very strong influence on member state strategies and economic instruments. A potentially significant area of development both at the centre and in member states relates to the ongoing work relating to environmental pressure points and sustainable development indicators. Both strands are closely related and depend on economic instruments, in part at least, for the purpose of translation into the more sophisticated regime of environmental control just referred to. That regime will necessitate effective, continuing reliance on subsidiarity and the relative freedom of transposition that is available through the directive, both of which will also permit due regard to other important variables such as the time likely to be needed in a member state to realise effective control of adverse impacts on environmental pressure points. As has been stressed already, economic instruments complementing regulatory requirements and sustainable development will play an increasingly important role here. However, beyond the formal structures both at the centre of the Community and in member states for the purpose of ensuring compliance with the law, there is a necessity for structures ensuring that sustainable development strategies are achieved. That task is of course rather less precise that than associated with ensuring that there is compliance with the law. Given the importance of sustainability in the equation of environmental control the evolution and development of effective markers is ever more important if the satisfaction of targets and objectives is to be objectively verified.

Central and local government structures The nature of verification can by definition be a relatively imprecise process despite the production of key indicators. This imprecision is seen very clearly in the intergovernmental arrangements which extend from the operations of a Cabinet subcommittee, through a network of so-called 'Green' ministers, to a Sustainable Development Unit in the Department of the Environment. Further development occurred towards the end of 2000 when the government announced the creation of a Sustainable Development Commission, whose terms of reference are to advocate sustainable development across all sectors of the United Kingdom, to review progress towards it, and to build a consensus on those activities required if there is to be further progress. Where, for example, the Commission identifies what it believes to be unsustainable policy, its function will be to raise awareness of that policy and its application. A specific initiative affecting local government is the Local Government Act 2000, which was referred to in Chapter Two. The Act requires any local authority covered by the Act to prepare a so-called 'community strategy' for promoting or improving the economic, social and environmental well-being of their area and contributing to achievement in the United Kingdom. Bearing in mind local authorities' important functions and responsibilities in relation to the environment, in relation to waste management for example, this statutory framework provides a good example of the evolving controls referred to above.

The dynamics of sustainable development Both sustainable strategies and economic instruments are crucial elements in realising the quality of the means by which legally prescribed targets and objectives affecting the environment may be achieved. The Local Government Act 2000 and the community strategies provided for there should bring together an awareness of targets and objectives prescribed by the law as well as those manifested in complementary terms for the purpose of sustainable development. The targets and objectives may be prescribed by Community law, while a member state could consider it appropriate to utilise an economic instrument which may be subject to legal enforcement. How that economic instrument is utilised is largely up to the member state which, in many cases, may wish to encourage local authorities to pursue this strategy, tied to any appropriate sustainable development objectives. For example, Directive 91/157[82] seeks to minimise pollution of the environment by lead, mercury and cadmium through the regulation of used batteries. The reaction of the United Kingdom was the creation of a voluntary 'producer responsibility' scheme. Whether such a scheme which, surprisingly, appears to have avoided challenge by the Commission is truly efficient in sustainable development terms must be the subject of evaluation at the policy formation stage. One of the critical variables in such institutional evaluation is the role of any economic instrument.

Producer responsibility for batteries The United Kingdom government having chosen a voluntary response to Directive 91/157 has opted for an approach based on an economic instrument which begs the question whether matters of effectiveness are necessarily dependent on enforceability in law. The fundamental question which no doubt troubled the Commission, is whether purely voluntary measures are capable of securing member state compliance with the relevant Community law. It may of course be argued that the structure and operation of the voluntary scheme (particularly if there is existing experience of such a scheme) are such that there is confidence in this respect. There is also the possibility that Commission hesitation in respect of such a voluntary scheme is overcome by member state confidence about satisfaction of sustainable development targets for the recycling of batteries. This of course stresses the critical need for convergence between Community legal requirements and member state targets and objectives arising from sustainable development strategies. Despite member state assertions about the likely effectiveness of a voluntary scheme, it is not unreasonable to make comparisons with a scheme that lies within and is referable to the relevant framework of law, operates wholly or in part through one or more economic instruments, and is explicitly tied to the targets and objectives of a sustainable development strategy. There is a cogent argument that, tied to the force of law, a scheme is likely to be more effective. Clearly the law's assistance is required if the scheme involves the imposition of a charge. This is the case with Sweden's charge relating to lead batteries where the revenue is fed into a system for the collection and disposal of spent batteries. Arguably, such a system is not economically feasible without financial underpinning. The scale of the charge (about 7 per cent of the retail price) is not a deterrent to the market and collection targets in recent years of 95 per cent have been met or exceeded.

Sustainable Waste Management

Two notable areas of law and policy here are reliance on so-called 'recycling credits' and (in relation to packaging waste), the 'producer responsibility' scheme. Recycling credits are governed by section 52 of the Environmental Protection Act 1990 in relation to the overall process of waste management. The producer responsibility scheme for packaging waste operates under regulations made through powers in the Environment Act 1995 but referable to the terms of Directive 94/62[83] on packaging waste.

Recycling credits These credits are intended to make available to recyclers the savings in disposal and collection costs which result from the recycling of household waste. Because generally there is no direct charge for the collection or disposal of such waste there had previously been no proper financial incentive to avoid costs associated with collection and disposal in favour of recycling. It is the recycling credit that provides the missing incentive. The nature of the transactions involved necessitate statutory support for the scheme. Accordingly, the subordinate legislation is subject to fairly regular amendment in order to adjust the amount of credit paid by local authorities to recyclers.

Producer responsibility for packaging waste Community law relating to packaging waste is concerned with effective, efficient packaging recovery. In part this is achieved in the United Kingdom through so-called 'packaging recovery notes' (PRNs). Revenue from the sale of PRNs is intended to be invested in new waste collection, sorting and reprocessing capacity for the purpose of fulfilling the United Kingdom's targets against Directive 94/62. PRNs are tradable certificates whose price is determined by the market in a voluntary scheme which enables participating companies to establish that they have facilitated packaging recovery. Each certificate (PRN) confirms that a prescribed amount of packaging waste has been reprocessed. The scheme is based on the assumption that each participant will purchase sufficient PRNs to meet annual recovery obligations.

Economic Instruments in the United States

The highest profile economic instrument in the United States is that which relates to emissions trading, which was described earlier in this chapter. Beyond this economic instrument the experience of environmental taxation is generally limited with any new developments and initiatives being spread between the federal and state government levels. Indeed, it cannot always be assumed that instruments introduced in the United States are designed and implemented with environmental priorities specifically in mind. Before other approaches to economic instruments are examined both at federal and state level, further consideration of tradable permits is necessary.

Tradable Permits

There are two main issues to be dealt with here. In the first place rather more background has to be added to the previous treatment of emissions trading. Thereafter the wider use of tradable permits will be considered.

Tradable permits and the Clean Air Act 1990   The federal Clean Air Act is concerned essentially in the present context with reductions in sulphur dioxide as a means of dealing with environmental acidification. Emission allowances provided for by the Act (which has been progressively amended since 1990) entitle those holding such allowances to emit one tonne of sulphur dioxide for each allowance issued by the Environmental Protection Agency. Fulfilment of that allowance means that it is exhausted and is cancelled. On the other hand, if any such allowance is not utilised it can be put into abeyance and used in the next year, sold on or transferred within a corporate group or even used for the construction of new and modification of existing plant. Of course there may be a state of affairs in which a particular operation exceeds an allowance, in which case it will be necessary to obtain additional allowances through sale or transfer.

Failure to comply with the statutory requirements here is potentially very serious given the enforcement possibilities whereby considerable fines may be levied in respect of what the Act defines as a felony rather than the less serious misdemeanour. As well as resort to criminal sanctions, the Environmental Protection Agency may issue civil proceedings against the operator responsible, seek injunctive proceedings or attempt to impose an administrative order which is enforceable with a large daily fine. Furthermore, an infraction may render the operator responsible liable to the withdrawal of allowances in the following year. Citizen suits are also provided for by the Clean Air Act, permitting actions for failure to enforce the law against federal and state functionaries, as well as operators alleged to be in breach of statutory requirements.

Clearly, the regulatory backbone of the Clean Air Act is supported by strong enforcement facilities. However, before the system of tradable permits can operate, the allowances are issued following a competitive auction. Most of the successful bids were from electricity generators although, as with the emerging ETS scheme in the United Kingdom, it is possible for campaigning organisations (for example) to purchase through a successful bid in order to cancel any allowances so obtained. Initially the arrangements under the Clean Air Act were characterised as involving only modest trades in the allowances issued, and relatively low prices for those allowances that were traded. Interestingly, many operators appeared to avoid the external market in favour of probably modest 'offset' through transfers within a corporate group, the installation of cost-effective technology to minimise atmospheric emissions, or the saving of allowances against the future reductions in the quantity of allowances in circulation.

Despite the practical limitations of this tradable permit regime under the Clean Air Act, emissions are said to have reduced quite significantly, by as much as 50 per cent when set against levels in 1980. However, the administrative burden of the accompanying regulatory framework is considerable. Implementation plans at state level can be complex, leading to uncertainty about the precise requirements to be applied. Trading arrangements can also be complex although it has been seen above that this may not be the only reason for evidence of reluctance to trade, through the 1990s, at least.

Other applications of tradable permits Various other applications of tradable permits occur in the United States. Some of the more significant examples are set out in this section. In the case of ozone-depleting chemicals, the requirements of the Montreal Protocol are manifested in arrangements whereby production rights have been allocated to existing producers by reference to production levels recorded in 1986. Among a number of complex regulatory requirements, including limited production increases for closely prescribed purposes, designated producers are permitted to transfer their production rights to other producers in signatory states. The Oxygenated Gasoline Program provides for credits. These credits can be earned by refiners and other process participants as a result of the introduction of additional oxygen to their respective products. At state level a fledgling scheme for water pollution rights has been open to trial for some years in certain states, such as Wisconsin. Discharge permits are issued to industries by reference to fractions of the assimilative capacity of the waterway in question and on the basis of reductions in excess of levels required by treatment technology norms.

Environmental Taxes

The federal ozone-depleting chemical tax is again related to obligations under the Montreal Protocol and operates as an excise tax against prescribed quantities of subject chemicals. Certain states apply a so-called 'severance' tax on mineral extraction. This tax may have an influence on decision-making about strategies for extraction although matters of timing may be influenced rather more by local property taxes which may operate by reference to the value of minerals as yet not exploited. A final example is the federal 'feedstock' tax which applies to inputs in the petroleum and chemical industries, but which is not is not ostensibly an environmental tax, rather a method of funding the 'Superfund' programme relating to the remediation of contaminated sites.

Notes

1   OECD (1994), *Managing the Environment: The Role of Economic Instruments*, p. 114.
2   *Ibid.*, p. 115.
3   OECD (1997), *Reforming Environmental Regulation in OECD Countries*, pp. 10–11.
4   *Ibid.*
5   OECD (1989), *Economic Instruments for Environmental Protection*, p. 120.
6   *Ibid.*, at pp. 15–16. *Cf.* n. 1, at pp. 17–21.
7   Hawke, N. (1997), 'Toxic Torts and Regulatory Standards in the Law of the United Kingdom and the European Union', 10 *Tulane Environmental Law Journal*, No. 2.
8   OECD (1998), *Improving the Environment through reducing Subsidies*, 'Part I: Summary and Policy Conclusions', at pp. 7–8.
9   *Ibid.*
10   Department of the Environment and Environmental Resources Ltd (1990), *Market Mechanisms: Charging and Subsidies*, at p. 59.
11   *Ibid.*
12   *Supra*, n. 1, at p. 69.
13   *Supra*, n. 10, at p. 54.

14   11654/99, Council Press Release 299, 2207th Council meeting: Environment, 12 October 1999, para. 12.
15   Cm 4345, (1999), The Stationery Office, London.
16   Luxembourg, 1997.
17   Luxembourg, 2001.
18   *Ibid.*, pp. 40–41.
19   OECD (1997), *Environmental Indicators for Agriculture*, pp. 27–9.
20   *Supra*, n. 16, at p. 87.
21   *Supra*, n. 17, at p. 40.
22   Ministry of Agriculture, February 2000.
23   European Environment Agency (2000), *Environmental Taxes: Recent Developments in Tools for Integration*, Environmental Issues Series, No. 18, Luxembourg.
24   *Ibid.*, p. 41.
25   *Supra*, n. 23 at pp. 48 and 74.
26   *Supra*, n. 23 at p. 74.
27   *Supra*, n. 23, at p. 44.
28   OECD (1993), at p. 26.
29   Chapter One, nn. 23–4.
30   Chapter Two, nn. 36–40.
31   COM (97) 9, OJ C224, 23.7.96.
32   OJ L316, 31.10.92.
33   *Supra*, n. 23, at p. 8.
34   *Supra*, n. 23 at p. 10.
35   OECD (1997), *Environmental Taxes and Green Tax Reform*, p. 7.
36   *Ibid.*, p. 8.
37   *Supra*, n. 23, at p. 8.
38   *Supra*, n. 23, at p. 15.
39   OJ L182, 16.7.99.
40   European Foundation for the Improvement of Living and Working Conditions (1998), *Employment and Sustainability: The U.K. Landfill Tax*, Luxembourg.
41   OECD (1994), *Environment and Taxation: The Cases of the Netherlands, Sweden and the United States*, p. 74.
42   *Supra*, n. 23, at p. 74.
43   European Environment Agency (1996), *Environmental Taxes: Implementation and Environmental Effectiveness*, Copenhagen, pp. 56–7.
44   Cm 1966 (1992), The Stationery Office, London.
45   OJ L257, 10.10.96.
46   Department of the Environment, April 2000.
47   *Supra*, n. 39.
48   Cm 4693, May 2000.
49   *Supra*, n. 1, at p. 103.
50   Environmental Protection Act 1990, s.153(4).
51   Interpretation Act 1978, s.5 and Sched. 1.
52   COM (2000) 87.
53   5th Report (Session 1999–2000).
54   *Ibid.*, para. 65.
55   *Supra*, n. 53, at para. 66.

56 HM Treasury (1997), 2 July.
57 Quoted by the House of Commons Environment Committee: *supra*, n. 53, at para. 63.
58 ENDS Report 312, pp. 33–4.
59 *Supra*, n. 23, at p. 65.
60 *Supra*, n. 23, at pp. 68–9.
61 *Supra*, n. 23, at p. 72.
62 *Supra*, n. 23, at pp. 60–61.
63 *Supra*, n. 31.
64 *Supra*, n. 23, at pp. 54–5.
65 *Supra*, n. 52.
66 ENDS Report 313, p. 48.
67 *Supra*, n. 14.
68 1st Report (Session 1999–2000).
69 *Ibid.*, at p. xx.
70 OJ L139, 25.5.94.
71 OJ L206, 22.7.92.
72 OJ L194, 25.7.75.
73 OJ L365, 31.12.94.
74 *Supra*, n. 39.
75 *Supra*, n. 23, p. 13.
76 *Supra*, n. 23, p. 14.
77 Chapter Four, nn. 86–90.
78 1st Report, Session 2000–2001.
79 *Ibid.*, para. 13.
80 *Supra*, n. 68, para. 48.
81 *Ibid.*
82 OJ L78, 26.3.91.
83 *Supra*, n. 73.

Chapter Seven

Modes of Environmental Control

Regulatory Control in Perspective

Previous chapters have shown that regulatory controls – often referred to as 'traditional' regulatory controls – represent the essential foundation of environmental control. However, Chapter Six showed that economic instruments demand increasing amounts of attention, usually because of their merit as complementary devices in support of regulatory techniques. The present chapter seeks to bring these two major forms of environmental control together, to see their relationship in rather more detail. At the same time, the opportunity is taken to look also at other devices deployed in aid of environmental control, such as self-regulation and voluntary, negotiated agreements. Having examined the range of controls available in the environment, the status and influence of Community law and policy is addressed. Thereafter the centre of the chapter is dominated by two themes relating to regulatory controls. In the first place consideration is given to the ways in which regulatory techniques have undergone adaptation in order to deal with increasingly sophisticated challenges. Secondly, attention is given to the trends which are evident in the light of some of these foregoing developments. The chapter ends with a consideration of voluntary, negotiated agreements and their essentially complementary role in environmental control.

The Range of Controls

The Nature of 'Control'

It may be tempting to see a reference to 'control' as indicative of an assumption of 'command and control' regulation. For present purposes it is necessary to see 'control' in wider terms, as that process through which environmental quality can be maintained and even enhanced through shades of intervention backed by law, duly implemented and enforced. Those 'shades of intervention' show that, increasingly, the Community and its member states have at their disposal techniques which may not necessarily be coercive in nature. To that extent, it may be said that attitudes to responsibility and accountability are capable of being translated through 'softer' law which may be manifested through a consensual private law of contract, for example. This may not necessarily suggest a total absence of coercion since there may be regimes in which advantages may accrue (as was seen in the previous chapter) where there is a willingness to contract. To that extent it cannot be said that the resulting transaction is truly voluntary. Nevertheless, this important example may be seen to be part of a larger picture in which hard law characterising (say) a regulatory regime or an environmental tax regime may be aimed, as a policy priority, at encouraging soft law responses which accord more directly with the polluter's (or the potential polluter's) own sense of responsibility and accountability. The success of such an approach in changing their priorities may be seen to be an important confirmation of achievement here. This matter of polluter priorities is of considerable moment when it is borne in mind that it is corporate activity which generates, or might generate, a good deal of the environmental damage adverted to here.

The Problem of Corporate Priorities

Since most of the jurisdictions referred to in this book operate in a culture of law where the company is owned by its shareholders and managed for the maximisation of their investment by the directors, it can be appreciated that, in theory at least, fulfilment of corporate objectives may be seen to marginalise priorities for the benefit of the environment in which the company operates.[1] Clearly, though, each such company is actually or potentially open to influence through the law or by virtue of other devices and techniques. Larger corporations may be amenable to shareholder and public pressure. Here, regulatory action is more easily deployed whereas in the case of other, smaller businesses, which may or may not be incorporated, their dissipation and relative lack of visibility make for all sorts of practical difficulties.

Practical Thresholds and Regulatory Adaptation

It is here that below a certain threshold, economic instruments may be deployed with success in ways that are denied to traditional regulation. This has been seen very plainly in previous chapters where reference has been made to the options available in order to implement and enforce Community law relating to the emission of volatile organic compounds, particularly in the case of large numbers of small businesses in the printing industry. This example is perhaps useful also for the purpose of showing how the regulatory pyramid is open to adaptation and change, both in relation to its own styles and emphases as well as in accommodating complementary devices for environmental control. For example, a legal framework may well be grafted in order to facilitate self-regulation through the encouragement of environmental management schemes. Whether those responsible for policy creation at the centre of the Community have always seen direct regulation of activity affecting the environment as being susceptible to adaptation and change is not beyond doubt. The reason for such doubt is the 5th Environment Action Programme which was discussed in Chapter One.[2]

Alternatives to Direct Regulation

The 5th Environmental Action Programme looked to a wider constituency of controls over activity adversely affecting the environment. Clearly driven by policy priorities in relation to sustainable development, this Action Programme raised awareness of alternative devices and techniques which might exert a rather more subtle influence on activity, particularly by polluters and would-be polluters, damaging or potentially damaging to the environment. As such, regulation is viewed as but one such device for environmental control. Other devices and techniques for environmental control have tended to be characterised as 'bottom-up' approaches, as explained towards the beginning of Chapter One. By way of a stark contrast, direct regulation has been characterised as a rigid 'top-down' approach. As such the general view of such regulation appears to have been one in which standard prescriptions backed by sufficiently robust enforcement requirements govern matters of efficiency and effectiveness in implementation. The result of policy development and refinement of statute design subsequently has seen an interesting mixing of regulatory and non-regulatory approaches which appears to confirm the central status of regulatory techniques, albeit refined by other approaches such as economic instruments. This development has been driven by numerous factors, not least of which are more sophisticated perceptions of environmental needs and priorities, the cultural variables affecting member state approaches to transposition, and the constitutional relationship between the Community and its member states. The increasing importance of non-regulatory approaches brings with it potential problems where relatively sophisticated devices and instruments are prescribed in detail by the centre, leaving member states little discretion for the purpose of their own cultural transposition, implementation and enforcement. It was seen in Chapter Six that this has not happened in relation to the economic instrument of environmental taxation where the Community remains largely paralysed, except in ensuring that member state taxes are consistent with rules governing the internal market, for example. Direct regulation and economic instruments are compared later in this section of the chapter.

The Advantages and Characteristics of Direct Regulation

It has been observed that the justification for direct regulation in the arena of the environment

> ... lies in market failures causing environmental externalities which are only automatically internalised in decision-making in perfectly competitive markets ... Therefore, the objective of environmental regulation is to change market behaviour in ways which are more closely consistent with behaviour when externalities are internalised, using methods which are feasible and cost-effective and which have acceptable distributional effects. However, this objective is often imperfectly achieved – in other words, regulatory failure occurs.[3]

Of course, such regulatory failure may occur on those occasions when policy priorities crystallised in the relevant legislation are simply too ambitious. It is clear, for example, that any attempt to seek compliance with air quality standards through legal sanctions against a company is doomed to failure both by virtue of the impossibility of enforcement and the constitutional limits of Community law. On the other hand, policy priorities have been pitched towards member state obligations in respect of air quality. Beyond member state duties in Community law in relation to air quality there are additional constraints in respect of ozone. Again the Community was aware of the fact that legislation here would bring the law – and the Community – into disrepute if attempts were made to impose limit values here since there would have been frequent failures to comply. Practical regulation therefore determined the need for a rather more cautious approach, which occurs in Directive 92/72.[4] This Directive omits to prescribe limit values for ozone, preferring instead to require the establishment of monitoring facilities from which data is distributed throughout the Community by the Commission.

Direct regulation and standardisation Policy priorities may point to the need for some certainty in the reduction of polluting emissions or discharges within a specifically defined period. A standardised response traditionally has been to impose a regulatory regime on the subject, polluting activity. That regime can be seen to have a standardised impact on member states, based usually on a model which borrows from the experience of one or more of those member states. The added merit of this model is that it has clearly defined structures which normally permit a clear view of compliance, as well as enforcement strategies. Arguably, that element of transparency in a regulatory regime is a matter of importance in allowing the public at large to see that those responsible for infractions are properly accountable and therefore subject to the law. However, it is arguable that direct regulation suffers from two constraints, one of which is peculiar to the Community, where directives require transposition by member states. Before looking at this matter, the first constraint is seen in the fact that direct regulation is information-intensive. In other words, effective direct regulation demands accurate, timely information for the purpose of ensuring compliance and, in the absence of such compliance, enforcement. However, there is a danger here in assuming that economic instruments are not information-intensive, which is not necessarily the case where (for example) the need for effective enforcement machinery is concerned. Information-intensiveness begs questions about the costs involved and who is to bear them, a matter addressed in the previous chapter where cost-recovery charging was discussed, as well as the extent to which those subject to regulation might take responsibility for monitoring and data collection and reporting. A second constraint is that legislation from the centre has a tendency to standardisation. This is undoubtedly the case where Community directives are concerned although it is difficult to generalise about the extent to which the peculiarities of member states, their regions and localities where implementation and enforcement is to occur, are catered for here. This matter has been addressed in previous chapters where the question of member state discretion in transposition, implementation and enforcement has been illustrated. The tendency to standardisation raises another question, about the nature and enforceability of the values and standards prescribed by environmental legislation.

The nature and enforceability of values and standards Although it is arguable that insufficient attention has been given to the peculiarities of member state regions and localities in Community environmental legislation the same criticism is not necessarily valid in relation to the legislative prescription of robust values and standards. A detailed treatment of these matters was provided in Chapters Two and Three. However, any serious shortcoming in this respect would put in doubt the enforceability of regulatory requirements. The fact remains, though, that robust requirements here depend both on the terms of Community legislation as well as member state transposition. For example, it is a matter for member state discretion whether enforcement is by means of criminal or civil law. It is here that member state compliance with Community law is critical in translating values and standards as they emerge from policy priorities affecting emissions, discharges or products. If for example, member state preference is in favour of enforcement through the criminal law in respect of values and standards for these purposes, there is a fundamental requirement that they are capable of effective enforcement against an individual or corporation. In the United Kingdom, a not unusual presumption is in favour of strict liability where causation will have to be established, but no evidence of the defendant's intention, recklessness or negligence. If this is the chosen approach the preferred offence is likely to be one of 'causing'. However, in practice, a favoured approach is one where an alternative offence of 'knowingly permitting' is added to the statutory formulation. If this is the case the burden of proof returns to the prosecution. This though is not to suggest that these are the only approaches: the foregoing options tend to represent a wide approach where the impact of enforcement may extend beyond Community values and standards, at least where strict liability is concerned. Specifically designed offences may be rather less complex where such values and standards are in issue: for example an offence comprising failure to comply with regulatory requirements in a licence, permit or other authorisation.

Direct Regulation and Economic Instruments Compared

Direct regulation has the distinct advantage of relative certainty, predictability and control. Where policy priorities are in favour of the need to reduce or minimise adverse environmental impacts, a standardised regulatory approach tends to bring the foregoing advantages where economic instruments such as environmental taxation are affected by variables which put those advantages in doubt. For example, how can there be certainty that a prescribed tax rate will have the desired effect if (say) there is no close organisational relationship between corporate financial and technical operations? If there is no straightforward method of applying a variable tax rate beyond a conventional linear tax arrangement, how might the differing conditions and characteristics of would-be polluters be allowed for? Where market-based economic instruments are in place what, if any, control can be exerted by the would-be regulator? For what purpose might such control be necessary here? These are but four questions which arise in any comparison for present purposes.

The case of pesticides A useful example here concerns the control of pesticides where it has been observed in a report from the OECD that most policies in its member countries involve intensive testing for registration, supported by regulatory limits on use, and residues.[5] It is pointed out[6] that regulatory instruments have, in most cases, been successful at preventing major disasters. However, registration is seen as involving substantial costs for the introduction of new and potentially less harmful products. Quantitative limits do not provide incentives for structural decrease in the use or adoption of alternative control methods. While economic and financial instruments are seen as being attractive in providing such incentives, practical difficulties are seen in the achievement of targets which are compatible with environmental and public health requirements. Finally, OECD point to the fact that problems of control here are compounded by a large variation in local and regional conditions affecting pesticide use.[7]

Further comparison While direct regulation may secure the foregoing advantages, economic instruments tend to bring efficiencies in relation to the information requirements which underpin regulation. It is through market-based mechanisms that polluters or would-be polluters manage their own information (say) for the purpose of determining the optimum tax level at which environmental management equipment might be applied most effectively. This important effect stresses again the sensitivity of response compared with the standardised response to direct regulation where more efficient companies may well find that their costs are arbitrarily increased. This marginalisation of efficiency is further stressed by the tendency of direct regulation to prescribe compliance with minimum requirements only. Indeed, unless this limited regulatory approach is avoided, those subject to regulation will be in a position to avoid any incentive for continuing improvement in environmental management. There are ways round this limitation: for example, there may be a continuing duty to secure application of 'best available techniques'. Whether or not this limitation is addressed through Community law, or the municipal law of a member state, there may be a continuing suspicion that those subject to regulation are able to secure so-called 'regulatory capture', where the regulator and the regulated are seen as being rather too close in their working relationship, a problem that will not be manifested where economic instruments are concerned. However, given the likely complementary role of economic instruments where direct regulation is concerned, it seems unlikely that 'regulatory capture' can ever be ignored, assuming of course that the close working relationship just referred to is necessarily a problem. This matter of 'regulatory capture' is one that has exercised those who observed the style and emphasis of environmental control in the United Kingdom prior to accession to membership of the Community. This is a useful point at which to outline that style and emphasis.

Pre-accession Environmental Control in the United Kingdom

Environmental control prior to Community accession by the United Kingdom was characterised as a system dependent on consensual negotiation between regulator and regulated without reliance on prescribed values, standards and targets and often advised by Circulars issued by the responsible departments of government. Much of the system of environmental control was built on a need to comply with 'best practicable means' where relevant guidance notes had no legal status. 'Best practicable means' was an ill-defined standard, largely by virtue of a need to rationalise two major variables: first, the technical capacity of an operator to eliminate or minimise emissions or discharges as defined by information held by the operator, and second, the economic and financial capacity to achieve elimination or minimisation. These arrangements usually rendered the regulator dependent on data and information held by the operator and, in turn, led to frequent accusations of too close a relationship: 'regulatory capture'. Infractions were not often enforced by criminal prosecution since the standard itself was so difficult to define by a regulatory body that was usually short of personnel for enforcement purposes. Although accession to Community membership introduced a far more disciplined regime based on detailed prescription of values, standards and targets for environmental control, the need for site-specific regulation for the purpose of integrated pollution control and, more recently, integrated pollution prevention and control, has once again raised suspicions of 'regulatory capture'. However, there is a cogent argument in favour of the proposition that environmental control techniques are developing in a rather more sophisticated manner, towards a more sustainable arrangement in which effective responsibility is ceded increasingly to the operator affected by a mix of regulatory control and economic instruments. Trends here are examined towards the end of this chapter.

Community Law and Policy Influences

It is not difficult to see how accession to Community membership resulted in a radical shift from what was, effectively, a voluntary regime of consensual agreement, to arrangements for environmental control founded on tightly prescribed values, standards and targets which, in turn, are usually transparent and assumed to be legally enforceable within the constitutional structure. The process of transposition in the United Kingdom, leading to implementation and enforcement, has resulted in another radical shift in the resultant style and emphasis of municipal environmental law. Given the common law traditions of the United Kingdom there seems little doubt that the consequences of accession were more far-reaching than they were in almost any other member state, with the possible exception of the Republic of Ireland. Beyond such structural impacts, accession to membership of the Community has shown that member states are often able to retain some cultural features of environmental control. Admittedly that has been less the case in relation to the United Kingdom, for the reasons just given. Nevertheless, legislation by directive has allowed in many cases an important cultural imprint while at the same time giving member states increasingly wider options in connection with implementation and enforcement. Various examples have been given already.

Cultural Features

Whether the cultural features in a member state are structural or substantive elements of environmental law, evolving Community law and policy on environmental control may see tensions developing in the process of transposition. Despite the advent of subsidiarity and the inherent characteristics of the directive, an increasing mix of regulatory and non-regulatory approaches may be seen to contribute to such tensions. In some cases, proceedings for noncompliance with Community law may be pursued by the Commission. To that extent it is arguably an exaggeration to suggest the appearance of such tensions amounts to a breakdown of law and policy on environmental control. Rather, the assumption is that member states and the Community continue to strive for harmonisation. To that extent there is a tendency towards dilution of certain cultural features in member states. However, the extent of post-accession movement in the approach to environmental control in the United Kingdom does raise a question about the status of so-called 'cultural' features in member states. Such features are undoubtedly subject to fast-moving developments in science, technology and economics as they affect perceptions of control techniques in relation to the environment. Nevertheless, there is undoubtedly a variable approach to the impact of evolving Community law and policy here. Some member states will be more resistant than others to the prospect of change and compromise in relation to cultural features affecting control of the environment. Nevertheless, the extent of that resistance will tend to reduce according to a number of well-recognised variables such as the existence of ambiguity in legislative drafting, the scale of application of subsidiarity, and the availability of options for transposition, implementation and enforcement.

Options for Transposition

The availability of options must be regarded as the most important facility for the purpose of maximising cultural features in environmental control. In addition to the examples referred to in earlier chapters and taken up again below, the following is also worthy of note.

The Sewage Sludge Directive Directive 86/278[8] on protection of the soil and the environment from the effects of sewage sludge application in agriculture deals with, *inter alia*, the need to ensure that sludge containing heavy metals is appropriately regulated according to two options available in member states. One of those options allows a member state to prescribe maximum limits in respect of the amount of sludge to be applied to defined areas, taking account of variable ranges for the subject heavy metals prescribed by the Directive. A second option refers to the maxima prescribed in the Directive for applications of heavy metals to defined areas. In earlier chapters reference was made to the Solvents Directive[9] but very little was said about matters of detailed implementation.

The Solvents Directive It was seen in Chapter One that Directive 99/13[10] provides for three methods of reducing solvent emissions, by means of (1) uniform emission limits; (2) schemes for solvent reduction; and (3) national plans. In the case of England and Wales regulatory control of many, if not all, of the subject processes has existed for some time, under the Environmental Protection Act 1990. To that extent, the impact of Directive 99/13 is necessarily limited. Nevertheless, it has been necessary to address the modes of control and regulation provided for by the Directive, as well as the transition to integrated pollution prevention and control (IPPC), bearing in mind that certain processes are subject to both regulatory regimes. These factors all contribute to a complex process of positioning environmental controls of solvents, despite the existence of a track record in this area in these jurisdictions. Despite the possibility of resorting to environmental taxation or a regime of tradable permits, the likelihood (at the time of writing) is that in England and Wales and, no doubt, in the remainder of the United Kingdom the preferred strategy will be direct regulation. Such a choice appears to be based on considerations of administrative cost as well as simplicity of application in view of the multiplicity of industries and companies undertaking the subject processes.

Where a process is subject to regulatory control already, the intention is to require the Environment Agency and local authorities responsible for regulation to impose the emission limits and controls prescribed by the Directive. This will be achieved through directions to the regulators under existing powers in section 7(3) of the Environmental Protection Act.

In the case of those processes subject to the Directive but not already regulated, wholly or in part, under municipal law, Community law appears to permit a measure of freedom in the style of implementation. The approach debated in England and Wales appears to involve a choice between full-blown regulatory authorisation, as opposed to what may be a simpler arrangement based on registration. The level of regulatory control probably depends on the amount of solvent utilised in a particular process. Registration can be described as a simpler arrangement by virtue of the application of so-called 'general binding rules' through which identical conditions can apply to similar installations. General binding rules will be discussed later in this chapter. However, resort to registration begs the question whether implementation and enforcement should be allied to 'best available techniques'. In other words, should any registered process be subject to IPPC standards under the Pollution Prevention and Control Act 1999? If that option is rejected, it remains open to those responsible for implementation to substitute a set of regulations under the European Communities Act 1972 where regulatory requirements might be otherwise defined. It seems clear from what has been said above, that there may well be an incentive built into any regulatory arrangement which is defined principally by the amount of the subject chemical used in the regulated process. The present example of the dynamic relationship between Community law and member state transposition of environmental controls throws up another dimension to this matter. That dimension relates again to the Solvents Directive, its inclusion (as one of the three foregoing options) of schemes for solvent reduction, and any previous regulatory culture in a member state now expected to implement and enforce this element of Community law.

Both under Part I of the Environmental Protection Act 1990 and the Pollution Prevention and Control Act 1999 dealing, respectively, with Integrated Pollution Control and Integrated Pollution Prevention and Control (IPPC) constituent regulations provide a formula indicating the method of calculating the amount of organic solvents used in a process. That formula is important in determining whether the threshold is crossed, exposing the process to regulatory requirements. If that threshold is not crossed the process will for this purpose fall outside regulatory control, otherwise referred to as a 'compliant coating': a reference to many of the relevant processes in the general area of coating processes and printing. The Solvents Directive makes no explicit reference to 'compliant coatings' although there are parallels with the Directive's option in favour of schemes for solvent reduction. There are reasons why marriage of the approach to 'compliant coatings' and Directive schemes for solvent reduction might be difficult, primarily because there is a statutory duty to account to the Commission in respect of equivalent emission reductions in relation to each installation where a subject process is to be found. Furthermore, there is an average implied by the Directive's solvent reduction scheme, which might not be met unless all subject processes can demonstrate solvent content below that level, which is unlikely in practice. Accordingly, this matter stands as an example of an occasion where cultural preferences in relation to environmental controls may be frustrated by an inability to fit previous practice into new Community directive requirements. Of course, the advent of new Community law may encourage a member state to reconsider regulatory and other environmental controls. This was the case in the United Kingdom when regulatory attitudes to the landfilling of waste had to be addressed when Community directives on Landfilling and IPPC came into force.

Regulatory attitudes to landfilling Although reference to the influence of Community directives on Landfilling and IPPC has featured in earlier chapters[11] it is necessary to provide a reminder of the extent to which Community law may provide room in which to allow a member state to undertake rationalisation of its range of environmental controls. This is nowhere better illustrated than in the present context where the United Kingdom government appears to be of the view that if landfill sites are subject to IPPC regulation, the end result will be better environmental regulation through greater clarity and consistency of approach. This view is expressed in the *Waste Strategy for England and Wales 2000*[12] along with the view that better integration of regulatory control will be allowed to the Environment Agency. Despite the merit of streamlining controls here, it appears that there are potential difficulties in the rationalisation proposed. For example, where a landfill operator has complied with statutory requirements under the Landfill Directive in connection with the control of leachate and methane gas is there justification for the regulator – the Environment Agency – to suggest that this removes any obligation on the operator to establish compliance with 'best available techniques', for the purpose of IPPC?

Aspects of Regulatory Control

Elsewhere in this chapter it has been stressed that traditional 'command and control' regulation remains an important and even an essential mode of environmental control. In addition to the recognition that economic instruments are complementary to regulatory control of the environment, there has to be an equally important recognition that regulatory techniques and devices are themselves capable of refinement and development. Already it has been seen, for example, that at member state level at least, incentive effects can be manifested through regulatory controls. Such effects appear to characterise what may be regarded as a growing sophistication of associated techniques and devices. Those regulatory techniques and devices may of course emerge from Community law itself, although it is probably more accurate to suggest that it is the cultural experiences of member states realised in the transposition of environmental directives which are rather more likely to be the vehicle for imaginative developments here. In turn of course it cannot be assumed that member state culture here is suitable for application in other member states. Nevertheless, to the extent that one particular culture is realised in transposition from a common root of Community law at least makes the prospect of application elsewhere in other member states an easier prospect than it might otherwise be. This section of the chapter takes up and examines seven issues: anticipatory regulation; variable regulation; the treatment of limits, standards and objectives; the control of diffuse sources of pollution; incentives in favour of regulatory control; triviality exemptions; and regulatory enforcement. Of these issues, arguably the most pressing concern relates to the perceived need to address pollution from diffuse sources, otherwise referred to as 'non-point source pollution' (NPSP). As well as being addressed later in this section of the chapter, NPSP will be dealt with in Chapter Eight where water quality and its protection from pollution are dealt with.

Anticipatory Regulation

This is an issue addressed previously, but worthy of repetition for present purposes. In the foregoing discussion of the options relating to implementation of the Solvents Directive in the United Kingdom, it was seen that controls have been in place for some time under the Environmental Protection Act 1990. Those controls have contributed greatly both to reductions of solvent emissions as well as hard experience of imposing regulatory controls in what is often characterised as a very diverse range of installations and processes.

In one sense however, previous experience of this sort may be counter-productive where a member state has a well entrenched infrastructure of environmental controls. The prospect of adaptation at transposition of new Community law may bring with it considerable difficulty. However, that difficulty may be minimised where policy creation at the centre of the Community takes considerable account of that member state experience, and control culture. This assumes though that lessons from what is described here as 'anticipatory regulation' have an impact on the making of policy and law at the centre of the Community. Where 'compliant coatings' and the Community's solvent reduction scheme under the Solvents Directive are concerned, it seems clear that constructive experience may be lost unless of course there is a later change in the relevant law, probably in the light of experience.

Variable Regulation

From the same source – the Solvents Directive – comes an illustration of 'variable' regulation, where member states, should they opt for this approach, will be able to account to the Commission by reference to the terms of a national plan, driven by different regulatory emphases among the target companies. Although lacking the standardised format of a rather more traditional regulatory framework, variable regulation offers a selective approach, reminiscent of a regime of tradable permits. Such a regime may indeed share some of the features of variable regulation, despite its overall character as a market-based instrument.

The Solvents Directive and sector selective approaches Returning to the Solvents Directive, variable regulation allows a selective approach by the regulator. That approach involves an appraisal of sectoral performance of installations subject to regulatory control. That appraisal may identify those installations with modest emissions in circumstances where it is determined not to be cost effective to require regulatory compliance. In order to balance the equation for the purpose of a national plan it will then be necessary for the regulator to turn to other parts of the sector in order to apply more stringent emission limits. Variable regulation is well characterised as a hybrid regulatory device. As such it has considerable limitations, not least of which is the cost of identifying and setting emission requirements to comply with a national plan under the Directive. In addition, industrial companies affected will undoubtedly consider variable regulation to be unfair and discriminatory. Indeed, the prospect of what appears to be a protective device for the benefit of less efficient installations will undoubtedly fuel feelings of discrimination here. This may not be the legislative intention behind Community law and policy but it may of course be clearly manifested at member state level through the style and emphasis of transposition and enforcement. There may of course be clear merit, politically and otherwise, in variable regulation being explicitly defined at the centre, through Community law and policy. This is the case in relation to Directive 91/271:[13] the Urban Waste Water Directive.

The Urban Waste Water Directive The essential approach of the Directive is to permit member states to designate so-called 'sensitive areas' which determines the need for a greater level of treatment compared with discharges to other waters.[14] Accordingly, where the Water Resources Act 1991 applies in the United Kingdom, variable regulation will characterise decisions by regulators on applications for licences to discharge effluent to controlled waters. The Act[15] stipulates the basis on which licensing decisions shall be made, including the need, as appropriate, to use conditions which are directed to matters of locality and standards of treatment prior to discharge.

The Treatment of Limits, Standards and Objectives

At the heart of regulatory control of the environment are the essential limits, standards and objectives which emerge from policy creation as priorities to be carried forward, usually with the force of law, through regulation or otherwise. Whether such limits, standards and objectives can be carried forward by economic instruments has been addressed already, in Chapter Six. The variety of control to be adopted will be determined by the nature of enforceability of these limits, standards and objectives. Objectives are a rather different species for present purposes since they provide the test of achievement arising from the implementation and enforcement of prescribed limits and standards. As such, objectives fall into two categories. The first of these categories sees an objective as a tightly defined regulatory limit while a second sees an objective as a broadly defined legislative or similar goal. In turn, reference to limits and standards tends to be the language of regulatory techniques and devices, where control is linked directly to what may be described as standardised coercion. By contrast, economic instruments are dependent on the coercive effect of the law only for the purpose of those failures which justify enforcement according to the statutory framework supporting such arrangements. Drawing a line in the design of such instruments between the culpable failure of the participating individual or company and a failure of the instrument in setting an insufficient level of tax, for example, may not always be easy in certain cases. Despite that inherent difficulty in the design process it is possible that regulatory control and economic instruments may share an interest in limits, standards and objectives as triggers or thresholds determining in particular matters of regulatory liability and what may be called 'incentive qualification' typifying the application of economic instruments in the environment. Nevertheless, in dealing with limits, standards and objectives in the remainder of this section of the chapter much of the emphasis will be on the regulatory parentage of these terms. There is however a need to be aware of two, interrelated points. In the first place, regulatory control and economic instruments are generally assumed to be complementary modes of environmental control. Second, that close relationship may in turn see an evolution where trends in the regulatory mode of control leads to further interstitial development of economic instruments. In terms of Community policy on the environment, such developments will depend very much on enlightened legislation from the centre taking account of member state experience and practice, an equally enlightened attitude to the application of subsidiarity and a continuing freedom for member states to develop accompanying law and policy on economic instruments and environmental taxes in particular. Against this background, this section of the chapter looks at three types of limit: absolute, percentile and average limits; common emission or discharge standards; quality objectives; and the development of alternatives to limits and objectives.

Limits The setting of limits from policy formation through to accompanying legislation is dependent on variables which will usually determine whether a limit is to be an absolute, average or percentile limit. Those variables are necessarily related to the incidence of adverse impacts of substances that are candidates for control. A particular substance whose environmental toxicity is established may be capable of serious impact on the environment and human health, in which case there is clearly a strong argument in favour of imposition of an absolute limit. On the other hand, a rather less toxic substance may be seen on evidence to have a variable presence in the environment, where high concentrations are countered by lower concentrations, suggesting perhaps that an average limit is appropriate. Finally, the presence of polluting substances in the environment may be seen to require a rather different approach to averaging, where high concentrations tend not to occur with any frequency but where there is justification for imposition of what is, in effect, a performance standard based on percentage compliance.

How do these approaches compare? There is little doubt that absolute limits compare well with average and percentile limits, for a number of reasons. In the first place, where absolute limits are prescribed by statute and are subject to strict liability enforced under the criminal law the enforcing regulator has little discretion but can apply relatively straightforward requirements where the only real challenge may be the need to adduce evidence of causation. Those straightforward requirements provide a clear trigger for what can be rapid enforcement action. However, considerable care is needed in setting absolute limits: for example it may simply not be practicable to expect compliance above certain levels given the state of knowledge, technology and likely associated costs. Nevertheless, there may be a strong policy preference in favour of absolute limits which seek to force technological improvement, for example. If this is the case, there may in turn be a policy priority in favour of providing grants or other support in order to encourage such improvement. Finally, percentile limits set at particular levels operate as performance standards. For example, a prescribed statutory requirement might be to the effect that a percentage (say 95 per cent) of samples taken should comply with a stated limit within the periods when they are taken. The outstanding advantage of this performance indicator is that it is particularly effective in identifying deteriorations in environmental media. The characteristics of these limits as outlined here cannot portray the use of limit values in Community legislation, where there are disparate approaches.

It was seen previously in this chapter[16] that the Sewage Sludge Directive provides a member state with two options in relation to applicable limit values. On the other hand, Community law has been criticised for its reliance on uniform limit values. This was the case with the Urban Waste Water Directive[17] where common standards are prescribed, despite varying local conditions, although there is recognition of the needs of 'sensitive areas' where more stringent treatment requirements apply. These common standards are in fact minimum standards affecting the collection, treatment and ultimate discharge of urban waste water. Although there is what appears to be a compelling argument in favour of limit values that might more sensitively reflect environmental quality objectives, a counter-argument is that uniform limit values avoid the complexities of what may be an enormous host of variables reflecting disparate environmental quality objectives. One final illustration of the deployment of limit values in Community legislation arises from Directive 76/464:[18] a Framework Directive. There are in the daughter directives certain common features, including features relating to limit values and their application. Taking Directive 84/156[19] on mercury discharges in certain industrial sectors as an illustration, limit values are dependent on defined sectors or processes set out in Annex I. Here the limit values (corresponding to a monthly average concentration or to a monthly maximum load) are set out in terms of quantities or concentrations. The former are subject to mandatory compliance. However, the latter should 'in principle ... not be exceeded'. Any such limit values normally apply at the point where waste waters containing the mercury leave the plant.[20]

Common emission or discharge standards Little more needs to be added to what has been said already about common standards. Reference has been made to the arguments, for and against, such an approach in the Urban Waste Water Directive[21] where the common standards are in fact minimum standards rather than maximum limit values. A cogent argument against such common minimum standards is the nature of much of the effluent discharged to the receiving waters. That effluent tends to be sewage effluent which normally has a high dispersal efficiency in receiving waters, pointing to the advantages of reliance on quality objectives.

Quality objectives The Water Framework Directive[22] provides two options for a member state seeking to regulate toxic substances such as mercury. On the one hand, it has been seen already that limit values may be applied. The alternative however, is the application of quality objectives through which a member state can implement and enforce specially tailored emission standards. Reference is made again to the regulation of mercury discharges governed by the daughter directive: Annex II to Directive 84/156[23] cross-refers to the quality objectives set out in Annex II to another directive on mercury discharges, Directive 82/176.[24] Among the quality objectives prescribed is one which refers to a maximum numerical concentration of mercury in a representative sample of fish flesh. It is open to a member state to determine the area affected by discharges affected by mercury concentrations and to select from among the quality objectives, of which that relating to concentrations in fish flesh is one, according to what is deemed appropriate in view of the intended use of the area, and the purpose of the Directive in seeking to avoid or eliminate all pollution.

The development of alternatives to limits and objectives The foregoing Directive 84/156 also provides an interesting contrast to the foregoing approach to regulation based on limit values and quality objectives. Article 3 of the

Directive stipulates that a member state is empowered to grant an authorisation in respect of a new plant only if there is application of standards corresponding to the 'best technical means available'. This term is not defined by the Directive: presumably its meaning will be determined by generally accepted industry-wide standards which are extant at the time. There are circumstances in which Community law here will allow an authorisation for new plant which does not comply with this standard, although Commission consent is required under the Directive.

The Control of Diffuse Sources of Pollution

Non-point, or diffuse, sources of pollution are necessarily more difficult to subject to regulatory control.[25] There is some recognition of this problem in Community law and policy: for example, Directive 84/156[26] on mercury discharges, described above. Article 4 of the Directive requires member states to draw up specific programmes addressing discharges from what are described as 'multiple sources' where the prescribed emission standards cannot be applied in practice. Member state programmes have to be communicated to the Commission. The purpose of such programmes is stated to be the avoidance or elimination of pollution and will include 'the most appropriate' measures and techniques for the replacement, retention and recycling of mercury. In practice, member states will tend to concentrate on those well-defined sources of mercury: hospitals, dental health establishments, laboratories and other non-industrial establishments using mercury.

Possible modes of control The distinct problem of controlling diffuse sources may well point to the merit of economic instruments affecting those tending to be responsible for such discharges to the aquatic environment. However, a development of such a mode of control seems a long way off at the time of writing.[27] For the moment there is little doubt that increasing success in many member states in dealing with pollution from point sources is revealing the incidence of pollution from non-point sources. The problem is no doubt exacerbated by agriculture as well as the growth in housing and industrial development. Where agriculture is concerned the incidence of eutrophic waters suggests inefficiencies in modes of environmental control affecting run-off from farms. As a result, and by way of just one example, phosphorus concentrations in vulnerable waters are often regarded as being environmentally unacceptable. The monitoring and conclusive identification of diffuse sources represents one critical challenge for the Community and member states.

Otherwise the central challenge is in creating modes of control to deal with the problem of diffuse sources. Cross-compliance is one possibility, where conditions for the receipt of subsidy in agriculture are tied to prescribed standards of integrated farm management and enforced accordingly. Land drainage may require more attention in the case of other sources, such as industrial development where measures to cope with run-off might be developed. Both options suggest a redrawing of regulatory requirements affecting new and existing agricultural and industrial development. Additionally, there may be some merit in the creation of taxes affecting pesticides and fertilisers, although their coverage in member states tends to be patchy. That these measures represent only part of the solution can be seen in references below to the development of law and policy on non-point source pollution (NPSP) in the United States and Canada.

Taxes on pesticides and fertilisers There is in member states adopting such taxes very little evidence of positive impacts on the problem of non-point, diffuse pollution. The effects of the pesticides tax applied in Denmark and Sweden were outlined in Chapter Six.[28] In Sweden a tax on fertilisers and their nitrogen and phosphorus content in particular has been in force since 1982 and extended to the cadmium content of phosphorus-based fertilisers in 1994. At its current rate, this fertiliser tax is calculated to reduce total nitrogen dosage by about 10 per cent although the impact on cadmium discharges is as yet unknown.[29] The tax is intended to raise prices and to depress demand for fertilisers, at the same time generating resources to address adverse environmental impacts. The impact of the tax has to be seen in the context of other agricultural reform although publicity and education initiatives accompanying the tax initiative may well have had a positive impact on perceptions of the adverse effects of fertilisers.[30] By way of contrast to a lack of developed modes of control in respect of diffuse pollution sources in the member states of the Community, federal law and policy in the United States has progressed rather further. The position in Canada appears to be rather different to that in the United States. It has been seen previously, towards the end of Chapter Two, that in Canada the federal government enjoys a far less dominant role in the creation, implementation and enforcement of environmental law and policy. Accordingly, the comparative section on NPSP in Canada looks at the evolution of law and policy from the perspective of one province – British Columbia – which has been particularly imaginative in developing initiatives on law and policy here.

Diffuse pollution source controls in the United States The federal Clean Water Act 1972 recognises the problem of diffuse pollution sources in sections 208 and 319. Another significant federal Act for this purpose is the Coastal Zone Management Act 1972. Both Acts have been subject to amendment for a number of purposes, not least the need to address NPSP.

Section 208 of the Act places a duty on states to target areas suffering what are referred to as 'substantial water quality problems' in order to facilitate waste treatment management plans prescribing, *inter alia*, processes through which pollution from activities such as agriculture and mining might feasibly be regulated. However, section 208 is notable mainly for the absence of enforcement machinery, suggesting that its role is essentially educative.

The Act of 1972 was amended in the present context in 1987 to make provision for what is referred to as the Section 319 Nonpoint Source Management Program. The starting point here is again the states' responsibility to identify sources which prevent attainment of water quality objectives within each of the jurisdictions and to report on measures to reduce, to the maximum extent practicable, the extent of pollution from them. State management plans are required to promote the adoption and application of 'best management practices': in practice any financial or other support from the Environmental Protection Agency for present purposes will be dependent on proof that they are so adopted and applied at state level. Again, the section 319 facility is voluntary although the financial, technical and other assistance available from the Agency provides important support in the development of strategies to tackle NPSP as well as assessments of the problem. A specific water quality protection project may qualify for financial support under section 319, covering up to 60% of the costs of dealing with NPSP. Funding is commonly provided in support of measures to address problems of NPSP in relation to agriculture where incentive effects may accrue, in contrast to Department of Agriculture whose programs often do not achieve such an effect.

As well as the Clean Water Act, the Coastal Zone Management Act 1972 also provides (again on a voluntary basis) facilities through which states can seek and obtain approval and support from the Agency in respect of enforceable programs for the protection and management of coastal resources. Agency support here depends on programs that are both comprehensive and specific in the regulation of land use and in the rationalisation of competing land uses. Such programs are now linked with the facilities provided by section 319, as a result of amendments to the Coastal Zone Management Act in 1990. As a result, the Coastal Nonpoint Source Pollution Control Program requires the 29 states with approved Coastal Zone Management Programs under the Act of 1972 to develop Coastal Nonpoint Pollution Control Programs, identifying measures for the control of diffuse pollution sources.

Urban run-off from storm waters is addressed by the 1990 amendment of the Coastal Zone Management Act, as well as by provisions of the Clean Water Act. One of those provisions is section 319 which was mentioned above. In addition, section 402 makes provision for the so-called 'storm water permit program'. This program demands possession of a permit in respect of any municipal separate storm sewer system provided for a large or medium-sized population, as defined by the legislation. The same permitting requirements apply to industrial premises and may also apply on an *ad hoc* basis where, whatever the category, storm water discharge is found to compromise the achievement of water quality objectives or is otherwise a material source of water pollution. The 'storm water permit program' is intended essentially to regulate the quality and the quantity of storm water discharge but does not mandate funds as such to the task. Instead, state governments are expected to resort to existing general budgets for the purpose. As a result provision may not be forthcoming or, if it is, it may be in an attenuated form. In these circumstances there have been created so-called 'stormwater utilities' in many counties and cities across the 50 states. A stormwater utility is a special assessment district generating funds necessary for stormwater management. Those benefiting from such management pay a fee which contributes to the cost of that management in the district.

Diffuse pollution source controls in Canada: the case of British Columbia
Unlike the position in the United States, Canadian provinces enjoy rather more autonomy from the federal government in relation to the creation, implementation and enforcement of environmental law and policy. This is well illustrated in the case of British Columbia which, in March 1999, published an action plan. In the present section an outline is provided of the main features of the developing law and policy. Among the initiatives, such as the deployment of economic instruments, is one which points to the need fully to implement existing statutes as well as identifying and addressing gaps and weaknesses in that legislation. Among the areas listed for action are the implementation of water quality provisions, the enhancement of agricultural waste management, the further development of on-site sewage management, the further development of strategies for effective stormwater management, and the management of forestry as it affects water quality. The array of different agencies involved in action to address NPSP is considerable. The provincial government has primary responsibility for land management, local authorities

have jurisdiction over the development of land within their respective boundaries, and various other provincial and federal agencies (not least the federal government) have jurisdiction over some matters affecting NPSP. The provincial government's action plan recognises that there is an important need for an efficient rationalisation as between these different actors, both vertically (say as between the federal government, the provincial government and constituent local authorities) and horizontally (say as between the Ministry of the Environment, Lands and Parks sponsoring the Action Plan and other provincial ministries with an interest). In addition there is a fundamental need to include private citizens and industrial interests such as those involved in forestry.

Three important and significant matters are addressed in the Action Plan. The first of these is the need to address potentially conflicting law and policy through horizontal strategies allowing effective rationalisation and coordination. For example transport law and policy may not easily be reconciled with the need to secure environmental policy preferences for the regulation of highway drainage. The second matter hints at the possibility that there may be consideration of a regime where exemptions from regulatory control could arise on those occasions where there is evidence of full compliance with Codes of Practice (say) in relation to drainage standards. The final matter is partially reflected in what has been observed already, namely the need to secure legislative harmonisation.

In crude terms, such harmonisation cuts in two directions, affecting both provincial and federal legislation. There is a considerable array of provincial legislation affecting NPSP. Not all of that legislation lies within the jurisdiction of the sponsoring Ministry of the Environment, Lands and Parks. In turn, the same applies to the eight federal Acts listed in the Action Plan. The intention, no doubt, will be to secure cooperation and coordination through the regional presence of the relevant federal agencies, such as Environment Canada. That process will no doubt require federal agencies to look at two main issues, the adequacy of their legislation in order to address the challenges of NPSP – the federal Fisheries Act deals with regulatory prohibitions on the deposit of deleterious substances affecting fisheries, for example – as well as the attendant policy on enforcement of such legislation or any necessary modifications and amendments.

Incentives in Favour of Regulatory Control

In Chapter Six it was seen that discounts in respect of the Climate Change

Levy in the United Kingdom have had the effect of encouraging certain industrial sectors to volunteer for inclusion in the regulatory arrangements for integrated pollution prevention and control (IPPC). Although not necessarily foreseen as an effect of the introduction of the Levy, nevertheless this occurrence stands as an important reminder of the synergy that may arise from a close working relationship between two of the dominant modes of environmental control.

Triviality Exemptions

Reference has also been made previously to triviality exemptions. Such exemptions serve a potentially important purpose in prescribing a minimum threshold below which regulatory control will not apply. Of course such a threshold might equally involve reduced regulatory control. However, for present purposes the first and more widely accepted view of the function of a triviality threshold is adopted. There are in the categories of Community environmental law examples of legislation which omit a triviality threshold: Directive 76/464,[31] for example. Accordingly, transposed legislation in member states will be obliged to demand control over any prescribed substance no matter how small its amount. Another area of Community law where no triviality exemption exists is in the IPPC Directive, Directive 96/61. The Directive itself contains no emission limits: rather the intention is that the applicable limits will be the minimum emission limits prescribed under other categories of Community environmental law, such as the Water Framework Directive. Despite the absence of reference in the IPPC Directive to a triviality exemption, what room (if any) is there for the implication of such an exemption? One attractive argument here is that the proportionality principle should facilitate exemption where a subject installation has very little adverse environmental impact. The objection to such an argument is that, in the absence of an express legislative indication, a principle of judicial interpretation cannot be deployed effectively in order to rewrite the statute book. A possible solution in these circumstances could be an arrangement through which a simplified regulatory process is created. In these circumstances, one possibility is that those processes and installations defined as operating below the triviality threshold would be subject only to a simplified regulatory process. This option involves the difficulty of defining where the threshold lies in the context of transposed legislation which is already characterised as involving a complex set of categories of installations and processes. In the face of such arguments, which are particularly relevant to transposition of the IPPC regime in the

United Kingdom, it will be seen below that the only likely concession for present purposes is resort to so-called 'general binding rules'.

Regulatory Enforcement

Regulatory enforcement may occur through application of civil and criminal law. Such enforcement may of course extend to the infrastructure supporting economic instruments. Under the laws applicable in the United Kingdom, there is a general distinction between statutory provision which is general in its terms, and provision which is targeted specifically at a failure to comply with regulatory requirements.

The criminal enforcement of unregulated activity In large part this is reflective of the need to ensure that unregulated activity is controlled through suitably coercive measures. Where polluting activity lies outside regulatory control or is undertaken in breach of regulatory requirements there may be a presumption in favour of criminal enforcement through offences of strict liability or offences where the burden of proof is on the prosecution to establish the *mens rea* of the perpetrator. In the former case of strict liability offences the onus of proof is usually reversed, bearing in mind the evidential difficulty in proving many cases of polluting activity. Despite this reversal of the onus of proof there will still be a need to establish causation, in itself a potentially difficult challenge to meet. This is not to suggest that civil enforcement of unregulated activity may not exist in the law of the United Kingdom, as will be seen below. However, before this matter is taken up, some reference needs to be made to the enforcement of regulated activity.

The enforcement of regulated activity Where noncompliance with a regulated activity occurs, this will usually be manifested as a failure to comply with a licence, permit or other regulatory authorisation or (more usually) conditions attached to it. It is of course open to a member state in transposing Community law to make its own choice of modes of enforcement here. It is open to the member state to determine that noncompliance is so serious that it justifies immediate resort to enforcement through the criminal law. More likely, though is a resort to civil enforcement where, ultimately, there may be resort to criminal enforcement (say) in respect of failure to comply with notices or orders served by the regulator on the perpetrator. This civil step is often crucial since it provides an important opportunity to impose requirements in respect of remediation or similar action in the face of the infraction. The perpetrator may seek to challenge the notice or order, in which case proceedings by way of an application for judicial review may be available. However, it is rather more likely that provision will be made by statute for an administrative appeal to a tribunal or a Minister in government. Whether such an appeal can be regarded as an exclusive remedy is a matter of policy preference which may be reflected in the drafting of the statute concerned. Overriding all of these possibilities however is a provision that may appear in statute whereby the regulator, considering that proceedings for a criminal offence would be ineffectual, may be empowered to apply straight to a superior court, usually for the purpose of obtaining injunctive relief.

The civil enforcement of unregulated activity   There are likely to be two principal options in this case. In the first place, statute may authorise enforcement measures (for example) on the ground that the defendant has been responsible for activities which should have been subject to regulatory control. Pursuit of the activity without the necessary authorisation, for example, may in turn provide the basis for prosecution under the criminal law. Alternatively, statute may provide an enforcement agency with civil powers to address some damage (or even a threat) to the environment. Typically, such a notice will be served on those occasions where it 'appears' to the enforcement agency that a pollutant has, or is likely to, enter the relevant environmental medium and, as such, the responsibility falls on the person served by virtue of his having caused or knowingly permitted the entry. Such a notice will in turn require remedial measures to be undertaken by the person served, with reserve powers allowing the enforcement agency to undertake works in default. There may be an administrative appeal against the notice and its terms. Ultimately though the civil notice will undoubtedly have the support of criminal enforcement where there is noncompliance with defined elements of the procedure overall. In certain instances, a court dealing with criminal proceedings here may itself have jurisdiction to require that remedial works are undertaken by the defendant. Any such works in default necessarily place an important and often costly responsibility on the enforcement agency.

Works in default   Statute will usually define very carefully the circumstances in which works in default may be carried out. In turn, statute will usually prescribe the processes to be satisfied for the purpose of recovering the costs. On occasions, such provisions will stipulate that the recoverable costs should be 'reasonable' costs: ultimately a matter for the court. To aid the process of cost recovery statute may also set out circumstances in which a person who, for example, has so acted as to commit an offence of 'causing' the pollution of a particular environmental medium is expressly liable for the loss, damage or injury accruing. Such a provision is particularly valuable since it can be used by the enforcement agency as a justification for cost recovery without necessarily taking the matter before the court.

The application of fines and charges in the regulatory enforcement process
Statute may reflect a policy preference in favour of an application of any fines levied following a successful criminal prosecution, in favour of the enforcement agency. If the fines levied are high there is a clear benefit to the agency and, no doubt, the process of environmental restoration. In some jurisdictions provision is made for so-called 'noncompliance' charges. There is particular experience of such charges both in the United States and Sweden. Swedish experience extends, for example, to application of a noncompliance charge in respect of sulphur dioxide emissions. Where there is a failure to comply with market-based tradable allowances, a noncompliance charge amounting to about 300 per cent of the expected market price for allowances is payable.

Regulatory Trends

This section of the chapter builds on what has gone before, in looking at the evolution of regulatory control affecting the environment. It has been suggested that, in part, the design and implementation of regulatory controls in member states is influenced, increasingly, by the growing need to apply complementary economic instruments. However, this is not the only driving force behind regulatory control. Enabling powers in Community law are particularly important in giving member states choices where regulatory style and emphasis are concerned. Indeed, there is evidence of national interest in regulatory reform affecting the environment.[32] Five matters of particular contemporary relevance in terms of the law are addressed here: general binding rules, risk monitoring and control, simplified permitting processes, self-regulation, and action plans. Not surprisingly, this list of items shows the extent to which regulatory initiatives in the environment extend across the Community and member states. Where member states are concerned, regulatory reform affecting environmental control is aided considerably by those elements of the constitutional relationship with the Community through which subsidiarity operates. Subsidiarity in turn is manifested in those areas of Community law which allow member state cultural preferences to be realised, encouraged in turn by those provisions which (as indicated above) give an opportunity to exercise a measure of choice.

General Binding Rules

The essence of general binding rules is that in the case of certain categories of process which are similar, and subject to regulatory control, standard conditions should be applied and enforced. General binding rules as a regulatory technique owe their origins to environmental law as developed in member states outside the United Kingdom and the Republic of Ireland. Such rules are capable of expediting the regulatory process and reducing associated costs where, as an option, those subject to regulation choose to be subject to standardised conditions affecting the operation of an installation.

Community law recognition of general binding rules Directive 96/61[33] – the IPPC Directive – recognises the potential utility of general binding rules, stipulating in Article 9(8) that member states may prescribe certain requirements for certain categories of installations in general binding rules, instead of including them in individual permit conditions, provided that there is an integrated approach to regulation, and that an equivalent high level of environmental protection is ensured. Directive 99/13[34] – the Solvents Directive – also recognises (in Article 5) the potential utility of general binding rules. The Directive stipulates that whichever option is chosen – individual, site-specific permit conditions or general binding rules – regulatory control must realise compliance with prescribed limit values or the requirements of an agreed scheme of reduction.

The application of general binding rules through transposition Drawing on recent experience of transposition of the IPPC and Solvent Directives in the United Kingdom, it is interesting to note the variables which affect choices of processes and installations to be subject to general binding rules, particularly in view of the absence of any historical, cultural reliance on this approach to regulatory control. Before those choices are examined, it is necessary to see how in one area – IPPC – transposed legislation already sets out the terms on which general binding rules will apply. That legislation is the subordinate legislation comprised in the Pollution Prevention and Control Regulations 2000.[35]

The Pollution Prevention and Control Regulations 2000 Regulation 14 empowers the Secretary of State to make general binding rules applicable to restricted categories of installation subject to regulatory control here: so-called 'Part A' installations. The exercise of the rule-making power here is based on the Directive's assumption that the application of such general binding rules will result in the same high level of environmental protection and integrated pollution control as would occur with site-specific permit conditions. Significantly, the regulation goes on to state that 'a regulator may, at the request of the operator' include in the permit authorising the operation of an installation a 'general binding rules condition' instead of a site-specific permit condition. In practice it may therefore be open to the regulator to accede to a request to compile a permit comprised entirely of general binding rules conditions. For a number of important enforcement purposes general binding rules conditions are assumed to have the same status as site-specific permit conditions. Two areas of operation are, at the time of writing, destined to be amenable to general binding rules: intensive livestock units, and dry-cleaning and surface cleaning, both regulated under the IPPC regime.

Intensive livestock units and dry-cleaning and surface cleaning operations The regulatory control of livestock units, dealing with pigs and poultry, of a critically prescribed size has not occurred hitherto in the United Kingdom. Although general binding rules are intended to apply to operations of this sort, the flexibility in the transposed statutory provisions outlined above is such that there may well be a mix of conditions. Where, for example, a livestock unit operates adjacent to a Site of Special Scientific Interest it may not be possible for the operation to be subject to a complete raft of general binding rules conditions. Transposition of the Solvents Directive may well see a lighter regulatory touch being applied in the case of dry-cleaning and surface cleaning, at least in the case of those installations operating within a limit of 5 tonnes of solvents used in any one year. That lighter touch would be seen in possible registration under the Pollution Prevention and Control Act 1999. As in the case of intensive livestock units, dry-cleaning and surface cleaning operations have not been subject to regulatory control in the United Kingdom hitherto.

Risk Monitoring and Control

As with a number of issues covered previously in this chapter, risk monitoring and control is in a state of evolution in many member states, including the United Kingdom. It is the situation in the United Kingdom at the time of writing which is the subject of this part of the chapter. Risk monitoring and control addresses the policy priority in favour of a perceived need to streamline the regulatory process, and to make it more cost-efficient. So-called 'operator and pollution risk appraisal' (OPRA) has been applied by the Environment Agency in the enforcement of integrated pollution control (IPC) under Part I of the Environmental Protection Act 1990 (now superseded by IPPC) and waste management licensing, under Part II of the same Act. OPRA is now applied to IPPC regulation. In the case of IPC regulation, a good deal of pollution monitoring has been undertaken by site operators under the terms of the authorisations granted. The output of data from that self monitoring has been audited by the Environment Agency and verified through check monitoring of sites.

OPRA OPRA is concerned essentially with arrangements whereby fees and the regularity of site inspection can be determined by reference to the assessment of risks as well as the standards of the operator's performance. This and any similar system of risk monitoring is open to criticism, based on a departure from site-intensive regulation, in favour of what is (arguably) an arbitrary, risk-based arrangement. This shortcoming is capable of mitigation perhaps, where the terms of a scheme like OPRA is as transparent as it can be made by the regulator. However, despite such transparency there is still a need to ensure that the consistency of regulatory monitoring and enforcement is maximised, albeit consistency will tend to be a rather more difficult goal to achieve in anything other than full, conventional regulation. Where a scheme such as OPRA is in force and operating as effectively as possible by reference to the foregoing constraints, there are several potential advantages for the purpose of deploying the regulator's scarce resources. In the first place, it may be possible to achieve more cost-effective regulatory control while at the same time deploying resources where they are most needed, often in areas of low compliance where greater incentives to improve that compliance may be generated. Against the background of this early development of OPRA other initiatives are being considered at the time of writing. Those initiatives cover risk monitoring by local authorities in connection with air pollution control and a scheme for operator monitoring assessment (OMA).

Local authority air pollution risk monitoring The development of a scheme here will again enable reconsideration of the fees charged and the regularity of site inspection by local authorities in connection with their air pollution control functions. In the first place the intention is to assess the level of risk posed by any particular operator under the terms of the authorisation granted. A number of variables should contribute to an assessment here. There may be a high incidence of enforcement action or threatened enforcement action affecting the operator's record, modest evidence of achievement in compliance with authorisation requirements for the upgrading of the technology in use on the site, and (say) proximity of that site to sensitive environmental features. These examples, cumulatively, would no doubt contribute to a modest score in this first part of the formula. However, the local authority will look also at two other sets of variables: organisational monitoring management by reference to the terms of the authorisation in force, and organisational management and training. As a result of a score compiled from these indicators the local authority will be in a position to determine the extent of regulatory supervision for the future.

OMA It has been seen already that a good deal of pollution monitoring is already undertaken by individual operators under the terms of an authorisation. Although an audit arrangement affects that self-monitoring, at the time of writing the Environment Agency is considering proposals for further assessing the quality of that activity. 'Operator monitoring assessment' (OMA) will be based on operator performance here, taking account of a range of factors such as the quality and reliability of monitoring facilities, management training and compliance records in relation to authorisations granted. As with OPRA, the intention is that scores from this process will determine the regularity and depth of check monitoring in pursuit of regulatory control.

Simplified Permitting Processes

It was seen previously that general binding rules allow the application and enforcement of standard conditions in relation to similar installations. In turn, such conditions may be applied by the regulator either wholly or in part, as a matter of discretion. Such a regime, applying to IPPC regulation for example, goes some way to facilitating a simplified permitting process, streamlining the regulatory process and reducing its associated costs. In practice, the policy preferences in favour of an application of general binding rules will tend to indicate the categories of installation or operation where they may apply. There may be cogent, practical arguments in favour of restricting simplified permitting or other regulatory processes to these limits. The practical reason for such limits may be seen in the complexity which affects the detailed definition of categories for the purposes of IPPC regulation, for example. In other words, policy priorities here are no doubt in favour of maximising simplicity rather than adding additional regulatory layers, rigidly defining certain processes as being exempt from control without the discretionary elements attending general binding rules as they apply to IPPC, for example.

Self-regulation

There is of course a certain measure of self-regulation under the environmental law of the United Kingdom, at least to the extent that there is (audited) self-monitoring of processes in certain areas of regulation. However, 'self-regulation' probably extends rather further than this. The critical question is how far, as a matter of policy, can self-regulation be permitted to extend? Elsewhere in this book environmental management systems have been addressed[36] as a potentially very important example of self-regulation. Such systems characterise self-regulation as an essentially voluntary process. To that extent, self-regulation may be seen to extend to almost any measure that is taken by a company or other organisation which extends beyond the requirements of the law governing the environment. As such it is not unknown for corporate policy to be in favour of greater transparency in relation to otherwise controversial operations. That transparency may take the form of additional, voluntary disclosures of information affecting the environment or undertakings to cut emissions in excess of the levels prescribed by existing regulatory limits. Encouragement of voluntary responses like these is clearly a worthwhile policy priority. Closely allied to this is the question whether economic instruments also can be characterised as encouraging such voluntary responses. Clearly, economic instruments have such a role, albeit voluntary corporate action is motivated by the incentive of cost-cutting, for example. Nevertheless, this view of economic instruments as devices inviting voluntary response remains valuable in terms of the further development of modes of environmental control, particularly where they continue to complement regulatory control.

Action Plans

Closely allied with voluntary measures are action plans, whose contents may be very specifically targeted towards all sorts of environmentally-beneficial measures, such as the problem of NPSP examined previously in this chapter. One further example will suffice here and it relates to the publication, in March 1997, of a United Kingdom Action Plan for the phasing out and destruction of

PCBs and dangerous PCB substitutes. The Action Plan arose from various sources, not least the Third International Conference on the North Sea, as well as Directive 96/59.[37] The Action Plan anticipated the progressive withdrawal of existing exemptions from the ban on the sale and use of PCBs, a requirement to register PCBs with a competent authority by March 16, 1998 (the target date for compliance with the Directive) and agreeing a date for destruction, a complete ban on supply, use and storage of PCBs from December 31, 1999 (subject to derogations in the Directive), and (finally) compilation of an inventory of equipment containing PCBs of more than a prescribed amount. The Action Plan refers to the need for action to prevent the direct discharge of PCBs to groundwater, rivers, drains and sewers during the elimination period. The Directive contains less stringent provisions than those in the Action Plan, largely as a result of a political compromise with those member states affected. Had the Action Plan targets been implemented in the United Kingdom they would have represented a significant voluntary move by a member state beyond the minimum requirements of the Directive. In the event, after considerable confusion about the status and effect of both instruments, the United Kingdom government ultimately implemented the rather less stringent requirements of the Directive. Nevertheless, the Action Plan is an important example of the voluntary, negotiated agreement which is dealt with next, in the final section of this chapter.

Voluntary, Negotiated Agreements

This final section of the chapter looks at the private law contractual approach as a mode of environmental control. At the outset it has to be observed that there is an enormous variety of applications of voluntary, negotiated agreements affecting matters of environmental control. As such, agreements are effectively another means of self-regulation in many cases. However, this mode of environmental control is beset with a number of constraints, which will be examined, below, along with the experience of the Netherlands. Of all the member states of the Community, the Netherlands is perhaps the biggest exponent of voluntary agreements as a means of achieving targets in the environment. Initially though, some examples of agreements are considered and categorised, taking account also of those referred to in Chapters Two and Six.

Categories of Environmental Agreement

Environmental agreements can most usefully be categorised by reference to a pyramidal structure, where the apex is represented by agreements concluded between sovereign states which may be freestanding or comprised within the framework of a convention or treaty which may or may not be equipped with enforcement measures. Below the apex are those agreements to which a sovereign state may subscribe when a convention or treaty is signed and ratified as a result of which that state may agree to legislate the terms of the convention or treaty through its own, municipal law. The convention or treaty may in turn provide for agreement on matters arising. This second category of agreement extends to include the process through which member states of the European Community accede to membership of that Community. A third category of environmental agreement within a state is tied to a regulatory regime governed by statute and is an essential element thereof, to the extent that it is a mandatory part of that regime usually for the purpose of realising or modifying prescribed targets or standards, facilitating access to financial or other benefits, or adjusting the balance between regulation and self-regulation. A fourth category is allied to the third, where an agreement is an informal arrangement, to the extent that it is not a formal part of the foregoing regulatory framework. This category begs the question whether the statutory regulator is empowered to enter such agreements in the absence of explicit legislative authority. The fifth category arises from activity surrounding the implementation and enforcement of economic instruments, where agreements may be seen as evidence of the incentives which tend to characterise such instruments as being effective. Agreements here will tend to be less constrained by questions whether statutory authority exists on the part of participating public agencies. Indeed, an agreement may fall into this category where it is concluded between (say) subsidiary companies in the same group, as a means of attracting benefits accruing from an economic instrument. A final, sixth, category covers those agreements between a government and (say) an industrial or other business sector.

The Categories Illustrated

The six categories above cannot be regarded as distinct and separate: clearly there are many points of overlap. For this reason, any attempt at categorisation has to be approached with great caution. Nevertheless, it is possible to appreciate the overlaps referred to through an illustration of the six categories.

The first and second categories really do not require illustration. The third category is well illustrated – as will be seen in Chapter Nine – by the regulatory arrangements in the Wildlife and Countryside Act 1981 whereby Community nature conservation law is transposed, implemented and enforced. Much of the emphasis of the municipal law here is on voluntary agreement for the protection of habitat. The fourth category is much less clearly illustrated and is far more likely to be an *ad hoc* arrangement separate from the regulatory arrangements. For example, a local authority may have granted an authorisation under Part I of the Environmental Protection Act 1990 in respect of air pollution, against the background of its general contractual powers in the Local Government Act 1972 whereby an agreement is concluded in which the company receiving authorisation undertakes to provide some community benefit which mitigates the local impact of its industrial operation. The fifth category is well represented in the references in Chapter Six to sectoral agreements through which discounts become available in respect of the Climate Change Levy in the United Kingdom. The final category overlaps with the fifth where, in particular, economic instruments may be concerned. However, there are other instances worth noting, as where the government of the United Kingdom agreed with farmers, agro-chemical companies and others in 1998 that there should be a postponement of the commercial cultivation of genetically modified crops. The Netherlands provides a very clear example of resort to environmental agreements in this context. Essentially, agreements are used in the Netherlands in order to seek achievement of the targets prescribed by the National Environmental Policy Plan. Those targets are entrenched in agreements with the relevant industrial sectors rather than with individual industrial companies. The experience of such agreements in the Netherlands does raise questions about their limitations as a mode of environmental control.

Environmental Agreements: Advantages and Disadvantages

The agreements just referred to in the Netherlands merit closer examination in one important respect. Although it might be assumed that such agreements between the government and particular industrial sectors are intended to be legally binding, the reality appears to be otherwise. The government's desire to preserve freedom of executive action appears to result in the agreements being regarded merely as statements of intent, in much the same way as such agreements between the Commission and other parties are so regarded. Such agreements in the Community lie outside Article 249 of the Treaty, although they may provide the basis for a Recommendation from the Commission under the terms of Article 211. In English law there is recognition of a limitation on the contractual capacity of certain governmental agencies where contracts have the effect of fettering future policy and other executive action. Both from a strictly legal and a practical political point of view such a limitation may have serious implications for the agreement as a mode of environmental control. In certain cases though, such a limitation may not be of great moment, as where a company simply requires evidence of a prescribed agreement simply for the purpose of triggering some benefit in relation to an environmental tax, for example. An attempt by government to renege on an agreement, no matter what its environmental objectives may be, might of course be regarded as counterproductive to the achievement of policy and other objectives. Such action by government would need to be based on clear, undisputed evidence if confidence is to be maintained in this approach to control of the environment. Furthermore, there is no doubt that voluntary agreements have the potential to bring the relevant issues closely to the attention of the parties. In turn a contractual commitment may be a more certain basis for compliance, compared with standardised regulatory approaches, for example. However, contractual agreements usually lack the transparency of those regulatory approaches as well as harbouring suspicions of what may be described as private dealing between the parties, whether or not they are parties also to a regulatory arrangement. This may be less of a problem where agreements are sectoral, where there is good definition of the subject companies and the targets to be achieved, all of which will tend to suggest that agreements are likely to be cost-effective, often because there has been prior, informed consultation.

Notes

1   See Hawke, N. (2000), *Corporate Liability*, Sweet and Maxwell, London. *Cf.* Chapter One, n. 99.
2   Chapter One, n. 1.
3   OECD (1997), *Reforming Environmental Regulation in OECD Countries*, pp. 10–11.
4   OJ L297, 13.10.92.
5   OECD (1997), *Agriculture, Pesticides and the Environment*, p. 8.
6   *Ibid.*
7   *Supra*, n. 5, at p. 9.
8   OJ L181, 4.7.86.
9   Chapter One, n. 24; Chapter Two, nn. 36–40; Chapter Six, nn. 29–30.
10   OJ L85, 29.3.99.
11   Chapter One, nn. 34–6 and Chapter Two, n. 29.

12 Cm 4693, May 2000.
13 OJ L135, 30.5.91.
14 Chapter One, n. 13. *Cf.* Chapter One, n. 40, Chapter Two, n. 31, Chapter Four, nn. 77–8; and Chapter Five, nn. 19 and 23.
15 Section 88 and Schedule 10.
16 *Supra*, n. 8.
17 *Supra*, n. 14.
18 OJ L129, 18.5.76.
19 OJ L74, 17.3.84.
20 *Ibid.*, Art. 3.
21 *Supra*, n. 17.
22 *Supra*, n. 18.
23 *Supra*, n. 19.
24 OJ L81, 27.3.82.
25 See, for example, J. van Dunné (ed.) (1996), *Non-point Source River Pollution*, Kluwer Law International, The Hague.
26 *Supra*, n. 23.
27 As to some examples of emerging approaches, see van Dunné, *op.cit.*, n. 25.
28 Chapter Six, nn. 25–6.
29 European Environment Agency (2000), *Environmental Taxes: Recent Developments in Tools for Integration*, Environmental Issues Series, No. 18, Luxembourg, p. 74.
30 European Environment Agency (1996), *Environmental Taxes: Implementation and Environmental Effectiveness*, Copenhagen, pp. 57–8.
31 *Supra*, n. 18.
32 See, for example, OECD (1997), *Reforming Environmental Regulation in OECD Countries*.
33 OJ L257, 10.10.96.
34 *Supra*, n. 10.
35 SI 2000, No. 1973.
36 See in particular, Chapter One, nn. 3, 4 and 33, and Chapter Two, nn. 42–4.
37 OJ L243, 24.9.96.

Chapter Eight

Developing Law and Policy for Pollution Control

The Dimensions of Law and Policy Development

The intention behind this chapter is to build on the content of previous chapters by focusing specifically on one area of law and policy – air pollution control – and considering the developmental variables by reference to experiences in the United Kingdom, the European Community, Canada and the United States. As such, the chapter divides into three sections, dealing with policies, strategies, standards and limits; the use of regulatory and other instruments for the purpose of implementation; and (finally), enforcement.

Policies, Strategies, Standards and Limits

The peculiar nature of policies and strategies affecting air pollution control is examined here, together with policy integration and the transition that occurs where those policies and strategies are realised as standards and limits. It will be seen that there is an almost inevitable overlap between these three areas. As a critical example, it is often the case that a policy or strategy affecting the environment can be characterised by reference to standards and limits as objectives in the application of environmental controls. Consequently, any suggestion that each area exists in its own right probably fails to take account of the realities.

The Nature of Policies and Strategies Covering Air Pollution

Policies and strategies on air pollution emerge from a wide range of sources and in this section of the chapter reference is made to an important example of an international convention on the subject, as well as Community policies and strategies, and also those developed in the United Kingdom, the United States and Canada. The opportunity is also taken to examine the environmental indicators which, increasingly, affect the development of policies and strategies in one specific area concerning the generation of greenhouse gases from agriculture. Interspersed throughout are references to the transition of policies and strategies to standards and limits for regulatory and other, related purposes.

International conventions One of the dominant conventions is the United Nations Convention on Long-range Transboundary Air Pollution, adopted in 1979 and in force on March 16, 1983.[1] Among the contracting parties are the European Community,[2] the United Kingdom, the United States and Canada. The objective of the Convention is the limitation and, as far as is possible, the reduction and prevention of air pollution, including long-range transboundary pollution. Added to the Convention subsequently are various pollutant-specific protocols. Among the protocols is one that addresses the emission of volatile organic compounds (VOCs), which came into force towards the end of 1997. Where the European Community is concerned, the policy appears to be in favour of signing such a protocol on its merits but, as in the case of the VOC protocol, postponing ratification until Community law is effectively implemented. Neither the European Community nor the United Kingdom signed a first protocol relating to sulphur dioxide emissions which came into force towards the end of 1987, although a second protocol on such emissions (in force towards the end of 1998) was signed and ratified by both these parties. Interestingly, this second protocol prescribes additional reduction targets which vary as between the participating states according to data on critical loads, a matter that is returned to, later in the chapter. As an effects-based instrument, this protocol distributes reduction targets by reference to those areas where resulting benefits can be maximised. However, a separate agreement between Canada and the United States is recognised as a basis for derogations from the target reductions in the protocol. Compliance reporting by the participating states indicates the scale of achievement, in many cases through measures which are characterised by a good deal of variety. In the case of member states of the Community, compliance reporting is of course based on the implementation and enforcement of Community law. Additionally, though, some of those member states' compliance with protocol targets is based on economic instruments which, very largely, are without the influence of the Community, as was seen in Chapter Six. In the next section, some general consideration is given to the policies and strategies of the European Community.

The European Community The Community has been an important participant in the negotiation and conclusion of various international conventions affecting air pollution. There is little doubt that the consolidated experience of the member states and the Community has contributed considerably to the design, development and implementation of effective international instruments in this context. It will be seen later in this chapter that that experience has given rise to devices and techniques which extend very widely across an area of environmental regulation and control which is characterised by its difficulty in coping with matters such as transboundary pollution and the reliable measurement of air pollutants, and their adverse impact on the environment. Indeed, this latter reference to adverse impacts may well characterise important future developments in Community policy and strategy. For the moment, though, the Community's position in relation to acidification is governed by data on critical loads, much influenced by the 5th Environmental Action Programme.[3] Emission limits for gases such as sulphur dioxide are prescribed by requirements under the Large Combustion Plants Directive[4] drawing significantly on the data in a Commission strategy document on acidification.[5] Beyond this position Community strategy is beset by considerable difficulties, not least of which is a policy ambition to extend the foregoing limit values beyond the constituencies covered by existing directives, particularly as a result of the second sulphur dioxide protocol referred to in the previous section. However, given the nature of the emissions and their adverse effects on the atmosphere it is difficult to see how such an extension of limit values might be effectively enforced when, ostensibly, they necessarily attract the force of law. This matter of enforcement continues to exercise the mind of the Community since there is evidence of difficulty in enforcing the prescriptions found in those directives whose concern has been to address ambient air quality.[6] That evidence again emphasises the margin of flexibility accruing from transposition in member states, as has been seen in earlier chapters where the constraints of Community law and policy in this context have been addressed.[7] The advent of integrated pollution prevention and control seeks to treat emissions to the atmosphere in an integrated fashion for regulatory purposes. Again, the question is whether this approach can be effective as the new regime is implemented and enforced in member states. Community policy addressing the adverse environmental impact of emissions from road vehicles is driven largely by the so-called 'Auto-Oil' programme through which the Commission seeks to initiate proposals in liaison with car manufacturers and fuel refiners. The programme and predecessor policies have sought to prescribe standards and objectives in relation to emission efficiencies in automobile engineering, fuel content, inspection and maintenance, by reference to cost-effective strategies. As a result evolving policies have given rise to prescribed vehicle emission limits and fuel content standards. All of these areas have been subject to continuing evolution through constant review and revision.

The United Kingdom The United Kingdom government's approach is based on a National Air Quality Strategy whose objective is the improvement of air quality by reference to health-based standards. The most recent Air Quality Strategy (2000) was dealt with in Chapter One, under the heading of 'Strategies'.[8] The Air Quality Strategy approach had been foreseen in policy terms in 1994. The policy and priorities behind the latest strategy of 2000 stress ambient air quality standards in respect of eight key pollutants. Stricter requirements may be recommended by the government's Expert Panel on Air Quality Standards although it is the Community's daughter directives which provide the foundations for prescribed requirements. As an example of the operation of this arrangement, the Expert Panel's air quality standard for nitrogen dioxide is 150 ppb (parts per billion) measured as an hourly average: the equivalent standard in Directive 85/203[9] is 105 ppb in respect of the limit value. The evolution of the National Air Quality strategy has been built on various developments, not just the science and technology of air quality standards *per se*. The 2000 strategy incorporates limit values for the protection of vegetation and ecosystems in the wider environment. In the case of ozone, objectives are not included in the framework for local air quality management, mainly by virtue of the fact that the pollutant arises from sources outside the United Kingdom. In the same way, local authorities have had no part to play in meeting objectives associated with nitrogen oxide and sulphur dioxide where stringent objectives have applied to secure the protection of vegetation and ecosystems by the end of the year 2000. Overall, the strategy is built on an effects-based approach and underpinned by sustainable development principles and the need to protect human health. The strategy is provided for by the Environment Act 1995 which obliges the Secretary of State to prepare, publish and keep it under review. In turn, the Environment Agency is obliged to have regard to the Strategy. It is further acknowledged by the Act that local authorities will assess local air quality and, as necessary, designate air quality management areas where standards or objectives are not being realised, or are being threatened. Designation of such an area further obliges the local authority responsible to produce an action plan identifying remedial measures deemed to be necessary.

The United States The dominant legislation for present purposes is the federal Clean Air Act 1970. The Act provides for national ambient air quality standards, national emissions standards for hazardous pollutants, and new source performance standards.

National ambient air quality standards are referable to those pollutants (carbon monoxide, lead, nitrogen oxides, ozone, particulates and sulphur oxides) found by the Environmental Protection Agency to have an adverse effect on human health, no matter what their source. Evidence of such adverse effects is prepared by the Agency, together with the devices and techniques which may be deployed in order to control atmospheric emissions. For these purposes so-called 'primary' standards are prescribed in relation to the protection of human health while so-called 'secondary' standards are prescribed by reference to rather wider criteria concerning the public welfare. Primary standards are determined by reference to the most vulnerable where atmospheric pollutants are concerned while secondary standards operate by reference a wide variety of factors, such as adverse effects on vegetation and ecosystems. Each standard is subject to constant, five-yearly, review in order to take account of evolving science and technology.

Emission standards for hazardous air pollutants, such as heavy metals and toxic organic pollutants, depend for their application on determination by the Environmental Protection Agency of 'maximum achievable control technology' in relation to 188 prescribed substances. Performance standards for emissions here depend on the Agency's prescriptions arising from the practices undertaken in the industries responsible. Against this background there are variable emission standards for new or existing plants or installations.

The process of implementation and enforcement of these standards centres on State Implementation Plans in each state which subdivides into regions for this purpose. Interestingly, the states here have an important measure of flexibility in implementation. Accordingly, any state has the opportunity to determine the nature and extent of regulation and control to apply, although any State Implementation Plan for a prescribed pollutant requires approval by the Environmental Protection Agency. Where there is default by a state, either through non-submission or submission of an inadequate Plan, the Agency is able to intervene and impose its own Plan. As in the European Community, ozone has proved to be a difficult pollutant to regulate and control. As a result, State Implementation Plans have had to be revised in order to indicate how a state will achieve attainment of standards according to the categorisation of areas as 'moderate' or 'extreme' (for example), within a prescribed period of time. Across the regions of any state it is likely that there will be variations in air quality: some regions will exceed federal standards, some will not. Although some of the classifications established by the Agency can be changed, strict limits are placed on changes in air quality. For example, a top quality Class I area covering a National Park, is permitted only *de minimus* increases in polluting concentrations to the atmosphere.

The Environmental Protection Agency's dominant control of air quality is seen also in New Source Performance Standards where prescribed categories of process may require stringent technological applications, for example, as a cost-effective incentive for investment in emerging techniques of emission control. The assumption here is that the Agency has a fully justified case for reliance on what may be technological innovation, which is a matter open to challenge before the court, in the absence of any state veto or challenge for this purpose.

National emissions and other related standards are also set by the Agency under the Federal Motor Vehicle Control Program, again by virtue of the Clean Air Act. Finally, the Acid Rain Control Program introduced under the Clean Air Act and described towards the end of Chapter Six is worthy of repeated mention here.

Canada For reasons explored in earlier chapters, it is clear that the constitutional relationship between the federal government and the provinces for present purposes is somewhat different – and less clear cut – than that in the case of the United States. It may therefore be suggested that the source of policies and strategies on the environment is also less well-defined than (say) in the United States and the European Community. International conventions are clearly very significant, along with federal government policy initiatives. It is clear however that provincial governments enjoy considerable freedom and autonomy in environmental policy such that that policy may be reshaped prior to standard and limit-setting in fora such as the Canadian Council of Ministers of the Environment (CCME). The political and other compromises manifested in the deliberations of CCME may be on a par with those which occur in the Environment Council of the European Community. The Canada-Wide Environmental Standards Agreement seeks to facilitate the continual development, improvement and attainment of standards referable to environmental quality across the country. The standards developed, such as those for particulate matter and ground-level ozone, are developed from a scientific foundation set against a risk-based approach but taking account also of other variables, such as socioeconomic factors and technical feasibility. In the implementation of such standards, CCME presumes that provincial governments will share expertise, avoid overlap and duplication, adopt effective and efficient measures and promote consistency. The standard relating to particulate matter, for example, takes account of relevant regional variables. Those variables take account of the fact that some areas of the country are adversely affected by transboundary air pollution from the United States, that high levels of background particulate matter and ozone occur naturally in some areas, and that smog conditions may differ considerably as between regions.

Greenhouse gases from agriculture Three greenhouses gases are attributable to agricultural activity: methane, nitrous oxide and carbon dioxide. The development and evolution of policy and, ultimately, law depends on the generation of an accurate, robust picture of the agricultural contribution of these greenhouse gases to the overall problem of managing emissions across the Community, for example. Indeed, the shape and emphasis of the law as a vehicle for standards and limits will depend crucially on a suitably sensitive reading and interpretation of so-called 'agri-environmental' indicators. Such indicators have the potential to provide reliable information on the environmental impact of agriculture, to furnish the policy creation process with this information, and to enable ongoing monitoring and evaluation.[10] Such indicators are likely to be able to explain the nature of what are undoubtedly complex linkages between agriculture and its environmental impact, as well as the variables which apply across the member states of the Community. In more general terms it is emphasised in a pilot study by the Commission of *Indicators of Sustainable Development*[11] that:

> The origins of these emissions are affected by climate and the type of energy used by a country, which depends on its industrial structure, its transport system, its forestry and agricultural sectors, and the consumption patterns of the population.[12]

More specifically, the Community, certain member state governments such as that of the United Kingdom, and the OECD have attempted to produce indicators for present purposes, as part of the policy creation process. In another Commission publication, *Environmental pressure indicators for the EU*[13] detailed indicators are provided in respect of anthropogenic methane for the purpose of monitoring total emissions of what is a greenhouse gas with a very high global warming potential.[14] The Commission goes on to observe evidence of a significant decrease in methane emissions from certain member states in the years from 1990 to 1998, where agriculture is a smaller part of the economy, where livestock numbers have declined, and where waste management is more efficient. In the case of nitrous oxide (mentioned also in Chapter One), the purpose of the indicator is the same: to monitor anthropogenic emissions of nitrous oxide, a majority of which come from intensive agricultural operations.[15] Agricultural soils are the main source of emissions, which appears to explain high *per capita* emissions in Ireland and Denmark according to the Commission. However, the Commission points to lower emissions in the Netherlands, stressing its strict manure management legislation, despite the fact that similarly strict controls exist also in Denmark. OECD appears to take the matter of agri-environmental indicators rather further in seeking to measure the release and accumulation of greenhouse gases by reference to a net balance of these gases, as generated by agriculture. As such the OECD approach is heavily influenced by the extent to which agricultural land may be regarded as a 'sink' for these gases.[16] Finally, in the United Kingdom, the former Ministry of Agriculture published its pilot indicators under the title *Towards Sustainable Agriculture*,[17] pointing out that agriculture is responsible for about 8 per cent of all greenhouse gases in the United Kingdom. While carbon dioxide is relatively insignificant, 37 per cent of United Kingdom methane emissions come from agriculture and 52 per cent of nitrous oxide emissions are from agriculture although both are shown to be declining for a variety of reasons, such as a declining cattle population. Against this background, there is an indication of those factors which influence the generation of greenhouses gases from agriculture and which, therefore can be addressed as 'driving forces'.[18] 'Driving forces' are those factors which give rise to changes in the environment: policy preferences in favour of intensive agriculture, for example. In turn, indicators can show the state of the environment as a result of its use and exploitation. Finally, policy and other responses arise from evidence of the extent of change in the environment where other factors are seen to be at work, such as policies on sustainability and organic cultivation.

Policy Integration

The reference above to greenhouse gas emissions from agriculture emphasises the significance in policy creation of horizontal effects, in this case between the environmental and agricultural sectors. That process of integration in the Community carries with it the question of which directorate will have responsibility for development of policy as well as the further development of that policy into standards and limits, many of which will have the force of law. Along this line of development questions will occur on the shape and emphasis of law or policy where, for example, an agri-environmental indicator shows low levels of greenhouse gas emissions from agriculture where manure and soil management in particular member states is of proven efficiency in addressing nitrous oxide emissions. Broader issues of environmental policy integration in the Community were dealt with in Chapter One. Elsewhere, in the United States, there has been a growing practice of policy integration flowing from federal legislation and encouraging links for these purposes between the Environmental Protection Agency and other (mainly federal) agencies. This is particularly the case in relation to the development of policy straddling energy and the environment where similar levels of integration are visible in Canada through federal – provincial arrangements.

Standards and Limits

Earlier in this chapter reference has been made to standards and limits, often in the context of policy and strategy development. In this section of the chapter standards and limits in relation to air quality are again examined but by reference to other specific issues. As such this section of the chapter concentrates on five matters: principal criteria, guide values and indicator limits, environmental improvement requirements, thresholds, and derogations.

Principal criteria Two principal criteria form the basis for the approach to regulatory control of air pollution in many cases: emission limits and quality standards. These are important foundations for regulatory control of air pollution and air quality, which will be separated out and examined, later in the chapter.

Taking emission limits first, there are numerous options grouped around what are standards or limits. Where standards are concerned, prescriptions may relate to identifiable sources or particular pollutants, or may require the management of those pollutants through the application of technology. Such standards may apply as a result of countrywide emission limits in respect of prescribed pollutants, or as a result of limits applying to particular processes, plants (as with integrated pollution prevention and control) or to particular industries. In turn, emission standards tend to be defined in a wide variety of different ways: in terms of parts per billion of flue gases assuming certain physical conditions, for example. Another potentially important variable involves possible discrimination between new and existing installations where, for example, the latter may enjoy a rather more relaxed emission standard pending closure or technological improvement. Numerous examples of these variables as applied in practice have been given in earlier chapters.

Quality standards referable to ambient air quality may include standards which relate to so-called 'critical loads'. In turn, the determination of standards here will tend to be closely allied to other calculations, relating to fuel content and quality, for example. In other words, there are important opportunities to determine ratios between ambient air quality and the means by which desired standards may be achieved through prescribed limits affecting the content of the target pollutants in fuels whose combustion contributes to atmospheric pollution. The critical quality standard is again open to different methods of calculation: concentrations may be determined on an annual or hourly basis, for example. The normal value in these cases is the maximum allowable value. Where critical loads are concerned, scientific justification will be used to provide the basis for targets, often subject to variables according to those elements of the environment to be accorded particular protection. However, resort to critical loads is by no means universal. Both the United States and the United Kingdom avoid reliance for the moment on critical loads, although in the United Kingdom, the emission limits on electricity generators are so based.[19]

Ambient air quality standards in the United States It was seen, above, that the United States relies, *inter alia*, on the creation and implementation of national ambient air quality standards which, in turn, operate by reference to primary and secondary standards. While these standards appear to have had considerable success in dealing with emissions of certain atmospheric pollutants, the difficulty of dealing with ozone is not surprising. In order to address the control of ozone pollution in urban areas in particular, powers under the Clean Air Act have been resorted to in order to designate numerous non-attainment areas. In such areas, new plant and major modifications of existing plant must satisfy the 'lowest achievable emission rate' which represents the most stringent limitation on emissions for that category of plant. Again the essential responsibility for determining strategy here falls on the states, through their state implementation plans. Given that a large number of small industrial companies contribute significantly to non-attainment of the national standard for ozone, there is a considerable regulatory problem. Designation of a non-attainment area for ozone depends on data from a single monitoring point in an air quality control region, indicating that the standard has been exceeded four times in a three year period. Amendments to the Clean Air Act provide for a permit program – the Operating Permit Program – applicable even to quite small businesses and capable of extending to the emissions which give rise to ozone non-attainment. The regulatory framework is such that each permit granted prescribes one consolidated parcel of limits on polluting emissions. The grant of the permit locally in each state brings with it a presumption that the grantee is in compliance with Clean Air Act requirements, at least as long as permit requirements are observed. Depending on the success of this regulatory extension, it may disprove the theory that economic instruments are the only efficient method of dealing with so many, disparate emissions. Nevertheless, such a regulatory extension will continue to depend on cumbersome statutory amendment should the arrangements require adjustment in due course.

Emission limits, quality standards and other approaches in the European Community Emission limits characterise several directives legislated under the umbrella of the Air Pollution Framework Directive: 84/360.[20] However, emission limits are just one of several methods of control adopted by the Community. Indeed, reference has been made in Chapter Two to the evolution of control methods,[21] and the later reliance on ambient air quality standards. Among the array of Community law on air pollution and air quality control it can be seen that progress towards adoption of 'critical loads' under the Large Combustion Plants Directive[22] is already in evidence in the United Kingdom largely as a result of the emerging requirements of a second protocol on sulphur dioxide emissions under the Convention on Long-range Transboundary Air Pollution. However, what is already a complex picture is further complicated by the Community's resort to a range of other methods, one of the more familiar being statutory prescriptions relating to the content and quality of fuels whose combustion contributes to emissions having an adverse effect on the environment. An even wider range of controls extending beyond production applies to substances whose exploitation is known to have an adverse effect on the ozone layer. The foregoing methods tend to be characterised by controls over atmospheric emissions *per se*. However, Community law controls affecting asbestos through Directive 87/217[23] operate as multimedia controls where requirements are triggered, whatever the medium through which asbestos might impact on the environment. The same general principle applies in relation to integrated pollution prevention and control where Directive 96/61[24] requires that regulatory control is inclusive of the whole installation no matter what emissions or discharges may accrue.

Guide Values and Indicator Limits

Guide values contrast limit values. The latter have characterised early Community law in relation to air pollution control, under Directive 80/779[25] for example, while guide values have been an accompaniment. As such, they have not been legally enforceable like mandatory limit values and member states generally have been reluctant to resort to more stringent guide values. This undoubtedly is the consequence of an ill-defined duty in Directive 80/779 attempting to require each member state to endeavour to implement these more exacting requirements. Clearly, Community law and policy is moving on, with the consequence that the Directive is destined for early repeal, along with its reliance on limit and guide values. However, if the guide value had any merit, it might have been found in the hope that such values would provide an incentive to member states to force standards for air quality upwards.

Environmental Improvement Requirements

The foregoing reference to Directive 96/61 directs attention to what is sometimes referred to as 'technology-forcing' regulation. Integrated pollution prevention and control and its reliance on 'best available techniques' obliges the regulator to ensure that authorisations are open to reappraisal on those occasions when there is evidence that an installation's emissions or discharges might be reduced without excessive costs. This important example is but one illustration of a range of possible regulatory approaches that might be prescribed by law for the purpose of securing continual improvement in any regulated operation. It is probably the case that most regulatory regimes are sufficiently widely defined to facilitate such improvement requirements.

Thresholds

The evolution of standards and limits in relation to air pollution control suggests in large part that many fixed limits here are probably beyond effective enforcement. Similar problems have been seen also in relation to attempts to impose enforceable limits on ozone. In the Community there appears to have been an awareness of the need to move to rather more subtle forms of environmental control. That movement has involved an appreciation of the function of thresholds which, for present purposes, can be seen to fulfil two important functions. In the first place, standard-setting may be undertaken by reference to variables represented by what may be described as 'acceptability thresholds' in relation to the environmental health dimensions of air quality standards, for example. The United Kingdom's Expert Panel on Air Quality Standards, in recommending a standard for sulphur dioxide in the atmosphere, suggested that that standard should be set by reference to effects on those suffering from asthma rather than those who are otherwise healthy. A second function however, is the adoption of thresholds as a trigger for dissemination of environmental health information, as where ozone levels become sufficiently critical according to accepted criteria: an 'alert' threshold.

Derogations

As a matter of Community policy it is quite possible that derogations may be permitted, usually on a temporary basis, from the requirements of Community law represented in a particular directive. The Large Combustion Plants Directive[26] for example allows a derogation where, in a member state, there is no technologically feasible alternative to the use of high sulphur indigenous coal. Nevertheless the Directive does contain an incentive to ensure that any such member state pursues an action plan for desulphurisation of affected installations. In some cases though, there are tight controls on any attempt to take advantage of derogations. The Solvents Directive[27] for example prohibits resort to any derogation otherwise provided for by the Directive where a solvent is a particularly toxic substance, as defined.

Regulatory and Other Instruments

Regulatory Instruments

In practice it is again not possible to separate regulatory from other modes of environmental control in relation to air pollution. As in most other areas of environmental law and policy there is an increasingly complementary relationship between regulatory and other instruments, such as economic instruments. In focusing initially on regulatory instruments it will be seen that their style and emphasis is dependent on reference to the sort of limits and standards considered earlier in this chapter. Policy may play a part in determining thresholds above which limits will be legally binding although there may be policy interest in even more ambitious limits. Those more ambitious limits have been referred to in earlier Community law as 'guide' limits. As such, guide limits were intended to provide an incentive in favour of more stringent air quality requirements. Whether they were successful in this ambition was a matter referred to above. Thresholds may be seen to operate in other ways too. For example, practical regulation may determine that only processes or installations of a certain size or capacity should be included in regulatory arrangements. Those more modest processes or installations might be excluded from regulation, but without prejudice to the possibility that they might be subject to economic instruments as a cost-effective method of addressing emissions. An alternative might of course be one of the more streamlined and less intrusive regulatory instruments such as registration and application of a regime of general binding rules.

Regulatory style: the Community and the United Kingdom An increasingly common approach to the regulation of air pollution in the Community is a statutory framework providing for the authorisation or other licensing of emissions or processes which fall within prescribed categories. The regulatory process will be based on the expectation of applications from those companies or other businesses falling within these categories prescribed by statute. These categories will usually include emissions from mobile sources. Failure to comply, or to comply with any authorisation or conditions attached to it, may trigger enforcement action as defined by the statutory provisions. Those provisions may also require the regulator to act as an enforcer in another respect, by acting in default to remedy any failure to comply (say) with requirements imposed by condition.

The conditions applicable will tend to fall into three general categories covering requirements specific to the site or installation, requirements emanating from priorities found in municipal law, policy or strategy and requirements emanating from applicable international conventions. Requirements specific to the site tend to comprehend matters of monitoring and compliance. Priorities in municipal law, policy or strategy may cover a multitude of different matters, some of which may, in the context of the European Community, impose more stringent requirements than those imposed by directive.

At the heart of this regulatory model are two fundamentals. In the first place there is an assumption that best available techniques will be applied to the subject process, and that, secondly, there will be continual improvement of the performance of the process subject to regulation, a matter that may be facilitated by a requirement for regular review of any authorisation granted. In addition there are complementary regulatory arrangements aimed (for example) at prescribing fuel and product quality relevant to air pollution and the promotion of air quality improvement although not necessarily governed by the same scheme of legislation carrying the main regulatory framework. The Pollution Prevention and Control Act 1999 (which does not presently extend to Northern Ireland) seeks to implement integrated pollution prevention and control whose regulatory framework follows the model just described very closely. The style and emphasis of that model for present purposes is seen in the Directive – Directive 96/61[28] – on integrated pollution prevention and control to which frequent reference has been made in previous chapters. This important area of Community law is of particular interest for present purposes in relation to regulatory style.

Normally, the assumption is that Community law will not prescribe detailed matters of style and emphasis in relation to the manner in which a member state may wish to transpose and implement regulatory arrangements. However, Directive 96/61 does seek to be rather more prescriptive in setting limits to regulatory requirements. For example, measures are expected from a member state to ensure that no subject installation is operated without the requisite authorisation. In turn, the authorisation must address all those requirements necessary to secure compliance with all of those matters which may be regarded as the fundamentals: decommissioning requirements and requirements in respect of efficient energy use, for example. Given the relatively radical nature of many of the provisions here governing integrated pollution prevention and control, it may be assumed that the Community has sought to avoid any uncertainties in transposition of the sort which have occurred previously in relation to other environmental legislation.

In England and Wales the Pollution Prevention and Control Regulations 2000[29] made under the authority of the Pollution Prevention and Control Act 1999 provide the detailed statutory framework for the regulation of polluting emissions to the atmosphere. Reference has been made to this legislation already[30] and certain of its regulatory features, such as those relating to general binding rules. More generally, the Regulations provide the focal point for Community limits and standards which are to be enforceable by the Environment Agency or local authorities according to a division of regulatory responsibilities. Regulatory controls of emissions may be supplemented on occasions by the issue of statutory directions to the regulators, requiring the application and enforcement of new Community statutory requirements. The regulators are obliged in the discharge of their functions here to achieve a high level of environmental protection or, if that is not practicable, to reduce emissions by reference to 'best available techniques'. Wide powers of review, suspension, enforcement and revocation of permits are included in the Regulations. A limited number of appeal rights to the Secretary of State are provided for. Criminal enforcement of regulatory requirements is included in the Regulations, as are rights for a regulator to seek injunctive relief where that regulator considers that criminal enforcement of an enforcement or suspension notice would be ineffectual.

Regulatory style: the United States Earlier in this chapter various elements of the application of the Clean Air Act were discussed. In this section of the chapter certain of those issues will be returned to, with particular reference to matters of implementation at state level. For this purpose one state will be used as an example: Virginia. The Clean Air Act sets a framework but it is at state level that the air pollution agency operates in hearing permit applications and, if necessary, enforcing regulatory requirements. This federal legislative framework provides states with the opportunity of developing their own implementation strategies through state implementation plans and associated regulations which are subject to federal approval by the Environmental Protection Agency. As such, the regulatory model is in many respects similar to that which exists in the European Community. However, there is a far more explicit recognition of the need for public participation in developing state implementation plans. Failure to obtain approval for such a plan, or a straight failure to submit any proposals, allows the Environmental Protection Agency to intervene and undertake implementation and enforcement of the Clean Air Act in the state concerned. The overarching functions of the Agency extend to research and development and powers to deal with interstate air pollution, among others. Regulatory permits were referred to previously: their unified operation has considerable merit where one company may be responsible for the emission of hazardous air pollutants, the emission of pollutants subject to the acid rain program as well as other categories of polluting emissions.

Regulatory style: State of Virginia, US The municipal air pollution control law of Virginia empowers the State Air Pollution Control Board to implement and enforce Clean Air Act programs as well as state programs, which may even add to and extend federal requirements. The Operating Permit Program extends to control those hazardous (toxic) air pollutants where the substances prescribed by the state are the same as those subject to federal prescription. At the time of writing, state permitting is based on five categories of permit: the so-called 'PSD' (Prevention of Significant Deterioration) permit; the Operating permit; the Existing Source Registration and Standards permit; the Minor New, Modified and certain Major Source Construction permit; and (finally) the Major New or Modified Source Construction permits in Non-attainment Areas.

The PSD permit is required for a new air pollution source, or the modification, relocation or reactivation of an existing source which will emit 250 tons per annum of any prescribed pollutant or combination thereof, or (in the case of one of 28 prescribed industries such as electricity generation or petrol refining) a source which will emit 100 tons per annum of a prescribed pollutant. Among the regulatory requirements is an obligation on the applicant to demonstrate that plant design incorporates the 'best available control technology'.

The State Operating permit applies to the owners and operators of any stationary source. In the case of hazardous air pollutants as prescribed by the Clean Air Act, applications are required from the owners and operators of any major stationary source, any source subject to 'maximum achievable control technology' and any source subject to New Source Performance Standards. A 'major' source here is defined as one that emits, or has the potential to emit, 100 tons or more of prescribed pollutants per annum or 10 tons or more per annum of any hazardous air pollutant, or 25 tons or more per annum of any combination of hazardous air pollutants. In non-attainment areas for ozone these threshold values are revised downwards. Permits have a life of five years and may be renewable.

The Existing Source Registration Standards permit applies to the owners and operators of any existing stationary source exceeding threshold values in respect of fugitive dust, odour or other prescribed pollutants, federally prescribed hazardous pollutants, standards referable to 'maximum achievable control technology' or standards prescribed by the state in respect of toxic pollutants. Registration is permanent, but subject to revision with changes in emissions, and transferable to any new owner of a subject plant.

The Minor New, Modified and certain Major Source Construction permit applies to a person or entity intending to construct a new source, or to modify, relocate or reactivate an existing source. The central regulatory requirement is that emissions will be controlled using the 'best available control technology' for prescribed pollutants, and 'maximum achievable control technology' for hazardous pollutants.

The Major New or Modified Source Construction permit in Non-attainment Areas applies to any person or entity intending to construct a new stationary source or to modify, relocate or reactivate an existing source emitting a pollutant which is prescribed as such for a non-attainment area. The permit remains in force until modified or replaced by an Operating permit, or the source is relocated. One of the central regulatory requirements is that emission control will be undertaken by reference to the 'best available control technology'. However, in the case of volatile organic compounds (VOCs), nitrogen oxides and (in two localities of Virginia, at the time of writing) carbon monoxide, control of emissions must be undertaken under the more restrictive terms of 'lowest achievable emission rate'. In order to avoid an increase in the total amount of prescribed pollutants in a Non-attainment Area, a new or expanding business is obliged to offset its emissions of VOCs and nitrogen oxides. Offsets may include emissions trading within the same Non-attainment Area.

Regulatory style: Canada   Against the background of the constitutional structures described above, the federal government has a generally limited jurisdiction in relation to air pollution and air quality. Under the federal Environmental Protection Act 1999, the federal government has statutory responsibility for the national fuel mark system, setting federal air quality objectives, emission guidelines and standards, vehicle emissions and international, transboundary air pollution control. In addition, federal responsibility extends to the application and enforcement of requirements relating to emissions under motor vehicle safety legislation. Where air quality objectives are concerned, values have, at the time of writing, been established for five pollutants. In the case of emission standards, values have been set for a variety of purposes, including vinyl chloride emissions from facilities manufacturing vinyl chloride and polyvinyl chloride. Agreements between the federal government and provincial governments may be concluded for a variety of purposes, such as the Acid Rain Reduction Program. The agreement between the federal government and the province of Nova Scotia, for example, is reflected in provincial measures (incorporated in the Nova Scotian Air Quality Regulations 1995) whereby an annual cap of 189,000 tonnes is placed on sulphur dioxide emissions from that province. These arrangements have to be seen against the background of the Canada-United States Air Quality Agreement dating from 1991.

Regulatory style: Province of Alberta, Canada   It is generally the provincial governments which undertake regulation of emissions from stationary sources. The regulator, Alberta Environment, is empowered to regulate the emission of substances into the atmosphere by virtue of the Environmental Protection and Enhancement Act 1993. Part IV of the Act prescribes a regulatory framework based on approvals and Codes of Practice against a background of general prohibitions affecting releases to the atmosphere. The Substance Release Regulations 1996 deal with four categories of release: visible emissions from stationary sources, particulate emissions from a wide variety of industrial and combustion processes, secondary lead smelter particulate emissions, and vinyl chloride releases from vinyl chloride and polyvinyl chloride plants. Interestingly, the Regulation identifies certain activities where substance release to the atmosphere is governed by Codes of Practice rather than regulatory approval. Where the requirement for Code compliance applies monitoring obligations are prescribed to ensure effective control of emissions. The industrial sectors selected are those using standardised industrial environmental protection practices, are not complex and have little potential to create adverse environmental impacts. Foundries, for example, are governed by the Code of Practice for Foundries. Where regulatory approval is required the assumption is that emissions will be minimised through the application of pollution prevention practices and the use of 'best available demonstrated pollution control technologies', taking account of the Alberta Ambient Air Quality Guidelines. Any approval granted will normally have a life of 10 years, although the regulator may substitute a shorter period. The holder of an approval may apply for an amendment at any time. The regulator may also take the initiative and propose an amendment. Approvals may be suspended, cancelled or transferred, the latter with written approval from the regulator. In some circumstances financial security may be required from a person granted an approval. Where this is the case and there is noncompliance with the subject approval, the security may be used for remedial purposes.

Economic and Other Instruments

Chapter Six provided a general background to economic instruments where it was seen that such instruments almost always complement regulatory control of the environment. Reference might usefully be made to the description of carbon taxes in certain Community member states in that chapter. The control of air pollution and the enhancement atmospheric quality are characterised by difficulties of implementation and enforcement and it is the difficulty of deploying more traditional regulatory devices that suggest the merits of economic instruments. Such instruments and their ability to internalise costs, which otherwise would fall on the environment, manifest the 'polluter pays' principle. However, it has been seen previously that there are all sorts of other variables which will tend to determine whether economic instruments are truly efficient. For example, it may be asked at what point an environmental tax is levied. It may be asked also at what rate that tax is levied. This second question begs a host of other questions, not least of which are those that focus on matters of valuation: what environmental damage should be taken account of and how should that damage be valued for present purposes? In the present area of environmental control the range of economic instruments extends beyond charges and other environmental taxes which are referable to emissions, to include charges and taxes levied on products such as fuels which have an adverse atmospheric impact. In some cases the policy preference may be in favour of the creation of artificial markets where, through what is usually referred to as 'emissions trading', it is possible (as was seen again in Chapter Six) to exert control over and internalise costs which otherwise would fall on the environment. Elsewhere in this section of the chapter, consideration will be given to other instruments which are of particular relevance to air pollution and atmospheric quality enhancement: agreements, environmental management systems and subsidies in particular.

Economic Instruments

A thumbnail sketch of economic instruments is set out below, focusing on the experiences of the European Community, the United Kingdom and Canada. However, reference should be made to Chapter Six where there is already a substantial section on economic instruments for present purposes. Particular note should be made of the Swedish nitrogen oxides charging scheme, emissions trading in the United States, the emerging emission trading scheme in the United Kingdom, the Climate Change Levy in the United Kingdom, carbon taxes in Finland, the Netherlands, Sweden and Denmark, and the European Community's 'facilitative' policy on economic instruments. The present section of this chapter will concentrate principally on issues not already dealt with in Chapter Six.

Economic instruments in the European Community Although much has been said already about the approach of the Community to economic instruments being characterised as a 'facilitative' policy, this is not entirely the case in one important area relating to the specifications of motor vehicles and the fuels used by them. Directive 98/70[31] introduced a prohibition on the marketing of regular unleaded petrol as well as prescribing standards for unleaded and diesel fuel, taking account of public health and environmental criteria. The Directive contains some measure of flexibility in permitting any member state to prescribe more stringent fuel standards where, in certain designated areas, there are seriously adverse air quality conditions. Various other directives have been aimed at prescribing emission standards for motor vehicles. Although the environmental basis of much of this Community law is beyond doubt, there has also been a certain preoccupation with the internal market, ensuring that undue competitive advantage cannot be sought by any one member state's motor manufacturing. Overall, therefore, these areas of

Community law and policy can be characterised as rather more direct than merely facilitative, combining limit values for emissions as well as a framework within which member states may for example offer tax-based incentives for those vehicles which demonstrate fuel and emission efficiency.

Economic instruments in the United Kingdom The government of the United Kingdom has had a policy in recent years whereby the duty payable on motor fuel has been subject to continual increase, year by year. In turn, there has been discrimination in favour of those varieties of diesel fuel with lower levels of sulphur, for example, as well as discrimination in favour of fuel-efficient vehicles through reductions in vehicle excise duty. These instruments are of course important additions to the government's emission trading scheme (ETS) and the Climate Change Levy, covered in Chapter Six. Schemes also exist giving favourable tax treatment to those projects which utilise energy-saving materials.

Economic instruments in the United States Emissions trading referred to in Chapter Six is undoubtedly the best known form of economic instrument in use in the United States. Beyond any federal initiative here, it was seen earlier in this chapter that individual states may utilise emissions trading for a variety of purposes. In the case of the State of Virginia, it has been seen already that emission set-off is applied in Non-attainment Areas for the purpose of minimising emissions of volatile organic compounds and nitrogen oxides.

Economic instruments in Canada Economic instruments are in an early state of development at the time of writing. However, both the federal and provincial governments have legislative powers in respect of economic instruments. In the province of Nova Scotia, for example, section 15 of the Environment Act 1995 empowers the Minister to establish programmes for the research, development and use of economic instruments and market-based approaches both for the purpose of environmental management and to achieve environmental quality objectives in a cost-effective manner. These powers will no doubt be considered as a vehicle for the development of law and policy on matters such as climate change in due course. In the meantime, one of the more significant economic instruments in relation to air pollution control operates in British Columbia where an emission fee is payable at a rate of $60 per tonne, accompanied by an annual administration fee of $1000 per permit. An incentive element operates to reduce the fee where it can be established that actual emission levels are below those prescribed by the permit. However, if emissions exceed the permit limit, a revision occurs with a commensurate increase in the fee payable.

Agreements and Understandings

It has been seen above that the Canadian federal and provincial governments may negotiate and conclude agreements in respect of air pollution and atmospheric quality so that limits, standards and objectives can percolate into municipal law at the local, provincial level. The federal government, using statutory powers, is able to regulate emission standards for motor vehicles which are either manufactured in Canada, or are imported from elsewhere. However, in practice, the approach has been to enter into a voluntary memorandum of understanding with motor manufacturers in order to ensure that the emission standards apply throughout the country. Such an understanding is rather different to a legally binding contract, and it seems that governments exert considerable influence in this way, in seeking to stress what they would regard as appropriate environmental standards without being bound contractually. Much the same situation occurs in the European Community where European car manufacturers, in 1998, put before the Commission an offer in respect of the carbon dioxide emission standards for all new vehicles commissioned in the Community from the year 2008.[32] However, it appears that this arrangement has a distinct, legally binding character, to the extent that after Council endorsement and approval by the Parliament, the Community has effectively bound itself not to legislate on matters such as vehicle carbon dioxide emissions and fuel efficiency during the life of the agreement. It is difficult to see how the Community can bind itself to such an agreement, no matter what the environmental context. Fundamentally it could be expected that any such agreement might be legally binding only if competence for this purpose was defined by the Treaty. It has been seen already, towards the end of Chapter Seven, that such competence is not so defined. Ultimately, a Commission recommendation is the usual conclusion to transactions of this sort, further confusing the question whether there can be any legally binding commitment at Community level. Even assuming that such a legally binding commitment is possible here at the centre, there is no certainty that it would be regarded as such by the member states.

Environmental Management Systems

In all of the jurisdictions considered in the present chapter, environmental management systems are actively encouraged. In the United States, the Environmental Protection Agency seeks to encourage companies to participate in ISO 14001 for the purpose of voluntarily enhancing standards of environmental management. Equally, in Canada ISO 14001 is adopted as an element of the national system of environmental standards. The European Community's own EMAS scheme which has been examined in earlier chapters[33] has had a modest start in member states like the United Kingdom. Nevertheless, the assumptions and expectations which flow from such an environmental management system have a potentially important relationship with emerging regulatory schemes such as that concerning integrated pollution prevention and control. IPPC is concerned with the totality of emissions and discharges from any one, regulated installation, as well as matters such as the efficiency of energy use, all of which will be encapsulated in the operation of an environmental management system. In turn, there will no doubt be cogent arguments in favour of more streamlined regulatory approaches where a company can demonstrate successful participation in EMAS, or ISO14001.

Subsidies

Reference can usefully be made to Chapter Six[34] where subsidies were considered in the context of economic instruments overall. Despite the fact that subsidies appear to be the antithesis of the 'polluter pays' principle, nevertheless, they are deployed increasingly for the purpose of encouraging environmental efficiency in dealing with emissions to the atmosphere. Subsidies may of course be applied indirectly through a system of tax allowances, as well being applied directly, through governmental grant-giving, for example. Subsidies may be seen to be particularly efficient where the product of a carbon tax, such as that applied in Denmark, for example, is used in order to facilitate investment in better technology. In some cases, the policy priority may be in favour of the need to modernise, in which case tax revenues will usefully be applied in order to allow new investment in up-to-date plant and technology.

Enforcement

The enforcement of air pollution legislation is such a disparate and difficult subject that it is necessary to explain at the outset the nature of the enforcement difficulty before going on to examine in outline the points at which enforcement opportunities arise. Those enforcement opportunities depend of course on the nature of the regulatory relationship which applies between the parties in question. Following an examination of these two issues, the remainder of this final section of the chapter proceeds to look at some interesting – and significant – manifestations of regulatory enforcement across the jurisdictions which have featured in this chapter. This includes consideration of so-called 'compliance assessment' which addresses the question whether it can be established that there has, or has not, been compliance as well as the question whether a regulatory regime might usefully provide assistance towards compliance rather than pursue enforcement to its normal conclusion. Also considered is what can be described as 'jurisdictional' enforcement, which returns to the widely configured possibilities that accrue from an area of environmental law that often stretches from the detailed requirements of municipal law through to the international treaties and conventions between nations or groups of nations. Across this axis there are important relationships which determine matters such as cooperative regulation as well as policy matters concerning the sometimes controversial matter of the distribution of regulatory responsibility. On some occasions, as in the United States, power and authority are very much at the centre although it is doubtful whether further distribution at state level can always be characterised as 'cooperative'. This issue as it affects enforcement will be addressed below in an examination of the policy of deterrence as it operates in the United States. Within the broader issue of 'jurisdictional' enforcement is included a consideration of the controls, and their enforcement, available in respect of ozone and ozone-depleting substances. Although the emphasis here is on the regulatory enforcement of emissions to the atmosphere and atmospheric quality, many of the issues mentioned are equally pertinent to other areas of environmental control.

Enforcement Difficulties

At the heart of enforcement difficulties in relation to air pollution law is the seemingly simple question, who in law is responsible for a polluting emission? Such a question is probably capable of a number of different answers, depending on the circumstances.

Point source regulation Arguably the easiest answer is the one that emerges from facts indicating that the source of the emission in question is a closely regulated site or installation where the authorisation is suitably specific on the matter of emission limits as well as the monitoring of emissions. Depending on the statutory powers available to the regulator there may be resort to the criminal law or resort to civil sanctions which might extend across the possibility of revocation, suspension or variation of the licence or permit granted. The question here comes down to what it is that the regulator has to prove. In practice the simplest option is that which demands enforcement of a failure to comply with the terms of that licence or permit. Explicit definition of trigger limits or standards backed by accurate monitoring data will be necessarily fundamental here. This enforcement process here is at least potentially efficient because the elusive nature of the environmental pollution is closely defined within an identifiable point source and the operation of the site or installation is clearly defined within the regulatory framework of the licence or permit. Beyond this set of facts the problems of enforcement raise a host of other, more difficult questions under the heading of 'non-point sources'.

Non-point source regulation It is the diffuse sources of air pollution that represent the real problems of enforcement confronting policy-makers, legislators and law enforcers. Diffuse sources range from the very small to the very large.

At the former end of the scale are those sources which can often be characterised as a 'statutory nuisance' where enforcement, usually by a local authority or even by an aggrieved individual, depends on proof that, in common law terms, the smoke or other emission was akin to a common law nuisance. Still at this more modest end of the scale are those emissions where statutory nuisance enforcement may not be appropriate, in which case the option may be prosecution where it can be established on the evidence that the defendant has 'caused or (knowingly) permitted' the subject pollution, for example. Proof of causation may be the simpler option here, bearing in mind that the requirement is that that defendant had 'control' of the activity that led to the smoke or other emission. That option is arguably the simpler option since there is no necessity to prove *mens rea* – guilty intention – on the part of the defendant if, as is likely, it is the criminal law that is in issue. Furthermore, it may be open to the court in these circumstances to reverse the onus of proof in respect of what is often referred to as an offence of strict liability. Although it will usually be the local authority that undertakes prosecutions of this sort, there may be no bar on private prosecution. Beyond enforcement in these foregoing categories problems of air pollution and the control of, and responsibility for, emissions throw up other challenges which trigger different approaches in regulatory law and policy. Law, policy and practice appear to expand from what has been described as point, or non-point, source emissions of relatively parochial proportions to concern for air quality management with the emphasis on state responsibility. Indeed, the graduation from one to another can usually be discerned quite clearly from the applicable statute law. Addressing diffuse sources has called for a rather wider-based approach such as legally binding restrictions on the production, distribution, use and disposal of those products whose make up is significantly responsible for the generation of emissions of hazardous pollutants. However, it should not be forgotten that economic instruments also may contribute to policy priorities in favour of emission control where (say) there is a necessity to deal with a large number of smaller sources or where, as in the Netherlands for example, installation of new and more efficient technology may be achieved through tax allowances.

Air quality management The nature of the emissions problem has expanded to an extent that the real concern is with the achievement of quality standards (usually in relation to certain problem pollutants) with responsibilities, often defined by statute, extending upwards from local government, through regional government (where it is part of the hierarchy), to national government and ultimately (again where it is part of the hierarchy) to a federal or other tier of government such as the European Community.

At this point there are two critical questions: how best to achieve a global or other widely-defined standard for air or atmospheric quality, and (if deemed necessary as a policy preference or priority) how best to define and fix legal or other responsibility, and its enforcement, on any one or more of the foregoing levels of government? This latter issue, whether it relates to member state liability in proceedings by the European Community, state liability to the federal Environmental Protection Agency in the United States or state liability under an international treaty or convention, is one that will normally be based on a clear policy priority. That priority is to ensure that the force of law is capable of securing accountability for noncompliance, at least on the assumption that those with rights to enforce can prove their case by reference to robust criteria based essentially on principles of causation. This though is not to suggest that the sole objective of such enforcement is a desire to impose financial penalties even though they may be part of the agreed parcel of sanctions, as is now the case in European Community law, for example. As will be seen later in this chapter, there may be a rather more supportive enforcement environment which may seek to address the underlying causes of the failure to comply. There may, for example, be a need for a state as a party to an international agreement to adjust regulatory or other controls within its jurisdiction in order to avoid future noncompliance. Whatever the context, limits, standards, objectives or targets will all contribute to agreed requirements for air quality management.

Those agreed requirements will often demonstrate the transboundary dimension of law and policy in the present context where ambient air quality standards are increasingly subject to sophisticated monitoring and measurement. However, the case of ozone, as one prominent example, shows that in this area of environmental law and policy the credibility of the law may be at stake where there are misguided attempts to impose liability and responsibility on a party who really has no control over transboundary sources. It is here that monitoring and measurement have an important role in providing warnings to the population where so-called 'alert' thresholds are breached. In this case it may be a party's failure to comply with legal requirements for the provision of that monitoring and measurement that results in an application of sanctions. Again, the control of ozone and ozone-depleting products provides an important example for this and wider purposes, extending from international conventional control right down to detailed municipal law and policy, as will be seen later in this section of the chapter.

Regulatory Enforcement

Enforcement policies   To the extent that regulatory requirements apply in areas such as integrated pollution prevention and control, enforcement policies will often be available. Such policies will indicate the criteria and variables which will relate to decisions by the regulator about the deployment of available civil and criminal remedies in the event of noncompliance. However, the relationship between the regulator and the regulated may allow a clear view of the extent to which any infraction will result in enforcement action being taken. This will be the case whether the relationship is at arm's length or is rather closer. This choice of regulatory style often refers to the distinction between an approach based on deterrence and one which can be described as resting on a strategy of compliance. These distinctive styles will be picked up and dealt with after consideration is given to the question of precautionary regulation.

Precautionary regulation   Whatever the characteristics of the regulatory relationship, there is always an outstanding question about how regulatory discretion might be used in order to deal with problems of atmospheric pollution on a precautionary basis, whether or not an emission is comprehended within the terms of a licence, permit or other authorisation. Whatever the context, enforcement carries with it a risk that statutory powers may not be sufficiently wide in order to accommodate precautionary action. In lawmaking terms, this raises the controversial question of how much enforcement power may be ceded to the regulator. The nub of the problem is whether that regulator can resort lawfully to statutory powers of enforcement where statistics show that it is very unlikely that an emission to the atmosphere will have a material and adverse effect on human health or the environment, and that view is shared by the scientists. Clearly, some statutory powers will be wide enough for this purpose, some not. It would be reassuring to believe that such distinctions are based on conscious policy choices. Within the European Community a directive may draw a line which indicates that transposition stops short of precautionary regulation which may seriously hinder a response to a legitimate environmental crisis. However, policy creation in the present context tends to be based on a careful evaluation of scientific evidence which, in turn, tends to be driven by precautionary assumptions. This can be seen in the recommendation of an air quality standard for ozone by the United Kingdom Expert Panel on Air Quality Standards:[35]

> The Panel have decided to recommend an Air Quality Standard for ozone in terms of a concentration with a specified averaging time. We have chosen a level of 50 ppb – appreciably lower than the concentration at which effects have been detected experimentally – in order to include a margin of safety. The Panel recommend that the 50 ppb level be measured as a running 8-hour average, since this most closely represents the exposures likely to be harmful to human health.[36]

Against this background there appears to be presumption against a policy preference in favour of very wide powers of regulatory enforcement. In practice, statutory powers tend to be tied to failures to comply with licences, permits or authorisations or conditions attached. Otherwise, more general powers outside such a regulated framework will tend to be subject to criminal enforcement, necessitating cogent evidence that the defendant caused or knowingly permitted the offending emission.

Compliance Regulation, or Deterrence?

Environmental regulation in the United States is characterised as depending on a policy of deterrence, in contrast to many others which depend on a rather more consensual approach dependent on strategies of compliance. This seemingly stark contrast occupies a good deal of what appears below, with a rather more detailed examination of the environmental enforcement regime in the United States appearing in the next main section of the chapter. For the moment though, four matters are considered: the nature of compliance strategy, the distribution of enforcement jurisdiction in the Canadian federal state, the associated problem of what is described as 'regulatory withdrawal', and (finally), the enforcement of transboundary regulation.

The nature of compliance strategy The essence of compliance strategy is that enforcement is based on an approach which does not necessarily involve full legal enforcement in respect an infraction. This is in stark contrast to what may be described as full legal enforcement, one of whose principal objects, as in the United States, is the achievement of deterrence.

An important illustration of compliance strategy is found in the Montreal Protocol on the Control of Substances that Deplete the Ozone Layer. Two areas of noncompliance here relate to production of proscribed substances in excess of prescribed limits, and unlawful trades in proscribed substances. Given the scale and extent of the Montreal Protocol it is not surprising that, in practice, enforcement is by no means easy. Clearly, the Protocol could well have been built on a formal process of identifying responsibility and thereafter imposing sanctions for proven infractions. Finding cogent evidence to establish such responsibility is undoubtedly difficult, at least as long as the infrastructure of the Protocol depends essentially on the submission of data by participating states. Against this background, a supportive policy applies in order to facilitate compliance by those states found to be in breach of their legal obligations.

Compliance strategy is well in evidence in the environmental law and policy of individual states. By way of illustration, in the Community, there are numerous examples of a policy preference for such a strategy in the laws governing air pollution. Towards the beginning of Chapter Seven it was seen that, prior to accession to membership of the Community, environmental control in the United Kingdom was characterised as 'consensual' and, given the frequent closeness of the regulator and the regulated, prone to the accusation of 'regulatory capture'. Although accession to membership of the Community has led to greater legal formality, the environmental regulator still tends to work fairly closely with those subject to regulation against a background of explicit enforcement policies and close consultation on strategies for transposition of Community environmental law. Evidence of a consensual approach to environmental control can be found in other Community member states. Air pollution law and policy in France shows a close collaborative relationship between the regulators and industrial associations which is driven by negotiation as a means of avoiding conflict. The spirit of agreement is also well evidenced in the Netherlands, as was seen in Chapter Seven. A final example shows that in Sweden, the environmental protection legislation actively encourages collaborative plant assessment in order to evaluate polluting processes overall, often against a background of general abatement strategies and action plans. Equally, there are many examples of compliance strategy in Canada.

The distribution of enforcement jurisdiction in the Canadian federal state
The Canada-Wide Accord on Environmental Harmonisation is an instrument under active development by the Canadian Council of Ministers of the Environment (CCME), whose status and functions were described towards the end of Chapter Two. The Accord is intended to develop working relationships for the purpose of policy development and programme management among the provinces and the federal government in relation to environmental regulation and control. Provincial governments are able to introduce more stringent standards than those agreed here as 'Canada-Wide Standards' although smaller provinces rely heavily on federal expertise and specialised resources here. Where consensus is not forthcoming in CCME, the provinces are able to apply their own standards.

Canada-wide standards have been developed under the Accord in order to provide for standardisation across the country, whilst recognising regional variations. Included here are standards for ozone, particulates, benzene and mercury, among others, all of which provide the essential benchmark for regulatory processes in the provinces.

A draft agreement on environmental monitoring and reporting is under development at the time of writing. An agreement on inspections and enforcement was accepted in principle in 2000. The objectives of this agreement include the achievement of a consistent, high level of compliance with environmental protection laws across Canada, particularly where there may be an overlap of federal and provincial enforcement jurisdiction. Whether or not an overlap exists, a smaller province may invite federal assistance. Nevertheless, the agreement recognises the continuing sovereignty of enforcement powers available to the federal and provincial governments where an infraction falls within these respective jurisdictions. In addition, provincial legislation may indicate that it is binding on the federal government. This is undoubtedly a sensitive and difficult situation in some cases where a provincial regulator seeks to take enforcement action. However, it would appear that such a statutory declaration is legally effective where a valid provincial function is in issue and there is no direct conflict between federal and provincial law.[37]

The foregoing agreements, including that on inspections and enforcement, have attracted controversy. In proceedings for judicial review, for example, it was argued in *Canadian Environmental Law Association v. Canada*[38] that the agreements under the Accord constituted a *de facto* transfer of authority to CCME, as an intergovernmental body, such that the federal Minister's accountability would be diminished, and that the Minister exceeded his lawful authority in signing such agreements. The court held that the agreements and their statutory foundation rendered them amenable to judicial review even though they could be regarded as agreements in principle, containing statements of political intention. Ultimately the court refused to intervene on issues raised, in the absence of essential facts.

Distribution of enforcement and, indeed, other regulatory functions may sometimes depend on judicial interpretation. This was indeed the case in proceedings before the Supreme Court of Canada in *Spraytech v. Town of Hudson*.[39] This was a case where a company – Spraytech – challenged the legality of a town's bye-law prohibiting the use of pesticides for purely cosmetic purposes. It was held that the bye-law was not *ultra vires* the enabling power since its purpose was to minimise pesticide use for the health of inhabitants, a purpose which fell squarely within that power. Apart from suggesting also that the bye-law was consistent with the precautionary principle examined earlier in Chapter Three, the Supreme Court found no conflict either with federal or provincial statutory provision on pesticides. In particular it was held that there is no barrier to dual compliance and no barrier to local, municipal provision covering pesticide use. Consequently there exists what was described as a 'tri-level' regulatory regime.

Regulatory withdrawal From the foregoing litigation it is clear that in Canada one point of controversy surrounding the Accord is the suggestion that constituent agreements may have the effect of federal withdrawal from environmental protection functions. While this is one example of so-called 'regulatory withdrawal' there are others. Both in Canada and elsewhere it may be suggested that withdrawal occurs on those occasions where the regulator opts in favour of negotiated agreements, as a result of which it may be assumed that transparency and public accountability are substituted with a private, discrete, contractual arrangement. This may well be the case where statutory powers appear to permit any such arrangement, albeit under the guise of self-regulation for enforcement purposes. Such withdrawal of environmental control from the regulatory framework may have important knock-on effects, at least to the extent that there are (for example) areas of accountability in law which depend on public law regulation rather than private law contracting. Depending on the law of the jurisdiction in question there may be regulatory obligations which trigger accompanying obligations under freedom of information legislation, for example. As a consequence information about enforcement activity may not reach the public domain if that activity is governed by a contract, unless of course the parties voluntarily agree. Manipulation of environmental controls and their enforcement may also lead to regulatory withdrawal where there is power to off-load functions and responsibilities to another level in the governmental hierarchy, again with other consequences of the sort just described.

The enforcement of transboundary regulation Given the transboundary issues which afflict law and policy on air pollution and air quality standards, it is hardly surprising that this complex topic raises equally complex matters of enforcement and enforceability. Nowhere is this better illustrated than in the arrangements which exist between the United States and Canada. The Air Quality Agreement of 1991 commits the two states to address transboundary air pollution. Initially the control of acid rain and sulphur dioxide exercised the agreement although attention has now turned also to the problems of other pollutants, such as ozone. Both states have enacted legislation in order to facilitate agreements and strategies where the primary legal responsibility lies on the respective federal governments. However, in terms of implementation and enforcement of detailed plans and strategies, the respective states and provinces undertake important functions. Although the respective federal governments have prime enforcement responsibilities, nevertheless the states and provinces may adopt facilities as a 'reciprocating jurisdiction'. In the case of the Canadian province of Nova Scotia, for example, where 85 per cent of air pollution emanates from outside its borders, the Environment Act 1994 makes provision for access to the courts of the province where pollution has originated, or may have originated, from the province. Where such litigation occurs the law of the province applies no matter where any loss, damage or injury is suffered.

The Policy of Deterrence in the United States

The deterrent core of Environmental Protection Agency enforcement policy is aimed essentially at the application of coercive sanctions prescribed by law which requires that cogent evidence is adduced. This suggests a generally different approach to enforcement that was seen earlier in the references to other states such as the United Kingdom, Sweden, the Netherlands and France.

The extent and effectiveness of deterrence by contrast has to be appreciated by reference to the essentially coercive nature of the remedies sought, as well as their scale. Culturally, this reliance on deterrence suggests a traditionally arm's length relationship between the regulator and the regulated. In turn, deterrence suggests an absence of a consensual or consultative approach to regulation and its enforcement. On the other hand in a very large jurisdiction there are no doubt strong policy arguments in favour of a standardised system of regulation, reinforced with strongly coercive enforcement. Indeed, the Agency appears to give considerable emphasis to annual enforcement records.[40]

Agency enforcement powers and their application The Clean Air Act contains a formidable array of enforcement powers for use by the Environmental Protection Agency as well as states acting under delegated authority. The Act shows that most infractions enforceable under the criminal law are in fact the more serious crimes known as felonies. Civil actions are also available against violators, as well as administrative orders and accompanying civil penalties, and injunctive proceedings. Citizen suits are also provided for.

Agency enforcement and the states As between individual states and the Environmental Protection Agency there can be considerable difficulties in relation to environmental control and enforcement in particular. Those tensions are caused by a number of factors, not least the attempts of the Agency to monitor and audit state enforcement performance. Given the deterrent emphasis of the approach to enforcement, another point of tension relates to the costs accruing against a state in relation to the totality of the process, stretching from initial regulatory responsibilities, through inspection and monitoring, to enforcement action before the courts. Standardised regulatory requirements under the Clean Air Act and other environmental legislation administered centrally provides another pressure point where states stress the absence of any effective discretion to mould regulatory requirements to regional characteristics and priorities. Enforcement will often provide further evidence of tension, to the extent that there is crucial disagreement between Agency and state on the essential approach to regulation as defined by statute, as well as the scale and emphasis of enforcement. In turn, it is not unusual to find Agency criticism of a state based on allegations of apparent willingness to permit violation either in the absence of enforcement or where it is considered that enforcement action is inadequate, given the nature and effect of the infraction. On occasions such tensions can result in prolonged litigation, as where a state might seek pre-emptive action before the court prior to federal intervention before the court in respect of an alleged infraction. Where the state has decided in favour of less stringent enforcement action it may be up to the court to decide that its statutory enforcement regime is less extensive than the federal regime and should not therefore prevail.[41] In other situations there is no doubt that the Agency has considerable power to prescribe enforcement requirements to be applied at state level. This is seen in an interesting example arising from Agency requirements for the revision of Virginia's State Implementation Plan for Nitrogen Oxides. The State of Virginia was identified, along with certain other states, as having a substantially inadequate Plan to comply with Clean Air Act requirements addressing the interstate transport of nitrogen oxides in quantities that contribute significantly to ozone non-attainment in one or more other states. As a result of the injunction to present a revised Plan it was necessary for the State of Virginia to include a description of accompanying enforcement methods.[42] Despite the foregoing tensions, the Agency has established a number of National Compliance Assistance Centres in order to provide support for those subject to regulation and who might, in turn, be subject to enforcement action.

Ozone Enforcement

Brief reference was made earlier in the chapter to the Montreal Protocol which provides a good example of international conventional regulation which provides a largely effective control regime through the municipal law of participating states. The Protocol provides a usually well-defined image of the activities which require control. In turn, it is really a matter for the participating states how they achieve enforcement of those controls: some states have even opted for voluntary agreements rather than traditional regulatory controls. However, the Protocol fulfils a crucial function in stressing the need for effective controls through robustly designed regulatory or other measures, as well as allowing the sharing of experiences which may suggest a need for a strengthening of that regulation. Where enforcement is concerned, however, there are two levels to be considered. In the first place there is the enforcement of primary obligations under the Protocol where compliance strategy is the main policy priority, as seen above. However, transposition of Protocol requirements through municipal law is essentially a matter for the participating state according to its own cultural priorities. This is especially true of the enforcement mechanisms in support of the regulatory or other requirements chosen to reflect compliance with the Protocol. That there is a fundamental link between these two elements almost goes without saying. A particular problem as the Montreal Protocol evolves relates to the development of supply controls affecting ozone-depleting substances.

The supply of ozone-depleting substances Regulatory or any similar control of supply is very much at the heart of the Montreal Protocol. However, where consumers are concerned there is a danger that unfulfilled demand may create incentives in favour of unlawful smuggling and other illegal importation, particularly where there has been a failure of educative initiatives. Those initiatives may well encourage exploration of effective – and lawful – means of managing unfulfilled demand. Such an extension is likely to be legislated in the European Community, which has ratified the Montreal Protocol. In the United States, the Environmental Protection Agency has considerable powers to deal with this problem of illegal importation.

Illegal importation under the US federal Clean Air Act Section 113 of the federal Clean Air Act confers on the Environmental Protection Agency considerable powers of enforcement, which are actively pursued. Sanctions include fines, imprisonment, and the withdrawal of regulatory permits. Among a considerable number of proceedings reported by the Agency just one example shows how the courts may deal with cases of unlawful importation of CFCs. This example involves seven cargo containers of CFCs containing 8,400 cylinders of refrigerant gas – dichlorodifluoromethane – being smuggled into the United States. Having pleaded guilty, one of the co-conspirators was sentenced to 22 months' imprisonment, three years' probation and a fine of $6,000.[43]

General regulatory and enforcement approaches In the United States it is federal legislation under the Clean Air Act which carries the most important areas of control although there is legislation in some states. In Canada, the federal government again has primary responsibility for implementation of the Protocol, under the Environmental Protection Act 1999 and related regulations, although each of the provinces has legislation for the purpose of detailed implementation. At Canadian federal level sanctions are based on fines and imprisonment whereas at provincial level there are examples of withdrawal of regulatory permits and benefits also. The European Union has legislated by Regulation, which imposes directly applicable obligations.[44] This legislation requires a member state to make its own municipal provision in relation to matters such as the penalties and sanctions for any manufacturer who is convicted of a prescribed offence. Some member states such as Denmark have additional municipal laws which are more stringent than Community law alone. However, a number of member states, including Denmark and the United Kingdom, have concluded voluntary agreements with the industries involved. Furthermore, some member states, again including Denmark, rely also on economic instruments in order to provide subsidies to encourage the development of alternatives to ozone-depleting substances.

Notes

1   For a general overview, see United Nations Economic Commission for Europe (1999), *Strategies and Policies for Air Pollution Abatement*, ECE/EB.AIR/65, Geneva.
2   See, for example, Decision 81/462, OJ L171, 27.6.81.
3   OJ C485, 18.3.92. *Cf.* Chapter One, n. 1.
4   OJ L336, 7.12.88.
5   COM (97) 88, 12 March 1997.
6   COM (95) 372, 26 July 1995.
7   See in particular, Chapter One, n. 1, and Chapter Two, nn. 24 and 32.
8   Chapter One, n. 55.
9   OJ L87, 27.3.85: to be replaced by a daughter directive under the Air Quality Framework Directive: 96/62 (OJ L296, 21.11.96).
10 OECD (1997), *Environmental Indicators for Agriculture*, p. 9.
11 Luxembourg, 1997.
12 *Ibid.*, at p. 65.
13 Luxembourg, 2001.
14 *Ibid.*, pp. 98–9.
15 *Supra*, n. 13, at pp. 100–101.
16 *Supra*, n. 10, at pp. 35–6.
17 Ministry of Agriculture, Fisheries and Food, 2000.
18 *Ibid.*, at pp. 40–41.
19 Chapter One, nn. 53–4 and Chapter Two, n. 31.
20 OJ L188, 16.7.84. *Cf.* Directives 88/609, 89/369 and 94/67.
21 Chapter Two, nn. 23, 24 and 32.
22 *Supra*, n. 4.
23 OJ L85, 28.3.87.
24 OJ L257, 10.10.96.
25 OJ L229, 30.8.80.
26 *Supra*, n. 4.
27 OJ L85, 29.3.99.
28 *Supra*, n. 24.
29 S.I. 2000, No. 1973.
30 See, for example, Chapter Seven, n. 35.
31 OJ L350, 28.12.98.
32 COM (98), 29 July 1998.
33 Chapter One, nn. 3, 4, 33 and 96; Chapter Two, nn. 42–4.

34   Chapter Six, nn. 8–9.
35   Department of the Environment, 1994.
36   *Ibid.*, at p. 9.
37   See, for example, Chapter Four, n. 97.
38   (1999) 88 A.C.W.S. 3d. 396.
39   Unreported, 28 June 2001.
40   See, for example, http://www.epa.gov/docs/ozone/enforce/record.html.
41   *United States v. Smithfield Foods Inc.* 972 Fed. Supp. 338 (1997).
42   http://www.deq.state.va.us/air/planning/noxsip.html.
43   http://www.epa.gov/docs/ozone/enforce/enforce.html.
44   See Chapter One, n. 20.

Chapter Nine

Developing Law and Policy for Amenity Control

Law, Policy and Landscape

While Chapter Eight looked at developing law and policy in relation to pollution control by reference to one area of such control – air pollution and air quality – the present chapter looks at one area of amenity law, landscape regulation. Landscape is undoubtedly a highly subjective issue where comparisons with other jurisdictions and their attitude to law and policy is that much more difficult, compared with the area of pollution control examined in Chapter 8. Much of the emphasis is on the attitude to law and policy as it emerges in England, and the European Community although reference is also made to the position in the United States and Canada. Where the United Kingdom is concerned there are considerable similarities in the approach to landscape regulation although devolution has allowed England to develop its own raft of law and policy. That law and policy and its development shows that concerns for landscape are found in many disparate areas including development control under planning legislation, nature conservation, agriculture and the coastline.

Landscape: a Framework for Policy Creation

What has emerged in recent times is the realisation that a concern for landscape can provide an holistic starting point for the purpose of determining policy priorities in the areas just mentioned and, in turn, for identifying the extent and emphasis of any role that might be played by the law. There is no doubt, however, that any examination of developing law and policy on landscape as an amenity is difficult, not only by reference its essentially subjective nature. Although the holistic qualities of landscape are extolled increasingly, in the European Community at least, the fact remains that it has often tended to be approached as a secondary element in law and policy terms. Arguably this approach is typified in relation to development control where landscape is often but one of a number of material considerations in the decision-making process. Where nature conservation is concerned landscape is necessarily subsumed in concerns about habitat. In the case of agriculture, landscape has assumed a status in the European Community that did not exist previously as long as there was almost total preoccupation with production priorities. As that preoccupation has reduced so the vacuum has been filled – in part – with opportunities to preserve and enhance the rural landscape. By way of contrast, the development of law and policy affecting coastal landscapes and their management appears to involve rather different considerations both within the European Community and beyond. For this reason the wider comparative developments relating to what is now known as Integrated Coastal Zone Management (ICZM) are dealt with later in this chapter.

Landscape and Agriculture

This meeting of issues concerning agriculture and landscape is a potentially important manifestation of the environmental policy integration (EPI) first addressed towards the end of Chapter One. All of this begins to show the disparate nature of developing law and policy as it affects landscape. It is against this background that the present chapter divides into five sections, covering characteristics, functions and values; environmental pressure points affecting landscape; strategies to address landscape protection and enhancement; the European Community's Rural Development Regulation; and regulatory and other forms of liability. This final section of the chapter will outline the factors and variables which may be relevant in valuing landscape, particularly where the law seeks to impose a remedy in respect of the damage or destruction of landscape features or where there are sustainable features of regulatory control which demand that such features – as externalities – are for example restored. Included in this final section of the chapter is a consideration of emerging regimes of environmental liability and, in particular, their application to damage and destruction of the unowned environment.

Characteristics, Functions and Values

Any attempt to portray the characteristics of landscape as an element of environmental regulation and control will always be difficult as long as landscape is an essentially subjective issue depending on national – and regional – variables. Within the European Community there seems little doubt that the treatment of landscape against this background stresses the importance of subsidiarity and the policy significance of maximising member state freedom of transposition according to national, regional and cultural characteristics and priorities. In other words, if there is one area of environmental control above all others that merits an approach which is not based on overall, generalised control, it is that which applies to landscape.

Characteristics

A particularly incisive view of the characteristics of landscape for present purposes is to be found in the following passage which recognises the increasing dominance of landscape considerations in measures where law and policy are concerned with agriculture:

> Landscape can refer to a way of describing agro-ecosystems and semi-natural habitats. An agricultural landscape can also refer to the visual character of the land including its intrinsic beauty, historical features, embodiment of cultural values, reflecting the past and present impact of land use. The specific value of landscapes depends on the pattern of land use, farm practices, composition of farming systems, and the distribution of habitats and man-made features like stone walls or historical buildings.[1]

The authors of this passage go on to stress that the development of environmental indicators to measure landscape and the impact of agriculture on that landscape is difficult because values here are often so subjective. Furthermore,

> Densely populated countries often consider it necessary to adopt an integrated approach to productive land use to achieve landscape conservation ... Other countries consider that landscape is connected to public and political preferences based on sociocultural attitudes and judgements and is not an environmental aspect of agriculture *per se.*[2]

This view would suggest that it is not easy to assume that policy integration will always characterise policy preferences here since there may be no desire to see landscape integrated into law and policy for the protection and enhancement of the natural environment. Whatever the policy preferences here, 6 per cent of Europe's land area is subject to landscape protection, albeit the law's protective capacity here is often characterised as being weak.[3] Within the European Community 51 per cent of the land area is devoted to agriculture which means that here, 'landscape' comprises an almost equal spread of agricultural and non-agricultural land use, geological and other natural features, built features, flora, fauna, and water, all of which are affected by prevailing climate patterns. Some of these features and characteristics will be in private ownership, others will exist as part of the unowned environment.

Functions

Within the European Community experience seems to suggest that an holistic approach to policy governing landscape has much to commend it. This seems to suggest that the function of policy evaluation based on landscape considerations is to encourage the rationalisation of other policies, such as those relating to biodiversity for example, while at the same time taking account of those local and regional characteristics referred to previously. In more pro-active terms, resort to such a landscape model may well facilitate policies which encourage the sustainable exploitation of natural resources, the protection and enhancement of biodiversity, as well as sustainable economic development. Although reference will be made, later in the chapter, to National Parks in England such provision represents an important policy example of the way in which economic development in a protected area may be allowed to continue, subject to compliance with landscape and other requirements.

Values

The value of landscape considerations as a basis for the evaluation of other policies, such as those relating to biodiversity, has been referred to, above. However, within the European Community there has been a very sharp appreciation of the way in which policy priorities in favour of the maintenance and improvement of landscape features can contribute to the vacuum left where traditional agriculture no longer exists, or is much reduced in scale as a result of reform of the Common Agricultural Policy. Some of these elements will be looked at in later sections of the chapter where matters such as the Community's Rural Development Regulation is examined. Indeed, there seems little doubt that the agri-environmental measures introduced by the Community in 1992[4] have most notably succeeded where landscape preservation and improvement have been supported. Generally, such value tends to be manifested in those circumstances where agri-environmental schemes in member states have targeted, very specifically, areas of landscape priority. This generally has been achieved by various means, examples of which will be set out, later in the chapter. However, there is little doubt that throughout the Community there has been an improvement in landscape quality where there has been conversion from arable cultivation to extensive grassland, for example. The application of support like this, targeted at landscape value and its improvement, may have other environmental benefits. Taking the last example again, the conversion to extensive grassland probably has the effect of 'fixing' nitrates in the soil, thus reducing the incidence of leaching to groundwater and, in turn, assisting in member state compliance with Community law in Directive 91/676 relating to the concentration of nitrates in drinking water.[5]

Environmental Pressure Points Affecting Landscape

Agricultural Pressures

A prominent example of adverse effects on landscape comes from contraction in farming activity. Where this occurs there will tend to be encroachment by forest and scrub. Such encroachment can in fact be very rapid, as where grazing is discontinued in upland areas, for example. However, at the other end of the axis, intensive farming and cultivation can also result in adverse effects for the amenity elements of the environment as represented by landscape. Indeed, it is here where the funding of agri-environmental initiatives may have little impact, bearing in mind the simple reality of the difference between high farm incomes and very modest payments under such initiatives. This however does not adequately represent the typical range of pressures on landscape.

Other Pressures and their Effects

Apart from agricultural intensification and abandonment, pressures also accrue from urban expansion, infrastructure development for transport and other similar facilities, tourism and recreation, the exploitation of natural resources, intensive commercial forestry and landfilling. Such lists do not really assist in identifying and addressing unsustainable land use affecting landscape. Such land use is well capable of resulting in serious scarring through erosion, desertification, flooding, and even rural depopulation, to mention but four. In turn there are likely impacts on biodiversity where natural and semi-natural habitats are reduced, fragmented or even destroyed. This can include loss of local character and visual attraction, as well as general diversity. In the specific case of agriculture, the main impacts have been characterised as involving a loss of linear features, a loss of broadleaved woodlands, changes in the general character of farmland, and standardisation of farm building design.[6]

Pressure Indicators for the Agricultural Landscape

The definition and quantification of pressures on the agricultural landscape is a matter of great complexity, partly by reason of the subjectivity which affects the subject. It is certainly a matter of great difficulty to arrive at criteria through which harm and benefit to the landscape can be defined. One possible approach is to estimate the value of landscape in monetary terms although, again, subjective judgements make this difficult to achieve. Alternatively, an inventory of physical features might be drawn up in order to track material changes. Although this is an approach used already, by the Countryside Agency in England in tracing the decline of hedgerows for example, it will always be a matter of dispute as to which features should be included in the inventory and whether any material change should be characterised as harmful or beneficial.[7] Despite the room for dispute, the fact remains that landscape features worthy of protection are routinely prioritised in planning policies, both in the zoning approach prevalent in the United States, for example, and in the approach based on broader discretion prevalent in the United Kingdom, for example. It should not be beyond the capability of policy makers and others to add calibration to an inventory for this purpose, according to defined criteria of harm or benefit. In turn, such policy prescriptions would no doubt win an important measure of popular support following publicity and opportunities for public participation and consultation.

Strategies for Landscape Protection and Enhancement

The term 'strategy' here is used to refer both to policy and law. Some reference is made to the treatment of landscape in the United States and Canada. The bulk of this section of the chapter however is taken up with an examination of law and policy affecting landscape as it exists in the European Community. Beyond the Community itself, the law and policy of individual member states is worthy of consideration. To that end brief reference is made to the cultural background against which Community law and policy is implemented and enforced through an examination of the law in Austria, a recent member of the Community, together with the Benelux Convention on Nature Conservation and Landscape. This is followed by a consideration of the law and policy in England and a general, comparative theme concerning landscape conservation as it arises in relation to coastal zone management. To begin with though, there is a thumb nail sketch of the rather different cultural emphasis affecting landscape in Canada and the United States. That sketch falls into two sections, one dealing with the planning and management of land in private ownership and the other dealing with the management of land in public ownership.

Law and Policy in Canada

The planning and management of land in private ownership Land use planning and regulation in Canada is essentially a provincial responsibility. Nevertheless, there are some federal programmes such as those relating to soil conservation which operate regionally and have an impact on land development and regulation. In practice, local authorities within each province will undertake the administration of land use planning and regulation under provincial government supervision. Appeals from local authority decisions will normally be determined by the provincial government. Strategic planning policy is also the responsibility of a local authority and it is through that policy that priorities can be addressed on the question of landscape and similar issues. Beyond land use planning and regulation the preservation and management of wildlife habitats is a federal responsibility in the hands of the Canadian Wildlife Service. Partnership agreements, which will often focus on the importance of landscape preservation, are entered into with public and private landowners, with particular emphasis on the private stewardship of agricultural land and forestry.

The management of land in public ownership Governmental competence in relation to the management of land in public ownership arises from the fact that certain land is in that ownership, as well as the fact of legislative authority found in the constitution. Public ownership of land in Canada is primarily provincial ownership which means that the provinces exert considerable influence in matters of environmental management. Nevertheless, federal government competence is much in evidence where landscape and habitat is of national significance. Land which is seen to be of such significance will usually be adjudicated as such by the federal government although agreement with a provincial government will also facilitate management of such land (as a national wildlife area, for example), usually by reference to federal policy on conservation which may or may not reflect any relevant international treaty or convention on nature conservation and related issues. Typically, wilderness of national or international significance will receive a protective designation through federal initiative, under the National Parks Act for example. Beyond these categories there are those areas of federal legislative competence, such as shipping and navigation, where it is quite conceivable that matters of landscape and nature conservation may be the subject of control where the management of Canadian waterways is concerned. Wetlands in particular may be affected by the operation of such waterways. If this is the case then, again, there arises a need to rationalise and coordinate matters of legislative authority. In this case where there may well be different branches of the federal government involved, the question is how best to rationalise these different jurisdictions involving, on the one hand, shipping and navigation, and, on the other, nature conservation affecting wetlands. Equally difficult though is the process of drawing a line below which federal competence does not apply. Where this is the case, provincial legislation on public land management involving matters such as landscape and nature conservation will be the governing regime.

Law and Policy in the United States

The planning and management of land in private ownership There is a distinct division of competence as between the federal government and the states in relation to land use planning. Nevertheless, there are examples of federal legislative initiative where states and municipalities within them may be encouraged or even required to regulate development on certain terms. Good examples of such arrangements are found in the federal Coastal Zone Management Act, which was outlined in Chapter Seven and appears again below where the matter of coastal landscape conservation is addressed, and the federal Endangered Species Act 1973. This latter Act will require land use planning decisions to restrict development which will adversely affect those habitats populated by prescribed species. Although land use planning is essentially a state responsibility it is usual for there to be delegation, as in Canada, to the municipalities and other local authorities in each state. Unlike Canada, however, the United States Constitution sets a very distinct limitation on decision-making in this and other related contexts. That limitation is found in the Fifth Amendment to the Constitution which, in broad terms, stipulates that any 'taking' of private property shall be accompanied by a payment of due compensation. This limitation depends of course on what may be regarded, in law, as a 'taking'. Clearly, compulsory acquisition of private property without compensation could not be regarded as lawful. However, in practice what is a 'taking' may not be so clear cut, as was seen in Chapter Four.[8] In addition to the statutory framework for land use planning in each state, valuable provision is made both at common law and by statute in the states for the creation of so-called 'land trusts' through which private ownership and public stewardship can combine in order to protect and manage valuable habitat and landscape.

The management of land in public ownership At federal level, various agencies have formal responsibility for the management of land in public ownership: the Bureau of Land Management and the National Park Service, for example. At state level also there is widespread concern for the management of land in public ownership which will be examined after consideration is given to the federal position.

The federal Bureau operates the National Landscape Conservation System which aims to protect some of the very important landscapes in the United States. For example, the System makes provision for National Conservation Areas: 13 areas totalling 14m acres facilitating conservation, use, enjoyment and enhancement of various natural and other features. Equally dissipated are the statutory foundations for such public land management. A very prominent area of statutory regulation and control is found in the Wilderness Act 1964 which provides for a scheme of preservation. That scheme triggers considerable restrictions on the use and development of wilderness land once it is so designated, in aid of recreation, habitat protection and landscape preservation, among other objectives. Reinforcement of this regime occurs in later legislation: the Federal Land Policy and Management Act 1976. Among other things, management of subject land by the Secretary of the Interior requires measures which will prevent unnecessary or undue degradation while other agencies involved in such land management are required to operate by reference to specific land management programmes. Part of the statutory background to public land management is the Coastal Zone Management Act, which will be returned to, below. The preservation of wetlands from undue reclamation and resulting agricultural development is dealt with by the Food Security Act 1985. The protection of ecosystems is dealt with under the Endangered Species Act which was referred to above. The Act allows for conservation as well as engagement with the relevant international conventions and treaties on nature conservation. The Fish and Wildlife Service undertakes much of the administration and enforcement of this legislation. At the heart of the enforcement process here is the restriction on a 'taking' of any species which is designated as being endangered. The Act has a potentially powerful impact to the extent that federally-based or federally-initiated functions must be undertaken so as to avoid adverse effects on endangered species.

At state level also there are numerous governmental schemes aimed at ensuring landscape and other forms of protection and conservation. One example again comes from the State of Virginia and its Natural Heritage Program, administered there by the Department of Conservation and Recreation. Conservation of biodiversity is at the centre of the Program, which comprises a number of different elements, such as stewardship. Natural Area Stewardship is one of the Program areas and is concerned with the long-term management of land, for the purpose of maintaining its natural resources and inherent natural beauty. To that end, the Department of Conservation and Recreation acquires, dedicates and manages natural areas of state-wide significance.

Law and Policy in the European Community

It is difficult to identify any explicit Community law and policy on landscape. One likely reason for this state of affairs is the potential difficulty of securing any coherent view of what 'landscape' comprises, an issue explored towards the beginning of this chapter. Nevertheless, the nature conservation law and policy of the Community sets out a number of implicit assumptions about the fundamental status of landscape. Interestingly, during its development and before enactment, Directive 92/43[9] – the Habitats Directive – contained provisions on landscape which were missing when it reached the statute book. Had deletion not occurred there seems little doubt that Community law on habitats would have been considerably more complex, largely by virtue of difficulties of definition which follow in the wake of the many subjective views on the issue. One further objection may well be the danger of a too narrow view of 'landscape' where the issue is addressed in law governing wildlife habitats, as a result of which those landscapes which are not so directly connected may be seen to be marginalised. Despite this absence of explicit law and policy on landscape, it is a subject that features increasingly in the agri-environmental law of the Community through measures accompanying the Common Agricultural Policy, as will be seen later in the chapter. In the same way, landscape may be an issue in the implementation and enforcement of Community law on environmental assessment. However, in each of these contexts it is necessary to stress the absence in law and policy of any greatly explicit reliance on landscape. Rather, landscape appears to have considerable importance in rather more subtle respects, either as a variable in determining the scope and nature of amenity protection or (more specifically) providing a reference point for law and policy on nature conservation.

The wider background to Community law and policy The Community has usually sought to subscribe to international treaties and conventions affecting nature conservation issues, such as the Berne Convention on the conservation of flora and fauna in their various habitats. As a result Community law and policy has seen further development, particularly in this case through the enactment of the Habitats Directive. One of the most powerful influences for present purposes was the Rio Convention on Biological Diversity which was signed by the Community and its member states, as evidenced in Decision 93/626.[10] In turn, the Community generated its own strategy for biological diversity.[11] These sources represent some of the fundamental foundations for Community legislation such as that represented by the Habitats Directive. This and the Birds Directive – Directive 79/409[12] – are the two essential planks of Community law and policy on nature conservation.

The Birds Directive and the Habitats Directive The Birds Directive relies significantly on landscape since the assumption is that the law in any member state will provide both a sufficiency of diversity and area in habitat terms. The law is defined essentially in terms of a duty on any member state to maintain populations at a level which correspond to ecological, scientific and cultural requirements but taking account also of economic and recreational requirements. As such, the expectation is that member states will actively manage habitats whether or not they occur in areas of protection, for example. Accordingly, there is the prospect that member states may actively engage in protective action benefiting landscape in the wider countryside. An example of the opportunity for pro-activity arose in the case of *Commission v. Germany*[13] ('the Leybucht Dykes' case) where dyke building received regulatory approval from a local authority in Germany for the purposes of coastal defences against incursion by the sea. The European Court of Justice considered that there could be justification for an infraction against the terms of protective Community law here where flood prevention was the essential objective of the works. The approach found in the Birds Directive is reflected in large part in the Habitats Directive where favourable conservation measures are aimed at the protection of habitat and species alike, and extended. Among the terms of the Directive is an expectation that each member state will endeavour to encourage landscape management through land use planning where subject features are of value to wildlife. However, it has just been seen that there may be circumstances in which landscape may require changes in other directions which – as in the case of flood prevention – may not accommodate nature conservation priorities.

Evaluation of Community law and policy It has been stressed already that Community law and policy on nature conservation is driven essentially by a concern for flora and fauna which is dependent on particular landscape features and characteristics. However, another critical dimension here relates to agriculture and the impact of farming on landscape, which is taken up in detail, below. For the moment though, agri-environmental law and policy in recent years has been driven by a perceived need to reverse the adverse impact on the countryside of a production-based Common Agricultural Policy. In other words, the effect on the countryside, its landscape and amenity of intensive and other forms of agriculture has not been open to correction by the market. What this means essentially is that there has been no effective internalisation of the environmental costs of agriculture. Attempts to provide so-called 'accompanying' measures through Community initiatives in agri-environmental schemes which member states could voluntarily subscribe to could not be represented as true internalisation. Indeed, the scale of these measures (now superseded by the Rural Development Regulation, which is referred to, below) can be characterised as being modest as well as being based on very few robust principles. Arguably there is need to move policy in the direction of the articulation and application of such principles. A list of those principles might include the precautionary principle and the 'polluter pays' principle, as well as rebuttable presumptions of reliance on 'best available technology' and restoration of landscape features. Any move in this direction will undoubtedly require careful rationalisation with the same or similar policy drivers in other, related legislation governing countryside amenity issues.

Law and policy in Austria Each province has jurisdiction over the law and policy governing nature conservation and landscape. As a consequence there are nine sets of legislation in force with no federal framework. Nevertheless, it is possible to characterise this body of legislation according to three concerns. In the first place, there is a regulatory requirement to notify certain projects prescribed by the legislation and in certain cases to obtain any necessary consent. This regulatory requirement extends to all non-urban areas. The regulatory framework for consents here will allow a grant of the necessary permit, licence or other authorisation after consideration of impacts on nature and landscape character, and the public interest in these matters. Restrictions may apply also in the case of those projects which are required only to be notified. A second concern is with habitat conservation, with particular reference to certain prescribed habitats such as Alpine areas and wetlands. Such areas receive general protection, usually without any specific designation, unlike other areas such as 'protected landscapes' and nature reserves. A final concern is with the conservation of flora and fauna, again based on both general protection and more specific protection, as where a particular species is endangered. Interestingly, when Austria acceded to membership of the European Community the Habitats Directive was amended to prescribe certain species – and habitats – peculiar to Austria and other states joining the Community at that time.[14] Following accession to membership, Austria has had to make progress to ensure that its municipal law will be compliant with Community law by the relevant target dates. Given that it is provincial law which predominates in this context, consideration of central government's status will be of importance, bearing in mind that Community law assumes that it is the member state itself which is legally responsible for ensuring compliance.

The Benelux Convention on Nature Conservation and Landscape Bearing in mind the shared borders between the three parties to this 1982 Convention, the Netherlands, Belgium and Luxembourg, it is hardly surprising that the purpose of the measure is stated to be the regulation of concerted action and cooperation among these states in the fields of nature conservation and landscape.[15] In turn, the intention of the Convention is to harmonise relevant policy principles and instruments as well as relevant laws. Perhaps most importantly here, the Convention states that there shall be information exchange and concerted action on new measures and developments to align or coordinate policies in relation to transboundary natural areas and landscapes of value. This objective is translated in various ways. For example, the Convention refers to the development of concepts for the protection and development of these transboundary areas and landscapes; the establishment of an inventory; the granting of protective status; and reciprocal consultation on development projects. Decision-making on these matters within the Convention is declared to be binding on the three participating governments. In turn it is declared that the three governments are obliged to take measures for the implementation of agreed programmes but without prejudice to the freedom of any participating government to implement measures which are more stringent than those agreed. However, provision is made for derogation from Convention obligations in certain prescribed circumstances.

Law and policy in England Policy priorities relating to landscape in England are manifested in a number of measures. Areas of Outstanding Natural Beauty (AONBs) are primarily concerned with the conservation of natural beauty.

The designation of such Areas – and National Parks – is provided for under the National Parks and Access to the Countryside Act 1949, albeit this legislation has been amended from time to time. Both designations are intended to maximise protection against adverse, inconsistent development through planning policy and control under the Town and Country Planning Act 1990. Essentially there is a need to ensure that any proposed development in such areas is compatible with conservation objectives before planning permission is granted. AONBs are designated as such because they are considered to represent the finest landscapes. In this respect the Countryside Agency acts as advisor to central government as well as being responsible for designation. Local authorities are obliged by the Countryside and Rights of Way Act 2000 to adopt management plans for AONBs in their areas. In the larger AONBs, which may straddle local government boundaries, conservation boards may be appointed for the purpose of producing and implementing these management plans. At the time of writing there are 37 AONBs in England, representing in excess of 15 per cent of total land area.

National Parks are designated for those areas considered to be of national importance in relation to landscape, biodiversity and recreational use. Designation is the responsibility of the Countryside Agency. One of the outstanding characteristics of National Parks – and AONBs – is that land is almost always in private ownership. Administration of a National Park is in the hands of the Park Authority which acts as the planning authority for the purposes of planning policy and control where, again, conservation will be the outstanding policy preference. General policy guidance in respect of development in National Parks and AONBs is issued by central government.

In the wider countryside much of the initiative for landscape conservation comes from European Community agri-environmental policy. The reform of the Common Agricultural Policy in 1992 saw the first concerted attempt to produce what were described as 'accompanying measures' whereby member states were free to adopt agri-environmental schemes, part funded by the Community. In essence, such schemes were aimed at reducing the production orientation of Common Agricultural Policy subsidies by linking environmental objectives, such as landscape preservation and improvement, to direct payments to farmers. These schemes have been replaced by new arrangements under the Community's Rural Development Regulation, described below. One of the most important manifestations of the Rural Development Regulation in England is the streamlining of the number of available schemes. As a result of that streamlining two major schemes now apply in England: Countryside Stewardship and Environmentally Sensitive Areas. Countryside Stewardship allows payments to farmers in return for the long-term management of important landscape in order to conserve and restore its features and to improve public access to them. An Environmentally Sensitive Area (ESA) can be designated where it appears particularly desirable to conserve, protect or enhance environmental features in such an area by the maintenance or adoption of particular agricultural methods. Once designated any person with an interest in agricultural land may apply for financial support in order to manage that land in accordance with an agreement struck with central government.

Landscape and Coastal Zone Management

Coastal landscapes are considered in this section of the chapter dealing with strategies, for two reasons. First, the environment of the coast contrasts with that part of the environment which is taken up with agriculture, raising concerns which are often materially different. Second, the approach to law and policy-making in various jurisdictions shows a widely differing attitude to strategies for control and regulation of this area of the environment. Despite such differing attitudes there are often sources of law, best characterised as sources of international law, that have to be addressed within a jurisdiction. On occasion these sources may be general in nature, such as the United Nations Law of the Sea, while on other occasions they may be more narrowly defined, where for example there is regional provision as with the Helsinki Convention on the Baltic Sea. Otherwise provision for coastal zone management in jurisdictions across the world is characterised by large differences of style and emphasis. Furthermore, landscape is but one element which is dealt with in these different approaches which tend to extend from one, coherent, coordinated statutory programme through to an apparent absence of any coordination between a disparate collection of statutory provisions which happen to apply to coastline. The outstanding approach to coastal zone management is seen in the United States and New Zealand. The Coastal Zone Management Act in the United States has been referred to already so in what follows, by way of a brief comparison of selected jurisdictions, reference is made instead to the way in which that federal legislation is implemented in certain states, again by reference to landscape and its conservation.

The United States 'Landscape' is not mentioned explicitly in the Coastal Zone Management Act, although there are references to natural resource protection and the management of coastal development. Of course the essential thrust of the Act is to provide financial incentives for coastal states to implement management programs. Where such programs are approved there is the opportunity to address other pressing environmental problems, such as non-point source pollution. Two programs which typify the approach to coastal ɔne management are those in California and Virginia. In California the Coastal Act provides the focal point for that state's program which is administered by the California Coastal Commission which undertakes important regulatory functions in the coastal zone in relation to a wide range of development. Among the targets for regulatory protection are terrestrial and marine habitat protection, visual resources and landform alteration. By way of contrast, in the State of Virginia, some of the particular concerns in its program relate to habitat protection and erosion and sediment control. The Department of Environmental Quality has primary responsibility for administering the program. However, unlike California, there is no one single statute governing its operation. Rather there are various statutes which apply, covering, *inter alia*, fisheries, subaqueous lands, wetlands, and dunes. Among the special projects undertaken here is one which relates to so-called 'sensitive lands', as well as one which relates to habitat protection.

The United Kingdom By way of stark contrast the United Kingdom has no overarching statute which governs coastal zone management. Instead there is an attempt to coordinate a mass of competing regulatory requirements which arise by virtue of a large number of statutory provisions. However, at the time of writing the two central government ministries in England mainly concerned, the Ministry of Agriculture and the Department of the Environment, have been subsumed into one new ministry, the Department of Environment, Food and Rural Affairs. Despite the potential for greater efficiency for present purposes, there are a number of other agencies which have relevant statutory functions here. Those agencies are the Environment Agency, English Nature, the Countryside Agency and, finally, the Crown Estate Commissioners who manage Crown property comprising land that is the foreshore together with the territorial sea bed. Not only is there a considerable array of regulatory agencies involved in coastal zone management, in addition, those agencies may or may not have regulatory and other responsibilities as between the land and the sea. As between terrestrial and maritime concerns there is an enormous amount of legislation in issue although in terrestrial terms there is little doubt that the most significant legislation is that which controls development affecting coastal zones: the Town and Country Planning Act 1990. Nevertheless, on either side of the foreshore proposed development, whether or not it is affected by the Act of 1990 and the need for planning permission, is increasingly likely to be subject to environmental considerations, some of which may be directed to landscape considerations. Accordingly, there may be a need for environmental assessment arising from Community legislation for example. In the same way, Community law is likely to impose constraints on coastal development affecting landscape in the interests of nature conservation.

New Zealand The Resource Management Act 1991 has rationalised the law as it affects coastal zone management by providing for a largely integrated and sustainable regime whose essential objective is to manage the likely effects of development. The vehicle for statutory control here is the national coastal policy statement, which is the responsibility of the Minister of Conservation, and accompanying regional statements both of which are referable to the area from the high water mark out to the 12 mile territorial limit. The regulatory pattern of the Act is variable so that while certain development may proceed unless proscribed by coastal policies and plans, other prescribed development may require a regulatory consent. For example, there are certain restricted categories of development or related activity that require the consent of the Minister, as where major coastal landscape features might be severely compromised by intrusive industrial development, for example.

Canada As is often the case in relation to environmental regulation and control, there is a division of responsibility as between the federal and provincial levels of government. For present purposes the emphasis in Canada, increasingly, is on marine resource and ocean management. Although the primary constitutional responsibility here is that of the federal government, it has been seen already that the provincial governments have responsibility for matters of planning control, albeit a function delegated to local authorities in the provinces. Against this background, the federal Oceans Act 1996 defines maritime zones by reference to the United Nations Law of the Sea Convention. The core of the Act however is a regime which seeks an integrated, sustainable form of control which is driven essentially by the precautionary principle. That control is achieved through appropriate management of defined areas covering estuarine, coastal and other marine ecosystems and includes the control of development on land in these areas.

France Planning law and the control of development dominates coastal zone management in France. The ministry responsible also has important functions in the control of navigable waters. Nevertheless, as in many other jurisdictions, other ministries in central government have responsibility for environmental protection, nature conservation and fisheries. Consequently, there is no guarantee of a coordinated approach to development which adversely affects landscape, in the absence of the coordination of policy and regulatory control. However, there is a potentially very powerful influence exerted in such cases through the functions and activities of the Conservatoire du Littoral which operates under the Rural Code. This public agency is concerned with the protection of the amenity of outstanding areas of coastline, lake shore and certain bodies of water, usually through agreed purchases of land in private ownership which is then often entrusted to local authority management. Coastal zone management also enjoys an elevated status under French planning law through the Loi Littoral, which requires that decision-making on development proposals complies with the nationally prescribed policy on planning for coastal areas extending to include territorial waters and the foreshore. Such policy tends to be very prescriptive and extends to cover some well-defined topics, such as the need to protect sensitive landscape and habitats. Despite the extent of planning control here, the planning ministry is also empowered to make special planning provision for defined areas of the sea and associated seashore.

Landscape and coastal zone management: a brief analysis As with the impact of agricultural development on landscape, so too with the impact of development and other activities on coastal landscapes, there is the potential for effective regulation and control in the interests of amenity. Both areas may be adversely affected by failure to integrate environmental and amenity considerations into the available controls. Those controls are likely to be dominated by planning controls which may tend to be more extensive where coastal development is concerned, compared with agriculture. Even where coastal development is concerned, there are likely to be uncertainties about the territorial scope of any planning law, although some jurisdictions are more expansive than others. Whether or not regulatory control is planning control there is an increasing trend in favour of environmental assessment of potentially adverse development although many jurisdictions have no coordinated arrangements as between a large number of statutory controls. Where coordination is realised as a policy priority there are important opportunities to crystallise further priorities such as sustainably integrated control and reliance on the precautionary principle. All of these priorities and principles are likely to play an important part in the law's role of managing coastal development which has to be rationalised with landscape preservation and enhancement. Sustainable policies may be usefully incorporated into the law where economic incentives are made available to the regulatory agencies responsible for decision-making here. Such an arrangement may well facilitate a more pro-active role in amenity and other environmental regulation. Indeed, such economic incentives may allow a number of pollution-based problems to be addressed in a way which allows the improvement of the local coastal environment overall.

The Rural Development Regulation

The Rural Development Regulation – Regulation 1257/99[16] – arose from the European Community's policy priorities found in a Commission Communication entitled *Agenda 2000: For a Stronger and Wider Union.*[17] In the agricultural context it was proposed that member states should prepare seven-year rural development plans. In turn, member states were to tie production payments to the satisfaction of environmental requirements, usually referred to as 'cross-compliance'.

The Status of the Regulation

We are concerned here only with amenity and landscape control. However, before that matter can be addressed it is necessary to look at the origins, status and effect of the Rural Development Regulation. There are significant matters of Community environmental law and policy which arise from the operation of the Regulation. What is interesting though is the fact that law and policy here emerges from that part of the Commission concerned with agriculture (D-G VI) rather than the environment (D-G XI). Furthermore, rather than legislating through the medium of a directive, the preference here is for a directly applicable regulation, in line with the traditional mode of delivery for law and policy on agriculture. The question that has to be considered is whether, given the environmental nature of the Rural Development Regulation, its effect is in fact similar to delivery by directive. Finally, it is the case that the Regulation represents an exercise in environmental policy integration (EPI), consistent with the 5th Environmental Action Programme, which was described at the opening of Chapter One.[18]

The Extent of the Regulation

The Regulation makes provision for the support of a large number of rural development measures which, in turn, are underpinned by various environmental requirements, where they are relevant. Such measures are nevertheless prescribed by reference to the fundamental objectives of the

Common Agricultural Policy. Articles 22 to 24 of the Regulation concentrate on additional agri-environmental measures beyond those prescribed by Regulation 2078/92[19] following an earlier attempt at reform of the Common Agricultural Policy. The Rural Development Regulation seeks to build on the experience of those earlier agri-environmental measures, as is evidenced by the need for commitments extending over at least five years, for example. Significantly, though, whereas adoption of agri-environmental measures by a member state under Regulation 2078/92 was voluntary, the new Regulation imposes compulsory take-up: one good reason at least for resort to a regulation rather than a directive. The specific issue to be addressed is the extent of the Regulation in facilitating effective management of rural amenity through support in member states for landscape conservation and enhancement by means of funded agreements with members of the agricultural community.

The Impact of the Regulation

Regulation 2078/92 was repealed by the Rural Development Regulation although a saving provision preserves schemes and agreements already approved and in force. Henceforth, the Regulation states that support will be available for agricultural production methods promoting sympathetic land use, environmentally-friendly extensification, conservation of high nature value farmed environments, upkeep of landscape and historical features, and the use of environmental planning in farming practice. A critically important cornerstone of the Rural Development Regulation is reflected in the requirement that any agreed commitments here must involve more than usual good farming practice: the farming community must be seen to provide services not already provided by other support measures in the Community.

The England Rural Development Plan and Landscape

The schemes contemplated by the Rural Development Regulation are likely to run for a period of seven years under the terms of the Plan for England. These schemes will be aimed at the conservation and improvement of the landscape, wildlife and the historic heritage of rural life, among others. As such the intention at the outset was to channel much of the support here through the Countryside Stewardship scheme, described previously in connection with law and policy in England. In turn, the ambition was to expand the area and range of habitats, species, landscape and historical features thereby contributing significantly to the targets prescribed by the United Kingdom's Biodiversity

Action Plan. A new scheme was proposed – the Hill Farm Allowance scheme – aimed at maintaining the social fabric of upland rural communities through measures including those that will support preservation of the farmed upland environment through sustainable management initiatives.

Countryside Stewardship and Environmentally Sensitive Areas These schemes, outlined previously, form an important basis of the Rural Development Regulation. Environmentally Sensitive Areas are designated in areas where there is perceived to be a valuable ecological or landscape benefit to be gained through the conclusion of management agreements. As such it might reasonably be observed that that benefit is manifested through reduced ecological damage as a result of incentives in favour of low-intensity farming. There seems little doubt that agri-environmental schemes predating the Rural Development Regulation resulted in some notable achievements which are now open to further development. However, such achievements in landscape conservation (in England at least) have to be balanced by the often limited objectives of funded management agreements. Previously those agreements were characterised by two levels, the lower and more modest of which required no further ecologically-damaging farming practices in sensitive locations. The more challenging level, which was not often taken up in practice, facilitated more positive landscape enhancement initiatives. In the wider countryside the same limitation appears not to have affected the operation of standard Countryside Stewardship agreements. Stewardship is concerned with seven English landscape types. One important element of agreements here relates to the landscape significance of hedgerows. Support is available for the restoration of hedges which are neglected, damaged or simply in a bad state of repair. Above all, though, Countryside Stewardship illustrates the strong relationship between landscape and ecology.

Landscape approaches as a policy priority The Commission's strong preference is in favour of scheme implementation which stresses the holistic advantages of landscape. Such an approach has the merit of allowing consideration of a full range of issues and processes in the landscape, thus allowing the realisation of measures of special merit in environmental terms. The landscape approach is seen as having advantages such as allowing reliance on local traditions and practices, the incorporation of features such as small farm woodlands, as well as the adoption of measurable targets. These policy priorities and the potential success of the Rural Development Regulation have to be seen against the background of expert views on the general effects of previous agri-environmental schemes affecting landscape. The Countryside Agency considers that valuable features were still being lost, albeit at a slower rate. Those features are characterised as diversity, local character, visual interest and biodiversity.[20] Such findings may tend to give rise to a fallacy, that support through schemes presently under discussion should be available only where there is evidence of deterioration or loss of cultural landscape features. However, as was seen earlier, in connection with previous experience relating to Environmentally Sensitive Areas, the support for amenity in landscape terms must address matters of enhancement also.

Enforcement Despite the fact that the Rural Development Regulation is directly applicable in member states, with immediate force of law, there is a necessity (recognised by the Regulation) that detailed enforcement machinery is required in those member states. For the moment, the mode of enforcement to be adopted by a member state is essentially within the discretion and judgement of that member state. At the centre of the supporting Community Regulation – Regulation 1750/99[21] – is a reference to 'threshold standards' which connote the need for compliance with general mandatory environmental requirements where agri-environmental support is approved under the terms of a member state's plan. In turn, these standards are referred to in the Regulation as 'verifiable standards'. The Rural Development Plan for England defines those verifiable standards as comprising three elements: compliance with existing environmental legislation, a list of verifiable standards included as conditions in all agreements carrying agri-environmental support, and encouragement to all those in receipt of such support to comply with the terms of the Codes of Good Agricultural Practice. This latter element is entirely voluntary and beyond any framework of coercive enforcement. Otherwise, the Plan for England is enforceable through municipal provision for the return of funding, wholly or in part, as well as through various criminal offences, all of which are found in the England Rural Development Programme (Enforcement) Regulations 2000.[22]

Regulatory and Other Forms of Liability

Reference has just been made to one form of civil or criminal liability in connection with member state enforcement of a very important aspect of Community law governing landscape, its conservation and enhancement in the context of agriculture. This final section of the chapter looks to develop a number of other themes of relevance to the situation where enforcement – civil or criminal – may be relevant to an effective realisation of law and policy on amenity, and landscape in particular. As such, this section covers two broad issues: the valuation and determination of environmental or amenity loss or damage, and the extent of liability in law for environmental or amenity loss or damage. These issues will be examined by reference to certain selected areas of comparative law in an area of liability which is difficult to define, bearing in mind that on many occasions loss or damage will be suffered by what is often referred to as the 'unowned environment' for which there is no market through which values can be determined for these purposes.

Valuation and Determination of Loss or Damage

Although much of the emphasis here is on *ex post facto* liability, later in this section there is reference to the basis on which compensation may be negotiated and concluded for the purpose of management agreements for the protection of natural features comprising flora and fauna. First though, reference needs to be made to the 'unowned environment'.

The unowned environment The central concern is the vulnerability of the environment – including its amenity features – to loss, damage or injury. Atmospheric pollution for example, is well capable of wreaking considerable damage on all sorts of natural features. This is well recognised in Community law where Directive 99/30[23] sets limit values for oxides of nitrogen and sulphur dioxide in order to protect vegetation and ecosystems. These values appeared in an earlier United Kingdom Air Quality Strategy as objectives for achievement by the year 2000. Existing categories of law are of course well used to addressing liability in respect of loss, damage or injury affecting private rights of property. Those private rights may well be protected by the law where the claimant can show a sufficiently specific interest in that property either for public or private law purposes. Beyond this usually well-defined category are numerous difficulties, some of which will be examined, below. Above all it must be assumed that there is no market for environmental or amenity features. Perhaps more fundamentally it may be asked who, if anyone, has sufficient *locus standi* to pursue proceedings in private or public law in order to seek redress in relation to some wrongdoing affecting environment or amenity. In certain cases international law may attempt to deal with the problem. The International Convention on Civil Liability for Oil Pollution Damage (the 'Brussels Convention') of 1969[24] refers for example to 'interests connected to a coastal state' referable, *inter alia*, to biological resources, fauna and flora. Such references provide an opportunity to argue that loss, damage or injury suffered by such resources are in fact losses suffered by the community affected, allowing enforcement action by those public agencies which represent such a community. However, any loss that may be recovered has to satisfy certain criteria.

Criteria for remedies in respect of loss, damage or injury Assuming that a claim affects the unowned environment, such as a critical landscape features in an area of coastline, whether that claim is successful will of course depend initially on whether the claimant such as a state or local government has sufficient *locus standi*. Where the court is satisfied on this matter, there are nevertheless other requirements to be satisfied. For example, it will have to be established normally that the claim is based in evidence of causation as well being a claim in respect of 'sensible' – material – loss, damage or injury. The next step of identifying and isolating the factors and variables which will quantify the extent of the liability is further complicated by the fact that although monetary compensation may be the obvious remedy, other remedies such as a requirement for removal of the cause of the loss, damage or injury or restoration or reinstatement of the environment may be prescribed by statute, for example. This section concentrates on compensation as a remedy. Other remedies such as reinstatement will be dealt with, below.

Compensation for environmental or amenity damage In an area of subjective, qualitative judgements it is clearly a matter of some difficulty to form a clear, reliable picture of the factors which may contribute to compensation liability. That compensation could well be based on a reduction of public enjoyment of damaged landscape features, for example. The reduction might be quantified initially by reference to certain identifiable negative impacts. However, it is likely that such impacts may be seen to affect economic, cultural and natural features, suggesting a complex, multifaceted process of calculation and quantification. A local fishing industry may for example be an agreed feature of economic and cultural importance, in which case income flows before and after the impact of an oil spill, for example, will be material to the calculation. Closely related will be socio-environmental impacts where (again) values may be available for inclusion in the equation. How each constituent value is treated is another area of difficulty. Are the constituent value rolled up into one, or are certain individual values susceptible to further refinement prior to 'roll-up'? For example, are certain, individual values open to a further question:

is there a critical value that the community at large would put on damage to certain amenity features? Of course, such calculations may arise before the event, often for the purpose of management agreements through which landscape and nature conservation objectives are to be protected within a statutory framework.

Compensation and management agreements   For this purpose a specific example is used as the basis for considering one approach to the matter of compensation. This example arises in the United Kingdom under the Wildlife and Countryside Act 1981 which relies to a large extent on a voluntary, compensated regime through which those with private landed interests are encouraged to achieve nature conservation management by agreement in Sites of Special Scientific Interest. It seems clear from this example that the stress and emphasis of these contractual arrangements for compensation can have a critical impact on the effectiveness of the management process affecting flora, fauna and landscape. Responsibility in England for management agreements falls on English Nature. Those agreements for present purposes have tended to fall into two categories: either such agreements are concluded on the basis of 'profits foregone' or positive management approaches. The former agreements are characterised by an undertaking by the owner or occupier affected to cease particular activities where compensation is attracted on the basis of profits foregone as a result. Such agreements have attracted considerable criticism, on two grounds: their additional cost, and their failure to facilitate positive site management. Following this diversion into management agreements, it is necessary to return to the broader issues introduced previously. Within those broader issues it is necessary to show how international and municipal law may address the matter of valuation and determination of loss, damage or injury to the environment and amenity. Initiatives by the European Community and the Council of Europe are also included. International law is illustrated through the Brussels Convention referred to previously[25] while the municipal law is that of the United States and Italy. Finally, the European Community's proposal (at the time of writing) and the Council of Europe's Lugano Convention on environmental liability are examined.

The Brussels Convention   The Convention's definition of 'pollution damage' is as follows:

> ... loss or damage caused outside the ship carrying oil by contamination resulting

from the escape or discharge of oil from the ship, wherever such escape or
discharge may occur, and includes the cost of preventive measures and further
loss or damage caused by preventive measures.[26]

A later protocol included a reference to 'impairment of the environment'.
Important litigation has occurred in relation to these conventional provisions.
A fuller description of the Convention is to be found in Chapter 3. One of the
more important decisions is that of the Court of Appeal of Messina, Italy, in
*General National Maritime Transport Co. and Others v. Patmos Shipping Co.
and Others (The Patmos)*.[27] Here the court was willing to compensate
environmental damage which was understood as covering everything which
'alters, causes deterioration in or destroys the environment in whole or in
part'.[28] This was a case where the motor tanker *Patmos* spilled oil following
a collision with another vessel in the Strait of Messina. The spill resulted in
oil pollution of part of the coast of Sicily as well as other maritime ecological
damage, for which the Government of Italy made a claim before the court.
The Court of Appeal in Messina concluded that the Convention extends to
shoreline damage and the related interests of coastal states: interests which
directly affect environmental values such as those relating to the conservation
of living marine resources and the fauna and flora. The equitable valuation
criteria were seen to be those which best coincided with the peculiar legal
status of the damaged property. Furthermore,

> The right to bring action to claim for the damage ... can accrue only to the State
> ... [which] protects the interests of the ecological, biological and sociological
> equilibrium of the territory, including the territorial waters ...[29]

The claim was successful and the court made an award to the government of
Italy in the exercise of its equitable jurisdiction.

The federal Oil Pollution Act of the United States This Act of 1990 deals with
liability issues arising from oil spills, as does the Brussels Convention. The
Act makes provision for liability in respect of the cost of removal of a source
of oil pollution, as well as making provision for liability for property damage.
Broad provision is also made in respect of economic loss suffered by those
who can establish a subsistence use of natural resources which are damaged
by an oil spill. The scope of the Act is extended still further since it is possible
to claim restoration and replacement costs, together with costs arising from
any resulting loss in the value of a natural resource affected, and any reasonable

costs of assessing the damage. However, claims are restricted to the federal government, any state, as well as any foreign government. Natural resource damage is also recoverable under the Comprehensive Environmental Response, Compensation and Liability Act 1980. Although the precise basis for compensating damage, loss or injury to natural resources is not perhaps as clear as it might be, the United States Court of Appeals in *Ohio v. US Department of the Interior*[30] has held that restoration costs should be the essential measure of damages. Within the overall statutory and constitutional context, the court relied on contingent valuation criteria where, for example, due weight may be given to inherent value of a feature by virtue of its status and existence. However, the court will be aware of the possibility that restoration may not be reasonable on the facts: restoration costs must be reasonable. This was the basis of another, earlier, decision of the Court of Appeals in *Commonwealth of Puerto Rico v. SS Zoe Colocotroni*[31] where the state government sought to recover for damage to an area of coastal mangrove wetland. At the first instance a district judge quantified environmental damage at $5.5m by reference to an estimated loss of 92m marine organisms. This figure was arrived at through prices found in a catalogue from a biological supply laboratory indicating a value for each organism set at $0.6. In rejecting this market value test on appeal, the Court of Appeals further rejected a proposal to remove all oil-affected mangrove in order to replace them with containerised plants. Using its reasonable cost test, the court saw this proposal as being too costly and prejudicial to the existing environment of the mangrove.

Italian Law 349 of 8 July 1986 It was seen previously that the court resorted to its equitable jurisdiction in the determination of compensation in the *Patmos* proceedings. Italian law addresses the calculation of compensation directly, in anticipation of those occasions where restoration costs are rejected, for example. Law 349 places the onus on the court for these purposes. Indeed, the law provides some important markers for the court, referring not only to restoration costs. Law 349 directs the judge's attention to other issues, namely the impossibility of precise quantification of compensation, the gravity of the perpetrator's conduct and the benefits accruing as a result of that conduct. It is against this background that the judge resorts to these equitable factors arising from the evidence before the court.

European Community and environmental liability At the time of writing the European Community is seeking to finalise a directive on environmental liability. This proposal has been examined previously.[32] In the present context it is necessary to underline the intention to legislate in order to impose strict liability covering different types of damage arising from dangerous activities regulated within the Community. The proposal is that the regime will extend to fault-based liability for biodiversity damage arising from dangerous activities. Biodiversity damage will be restricted to Natura 2000 sites. Any compensation payable will come with the requirement that it be applied for remediation of the environmental damage in question. However, there appears to be no indication in the proposal of what may be regarded as appropriate standards of remediation. Civil liability in respect of harm to the environment is also provided for by the Council of Europe's (Lugano) Convention on Civil Liability for Damage resulting from Activities Dangerous to the Environment.[33] Strict liability is also the basis of this Convention which has had only limited support to date. Apart from a wide definition of environmental damage, the Lugano Convention also contains a detailed indication of those occasions when restoration is deemed to be 'reasonable'.

The Extent of Liability

A lot of the emphasis hitherto has been on the civil enforcement of law governing environmental amenity affecting areas like rural and coastal landscape. There is of course the possibility that criminal sanctions might be adopted as an aid to law enforcement here. In the European Community for example, member states are for the moment free to determine the style and emphasis of enforcement. In the United Kingdom, the Countryside and Rights of Way Act 2000 typifies this freedom of choice in the way in which protected sites are treated. Criminal sanctions may not always be accompanied by measures requiring restoration or, indeed, specially tailored measures for compensation. Indeed, with the exception of some areas of law, such as that in Italy, there appears to be a certain reticence about any requirement that the court should be obliged to quantify compensation in what is, admittedly, a difficult area. That same Italian law (Law 349) examined previously appears to extend to allow an application to the court to impose a prison sentence following conviction for causing environmental damage, with a further power to suspend the sentence pending satisfaction of an order for the payment of compensation or restoration of the damaged feature.

Notes

1   OECD (1997), *Environmental Indicators for Agriculture*, p. 40.
2   *Ibid.*, pp. 40–41.
3   European Centre for Nature Conservation (1996), 'Pan-European Biological and Landscape Diversity Strategy': http://www.ecnc.nl/doc/europe/legislat/strafull.html.
4   Hawke, N. and Kovaleva, N. (1998), *Agri-Environmental Law and Policy*, Cavendish Publishing, London.
5   OJ L375, 31.12.91. *Cf.* Chapter Three, nn. 39 and 51, and Chapter Four, n. 64.
6   Baldock, D., Bishop, K., Mitchell, K. and Phillips, A. (1996), *Growing Greener: Sustainable Agriculture in the U.K.*, CPRE and WWF, London, pp. 112–14.
7   *Supra*, n. 1, p. 41.
8   Chapter Four, nn. 99 and 100.
9   OJ L206, 22.7.92.
10   OJ L309, 13.12.93.
11   COM(98) 42, 4 February 1998.
12   OJ L103, 25.4.79.
13   [1991] ECR I–883. *Cf.* Chapter Four, nn. 61–3.
14   OJ L1, 1.1.95.
15   http://sedac.ciesin.org/pidb/texts/benelux.landscape.protection.1982.html.
16   OJ L160, 26.6.99.
17   COM (97)2000, July 15, 1997.
18   Chapter One, nn. 1 and 2.
19   OJ L215, 30.7.92.
20   Countryside Agency (1998), Research Notes Issue CCRN 9.
21   OJ L214, 13.8.99.
22   S.I. 2000, No. 3044.
23   OJ L163, 29.6.99.
24   973 United Nations Treaty Series 3.
25   *Ibid.*
26   *Supra*, n. 24, Art. 1(6).
27   Joined Cases 391 to 393, 398, 426, 459, 460 and 570/1986, Court of Appeal, Messina, Civil Section, 30 March 1989. Unapproved translation in possession of the author.
28   *Ibid.*, p. 57.
29   *Supra*, n. 27, at p. 61.
30   880 F.2d 432 (DC Circ. 1989).
31   628 F.2d 652 (First Circ. 1980).
32   EU Document 6055/00. *Cf.* Chapter Three, nn. 45 and 46.
33   32 ILM (1993) 1228.

Chapter Ten

Case Study

Introduction

The case study contained in this final chapter is concerned with the development of a large pulp mill on an estuarine site. It will be assumed that the location for the development is England. The proponent company has earmarked the site with particular reference to accessibility to water resources as well as facilities which will permit reliance on sea transport for a significant proportion of movements in and out of the proposed installation. The development proposal is unusual in the United Kingdom since the intention is to construct and operate a pulp mill without any associated paper-making capacity. A majority of the pulp will be transported by sea to paper-making facilities operated by other companies in the group as well as to other customers in the high quality paper-making industry.

A Pulp Mill on an Estuarine Site

The Site and its Environs

The site of a proposed pulp mill is an estuarine site approximately half a mile inland from the coast. If approved, the pulp mill will be situated within one mile of a small commercial port operated by a harbour authority. The area is predominantly rural and is dominated by gently rolling hills which reach to within a mile of the sea shore. The small commercial port is dominated by the export of stone by sea. The stone is quarried one mile away and is transported to the port by large conveyor belts. Within the port area there are various light industrial factories.

The timber for the proposed pulp mill will be imported directly by sea from Scotland and Scandinavia. Some of that timber will be ready chipped: the remainder will be whole timber for chipping on site. Oil to fire the pulp manufacturing process together with the constituents for the on-site production of bleaching agents will be delivered by road. An existing minor road will require widening between the junction with a main, trunk road and the site, a distance of approximately one mile. The dry pulp slabs will be exported by sea directly from the mill. Seaborne imports and exports to and from the site will be facilitated by the construction of two tidal berths capable of taking low air-draught coasters of up to 4,000 tonnes, gross thus restricting the amount of dredging required. It is anticipated that no more than four vessels per week will use the berths, in order to unload timber or wood chips, and to load dry pulp slabs for export. The construction is to be funded by another proponent and undertaken in collaboration with the harbour authority, assuming that consent is forthcoming from the Secretary of State under the Harbour Works (Environmental Impact Assessment) Regulations 1999. This will occur in advance of any decision on the pulp mill development since the land may be earmarked for other industrial development if the pulp milling is rejected.

For the building of the berths the intention is to purchase and use stone from the nearby quarry. Capital dredging will be necessary to create the berths. According to initial engineering surveys by the proponent the spoil produced by dredging will be gravel and sand which can be reapplied within the estuary, in order to maintain estuarial dynamics, and on the coast outside the estuary for beach recharge. However, 25 per cent of the spoil will be surplus to these requirements and regulatory consent will be required for its dumping at sea.

The mill will look out over the widening mouth of the estuary and towards the far shore which is dominated by an area of Special Scientific Interest declared some years ago under the Wildlife and Countryside Act 1981. The SSSI follows the shoreline around to the site of the proposed pulp mill but does not overlap with it or with the limits of the proposed new berths for shipping servicing the mill. The SSSI designation has been advised previously by English Nature to various statutory agencies, including the local planning authority. More recently the area of the SSSI has been declared a 'Special Protection Area' (SPA) under Directive 79/409: the Birds Directive. This is in recognition of the site's importance – its mudflats in particular – as a habitat for many migratory species.

At the entrance to the estuary from the sea is a channel sufficiently deep to allow navigation by coastal dry cargo vessels. Capital dredging of the channel will extend from the seaward end of the estuary, up to the proposed new berths at the front of the proposed site of the pulp mill. However, maintenance dredging will not thereafter be required if consent is obtained to install a sluice across the mouth of the river which drains in to the estuary. Sluicing on a regular basis will keep the berths, and the channel to the sea, clear of sediment and navigable within the proposed limits.

The manufacturing process (as detailed below) will necessitate an abstraction of water from the river. It is anticipated that abstraction will occur sufficiently far upstream to avoid saltwater contamination in quantities which will not adversely affect sluicing. It is anticipated that it will be necessary to discharge treated effluent into the estuary, normally within an hour on either side of high tide.

A line drawn at the mean low water mark between the two spurs of land forming the mouth of the estuary represents the limit of jurisdiction for the local sea fisheries committee. The sea fisheries committee has had a general concern for some time about the state of shellfish stocks on the seaward side of the line. This concern is shared by local shellfishermen who rely on an area designated under Directive 79/923 for the purpose of protecting water quality for shellfish. The designated area extends for several square miles beyond of the mouth of the estuary. Apart from harvesting shellfish in this area the shellfishermen actively cooperate with the local sea fisheries committee which manages the designated area under its statutory powers.

The Pulp Manufacturing Process

In addition to the features already set out above, the proponents describe the process as a combined mechanical, thermal and chemical process that leads to the production of dry slabs of pulp which is shipped to consumers, primarily for use in high quality print applications. Given that this market will predominate, the manufacturing process will concentrate primarily on softwoods whose long fibres give added strength to paper which can also be bleached to a brilliant white. The so-called 'kraft' process is to be used for cooking and whitening the pulp. Woodchip is to be screened, cooked, washed, re-screened and bleached before moulding into sheets of pulp for drying and dispatch. In order to minimise the adverse impact of effluents from the process and to maximise bleaching efficiency it is proposed to adopt an elemental chlorine-free (ECF) bleaching operation using chlorine dioxide as the bleaching agent. Because chlorine dioxide is chemically unstable it is proposed to produce this bleaching agent on site at a rate of approximately 20 tons per day. The final bleaching solution will comprise a mixture of chlorine dioxide and water abstracted from the river draining into the estuary. The abstracted water may require pre-treatment for this purpose, particularly where turbidity occurs at certain times of the year. In addition, abstracted water will require chilling in order to allow absorption into a solution of chlorine dioxide. For this purpose it is proposed to install an absorption chiller which will be fired by steam in order to refrigerate abstracted water and maintain it at its optimum temperature. The steam will be generated by boilers fed with wood chip rejected in the initial screening process. Excess steam will be used for other miscellaneous requirements on the site, such as heating and drying. Two other by-products are the bark stripped from timber before chipping, and turpentine which comes from the cooking process. The bark is to be collected and batched for sale to local tanneries while the turpentine is to be decanted and sold to local chemical processors. These by-products will be transported by road from the site.

The Environmental Impacts of Pulp Manufacturing

In order to appreciate the environmental impacts of pulp manufacturing, it is necessary to look at the media likely to be affected, as well as the likely manufacturing options open to the proponent of any new mill development. Accordingly, this section of the chapter looks at the manufacturing options as well as the impacts likely to arise from water, waste and air pollution. Consideration is given also to the characteristics of the best technological profile of a pulp manufacturing operation, for two reasons. In the first place the regulatory requirements which will apply to such installations – IPPC – insist on an application of the 'best available technology': a significant contrast. Secondly, in focusing on the best technological profile there is a further opportunity to stress the main environmental pressure points where pulp manufacture is concerned, as well as the measures to address them if cost was not a consideration.

Manufacturing options The proponent will approach pulp manufacture on the site using the 'kraft' process whereas 'mechanical' processing shreds timber into pulp through grinding, which may or may not involve the application of heat to the process. While the advantage of this process is that 90 per cent of the timber can be utilised the end product is paper of lesser strength by virtue of weaker fibres, whereas the 'kraft' process utilises no more than 50 per cent of the timber used. Nevertheless the mechanical process may allow bleaching without resort to chlorine-based chemicals. Another disadvantage environmentally is that considerably more water and energy is required by the mechanical process. At the other end of the process, even where a large pulp mill uses the best conventional effluent treatment processes up to five tonnes per day of ill-defined substances with adverse biodegradability may be discharged into the aquatic environment.

The 'kraft' process is often referred to as chemical pulping where sulphur is used in order extract the fibre from timber. The sulphur used in the process results in the malodorous character of much pulp manufacture. The malodorous effects come from the manufacturing as well as from the storage of the considerable quantities of sludge produced by the 'kraft' process. The end product is a dark pulp which has to be bleached, usually with chlorine-based chemicals referred to previously.

Consideration of manufacturing options in relation to IPPC regulation necessarily demands attention to energy consumption. For example, how might heat recovery occur on site? As a major energy consumer, pulp milling requires careful consideration of energy sources bearing in mind the need to minimise the emission of greenhouse gases. In turn, consideration will have to be given to the approach adopted to the 80 per cent discount available under the Climate Change Levy in relation to the minimisation of emissions.

Impacts on the aquatic environment The consumption of water on a scale required by a large pulp mill can adversely affect local habitat where water levels are reduced and water temperature is increased. At the other end of the process the sludge generated by the 'kraft' process in particular probably contains hormone disruptors which may affect the health and spawning habits of fish and shellfish, which may also be affected by changes in acidity and alkalinity. Accordingly there is a need to ensure the greatest technological efficiency in effluent treatment as well as in the storage of pulp sludge. However, in the receiving waters, the higher the concentration of seawater, the greater the likelihood of neutralising excess acidity or alkalinity. A further and related problem occurs where organic waste such as lignin and wood fibre are discharged from the manufacturing process. Lignin (which produces a brown discolouration of water) is a polymer which is separated chemically from the cellulose in timber which is required for pulp production. Both lignin and wood fibre can have an adverse effect on waters where sunlight will tend to be reduced, together with photosynthesis: the resulting oxygen deficiency can have a serious effect on plant and animal life in the water affected. Pulp mills will rely on their own or municipal water treatment facilities although the distance of the site from municipal facilities suggests an on-site treatment facility in the present case. Whichever option is chosen there will be concerns about the efficiency with which the persistent chemicals (which are often ill-defined) are broken down. As a consequence there is likely to be difficulty in monitoring, suggesting a need for sometimes onerous direct toxicity testing.

Waste pollution The often large quantities of sludge generated by the 'kraft' process in particular pose a considerable problem for the pulp manufacturing industry. The sludge may include many different compounds, including heavy metals, dioxins and organochlorines. Elements of the sludge such as lignin and wood fibre may of course escape into the aquatic environment, leading to the impacts just described. Management of the sludge presents various options although which option is to be preferred depends on local circumstances in determining the 'best practicable environmental option'. Essentially, the sludge may be landfilled, incinerated or spread on agricultural land although it will normally require de-watering prior to consignment to any of these destinations. Pending consignment (either by sea or by road if incineration on site is not feasible), management of the sludge will be crucially important. Stockpiling, for example, will usually require surface areas to be impermeable in order to avoid threats to vulnerable groundwater, for example. In addition, berms or bunds will be required, as an aid to containment for the protection of ground and other waters. Other options will have to be addressed, as well as strategies for recovery and disposal. The state of the site will require early evaluation in terms of requirements which will apply in relation to site restoration when pulp milling is discontinued. Odour problems also require solution: limitation on the duration of storage in the open is one possibility.

Air pollution Emissions from pulp manufacturing are likely to contain hormone disruptors as well as carcinogenic chemicals where incineration is used for the treatment and disposal of sludge. Nevertheless, on-site the likely persistent, toxic nature of such emissions can be appreciated by reference to the use of chlorine dioxide in the bleaching process and their combination with organic compounds in timber. The product – organochlorines – in incinerated, de-watered sludge represents a significant concern in relation to the public health, for example. Where incineration is regarded as the best practicable environmental option, the remaining issue is how the resulting ash is to be dealt with, given the possibility of the toxins remaining.

The best technological profile The best technological profile (BTP) for a modern pulp manufacturing operation can usefully concentrate on three features and their contrast with the profile demanded by the Environment Agency for the purpose of an IPPC permit application. In the first place, the operation would not be dependent on chlorine-based chemicals for the purpose of bleaching and would not be dependent on discharges to water, emissions to the atmosphere and the need to manage pulp sludge and other wastes. BTP would in turn characterise pulp manufacture as a sustainable 'closed-loop' operation without adverse environmental impact. Thirdly, the foregoing BTP elements would be aided by the substitution of oxygen-based bleaching processes involving only a marginal deterioration in paper quality. When compared with the features of the proposed pulp manufacturing development previously described, it will be noted that the proponent will rely on ECF. However, continued reliance on chlorine-based bleaching has to be balanced with an acknowledgement that modern technology will usually allow most of the chemicals in use to be isolated and recovered within the installation. By-products also may be captured and sold on, while woodchips can be utilised in order to power steam generation for the purposes already described. Against this background it would appear that the most challenging feature of pulp manufacture is the management of the sludge, particularly in view of the quantities generated by the 'kraft' process. Although de-watered sludge may be landfilled or incinerated, the other option is land-spreading. The justification for land-spreading may be that there is nitrogen enrichment of the soil, bearing in mind that such spreading may be exempt from waste management licensing where it can be established that there is benefit to agriculture or ecological improvement, as is the case under the Waste Management Licensing Regulations 1994 applicable throughout the United Kingdom.

The Issues

The foregoing facts suggest that the following areas of law are likely to be of particular significance in considering the likely impact of the proposed construction and operation of the pulp mill:

- development control and environmental assessment requirements under the Town and Country Planning Act 1990 and the Town and Country Planning (Environmental Impact Assessment) Regulations 1999;
- authorisation under the Pollution Prevention and Control Act 1999;
- nature conservation requirements under the Wildlife and Countryside Act 1981 and related legislation.

In addition, the following matters will be considered towards the conclusion of this case study:

- protection and management of shellfisheries on the seaward side of the estuary entrance;

- development of berths and the dredging of the channel from the mouth of the estuary under a separate scheme.

Development Control and Environmental Assessment

The building of the pulp mill will require planning permission under the Town and Country Planning Act 1990. However, in anticipation of a decision of the development control authority (usually the local authority) there will be a need for an environmental assessment of the project under the Regulations of 1999. Pulp mill construction is referred to as an Annex 1 development under Community law, in Directive 85/337, transposed in the 1999 Regulations. Consequently there will be a requirement for a mandatory environmental assessment. However, the decision-making process relating to the application for planning permission must be effectively engaged with the assessment presented by the proponent. This fundamental requirement, which may be directly enforceable by third parties in law, demands that the relevant information is presented in a single and accessible compilation, not only for the purpose of better informing the decision-making, but also for the purpose of being available to the public in order to permit representations to be made about the proposed development. Community law will not permit any retrospective dispensation with these fundamental requirements. Any such dispensation found to be contrary to Community law in this respect would undoubtedly result in a decision to grant planning permission being quashed by the court.

Information required of the proponent The mandatory environmental assessment demands that the following information be submitted: a description of the pulp mill project accompanied by information on its location, design and size; data necessary to isolate and assess the principal effects of the mill on the environment; identification of measures intended to avoid, minimise or otherwise deal with, significant adverse effects of the proposed development; an outline of principal alternative approaches with reasons from the proponent for the choice of approach made; and a nontechnical summary of the foregoing. Many of the features of pulp manufacture set out above, together with the advantages and disadvantages of different approaches, will no doubt feature in an environmental statement submitted by the proponent in the present context, albeit in rather more technical terms. In addition, other environmental factors to be explored, below, will no doubt be featured also. Where consent has been granted by the Secretary of State for the building of the new berths under the Harbour Works (Environmental Impact Assessment) Regulations 1999 reference will be made to the environment characteristics (and relevance) of that development to the present proposal for a pulp mill. Had another proponent not been involved in development of the berths for shipping access to the site, this element of the overall development would no doubt have been subsumed under the general environmental assessment being undertaken here as a precursor to any grant of planning permission and any application for an IPPC permit. The Secretary of State has responsibility for development control decision-making either on appeal, or because a decision is 'called-in' from a local planning authority, as well as responsibility for environmental assessment and decision-making under the Harbour Works Regulation: these factors and powers over environmental assessment generally would be a powerful argument for concentrating all decision-making except that relating to the IPPC application in the hands of one person.

Planning and pollution control Given that the Environment Agency acts as the regulatory agency in dealing with proposals like the present which fall within the IPPC regime, it is clear that there is an important relationship with the development control decision-making process for the site which is normally in the hands of the local authority for the area. Planning policy guidance from central government here (known as 'PPG 23') indicates a need to avoid duplication as between development control and pollution control decision-making. Essentially, development control is concerned with matters affecting the use and development of the site for which the application for planning permission has been submitted by the proponent. In other words, the real concern is with the rationalisation of competing uses of land. In the present context the fundamental tension may be seen to be that which affects a major industrial use with surroundings which are non-industrial and in some respects, particularly sensitive. A critical issue will be whether conditions attached to any grant of planning permission might minimise the adverse impact of the development on the surrounding area, the uses (if any) to which land in that area is put, as well as its landscape and amenity. By way of an example, it will be recalled that one of the problems associated with pulp manufacture relates to the storage of malodorous sludge. However, if the local planning authority considers imposing a condition which restricts open air storage, for example, PPG 23 might be pointed to in order to indicate that such a matter is really one for the Environment Agency under the IPPC authorisation process, which is addressed, below.

Planning and nature conservation When declared under the Wildlife and Countryside Act 1981, the SSSI in the estuary will have been notified to the local planning authority which is therefore obliged to regard the designated area as a legally material consideration in decision-making on applications for planning permission. In the present case, the proposal for the construction of a pulp mill is undoubtedly material to the decision, bearing in mind the possible scale and impact of the manufacturing operation, as well as the harbour development and (eventually) the shipping traffic. Had the proponent's site overlapped with the area of the SSSI there would have undoubtedly been a management agreement in existence, containing a contractual obligation to undertake certain management practices on the land in order to preserve or enhance its nature conservation value. The fact that the site of the SSSI has now been designated as a Special Protection Area introduces an additional protective dimension, which is discussed below, in the section on potential significant effects on the environment. In more general terms though, the local planning authority is obliged by the Town and Country Planning Act 1990 to have regard to any development plan which is applicable, as well as any other material considerations. Those material considerations may well include nature conservation issues, given the location and status of the site chosen for pulp milling. Planning Policy Guidance on Nature Conservation (PPG 9) will assist the local planning authority in its decision-making. Given the scale of the proposed pulp mill it seems likely that any one or more development plans may well be relevant in indicating the nature (and terms) of policy preferences in respect of such a large manufacturing operation in such a location. The likelihood of planning permission being granted, albeit subject no doubt to a formidable array of conditions, may not necessarily depend on positive indicators in the appropriate development plan. There are procedures under the Act of 1990 whereby development may be approved, contrary to the terms of the development plan.

A decision The local planning authority or, if the decision has been called-in, the Secretary of State will have relied heavily on the mandatory environmental assessment which should have included reference to the impact of the harbour development described below, on the assumption that it was pursued separately and in advance. If planning permission is granted, the decision-maker should be able to point to the advantages of the environmental assessment in improving the quality of definition of the variables affecting the decision. Any planning permission that is granted in these circumstances will undoubtedly be subject to conditions. However, there is no doubt that if the constraints in planning and environmental terms are too great, the only effective option is a refusal of planning permission. If that is the decision of the local planning authority (or there is a conditional grant of planning permission) there is an appeal to the Secretary of State, whose decision may be further informed by a public inquiry. A grant of planning permission is of course necessary for an application for a permit under the IPPC regime, which is discussed next.

Authorisation under the Pollution Prevention and Control Act 1999

Assuming that an appropriate planning permission is obtained against the background of an acceptable environmental assessment, consideration can be given to an application for a permit under the Pollution Prevention and Control Act 1999. Integrated pollution prevention and control (IPPC) requirements from Community law are transposed through this Act, together with the accompanying subordinate legislation, the Pollution Prevention and Control (England and Wales) Regulations 2000. The Schedule to the Regulations shows that an industrial installation producing pulp from timber is a Part A(1) installation whose IPPC regulation is the responsibility of the Environment Agency. Given that the development of the site through the building of a pulp mill is still a proposal it is necessary at the outset that the operator of the installation is identified. Such a person is defined by the Regulations as the person who will have control over the operation. Indeed, unless the regulator is satisfied that it is the applicant who will have control or ensure compliance no permit can be granted. Typically the proponent will be a company. It is that company which will hold the permit should an application be successful.

Essential priorities in the IPPC regulatory process   In dealing with an application for a permit here, the Environment Agency will look for a selection of techniques which achieve protection of the environment, achieving a balance between environmental benefits and the costs to be incurred by the proponent. Through what is a unified regulatory process for pollution control, the regulator looks for a systematic development of proposals which can be tested against the criteria generically referred to as 'best available techniques' while taking account of local conditions. Initially the question is what the installation itself can reasonably achieve before consideration is given to the capacity of the local environment, often in a precautionary sense. Potential significant effects on the environment are addressed, below. In the meantime an investigation of what the installation can reasonably achieve may show that standards, targets and limits prescribed by law may be replaced in any permit granted by the

Environment Agency with more stringent limits affecting discharges to the aquatic environment, for example. The regulatory process is driven also by an expectation of continuous improvement in the process concerned, as an element of the priority to achieve sustainability. Some, but not all of the foregoing judgements will be made by reference to technical guidance affecting the pulp and paper sector published by the Agency and based on BAT reference documents published by the Commission. As a result an increasingly standard structure and methodology is available, ensuring that the municipal Pollution Prevention and Control Regulations are followed.

BAT and the core pulping operation Process descriptions are demanded by the Environment Agency as part of the application process. Those descriptions will require identification of the plant and chemical reactions which will be material in terms of environmental impacts. The systems to control operations (including emergency measures and abnormal conditions) will require clear definition, together with details of production capacities, energy ratios, venting measures, maintenance schedules, and energy management with or without reliance on a Climate Change Levy agreement. It has been seen already that a variety of other characteristics of the proposed pulping operation will require consideration against BAT guidance in anticipation of the permit application. Reference has been made to the considerable difficulties raised by the management of pulp sludge. Clearly the options already referred to will form an important basis for the finalised application. However, having identified a preferred option and its merits by reference to BAT guidance it will be necessary to address also the detailed handling of such wastes from the manufacturing process. Among the issues of relevance here are the quantity, nature and origin of such critical wastes, as well as the destination, frequency of collection, mode of transport and method of treatment, according to the general option chosen, whether that is disposal or recovery. If sludge is to be sent off-site (say) for incineration it will be necessary to identify storage arrangements away from watercourses and sensitive boundaries prior to transportation, the maximum capacity of storage areas, the security and integrity of dewatering processes, and the quantities involved before and after dewatering. Additionally and for the purpose of the duty of care arising under the Environmental Protection Act the proponent will need to detail management arrangements for the waste as it is transported from the site, through to the point of incineration or landfilling, whichever option is chosen.

Potential significant effects on the environment The proponent will have to demonstrate the impact on the receptors of any polluting activity from the installation both where they exist in the local and in the wider environment. Centres of urban population are an obvious concern although a variety of different receptors may be vulnerable to odour, noise or other pollution from the proposed installation. Otherwise there is a considerable list of environmental media to be considered, including flora and fauna within a protected site such as the nearby SSSI and SPA, the waters within and beyond the estuary, groundwater, landscape, and the atmosphere. The pathways linking the polluting activity of the installation with those media will in most cases require identification and definition. Thereafter the proponent will have to draw together these impacts, in terms of the installation's total emissions, for the purpose of setting them against objectives, standards and targets whether prescribed by law or otherwise. One useful example of the way in which Community law and policy percolates down through the transposed law of the member state into the regulatory process itself relates to waste management, as will be seen in the following section. Before that matter is addressed, one further issue concerning the status of the SSSI and the recently designated SPA requires attention. In looking at the proponent's assessment here, the Agency may conclude that there will, indeed, be a significant effect on the SPA, as a result of an authorisation of pulp milling on the site. That conclusion will necessarily be based on the Agency's view of the conservation objectives of the SPA. The statutory obligation on the Agency is to undertake what is referred to as an 'appropriate assessment' of the impacts. That assessment cannot rely on the assessment already supplied by the proponent as part of the application for the IPPC permit although there is no reason why the proponent's data should not be used. Overall, the so-called 'appropriate assessment' may be less onerous when it is borne in mind that when the application for planning permission was being considered, this matter will have been before the local planning authority.

Statutory waste management objectives The Environment Agency is required by the Waste Management Licensing Regulations 1994 to exercise its functions by reference to the objectives set out in Schedule 4 to those Regulations. It has been seen already that there are three essential options open to the proponent in relation to the pulp sludge generated by the manufacturing process: land filling, incineration and land-spreading. In looking at those options, the Agency is required by the Regulations to ensure that recovery or disposal occurs without endangering human health and without resort to methods or processes which will result in environmental harm. Such environmental harm is seen in terms of risk to water, air, soil, plants or animals, or nuisances created by noise or odour, or adverse effects on the countryside or places of special interest. Application of BAT principles and guidelines through the application process should usually address the risks associated with these areas of concern. Nevertheless, the applicant may need additionally to deal with the relevant terms of other policies, such as local authority policies in relation to waste as contained in waste local plans, for example.

A decision The Environment Agency will be aware of the terms of the earlier grant of planning permission, as well as the terms of the environmental assessment that was conducted. It is the latter which may be of some direct relevance at this IPPC stage. The Agency may grant the permit sought unconditionally, or subject to conditions, or reject the application. If a permit is granted it is almost certainly going to be subject to a considerable list of conditions, some of which will seek to rationalise identified environmental impacts, as well as seeking to ensure ongoing improvements in the efficiency of the pulp-milling installation on the site.

The Protection and Management of Shellfisheries

This matter is selected for particular attention despite the fact that it will have been taken account of, albeit as part of the wider environmental impact. Locally, the Sea Fisheries Regulation Act 1966 provides for the powers and functions of Sea Fisheries Committees which regulate fisheries along the coast of England and Wales, up to six miles out. An important function is the making and enforcement of bye-laws for the management and conservation of fisheries in each designated sea fisheries area. Later legislation – the Sea Fisheries (Wildlife Conservation) Act 1992 – requires each Committee to have regard to the conservation of marine flora and fauna and to endeavour to achieve a reasonable balance between this consideration and other considerations to which it is required to have regard.

Directive 79/923 The Directive is concerned with the quality of shellfish waters. Values are prescribed by the Directive in relation to the water quality to be attained. Monitoring undertaken by the statutory agencies in this designated area has not indicated any failure to comply with these mandatory values, although data recently has suggested that that compliance is increasingly under challenge despite initiatives whereby, under Directive 91/271 (the Urban Waste Water Directive), these waters have been designated as 'sensitive'. As a result increased investment in sewage treatment nearby may perhaps contribute to an improvement. Furthermore, the Environment Agency will regard the effluent discharges from the proposed pulp mill as being 'qualifying discharges' in precautionary terms for the purpose of the designated waters. Designation of waters under the Directive is the responsibility of the Agency which, for the purpose of the IPPC application, will need to take into account the effect of the effluent on the shellfish waters.

Directly effective rights under Directive 79/923 It has been seen already that local shellfishermen have a very close connection with the designated waters (and the work of the local sea fisheries committee), which they depend on for their livelihood. The Environment Agency, in considering the IPPC application, is aware of the probability of those shellfishermen being able to secure compensation in respect of directly effective rights arising under the Directive, according to recent pronouncements of the English courts. This would be a distinct possibility if monitoring data suggests that water quality for shellfish is failing and that that failure is attributable to an absence of regulatory action to check deterioration of water quality below mandatory levels prescribed by Community law. This prospect represents a real concern for the Agency in addressing its decision whether to grant a permit for pulp milling in the immediate vicinity.

Harbour Development and Estuarial Dredging

This development is assumed to proceed in advance of the foregoing application for planning permission and application for IPPC authorisation and at the initiative of a proponent who is not the proponent seeking to development a new pulp mill, described above. The area of the estuary falls within the area of the statutory harbour authority which operates the small port nearby. Accordingly, development of the berthing facilities for the proposed pulp mill will come under the jurisdiction of that authority according to its powers and functions set out in the Harbours Act 1964, and related legislation. For present purposes however, the regulatory framework of central importance is the Harbour Works (Environmental Impact Assessment) Regulations 1999, a responsibility (since 2001) of the Department for Environment, Food and Rural Affairs (DEFRA). Since the proposal is to dredge in waters that are regarded as being navigable, regulatory consent is required from the Secretary of State under the Coast Protection Act 1949. The application for planning permission and the Harbour Works (Environmental

Impact Assessment) Regulations carry a far-reaching set of regulatory requirements.

The Harbour Works (Environmental Impact Assessment) Regulations The proponent may well choose to seek a prior opinion on the question whether the proposed construction falls within Annex I or II of Directive 85/337 on Environmental Assessment. Annex I development will attract a mandatory assessment whereas Annex II development will attract an assessment only where it is seen as having 'significant effects' on the environment. Where the proponent makes such a request, that request must be accompanied by a plan identifying the location of the new berths, a brief description of the nature and purpose of the harbour works and their possible environmental effects, plans and sections showing the lines, situation and levels of the proposed works, as well as any other information deemed relevant. In giving an opinion the Secretary of State is required to indicate the extent of the information which the proponent would be obliged to supply for present purposes.

A decision The Secretary of State may take the view that the scale and impact of the proposed harbour works for the construction of the new berths is such that there is no requirement for a mandatory assessment. Nevertheless, it may be speculated that the nature of the estuary in nature conservation terms, as well as the overall landscape, may render the decision a difficult one, as between Annex I and II of the Directive. These and other related factors are prescribed by the Regulations as 'selection criteria'. Of particular relevance in the prescribed criteria are references to the characteristics of the project: size, the use of natural resources and the generation of nuisances in the construction and operation of what is a small port; the location: sensitivity of the geographical area by reference to, *inter alia*, existing land uses, designated areas of nature conservation, and valued landscape; and (finally) the characteristics of the potential impact set against the foregoing characteristics and location as forecast by the proponent: the extent of the impact, its complexity and frequency.

Information requirements affecting the proponent Where the proponent decides to proceed following the prior opinion of the Secretary of State various categories of information will have to be supplied. A description of the project will have to include its physical characteristics, land use requirements during construction and operation, production processes such as reliance on locally-quarried stone, and an estimate of expected residues and emissions such as the impact of piling during construction, and noise and light when the berths are in use. The proponent will be obliged also to outline the main alternatives considered and the reasons for the eventual choice, taking account of environmental effects; to describe aspects of the environment likely to be significantly affected, such as flora, fauna, soil, water and landscape and the interaction between them; to describe any likely significant effects covering matters such as direct, indirect, secondary and permanent impacts; to describe measures to be taken by the proponent to prevent, reduce, remedy or offset any significant adverse effects on the environment; and to provide a nontechnical summary of the information provided.

Public participation Prior to the supply of the foregoing information, the proponent is required to provide public information of the details of the proposed development as well as indicating that interested parties may make representations. Subsequently, the Secretary of State, as the decision-making authority, is required to direct the proponent to provide copies of the environmental statement to those bodies appearing to be likely to have an interest in the proposed development by virtue of their environmental responsibilities. This obligation extends to the harbour authority also. All of these bodies will be consulted by the Secretary of State before a decision on the merits of the proposed development is arrived at. There is a discretion also for the Secretary of State to convene an inquiry into the proposal. Only after the conclusion of these steps (including any inquiry) will the Secretary of State be competent to arrive at a decision, to grant consent unconditionally or subject to conditions, or to refuse such consent. The decision must be made available for public scrutiny.

Wider impacts of the decision If, in anticipation of any grant of planning permission for the development of a pulp mill (with the attendant environmental assessment) and the grant of any IPPC permit, the Secretary of State decides to grant consent for the development of shipping access to the site there may be considerable efficiencies to be realised. As already anticipated, the proponent here may seek to collaborate commercially both with the proponent of the pulp mill and the harbour authority. In these circumstances the environmental assessment will feed directly into the other regulatory processes. However, should the pulp mill development be refused, the berths will no doubt service some other development on the site.

Bibliography

Baldock, D., Bishop, K., Mitchell, K. and Phillips, A. (1996), *Growing Greener: Sustainable Agriculture in the UK*, CPRE and WWF, London.

Buller, H. (1998), 'Reflections across the Channel', in P. Lowe and S. Ward (eds), *British Environmental Policy and Europe*, Routledge, London.

Commission of the European Communities (1989), *Strategy for Waste Management*, SEC(89)934.

Commission of the European Communities (1994), *Proposal for a Directive on Bathing Waters*, COM(94)36.

Commission of the European Communities (1997), *Agenda 2000: For a Stronger and Wider Union*, COM(97)2000.

Commission of the European Communities (1997), *Environmental Taxes and Charges in the Single Market*, COM(97)9.

Commission of the European Communities (1997), *Indicators of Sustainable Development*, Luxembourg.

Commission of the European Communities (1999), *Towards Environmental Pressure Indicators for the E.U.*, COM(1990)772 Final.

Commission of the European Communities (2000), *Green Paper on Greenhouse Gas Emission*, COM(2000)87.

Commission of the European Communities (2000), *The Precautionary Principle*, COM2000/1.

Commission of the European Communities (2000), *The Standardised Reporting Directive*, Luxembourg.

Commission of the European Communities (2000), *White Paper on Environmental Liability*, Document 6055/00.

Commission of the European Communities (2001), *Environmental Pressure Indicators for the E.U.*, Luxembourg.

Department of the Environment (1990), *This Common Inheritance, Britain's Environmental Strategy*, Cm1200, HMSO, London.

Department of the Environment (1992), *Guidance on The Implementation of The Environmental Information Regulations*, Department of the Environment, London.

Department of the Environment (1992), *Planning, Pollution and Waste Management*, Department of the Environment, London.

Department of the Environment (1993), *U.K. Strategy for Sustainable Development*, Department of the Environment, London.

Department of the Environment (Expert Panel on Air Quality Standards) (1994), *Ozone*, HMSO, London.

Department of the Environment (1998), *Packaging Waste*, Department of the Environment, London.

Department of the Environment (1998), *Policy Appraisal and the Environment*, Department of the Environment, London.

Department of the Environment (1998), *Review of Water Abstraction Licensing*, Department of the Environment, London.

Department of the Environment (1998), *The Shellfish Waters Directive*, Department of the Environment, London.

Department of the Environment (1999), *A Better Quality of Life*, Cm4345, The Stationery Office, London.

Department of the Environment (1999), *Sustainable Development: The U.K. Strategy*, Department of the Environment, London.

Department of the Environment (2000), *Air Quality Strategy for England, Scotland Wales and Northern Ireland*, Cm4548, The Stationery Office, London.

Department of the Environment (2000), *Economic Instruments in Relation to Water Abstraction*, Department of the Environment, London.

Department of the Environment (2000), *The Implementation of Council Directive 1999/31*, Department of the Environment, London.

Department of the Environment (2000), *Waste Strategy for England and Wales 2000*, Cm4693, The Stationery Office, London.

Department of the Environment and Environmental Resources Ltd (1990), *Market Mechanisms: Charging and Subsidies*, Market Resources, London.

Environment Agency (1996), *Taking Account of Costs and Benefits*, Sustainable Development Publication DS3, Environment Agency, London.

Environment Agency (1999), *Controlling Pollution from Existing Coal- and Oil-fired Power Stations*, Environment Agency, London.

Environment Agency (2000), *Consenting of Dangerous Substances in Discharges to Surface Waters*, Environment Agency, London.

European Centre for Nature Conservation (1996), *Pan-European Biological and Landscape Diversity*, ECNC, Geneva.

European Environment Agency (1996), *Environmental Taxes: Implementation and Environmental Effectiveness*, EEA, Copenhagen.

European Environment Agency (2000), *Environmental Taxes*, Environmental Issues Series, No. 18, EEA, Luxembourg.

European Foundation for the Improvement of Living and Working Conditions (1998), *Employment and Sustainability: The U.K. Landfill Tax*, Luxembourg.

Franklin, D., Hawke, N. and Lowe, M. (1995), *Pollution in the U.K.*, Sweet and Maxwell, London.

Haigh, N. (ed.) (2000), *Manual of Environmental Policy*, Institute for European Environmental Policy, London.

Hawke, N. (1997), 'Toxic Torts and Regulatory Standards in the Law of the United Kingdom', *Tulane Environmental Law Journal*, Vol. 10, No. 2.

Hawke, N. (2000), *Corporate Liability*, Sweet and Maxwell, London.

Hawke, N. and Kovaleva, N. (1998), *Agri-environmental Law and Policy*, Cavendish Publishing, London.

House of Commons Environment Committee (Session 1996–97), *Water Conservation and Supply*, 1st Report, HMSO, London.

House of Commons Environment Committee (Session 1999–2000), *The Environment Agency*, 6th Report, HMSO, London.

House of Commons Environment Committee (Session 1999–2000), *U.K. Climate Change Programme*, 5th Report, HMSO, London.

House of Commons Environmental Audit Committee (Session 1999–2000), *E.U. Policy and the Environment: An Agenda for the Helsinki Summit*, 1st Report, HMSO, London.

House of Commons Environmental Audit Committee (Session 2000–01), *Environmental Audit: the First Parliament*, 1st Report, HMSO, London.

House of Commons and House of Lords Joint Committee on Statutory Instruments (Session 1993–94), 10th Report, HMSO, London.

House of Lords Select Committee on the European Communities (Session 1991–92), *Carbon/Energy Tax*, 8th Report, HMSO, London.

House of Lords Select Committee on the European Communities (Session 1991–92), *Implementation and Enforcement of Environmental Legislation*, 9th Report, HMSO, London.

House of Lords Select Committee on the European Communities (Session 1992–93), *Fifth Environmental Action Programme: Integration of Community Policies*, 8th Report, HMSO, London.

House of Lords Select Committee on the European Communities (Session 1993–94), *Remedying Environmental Damage*, 3rd Report, HMSO, London.

House of Lords Select Committee on the European Communities (Session 1994–95), *Bathing Water Revisited*, 7th Report, HMSO, London.

House of Lords Select Committee on the European Communities (Session 1997–98), *Community Environmental Law: Making it Work*, 2nd Report, HMSO, London.

House of Lords Select Committee on the European Communities (Session 1997–98), *Community Water Policy*, 8th Report, HMSO, London.

House of Lords Select Committee on the European Communities (Session 1997–98), *Sustainable Landfill*, 17th Report, HMSO, London.

House of Lords Select Committee on the European Communities (Session 1998–99), *Waste Incineration*, 11th Report, HMSO, London.

Kimber, C. (2000), 'Implementing European Environmental Policy and the Directive on Access to Environmental Information', in C. Knill and A. Lenschow (eds), *Implementing E.U. Environmental Policy*, Manchester University Press.

Kramer, L. (2000), *E.C. Environmental Law*, Sweet and Maxwell, London.

Lowe, P. and Ward, S. (1998), 'Domestic Winner and Losers', in P. Lowe and S. Ward (eds), *British Environmental Policy and Europe*, Routledge, London.

Ministry of Agriculture (2000), *Towards Sustainable Development: A Pilot Set of Indicators*, Ministry of Agriculture, London.

Morphet, J. (1998), 'Local Authorities', in P. Lowe and S. Ward (eds), *British Environmental Policy and Europe*, Routledge, London.

National Rivers Authority (1994), *Bathing Water Quality*, Water Quality Series No. 22, NRA, London.

National Rivers Authority (1994), *E.C. Freshwater Fish Directive: U.K. Implementation*, Water Quality Series, No. 20, NRA, London.

Organisation for Economic Cooperation and Development (1989), *Economic Instruments for Environmental Protection*, OECD, Paris.

Organisation for Economic Cooperation and Development (1993), *Taxation and the Environment*, OECD, Paris.

Organisation for Economic Cooperation and Development (1994), *Environment and Taxation*, OECD, Paris.

Organisation for Economic Cooperation and Development (1994), *Managing the Environment: The Role of Economic Instruments*, OECD, Paris.

Organisation for Economic Cooperation and Development (1997), *Agriculture, Pesticides and the Environment*, OECD, Paris.

Organisation for Economic Cooperation and Development (1997), *Environmental Indicators for Agriculture*, OECD, Paris.

Organisation for Economic Cooperation and Development (1997), *Environmental Tax and Green Tax Reform*, OECD, Paris.

Organisation for Economic Cooperation and Development (1997), *Reforming Environmental Regulation*, OECD, Paris.

Organisation for Economic Cooperation and Development (1998), *Improving the Environment through Reducing Subsidies*, OECD, Paris.

Royal Commission on Environmental Pollution (1988), *Best Practicable Environmental Option*, Cm310, The Stationery Office, London.

Royal Commission on Environmental Pollution (1992), *Freshwater Quality*, Cm1966, The Stationery Office, London.

Royal Commission on Environmental Pollution (1993), *Incineration of Waste*, Cm2181, The Stationery Office, London.

Royal Commission on Environmental Pollution (1994), *Transport and the Environment*, Cm2674, The Stationery Office, London.

Royal Commission on Environmental Pollution (1998), *Setting Environmental Standards*, Cm4053, The Stationery Office, London.

Royal Commission on Environmental Pollution (2000), *Energy – The Changing Climate*, Cm4749, The Stationery Office, London.

Van Dunné, J.M. (ed.) (1996), *Non-point Source River Pollution*, Kluwer Law International, The Hague.

United Nations Economic Commission for Europe (1999), *Strategies and Policies for Air Pollution Abatement*, ECE/E13.AIR/65, UK, Geneva.

United Nations Environment Programme (1998), *Policy Effectiveness and Multilateral Environmental Agreements*, UN EP/98/6: Environment and Trade Paper 17, UN, Geneva.

Index